D1403667

NEED TO KNOW

Also by Timothy Good

TIMOTHY GOOD

NEED TO KNOW

UFOs, the Military and Intelligence

PEGASUS BOOKS
NEW YORK

NEED TO KNOW

Pegasus Books LLC
80 Broad Street
5th Floor
New York, NY 10004

Copyright © 2007 by Timothy Good

First Pegasus Books edition 2007

Library of Congress Cataloging-in-Publication Data is available.

ISBN: 978-1-933648-38-5

10 9 8 7 8 6 5

Printed in the United States of America
Distributed by W. W. Norton & Company, Inc.
www.pegasusbooks.us

Dedicated to

MAJOR L. GORDON COOPER

(1927–2004)

Contents

Acknowledgments

It would be impracticable to thank all those who have contributed directly or indirectly to the production of *Need to Know*, but I would like to record my thanks in particular to the following individuals and organizations:

Jan Aldrich; Johan Andersson; Don Berliner and Robert J. Durant; Larry Bryant; Rhiannon Burruss; John Callahan; Grant Cameron; Franklin Carter; the Center for UFO Studies and the *International UFO Reporter*; the Central Intelligence Agency; Bill Chalker; *China Daily*; the Chinese Air Force; Ronald C. Claridge DFC; David Clarke and Andy Roberts; the Defense Intelligence Agency; Copyprint Bromley, especially Joanne, Karly, Mike, Simon and Victoria; Philip Corso Jr; Glenn Dennis; Robert F. Dorr; Frederick C. Durant; Ethan Eisenberg; the Federal Bureau of Investigation; Flight Data Center; *Flying Saucer Review*; Fortean Picture Library; Raymond E. Fowler; René Giraud; Jay Gourley; Jean Gabriel Greslé; Dr Richard Haines; Richard H. Hall; C. M. Hanna; Jan Harzan; David J. Hastings; Georgina Howell; Tim Iahn; the Indian Air Force; Japan Airlines; Philip Jarrett; Anthony L. Kimery; George Knapp; Andrzej Krzewski; the *Los Angeles Times*; the Ministry of Defence; Jean-Pierre Morin; the Mutual UFO Network and the *MUFON UFO Journal*; the National Archives, London, and the National Archives, Washington, DC; the National Security Agency; *Newsweek*; *New York Times*; Sid Padrick; Dr Hal Puthoff; Gian J. Quasar; Nick Redfern; Madeleine Rodeffer; the Royal Air Force; Bradford Runyon Jr; Mike Sacks; Robert Salas and James Klotz; John F. Schuessler; L. Schultz; Esen Şekerkarar; *Time*; Tim Shawcross; Margaret Sheppard; Arthur Stansel; Carlton Stowers and the *Dallas Observer*; Clas Svahn; *UFO Magazine*; Rebecca Ullrich; the US Air Force; the US Army; the US Navy; Dorothee Walter; the *Washington Post*; Fred Whiting and the Fund for UFO Research; Steve Williams; John Timmerman; *UFOBC Quarterly*; UPI Newspictures; the US Information Service.

I am especially indebted to Rear Admiral Joe Barth, USN (retired), former Commanding Officer, USS *Forrestal*, for assistance in resolving my queries about aircraft carrier operations; Dermot Butler and Carl Nally for their first-class research into the disturbing Dublin/Irish Sea air incidents

of 2004–5; Ingrid Connell and Georgina Difford, my editors at Sidgwick &
Jackson, for their forbearance in the face of the many problems that beset
us; Kate Eshelby, my publicist at Sidgwick & Jackson; Lucius Farish, for a
great deal of help and encouragement, and for his UFO Newsclipping
Service; Captain Robert Filler, USAF (retired), for his account of a UFO
interception in California in 1961; Bill Gunston OBE, not only for his
foreword, but for an enormous amount of help in checking my manuscript
and the page proofs; Michael David Hall and Wendy Connors, for a lot of
data from their monumental work, *Captain Edward J. Ruppelt: Summer of
the Saucers – 1952*; Terry Hansen, for the use of much material from his
brilliant book, *The Missing Times*; Leslie Kean, for extracts from her article
on the Kecksburg, Pennsylvania crash-retrieval case of 1965, as well as
additional information; Jon 'Andy' Kissner, to whom I am especially
grateful for so generously providing me with a wealth of information from
A Peculiar Phenomenon, his groundbreaking manuscript detailing the
shocking events of 1947; Dr Lynne Kitei, for extracts from her book, *The
Phoenix Lights*; James M. Kopf, USN (retired), for his testimony on the
USS *John F. Kennedy* incident of 1971; Don Ledger and Chris Styles, for
extracts from their book, *Dark Object*, and for additional information; Dr
Roger Leir, for so kindly and unstintingly allowing me to reproduce such a
lengthy segment from his astonishing book, *UFO Crash In Brazil*; Nikolay
Lebedev, for his superb research into Russian military cases; my agent
Andrew Lownie, as always; Clark C. McLelland, who so generously allowed
me the use of much material relating to his extraordinary experiences while
working with NASA; Commander Will Miller, USNR (retired), for his
testimony on the UFO/USO incident witnessed on board the USS *Leary* in
Vietnam, and for additional help; Roberto Pinotti and Alfredo Lissoni, for
material from their book, *Mussolini e gli UFO*; Nick Pope, for much advice
and help, as well as for quotations from his book, *Open Skies, Closed Minds*;
Scott and Suzanne Ramsey, for so much of their material on the 1948
Aztec, New Mexico case; Chris Rolfe and UFO Monitors East Kent, for
their research into the Burmarsh, Kent incident of 1997; Dr Irena Scott, for
numerous extracts from her remarkable book, *Ohio UFOs (and many
others)*; Joan Woodward, for copious extracts from her article on the
Washington, DC sightings of July 2002, and for additional input. And, as
ever, my very special gratitude to those who have helped enormously, but
must remain anonymous.

Finally, my apologies in advance for any omissions of credit.

Foreword

BILL GUNSTON OBE

I have known Timothy Good for many years, and I am delighted that he asked me to contribute the foreword to his latest book.

Of course, before doing this I read the text. His previous books on the subject – mostly bestsellers – left the reader thinking, 'Well, it's all pretty convincing, and Good has put together a formidable package of evidence – but it simply *can't be true!*'

The very idea of vehicles from another planet visiting us seems outrageous. Such beings would have had to come from a civilization much more advanced than our own. We know (or think we know) that they could not have come from anywhere in our solar system, and the nearest stars are light years away.

What about such objects actually landing on our planet's surface? Even more seemingly incredible, who can believe the story of 'little green men' coming to see us, speaking perfect English?

Whoever they are, our visitors have studied us (and our radio broadcasts) long enough to learn terrestrial languages, especially English. They might never have actually come to visit, had we never shocked them by our actions. That we did shock them is evident from the fact that their visits increased dramatically soon after the start of nuclear warfare, and that they alighted close to the place where the first atom bomb was detonated.

With this new book, Good has the advantage of a wealth of new documents and oral evidence. But we really do not need to rely on this. Let us study the question from another angle, and suppose that, for whatever reason, the whole notion of flying saucers and extraterrestrial visitors has always been a gigantic hoax. For this to be the case, one is faced with formidable difficulties:

— On literally hundreds of occasions someone (who?) would have had to get anything up to thousands of people to say that they had themselves seen and heard extraordinary phenomena, the details of which all would have had to agree.

— Large numbers of (mostly very intelligent and highly trained) people in

various armed forces and government posts would have had to devote a
great deal of effort pretending to clean up fictitious landing sites and
transport non-existent items to secure laboratories for further
examination and storage.
— Even greater numbers of supposedly reliable witnesses, such as fighter
pilots, warship crews and airline captains, would have had to agree to
invent seemingly incredible tales of alien encounters, and then pretend to
be deeply shocked by them.
— Not least, the agency responsible for perpetrating this fraud would have
had to convince thousands of people *in countries all over the world* to go
along with the great hoax, and to pretend to have witnessed non-existent
events, and to do so in such a way that there were no disagreements or
dissenters.

Of course, from the start of UFO phenomena there were indeed plenty
of dissenters. Large numbers of employees of the national governments
were simply told to provide a cover story, even when the official explanation
of the phenomena was clearly nonsense. Other would-be experts just took
it upon themselves to debunk what appeared to them to be stories that
were beyond belief.

They will find this book disturbing.

Bill Gunston, an Officer of the Order of the British Empire and a Fellow of the Royal
Aeronautical Society, is one of the world's leading aviation historians, with nearly 400
books – not including co-author or team efforts – to his credit.

Born in London in 1927, he was educated at Pinner County School, where in his
spare time he was Flight Sergeant in the school Air Training Corps squadron, and for
several months librarian of the London Philharmonic Orchestra.

He joined the Royal Air Force and was sent to University College, Durham
(1945–6), then served as a pilot for three years, flying many types of aircraft, ending
with the Vampire jet fighter. On leaving the RAF, he joined the staff of *Flight* magazine,
and was appointed Technical Editor in 1955. He has written several thousand magazine
articles. Since 1969 he has been part of the team producing *Jane's All the World's
Aircraft*, and he is Editor of *Jane's Aero-Engines*.

Bill Gunston married his *Flight* secretary, Margaret Anne, a glider pilot. They have
two daughters, who were international swimmers.

INTRODUCTION

Evidence for the existence of unidentified flying objects – per se – is indisputable. Millions of sightings have been reported throughout the world. That up to 90–95 per cent of all these reports can probably be explained in conventional terms is also not in dispute. But that still leaves tens of thousands of unexplained cases, including the many thousands reported by military and civilian pilots, army and naval officers, astronauts and astronomers, whose testimony is often supported by radar, sonar, and sometimes by film and photographs. In my estimation, many such cases are likely to represent genuinely anomalous craft or phenomena.

The attitude of the media, in the face of the massive amount of evidence available, is puzzling. 'UFOs do not exist,' proclaimed an editorial in *The Times* in 2005.[1] Based on an article by David Charter in *The Times* of the same date, the editorial commented on the Ministry of Defence's declassification of a large batch of papers on UFOs, under provisions of the UK Freedom of Information Act which came into force in January 2005. Charter wrote that 'it has taken the Ministry of Defence 54 years to release secret papers ruling out the existence of UFOs'.[2] Nonsense.

The Times is behind the times. Most news coverage of the 2005 release was positive. In the *Independent*, for example, Robert Verkaik cited the reports included in the MoD releases of unidentified flying objects sighted by RAF personnel, British Airways pilots and senior police officers.[3] 'Until recently, even the tabloids regarded "flying saucers" as a joke,' commented science reporter Robert Matthews. 'Now newspapers like the *Financial Times* and *Independent* are filing Freedom of Information (FOI) requests to compel official sources to reveal what they know.'[4]

The much-heralded release of a large batch of UFO files in 2005 was not unprecedented: the MoD has declassified a number of documents over the years, either periodically (such as after thirty or fifty years), or as the result of requests from members of the public for information on a specific incident. In the United States, where the Freedom of Information Act became law in 1966, tens of thousands of UFO-related documents have been released by the armed services and intelligence agencies (most of which had previously denied having any documentation on the subject). Other countries, such as Canada, France, Italy, Russia and Spain, have also declassified files. Many of these documents were revealed for the first time in my book *Above Top Secret*, published in 1987.[5] In May 2005, the Brazilian Air Force held meetings with a committee comprising the country's leading UFO researchers and agreed to declassify more of its files on the subject. However, as elsewhere, the most sensitive information on the subject continues to be exempt from disclosure, in the interests of national security.

The Times editorial contends that astronomers 'now agree that there is no evidence for the visitation of Earth by aliens, and that the obsession with UFOs has delayed legitimate research into the possibility of life elsewhere'. Many astronomers do indeed take this position – but very few are experts on UFOs. Astronomers focus mostly on planets, moons, comets, asteroids, stars and the search for extraterrestrial intelligence (SETI) in our galaxy and beyond. UFOs most often are reported within Earth's atmosphere. Yet in this respect, a 1977 survey of members of the American Astronomical Society by Peter Sturrock of Stanford University is revealing. Of those who responded (1,356 out of 2,611), 53 per cent said UFOs 'certainly' deserved scientific study.[6] More significantly, sixty-two respondents said they 'had witnessed or obtained an instrumental record of an event that they could not identify and which they thought might be related to the UFO phenomenon'.[7]

In a recent peer-reviewed article, scientists Deardorff, Haisch, Maccabee and Puthoff re-evaluate the present assumption that extraterrestrials or their probes are not in the vicinity of Earth, arguing instead that 'some evidence of their presence might be found in certain high-quality UFO reports' (examined briefly). They also address the frequently raised notion that vast interstellar distances preclude visits by ETs.

> The extraterrestrial hypothesis (ETH), that intelligent life from 'elsewhere' in the universe could be visiting Earth, has become less implausible through suggestions that the velocity-of-light constraint – 'they can't get here from there' – is not as restricting as had been assumed previously. This restriction has its origin in the special theory of relativity, which we do not question. However, within the context of general relativity, there are three approaches which may permit legitimately bypassing this limit, given sufficiently advanced (perhaps by millions of years!) knowledge of physics and technology.

The authors discuss exotic methods of space travel, such as 'wormholes', 'warp drive' and the use of 'additional dimensionalities'. Though conceding the seemingly insurmountable obstacles, given our current technology, they point out that 'ET knowledge of the physical universe may comprise new principles which allow some form of faster-than-light travel. This possibility is to be taken seriously, since the average age of suitable stars within the "galactic habitable zone", in which the Earth also resides, is found to be about 10^9 years older than the Sun, suggesting the possibility of civilizations extremely advanced beyond our own.'[8]

Eric Jones of the Los Alamos National Laboratory has calculated that space-faring civilizations capable of reaching velocities of just one-tenth the speed of light could theoretically colonize the entire galaxy within 60 million years.[9] A corollary is that our galaxy could already have been teeming with technologically advanced civilizations aeons ago.

Attitudes may be changing, though the national media typically continues to refer pejoratively to UFO researchers as 'believers', 'buffs' or 'conspiracy theorists'. The fact that thousands of scientists worldwide take this multidisciplinary subject seriously – or have authored books on it – is usually overlooked. A list of doctorates for members of the Mutual UFO Network (MUFON), for example, included: physical sciences (127); medical sciences (120); biological sciences (43); earth sciences (22).[10]

Reviewing a tendentious 1996 PBS/NOVA television documentary on alien abductions that featured the late Dr John Mack, Professor of Psychiatry at Harvard Medical School and a MUFON consultant, Dorothy Rabinowitz of the *Wall Street Journal* wrote: 'Dr Mack, who gives credence to the alien-encounter experience, will likely not be pleased with this film, which proceeds to demolish the claims of the various hucksters, charlatans, assorted exhibitionists and garden variety nitwits immersed in humbug about alien abductors . . .'[11]

In December 2004, a retired Chilean Air Force general, Ricardo Bermúdez, announced the foundation of a degree course on 'anomalous aerial phenomena', which he would direct, to be held at the University of Chile. With a faculty of specialists including Klaus von Storch, Chile's first astronaut, the academic programme was declared 'a necessity for these times' and a counter to media sensationalism on the subject. 'Ufologists' would be excluded. 'Something is happening in our world,' said Bermúdez. 'We don't know what it is, but the fact is that it can no longer go unnoticed by governments and the scientific establishment.'[12]

It is largely owing to a prevailing sensationalist or debunking attitude of many national newspapers and scientific journals that scientists are reluctant to openly acknowledge their interest. This is less the case in China. In *Beyond Top Secret*, I devoted a chapter to encounters reported by military and civilian pilots and other credible observers in that country, and discussed how the subject is treated more seriously in the academic community. In 1992 the China UFO Research Association, which is affiliated to the China Association for Science and Technology, had 3,600 full members as well as 40,000 research associates.[13] Most of China's UFO researchers are scientists and engineers, and many UFO groups require both a college degree and published research for membership. 'In the US, scholars investigating this are under pressure and have been derided,' explained Sun Shili, a former foreign ministry official and head of the Beijing UFO Research Society, in 2000. 'But in China, the academic discussion is quite free, so in this area American academics are quite jealous of us.'[14]

Not all scientists, however – including those in China – are free to discuss their UFO research, since many work for the military/intelligence community and hold high security clearances. Terry Hansen, a science journalist who is the author of *The Missing Times*, an erudite study of American media complicity in the UFO cover-up, previously believed that the resistance displayed by establishment science towards examining UFO data could be explained mainly by 'an innate tendency of scientists to reject surprising discoveries'. Later, Hansen concluded that such resistance has more to do with federal government policies, as we shall learn in the final chapter.[15]

In 1950, a Top Secret Canadian government memorandum revealed that, 'The matter is the most highly classified subject in the United States Government, rating higher even than the H-bomb'.[16] And as Rear Admiral Roscoe Hillenkoetter, a former CIA director, noted in 1960, 'Behind the scenes, high-ranking Air Force officers are soberly concerned about the UFOs. But through *official secrecy and ridicule*, many citizens are led to believe the unknown flying objects are nonsense.'[17] (My emphasis.)

'Despite the tendency of the elite news media, particularly in recent years, to avoid coverage of the UFO issue,' Hansen points out, 'Americans show an increasing scepticism about the official version of reality they present.' He cites a *Time* magazine/CNN poll released in 1997, which revealed that 80 per cent of the 1,024 adults polled responded that they believed the US Government was hiding knowledge of extraterrestrials; 64 per cent said they thought aliens had contacted or abducted humans, and 37 per cent believed that aliens had contacted the US Government![18]

Because *Need to Know* chronicles the worldwide military and intelligence involvement with the UFO problem since the 1930s, and most of my books are currently out of print, I have alluded to, and updated where appropriate, some cases from previous books. I also felt it essential to include a great deal of material from the 1940s and 1950s – a period crucial to our understanding of both the development of the problem and the response to it by the military intelligence community. Much of this material will be new – even to aficionados.

Moreover, much of the material is disturbing. It is no wonder that governments are so reluctant to release information. Many readers will be shocked to learn that early military action against UFOs led to an unprecedented number of military and civilian aircraft crashes worldwide; that hundreds of pilots have either lost their lives or simply disappeared during interceptions of UFOs; and that we are in conflict with some extraterrestrial species.

In the past few decades, I have acquired a great deal of information from my contacts around the world, to the extent that I now feel able to speak with authority about a number of the seemingly outrageous stories that appear in this and previous books. Some of these sources have been, or are currently, involved in official and unofficial programmes that deal with the UFO/alien problem. They have stressed that gradual disclosure of the facts is the best way forward. I have been encouraged to come out with this information, even though it is disturbing because eventually we will have to come to terms with the truth – however unpalatable.

Need to Know is dedicated to the memory of L. Gordon Cooper, the pilot, astronaut and UFO researcher, who passed away in 2004. 'Gordo' took his first flight at the age of five, learned to fly at eight and went solo when he was twelve. During his distinguished military flying career he flew many types of aircraft, including two of my favourites – the F-86 Sabre and F-102 Delta Dagger jets. As a second lieutenant stationed at Neubiberg Air Force Base, Germany, in 1951, he saw his first UFOs – unknown saucer-shaped craft that overflew the base for several days. Cooper and his squadron mates were scrambled to intercept, but their F-86s were incapable of flying high enough (Chapter 11). In 1957, while assigned as test pilot and project manager of the fighter section at the Experimental Flight Test Engineering Division at Edwards Air Force Base, California, a flying saucer literally landed on the dry lake bed, filmed by cameramen (Chapter 15).

Cooper was the youngest and most laid-back of the seven Mercury astronauts, and his first trip into space – a twenty-two-orbit flight in May 1963 – led to ceremonies at the White House and a parade through New York City involving 2,900 tons of ticker tape! He retired from NASA and the Air Force in 1970 as a 'full bird' colonel (having turned down promotion to general because he would no longer have been allowed to fly single-seat aircraft).[19] Though we corresponded a couple of times, I never met this courageous, modest, yet outspoken man, whom I admired so much.

'What will it take?' asks Cooper in his autobiography. 'Must a UFO land at the Super Bowl to get the world's undivided attention?'[20]

It is to be hoped that the evidence contained in *Need to Know* will stimulate serious, if not undivided, attention to this controversial, disturbing, yet exciting subject – the most highly classified secret on Earth.

REFERENCES

1. 'Pie in the Sky', editorial, *The Times*, 4 February 2005.
2. Charter, David, 'How Britain's X-Files said that UFOs were just a waste of time', *The Times*, 4 February 2005.
3. Verkaik, Robert, 'Uncovered at last: the sightings of strange flying objects found in Britain's X-Files', *Independent*, 22 January 2005, p. 17.
4. Matthews, Robert, *Focus*, No. 150, May 2005.
5. Good, Timothy, *Above Top Secret: The Worldwide UFO Cover-up*, Sidgwick & Jackson, London, 1987.
6. Sturrock, Peter A., 'Report on a Survey of the Membership of the American Astronomical Society Concerning the UFO Problem', *Journal of Scientific Exploration*, Vol. 8, No. 1; 2; 3, pp. 1–45; 153–95; 309–46 (1994).
7. Ibid., p. 3.
8. Deardorff, J., Haisch, B., Maccabee, B. and Puthoff, H.E., 'Inflation-Theory Implications for Extraterrestrial Visitation', *Journal of the British Interplanetary Society*, Vol. 58, pp. 43–50 (2005).
9. Jones, Eric, M., 'Discrete Calculations of Interstellar Migration and Settlement', *Icarus*, Vol. 46, pp. 328–36 (1981).
10. Mutual UFO Network (MUFON), P.O. Box 369, Morrison, CO 80465-0369, USA. www.mufon.com and mufonhq@aol.com
11. Rabinowitz, Dorothy, 'TV: Talk-show wars; Alien abductors; Black-listed actors', *Wall Street Journal*, 12 February 1996, p. A12.
12. *Inexplicata*, The Journal of Hispanic Ufology, 28 December 2004.
13. Good, Timothy, *Beyond Top Secret: The Worldwide UFO Security Threat*, Sidgwick & Jackson, London, 1996, pp. 209–22.
14. Rosenthal, Elisabeth, 'In UFOs, Beijing finds an otherworldly interest it can live with,' New York Times Service, *International Herald Tribune*, London and Paris, 12 January 2000.
15. Hansen, Terry, *The Missing Times: News Media Complicity in the UFO Cover-up*, XLibris Corporation, 2000, pp. 298–9.

16. Memorandum (Top Secret) to the Controller of Telecommunications from W.B. Smith, Senior Radio Engineer, Department of Transport, Ottawa, 21 November 1950.

17. *New York Sunday Times*, 28 February 1960.

18. 'Poll: US hiding knowledge of aliens', CNN website, 15 June 1997.

19. Cooper, Gordon with Henderson, Bruce, *Leap of Faith: An Astronaut's Journey into the Unknown*, HarperCollins, New York, 2000.

20. Ibid., p. 200.

> As an RAF Fighter Controller you are
> responsible for guiding the pilots to their
> target, as well as anticipating how the
> target might react.
>
> You have to make split-second decisions
> that will place your pilots in a position where
> they can make positive identification.
>
> Whether it is reporting on unidentified
> objects, guiding fighter pilots, or check-
> ing on thousands of man-made objects
> orbiting the earth - Fighter Controllers
> are maintaining the defence of their
> country in one of the most high-pressure
> environments there is.

An extract from a full-page Royal Air Force advertisement for recruiting
fighter controllers, which appeared in the *Daily Express* (25 July 1991), headlined
'UFO or VIP?' *(Royal Air Force)*

An extract from the executive summary of an over-460-page Scientific & Technical
Memorandum by the UK Defence Intelligence Analysis Staff, entitled
Unidentified Aerial Phenomena in the UK Air Defence Region (2000),
code-named Project Condign, and mostly declassified in May 2006.
UFOs are designated here as UAPs. *(Crown Copyright)*

> • The flight safety aspects of the findings should be made available to the appropriate
> RAF Air Defence and other military and civil authorities which operate aircraft,
> particularly those operating fast and at low altitude.
>
> In so advising:
>
> - It should be stressed that, despite the recent increase in UAP events, the
>   probability of encountering a UAP remains very low.
>
> - No attempt should be made to out-manoeuvre a UAP during interception.

UK EYES ONLY
UK RESTRICTED
UNCLASSIFIED
SECRET

11

PART ONE

1930–49

1. DAWN OF AN ERA

Officialdom began to pay attention to aerial phenomena at the outbreak of the First World War in 1914. In Australia, for example, strange aircraft, accompanied by 'machinary hums' and odd lights, were reported in northern New South Wales, Australia.[1] Such reports must be seen in context with that war, of course, involving as it did the use of military aircraft for the first time. However, more serious attention was paid in 1920, when unexplained lights were seen in the sky around the entrance to the Bass Strait, Australia, around the time a ship, SS *Amelia J.*, had disappeared. The search aircraft sent to investigate also disappeared without trace.[2]

The Bass Strait is one of a number of areas – such as the Bermuda Triangle and the Great Lakes area in North America – where many aircraft and ships have mysteriously disappeared. In 1930, witnesses at Warrnambool, Victoria, on the north shore of the Bass Strait, reported sightings of unidentified 'aircraft', and the Royal Australian Air Force dispatched Squadron Leader (later Air Marshal) George Jones to investigate. No evidence could be found that the aircraft were either Australian or foreign. On the morning of 19 October 1935, a four-engined Qantas Empire Airways D.H.86 airliner, the *Miss Hobart*, disappeared inexplicably in the Bass Strait. Strange lights were seen in the sky that night and three nights later, not far from where the plane reported its last position.[3]

In 1933, mysterious but conventionally shaped, unmarked aircraft were sighted over Scandinavia and, to a lesser extent, the UK and USA. Often seen flying in hazardous weather conditions, the 'ghost aircraft', as they were called, frequently circled low, projecting powerful searchlights on to the ground. Although engine noises accompanied the sightings, the aircraft sometimes described low-level manoeuvres in complete silence.

'. . . there can be no doubt about illegal air traffic over our secret military areas,' said Major-General Reuterswaerd of the 4th Swedish Flying Corps. 'Who or whom are they, and why have they been invading our air territory?'[4]

An Italian government report – dating back to 1936 – was leaked sixty years later to researcher Roberto Pinotti. Purportedly written by 'Andrea', an Italian secret service agent, the report describes observations of unknown flying craft seen near Venice on 17 August 1936:

> It was a metallic disc, polished and reflecting light, with a diameter of ten to twelve metres. Two fighters from a nearby base took off, but were unable to reach it ... It didn't emit sound, which would lead one to consider an aerostat. But nobody knows of balloons that can fly faster than the wind. I know for sure that it was seen by other aviators ... Then, after approximately at least an hour and after passing over Mestre, it was seen as a sort of metallic tube, grey or slate.

Benito Mussolini – *Il Duce* – the Fascist dictator (himself a pilot) took a great interest in this and other sightings at the time, and a report on the incident was also sent to Count Ciano, Mussolini's son-in-law and Italy's Minister of Foreign Affairs.

A sketch by a confidential informant was redrawn by Andrea, who explained that:

> [The main object] was described like a kind of aerial torpedo, with very clear windows ... and alternating white and red lights. [The two other objects] were two 'hats', hats like those used by priests: wide, round, with a dome in the centre, metallic and following the torpedo without changing their relative positions ... the prefecture has opened an inquiry, but you can imagine that it will make little inroad ... The *Duce* has expressed his worries, because he says that if it were a matter of real English or French aircraft, his foreign policy would have to start all over again.

Pinotti and his colleagues received this, as well as many other extraordinary documents, including handwritten notes and telegrams, on original paper bearing the seal of the Senato del Regno (Senate of the Realm), which are published in a book co-authored by Pinotti with Alfredo Lissoni.[5] But Pinotti was not the first to receive the series of documents. Earlier, packages had been addressed to the Bologna newspaper *Il Resto del Carlino*, for instance, containing a dossier of thirty-four photocopied pages covering various sightings in Italy between 1933 and 1940 – including reports from what was then the Royal Italian Air Force, with the recommendation, 'Say nothing to *Il Duce*'. Three telegrams related to instructions for the recovery of a flying disc which supposedly had landed in an unnamed location (believed to be near Milan) on 13 June 1933, and counter-intelligence measures including press censorship (see p. 15).

There are frequent references in the documents to a top-secret group –

Gabinetto RS/33 – reportedly dealing with the collection, investigation and even suppression of information relating to *velivolvi sconoscuti* (unknown aircraft). Headed by Mussolini, Ciano and airman General Italo Balbo, RS/33 is said to have included several prominent aeronautical engineers, astronomers and scientists, directed by none other than Guglielmo Marconi, the great inventor, although he never played an active role in the cabinet, preferring to delegate to the astronomer Gino Cecchini. RS/33 had links with OVRA, the Fascist secret police, and Agenzia Stefani, the regime's news agency in charge of disseminating propaganda.[6] As Pinotti elucidated for me:

> ... All this re-writes the history of 'official' ufology, which started secretly in Italy under Mussolini with the RS/33 (*Ricerche Speciale* [Special Research] 33) Cabinet in 1933 to study the '*Velivoli Non Convenzionali*' (unconventional aircraft) after a possible UFO crash near Milan, and a definite 'reverse-engineering' approach to 'copy' what the Fascists considered to be purported English or French secret aerial spy devices. The Italian studies led to different concepts of round flying machines, to be used by the Germans at the end of WWII.[7]

Pinotto told me that the documents he received – originating with the nephew of a member of the RS/33 Cabinet – were authenticated by forensic analysis involving chemical tests on the paper and ink, conducted by Antonio Garavaglia, a top Italian forensic consultant. Checks for historical accuracy by historian Andrea Bedetti, an expert on Italy's Fascist period, indicate authenticity.[8] Alfredo Lissoni discovered additional evidence in the archives of the Prefeturra (Civil Governor's office) in Milan: about 500 telegrams sent to the Prefeturra between 1933 and 1938, at least nine of which exclusively concerned *velivoli non identificabili* (unidentifiable aircraft).[9]

Alfredo Lissoni has unearthed a fascinating reference from a speech by Mussolini to the Federation of Fascist Combatants on 23 February 1941: 'The United States are far more likely to be invaded, not by soldiers of the Axis, but by the not so well known but warlike inhabitants of the planet Mars, who will come down out of space in their unimaginable flying fortresses.'[10]

This was almost certainly the first official reference to alien spaceships – and one that turned out to be prescient. A year later, an extraordinary incident led some American military leaders to wonder if they were indeed being invaded by beings from elsewhere.

REFERENCES

1. Information supplied by Bill Chalker.
2. Norman, Paul, 'Countdown to Reality', *Flying Saucer Review*, Vol. 31, No. 2, 1986, pp. 13–22.
3. Ibid.
4. Keel, John A., 'Mystery Aeroplanes of the 1930s', Part II, *Flying Saucer Review*, FSR Publications Ltd., PO Box 585, Rickmansworth, WD3 1YJ, UK, Vol. 16, No. 3, 1970, pp. 10–13.
5. Pinotti, Roberto and Lissoni, Alfredo, *Gli 'X-Files' del Nazifascismo: Mussolini e gli UFO*, Idea Libri S.r.l., Rimini, Italy, 2001.
6. Lissoni, Alfredo, 'UFO Cover-up by Mussolini!', *Flying Saucer Review*, Vol. 46, No. 3, 2003, pp. 13–14, translated by Gordon Creighton from *Il Giornale dei Misteri*, No. 353, March 2001.
7. Letter, 7 August 2005.
8. Lissoni, op. cit., p. 15.
9. Pinotti and Lissoni, op. cit.
10. *Giornale d'Italia*, 25 February 1941, cited by Lissoni, op. cit., p. 16.

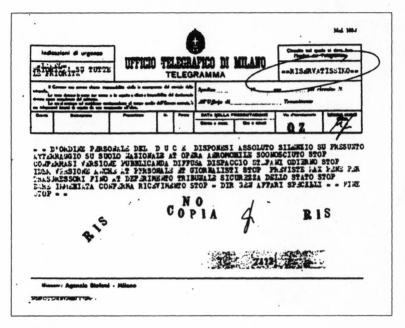

A 'highly confidential' Italian Government telegram dating back to June 1933 from the Director of Special Affairs: 'On the personal order of *Il Duce*, absolutely no mention is to be made of the alleged landing of an unknown aircraft on national soil – the same applies to today's news due for publication by the Stefani Agency [and] individual journalists – Maximum penalty for non-compliance will be enforced by the Tribunal for State Security.' *(Roberto Pinotti/Alfredo Lissoni)*

2. SECOND WORLD WAR

In the early hours of 25 February 1942, the city of Los Angeles was alerted by air-raid sirens and searchlights probing the sky, provoking fear that a Japanese invasion was imminent. Pearl Harbor had happened less than three months earlier, and on 24 February a Japanese submarine had attacked the coast from the Santa Barbara Straits, north of Los Angeles. (The secret memorandum to President Franklin D. Roosevelt signed by General George C. Marshall, Chief of Staff, describing these events, appears on p. 31.)

According to thousands of witnesses, a large unidentified object remained stationary while anti-aircraft shells burst around it and against it, as may be seen in a press photograph taken at the time (see plates). A *Herald Express* staff writer said he was certain that many shells burst directly in the middle of the object and he could not believe that it had not been shot down. The object eventually departed at a leisurely pace over the coastal cities between Santa Monica and Long Beach, disappearing after twenty minutes. The air alarm had lasted for nearly five hours.[1]

John E. Seidel, a carrier for the *Los Angeles Times*, recalls that the first edition of the newspaper that morning was delayed so that a first-page supplement could be added stating that 'foreign' aircraft had been in the air and that: 'At 5 am, the sheriff's office announced that an airplane has been shot down near 185th Street and Vermont Avenue. Earlier, the Fourth Air Force in San Francisco announced that at least one plane had been downed in the raid.' The supplement did not appear with later editions, nor did any reference to the downed plane appear again. Seidel subsequently learned that a plane – said to be American – had indeed crashed near 185th and Vermont, but the Army quickly removed the wreckage and cleaned up the area.[2] Is it possible that one or more of the unknown machines had been shot down? There is evidence that alien craft were recovered on several occasions during the Second World War, as will be seen later in this chapter.

The Los Angeles air alarm, the first milestone in the relatively recent history of the UFO phenomenon, generated headline news in the US, but with the world plunged into war on an unprecedented scale, official and public interest swiftly waned.

Following reports by fishermen of strange lights seen in the Bass Strait in the summer of 1942, a Royal Australian Air Force aircraft on flying patrol off the Tasman Peninsula late one afternoon was approached by an unidentified object which came out of a cloud bank. The pilot described the object as 'a singular airfoil of glistening bronze colour', about 150 feet in length and 50 feet in diameter, with what seemed like a dome on top that reflected sunlight. The UFO flew alongside the plane for a few minutes, then suddenly turned away 'at a hell of a pace'. It turned again, then dived straight into the ocean, throwing up 'a regular whirlpool of waves' and vanishing as though it had submerged like a submarine[3] – thus effectively becoming an 'unidentified submergible object' (USO).

Several reports from 1942 – declassified fifty years later by the Ministry of Defence – relate to sightings of unusual aircraft seen by RAF crews. A secret memo dated 3 December 1942 (see p. 32), from Headquarters, No. 5 Group, to Headquarters, Bomber Command, begins: 'Herewith a copy of a report received from a crew of a Lancaster after a raid on Turin. The crew refuse to be shaken in their story in the face of the usual banter and ridicule.' The report by the crew of aircraft 'J', No. 61 Squadron, based at RAF Syerston in Lincolnshire, describes the encounter on the night of 28/29 November:

> The object . . . was seen by the entire crew of the above aircraft. They believe it to have been 200–300 feet in length and its width is estimated at 1/5th or 1/6th of its length. The speed was estimated at 500 mph, and it had four pairs of red lights spaced at equal distances along its body. These lights did not appear in any way like exhaust flames; no trace was seen. The object kept a level course.
>
> The crew saw the object twice during the raid, and brief details are given below:
> (i) After bombing, time 2240 hours, a/c [aircraft] height 11,000 feet. The aircraft at this time was some 10/15 miles South-West of Turin travelling in a north-westerly direction. The object was travelling South-East at the same height or slightly below the aircraft.
> (ii) After bombing, time 2245 hours, a/c height 14,000 feet. The aircraft was approaching the Alps when the object was seen again travelling West-South-West up a valley in the Alps below the level of the peaks. The lights appeared to go out and the object disappeared from view.

The report adds that the pilot of the aircraft, a Captain Lever, saw 'a similar object about three months ago North of Amsterdam. In this instance it appeared to be on the ground and later travelling at high speed at a lower level than the heights given above along the coast for about two seconds; the lights then went out for the same period of time and came on again, and the object was still seen to be travelling in the same direction'.[4]

FOO-FIGHTERS

More typically in this period, many Allied and Axis airmen (including Japanese) began reporting sightings of small, apparently remotely controlled objects which followed and sometimes buzzed aircraft during missions. Among the US Army Air Forces (USAAF), rumours spread that the Germans had introduced a new weapon designed to interfere with the ignition systems of bombers' engines but, since the 'foo-fighters' (as they were nicknamed by pilots of the 415th Night Fighter Squadron) never engaged in hostile action – even though they posed a threat – most flight crews became convinced that the objects were some type of psychological warfare device (see p. 33). The US Eighth Army Air Forces ordered a full investigation, but was unable to arrive at a satisfactory solution.[5]

On the night of 26/27 May 1943, during a raid on Essen, Germany, involving up to 500 aircraft, an RAF Halifax four-engine bomber encountered a structured craft similar to the one reported over Turin six months earlier. Flight Sergeant G.N. Cockcroft, co-piloting, recalled the incident: 'It was in the two or three minutes before our final run-in, when we were at approximately 18,700 feet when we saw in front, but slightly to port and about the same height, a long cylindrical object, silver gold in colour, very sharply defined, hanging in the sky at an angle of approximately 45 degrees. There were, evenly spaced along the length of the object, a number of portholes.'

First to observe the object was the captain, Flight Sergeant Ray Smith (Royal Canadian Air Force), who alerted Cockcroft, as well as the bomb-aimer, flight engineer, mid-upper gunner and wireless operator. The navigator and rear gunner, preoccupied with ensuring that the Halifax stayed on course and didn't get shot down, did not witness the incident. 'I think the first reaction of most of us was amazement,' said Cockcroft, 'because the object just had no right to be there.'

The speed it attained seemed to us completely incredible. It was certainly in the thousands of mph! As it accelerated, the outline became blurred and the shape foreshortened. The size is more difficult to judge but it was very large, certainly very much bigger than our own aircraft, appearing at least as long as a king-sized cigarette or small cigar at arm's length. We then completed our bomb run and returned to base. The intelligence officer debriefing us was given a description of this object, but we were unable to judge what importance was attached to it by the authorities . . .[6]

Multiple unknown flying objects were often encountered by aircrews. On 14 May 1943, during a raid on Germany, USAAF 348th Group bombers reported 'a cluster of disks in the path of the formation near Schweinfurt' at a time when no enemy aircraft were above. The air intelligence report continues:

Discs were described as silver coloured – one inch thick and three inches in diameter. They were gliding slowly down in very uniform cluster. A/C [aircraft] 026 was unable to avoid them and his right wing went directly through a cluster with absolutely no effect on engines or plane surface. One of the discs was heard striking tail assembly but no explosion was observed . . . Also observed 2 other A/C flying through silver discs with no apparent damage. Observed discs and debris 2 other times but could not determine where it came from.[7]

America's Office of Strategic Services (OSS) – the forerunner of the CIA – headed by Major General William ('Wild Bill') Donovan, took an interest in reports such as these. At first convinced that they were German pilotless probes, investigation by OSS agents in Europe proved otherwise, and Donovan and his staff decided that the foo-fighters were unusual but harmless phenomena.[8]

According to information disclosed to the respected investigator Jacques Vallée by a former engineer with US intelligence in Germany, the Americans were already aware by 1943 that unknown flying objects – specifically the 'foo-fighters' – could interfere at a distance with internal-combustion engines. Investigators at the time suspected that electrostatic effects were the cause. A secret investigation into the phenomenon was conducted in 1943 by the then National Bureau of Standards, directed by Professor Hugh L. Dryden, a distinguished aerodynamicist.[9] In 1944, American planes returning to England from bombing missions over the Continent were plagued repeatedly by engine cut-outs. 'The engines would suddenly become very rough, cutting in and out,' author Ralph Blum learned from a source attached at the time to the Technical Intelligence Division of the US Strategic Air Force.[10]

OTHER AERIAL PHENOMENA

While sightings of foo-fighters continued, other types of unusual, larger craft or phenomena also continued to be encountered during the war. Gordon W. Cammell, a New Zealander who flew for more than twenty years as a pilot with the Royal New Zealand Air Force and the RAF, describes an encounter in May 1943:

> I was the captain of a Lancaster bomber aircraft, and as we crossed the English Channel upon returning from a bombing raid over Germany, I and all of my crew saw what appeared to be a huge orange ball on or near the sea, seven or eight thousand feet below us. It appeared to be stationary as we observed it for about 10 minutes, and its light intensity was bright and constant. We decided that it was not an aircraft or ship on fire, since we could not see flames or changing reflections on the water. After landing back at our base at RAF East Wretham, Suffolk, we reported our sighting to the debriefing officer, who also had no idea of what we had seen.[11]

According to a semi-humorous item in an RAF news sheet, classified secret, an unknown aircraft was observed during a USAAF daylight bombing raid on Emden on 11 December 1943. Visibility was good and the weather was clear. The report is cited by the editor:

> An unidentified object was seen in the target area. It was about the size of a Thunderbolt and passed 50/75 yards beneath the formation. It flew STRAIGHT AND LEVEL (No chaps it was not a [Lancaster] gone mad) at a terrific speed, leaving a streak like a vapour trail which was all white and which remained visible for a long time. The object passed so quickly that the observer could not determine it more accurately.[12]

The only conventional aircraft at the time that might fit the description was the Messerschmitt Me 163B Komet, a tail-less, rocket-powered interceptor fighter with a maximum speed of 596 mph, trailing a white exhaust. However, although the Komet first flew in 1941, it did not enter service until June 1944 and first intercepted B-17 Flying Fortress daylight bombers on 16 August that year[13] – well after the incident described. Nonetheless, it is possible that the American bomber crews saw one of these extraordinary aircraft.

During a mission to Romania in 1944 (date unspecified) to bomb oil refineries used by the Germans, a Soviet Air Force bomber experienced a shocking encounter with a highly unusual craft. Boris Surikov and his commander, Major Bajenov, were flying at an altitude of 5 kilometres over south-west Ukraine when a large, elliptical-shaped object flew towards them. 'We'd read in the newspapers about new German weapons, but we'd seen nothing like this,' said Surikov.

> What happened was that our heavy plane [probably a Tupolev Tu-2], of 14.5 tonnes, started shaking, the oil pressure rose, and when I leaned towards the window I felt a strong electrostatic charge. I was worried that the plane would burst into flames. It passed us and disappeared, but our plane was still affected: I looked at the wings, and they were covered in electrical discharges. The whole plane was fluorescent and the wings were glowing like a rainbow.

Believing the aircraft to be in real danger of catching fire, Major Bajenov gave orders to jettison the 2-tonne bomb load in south-west Ukraine instead of in Romania. The pilots mentioned nothing about the incident during their debriefing, merely 'confirming' that they had successfully bombed the refineries.

Surikov described the unknown craft as similar in some respects to the space shuttles. 'It lit up the air around it. It looked like a localized sunset, but in the centre was a strange-looking flying object ... It was larger and longer than our Buran space shuttle – I think about twice as long.'

Surikov, who years later became the Soviet chief military authority on weapons of mass destruction, asked scientists for their opinion on the phenomenon. 'I was told that one could not rule out the possibility that the electrification of the plane was due to the close proximity of a UFO with a new type of propulsion system which ionized the atmosphere,' he related.[14]

Ronald R. Claridge, a holder of the Distinguished Flying Cross, served as a wireless operator on Lancaster bombers with No. 7 Squadron, RAF, in the Second World War. On 11 August 1944, his aircraft, as master bomber, had led a raid on the oil refineries at La Pallice, France. 'We were returning to our base at Oakington [Cambridgeshire] and still flying over France, which was a hotbed for German fighters, so we were very alert,' wrote Claridge.

> I was the radio and radar operator and as such was concentrating on my 'Fishpond' screen looking for the blips of German fighters. The first I knew that anything untoward was happening, my screen went blank – I thought it was an electrical failure. I was reporting this to the skipper when he shouted over the intercom, 'What the hell is that?'

I moved into the astrodome, which gave 360-degree vision. I stood looking into the night. On our starboard side was a sight I have never forgotten. By this time our Lancaster was flying straight and level. There was a string of lights which stretched ahead and behind us for what seemed miles. The lights along our side were the largest and brightest, fading into the vast distance. We could only hear our own engine noises and there was no turbulence – only the lights.

As my night vision improved I saw a grey saucer-like object emerge as part of the lights. It is still difficult to describe its size . . . I am an artist and I painted what I saw. Our Lancaster was a large aeroplane but the only comparison I can make is that we were but a dot on a sheet of foolscap paper. We all watched this object for about three minutes. We watched it shoot away – it was just a flash of light and the vast size was gone in less than a second, without any noise or turbulence.

There was a silence among the crew, and I can only give my own reactions. I seemed to know whatever it was had been watching us. I was left with a feeling of complete calm and the feeling that I was finished with war – which I must say never left me. I was a Warrant Officer: we finished our tour after four more Operations and as far as I was concerned I finished my active service then. It was some time before I thought we had met the ultimate weapon – no one left willing to fight in future wars!

I often wonder if this encounter had any effect on our lives. Personally I believe it did. I remember that during those few minutes I felt no fear whatsoever. And why did our gunners not open fire?

When the crew returned to Oakington, it seemed that more intelligence officers than usual were present at the debriefing. 'They just took notes of our experience and did not seem at all surprised at what we reported, and we were not even debriefed about the raid,' Claridge explained. 'One thing I remember is that we were told not to discuss what we had seen, even among ourselves, and I think we respected this.'[15]

FIGHTER PLANE ATTACKS 'BALLOON'

In November 1944 the Japanese began launching 'Fugo' balloon bombs against western North America. Of the 15,000 built, 9,300 were deployed, carried across the Pacific by high-altitude winds.[16] Relatively few actually reached the US, however, and those that did caused little damage – the most potentially serious event occurring in March 1945 when a Fugo crashed into some high-tension power lines in Washington State, causing power failure over a wide area, including the plutonium-production factory at Hanford, where work had to be suspended for three days.[17] The only casualties were six people, who were killed in June 1945 when they tampered with a bomb near Lakeview, Oregon.

When numerous circular flying objects were seen in the summer of 1945 by citizens and military personnel in the vicinity of the USAAF base at Selfridge Field, Mount Clemens, near Detroit, Michigan, it was naturally assumed that the Japanese were responsible, though it later transpired that the last Fugos landed in June, and very few made it as far east as Michigan. Many American as well as Royal Canadian Air Force and Navy pilots had been involved in attacking the 33-foot-diameter balloons, with their suspended payload of five bombs, four incendiaries and a 33-pound anti-personnel bomb. Comparatively few had actually been shot down, however. So, when three or four balloon-like objects appeared directly over the airfield in July, the base commander asked for a volunteer to attack them. Jean Kisling, serving with a Free French Air Force detachment as an instructor on P-47D and P-47N Thunderbolt fighters, valiantly accepted the challenge.

'I was the only one to say yes!' Kisling told me. 'So I took off and I climbed. It was impossible to judge the distance of these things – they were very high. I climbed to well beyond the service ceiling of the P-47D – and eventually got one of them in my gunsight.' Opening fire with the P-47's wing-mounted eight .50-calibre machine guns, he was astonished at what happened next. 'The moment I fired, it suddenly shot off sideways – on edge – having at first appeared as a sphere. And it left a contrail. This was no balloon!'

On landing, Kisling was fêted like a hero. He also recalls the pain in his arms 'from decompression – having flown so high'.

A Frenchman thus became the first pilot in America, as far as I know, to attempt to shoot down an unidentified flying object. Kisling was lucky to survive. Some days later, a fighter plane – he thinks it might have been a jet – sent to intercept a similar object, exploded and crashed near Denver, Colorado, killing the pilot.[18]

'PREPARE FOR A DITCH!'

On 28 August 1945, USAAF intelligence officer Leonard Stringfield was one of twelve Fifth Air Force specialists on board a transport aircraft flying from Ie-shima to Tokyo via Iwo Jima, assigned to occupy Atsugi airdrome, near Tokyo. As the aircraft, a Curtiss C-46 Commando, approached Iwo Jima at around 10,000 feet in a sunlit sky, Stringfield was startled to see three teardrop-shaped objects from his starboard-side window:

> They were brilliantly white, like burning magnesium, and closing in on a parallel course to our C-46. Suddenly our left engine feathered, and I was later to learn that the magnetic navigation-instrument needles went wild. As the C-46 lost altitude, with oil spurting from the troubled engine, the pilot sounded an alert; crew and passengers were told to prepare for a ditch!
>
> I do not recall my thoughts or actions during the next, horrifying moments, but my last glimpse of the three bogies placed them about 20 degrees above the level of our transport. Flying in the same, tight formation, they faded into a cloud bank. Instantly our aircraft's engine revved up, and we picked up altitude and flew a steady course to land safely on Iwo Jima.[19]

The incident led to Stringfield's life-long interest in the UFO subject. I knew Len as an honest and diligent investigator, which for me lends added credibility to the case. Furthermore, many similar incidents, cited throughout this book, involve serious – and sometimes disastrous – effects on aircraft.

CRASH-LANDINGS

Periodically, the myth is revived that Nazi Germany was responsible for the unidentified phenomena or craft reported in the Second World War. As any aviation historian will confirm, it is a fact that the Germans were working on all manner of unusual aircraft – including circular-planform designs – during the last few years of the war. However, there is no reliable evidence whatsoever that they produced craft with such extraordinary performance characteristics, reported all over the world, and in such large numbers, since 1942 and earlier. Had this been the case, Germany would have won the war. Another point is that several exotic craft are said to have

crash-landed during the war. A summary of those, and two supplementary
new cases, follow.

The earliest reported event, as far as I am aware, is said to have taken
place in the spring of 1941. According to Charlotte Mann, her grandfather
Reverend William Huffman was called out one night to an aircraft crash
site about 15 miles from Cape Girardeau, Missouri. On returning, he told
the family that it was not any kind of aircraft he had ever seen; it lay
broken and scattered all around, though one large piece was still intact and
appeared to have a rounded shape with no edges or seams and a very shiny
metallic finish. Charlotte gave Leonard Stringfield more details:

> There were some police officers, plain-clothes and military men. There
> were three bodies, not human, that had been taken from the wreckage
> and lain on the ground. Grandfather said prayers over them ... they
> didn't appear to have any injuries [and] they were covered from head
> to foot in what looked like wrinkled aluminium foil ...
>
> There were several people with cameras taking pictures of every-
> thing. Two of the plain-clothes men picked up one of the little men,
> and held it under its arms. A picture was taken. That was the picture I
> later saw ... one of the military officers talked to granddad and told
> him he was not to talk about or repeat anything that had taken place,
> for security reasons, and so as not to alarm the people. [But] granddad
> returned home and told his family ... he never did talk about it after
> that.

Huffman later acquired a copy of the photo of the alien being, which
Charlotte saw. It showed a being about 4 feet tall with a large head and
long arms. 'He was thin and no bone structure was apparent; kind of soft-
looking. He had no hair on his head or body, with large, oval, slightly
slanted eyes, but not like an oriental from left to right, more up and down.
He had no ears at all and no nose like ours. There appeared to be only a
couple of small holes ... His mouth was as if you had just cut a small
straight line where it should have been ...'

If this event occurred, one is left wondering why no more witnesses
have come forward. Were they all intimidated?

According to Dr James Harder, a former professor of civil engineering,
an unusual craft may have been recovered from the Sonoran Desert in
Mexico late in 1941. The recovery was effected by a team from the US
Office of Naval Intelligence (ONI). One member of the team brought back
some photos showing the craft and small bodies. Dr Harder told me that
he had interviewed a relative of the witness who, though only ten years old

or so at the time, managed to see the photos. The dead bodies looked 'spindly' she said, and were about 3.5 feet tall.

Another event is reported to have occurred at Exelgroud, near Gdynia, north of Gdańsk, on the Baltic coast of Poland, on 18 July 1943. Daniel Léger, conscripted by the Germans for work at a labour camp in Exelgroud, came across a highly unusual aircraft, partially embedded in sand dunes. Shaped like a 'colonial hat', it was estimated to be about 6 metres in diameter. Several square portholes with rounded edges were spaced on the upper section. No insignia, seams, weldings or connections were apparent. Beside it was a woman – presumably the pilot – trying to free the craft from the sand. She seemed to sense Léger's presence.

Dressed in a tight-fitting, one-piece dark brown suit, she appeared to be about 1.75 metres tall, with long blonde hair, a slim waist and broad hips. Léger assumed she was a German Air Force pilot, since a number of Luftwaffe pilots were based in Exelgroud at that time. Her features were regular, with white skin and slightly slanted, Asian-like eyes. She addressed Léger in an odd language he could not understand.

Shortly afterwards, when the sand had been cleared, the aviatrix boarded her craft. A slight rumbling sound could be heard and two rings on the craft began to rotate, one clockwise and the other anti-clockwise. A dark stripe separating the rings became luminous and began to vibrate, at which point the craft rose from the ground slowly, then suddenly accelerated at a speed far higher than any German aircraft with which Léger was familiar. The witness is rated highly by Jean Sider, one of France's leading researchers.[20]

In the spring of 1944, it is claimed that a UFO came down at Kaneohe Naval Air Station on the island of Oahu, Hawaii. The claimant, a young construction engineer with Headquarters Company 112, US Navy Sea Bees, reported seeing a grounded, silver object with a smoothly 'pock-marked' surface, surmounted with 'a transparent dome containing a gold-coloured device which spun at various speeds'. The claimant was interrogated by federal investigators who asked specific questions in a way that indicated knowledge of a previous event.[21]

In August 1945, nearly five weeks after the world's first atom bomb was detonated at the Trinity site in New Mexico's Jornada del Muerto Desert on 16 July 1945, two young boys, José Padilla and Reme Baca, were doing various chores on the Padilla Ranch at San Antonito, near San Antonio, New Mexico, when they saw a brilliant light, accompanied by a crunching sound. Eventually, they came upon a long gouge in the earth, at the end of which lay a dull grey avocado-shaped craft, with a protuberance towards one end, which could be seen through the smoke from its burning wreckage. Scattered among the debris were pieces of shiny tin-foil-like metal. A piece that had become lodged under a rock unfolded itself instantly. It was kept at the ranch home for a number of years.

Through a gash in the side of the craft came signs of movement. Strange humanoid creatures were moving around in quick, darting movements, making squeaking sounds.

It was getting late, so the boys headed back on their horses to the ranch home to tell Faustino Padilla what had happened. He reacted somewhat casually, saying that he and others would check it out in a day or two – an odd reaction to an air crash and injured occupants (wherever they came from). Two days later Padilla Sr, accompanied by State Policeman Eddie Apodaca, headed for the crash site in two vehicles, directed by the boys. As the terrain became increasingly rough, the group hiked the rest of the way. At first, nothing could be seen, as the craft had been covered with dirt and debris. The creatures had gone, and the huge debris field had been largely cleared and raked over, although the craft remained where it had come to rest. Evidently the Army had learned of the incident.

A Sergeant Avila turned up at the ranch home later and explained that an 'experimental balloon' had come down on the Padilla property and they needed to bring in some equipment to remove it. A crane and low-boy trailer were used in the recovery operation, which lasted several days. Periodically the boys watched what was going on from a secluded position. One night, when the craft was, surprisingly, unguarded, José Padilla clambered on to the low-boy, went inside the craft and prised a 'souvenir' from what appeared to be a bulkhead.

In Seattle, I carefully examined and photographed the souvenir. It appears decidedly terrestrial, a point conceded by the witnesses. Looking like a bracket of some kind, it is 12 inches long, weighs 15 ounces and contains a number of holes for fasteners of some kind. A section cut off for analysis, as well as acid tests, reveal the metal to be 200-series aluminium, or similar. A smaller, semi-circular piece, believed by the witnesses to have come from the craft, was found years later at the ranch entrance. Tests indicate 330/380-series aluminium (or similar).[22]

*

The proliferation of sightings in the Second World War was not coincidental. I have no doubts that the reason for this lay in the inauguration of the nuclear age on Earth, necessitating increased surveillance and strategic reconnaissance by advanced intelligences. In my opinion, it is probable that some of these intelligences reside on Earth or use it as a base, which would explain their concern for the welfare of the planet, per se. I believe that these intelligences have had space-travel capability for millennia – and I have no doubt that species of quite different extraterrestrial origins are also coming here.

In a report by the US Air Force's second official UFO investigation, Project Grudge, in 1949, intelligence specialists speculated on the correlation between the dawn of the nuclear age and the increase in visits:

'Such a civilization might observe that on Earth we now have atomic bombs and are fast developing rockets. In view of the past history of mankind they should be alarmed. We should, therefore, expect at this time above all to behold such visitations . . .'[23]

REFERENCES

1. Collins, Paul T., 'The UFOs of 1942', *Exploring the Unknown*, No. 48, September 1968.
2. Letter published in *Air & Space* (Smithsonian), February/March 1990, p. 8.
3. Chalker, Bill, 'Australian A.F. UFO Report Files', *The APRO Bulletin*, Vol. 30, No. 10, 1982, pp. 6–7.
4. The National Archives, ref: AIR 14/2076, 'A Note on Recent Enemy Pyrotechnic Activity over Germany'.
5. *Just Cause*, PO Box 218, Coventry, CT 06238, No. 32, June 1992.
6. British UFO Research Association (BUFORA) files, cited by Clarke and Roberts in *UFO Magazine* (UK), January 2003, p. 9.
7. The National Archives, AIR 40, 'Annex[e] to Intelligence Report Mission Schweinfurt, 16 October 1943'.
8. Smith, Warren, *UFO Trek*, Zebra Books, New York, 1976, p. 220.
9. Vallée, Jacques, *Forbidden Science: Journals 1957–1969*, North Atlantic Books, Berkeley, California, 1992, p. 309.
10. Blum, Ralph with Blum, Judy, *Beyond Earth: Man's Contact with UFOs*, Corgi Books, London, 1974, p. 67.
11. Cammell, Gordon W., 'Memories of UFO Sightings Fresh After 50-plus Years', *UFO Magazine* (US), Vol. 12, No. 1, January/February 1997, p. 17.
12. The National Archives, AIR 14/2076, 'BANG ON, 115 Squadron Gen. News Sheet, Number 1, December 31st 1943'.
13. Mason, Frances K., *The Illustrated Encyclopedia of Major Aircraft of World War II*, Aerospace/Temple Press, Feltham, Middlesex, 1983, p. 108.

14. Interview with General-Major Boris Surikov by Lawrence Moore and Livia Russell, Moscow, February 1994. Part of this interview was shown in *Network First: UFO*, produced, written and directed by Lawrence Moore for Central Productions, 1994.
15. Letters from Ronald R. Claridge, DFC, AEA, to Alex Turner, 23 September/8 October 2003, given to the author.
16. Mikesh, Robert C., *Japan's World War II Balloon Bomb Attacks on North America*, Smithsonian Institution Press, Washington, DC, 1997.
17. Covington, John, 'Fugos: Japanese Balloon Bombs of WWII'. www.seanet.com/-johnco/fugo.htm
18. Personal interviews, Paris, 2000, 2004 and 2005.
19. Stringfield, Leonard, *Situation Red, The UFO Siege*, Doubleday, New York, 1977, pp. 9–10.
20. Good, Timothy, *Alien Base: Earth's Encounters with Extraterrestrials*, Century, London, 1998.
21. Worley, Don, 'UFO Occupants: The Heart of the Enigma'. *Official UFO*, Vol. I, No. 2, November 1976, pp. 15, 46.
22. Personal interviews, Seattle, 6/7 June 2004, and numerous subsequent communications with both witnesses.
23. Valley, Dr G.E., 'Some Considerations Affecting the Interpretation of Reports of Unidentified Flying Objects', Appendix D, *Unidentified Flying Objects: Project 'Grudge'*, Air Materiel Command, Intelligence Department, Headquarters, Wright-Patterson Air Force Base, Dayton, Ohio, August 1949. Originally classified Secret.

OCS 21347-86

~~SECRET~~

February 26, 1942

MEMORANDUM FOR THE PRESIDENT:

The following is the information we have from GHQ at this moment regarding the air alarm over Los Angeles of yesterday morning:

"From details available at this hour:

"1. Unidentified airplanes, other than American Army or Navy planes, were probably over Los Angeles, and were fired on by elements of the 37th CA Brigade (AA) between 3:12 and 4:15 AM. These units expanded 1430 rounds of ammunition.

"2. As many as fifteen airplanes may have been involved, flying at various speeds from what is officially reported as being 'very slow' to as much as 200 MPH and at elevations from 9000 to 18000 feet.

"3. No bombs were dropped.

"4. No casualties among our troops.

"5. No planes were shot down.

"6. No American Army or Navy planes were in action.

"Investigation continuing. It seems reasonable to conclude that if unidentified airplanes were involved they may have been from commercial sources, operated by enemy agents for purposes of spreading alarm, disclosing location of antiaircraft positions, and slowing production through blackout. Such conclusion is supported by varying speed of operation and the fact that no bombs were dropped."

DECLASSIFIED
E.O. 11652, Sec. 3(E) and 5(D) or (E)
OSD letter, May 3, 1972
By ___ NARS Date 4-9-74

(Sgd) G. C. MARSHALL

Chief of Staff.

~~SECRET~~

akn

A previously secret memorandum from General George C. Marshall to President Roosevelt, giving details of the Los Angeles air alarm in February 1942.

(The National Archives, Washington)

From: R.A.F. Station, SYERSTON.

To: Headquarters, No. 5 Group.
        (Attention Major Mullock, M.C., F.L.O.)

Date: 2nd December, 1942.

Ref: Syn/414/A/Int.

S E C R E T

3B.

Report by the Crew of 61 Sqdn. a/c 'J', Captain W/O Lever,
of object seen during raid on TURIN, night of
November 28/29th, 1942.

The object referred to above was seen by the entire crew
of the above aircraft. They believe it to have been 200-300 feet
in length and its width is estimated at 1/5th or 1/6th of its
length. The speed was estimated at 500 m.p.h., and it had four
pairs of red lights spaced at equal distances along its body.
These lights did not appear in any way like exhaust flames; no
trace was seen. The object kept a level course.

The crew saw the object twice during the raid, and brief
details are given below:-
    (i)   After bombing, time 2240 hours, a/c height 11,000
            feet. The aircraft at this time was some 10/15 miles
            South-West of Turin travelling in a north-westerly
            direction. The object was travelling South-East at
            the same height or slightly below the aircraft.
    (ii)   After bombing, time 2245 hours, a/c height 14,000
            feet. The aircraft was approaching the Alps when
            the object was seen again travelling West-South-West
            up a valley in the Alps below the level of the peaks.
            The lights appeared to go out and the object
            disappeared from view.

The Captain of the aircraft also reports that he has seen a
similar object about three months ago North of Amsterdam. In this
instance it appeared to be on the ground and later travelling at
high speed at a lower level than the heights given above along
the coast for about two seconds; the lights then went out for the
same period of time and came on again, and the object was still
seen to be travelling in the same direction.

J.R. .... F/Lt
for Group Captain Commanding,
    R.A.F. Station, SYERSTON

A previously secret report on a sighting by the crew of a Royal Air Force Lancaster
bomber during a raid on Turin in November 1942, and an earlier sighting by the
Captain. (*The National Archives, London*)

Foo-Fighters

Lt. Donald Meiers of Chicago was flying a Beaufighter on an intruder mission over Germany.' He was braced to meet Nazi planes or anti-aircraft. Suddenly an eerie light split the darkness around his plane. Looking up from his instrument panel, the horrified lieutenant saw two red balls of fire cruising alongside his wingtips. Thinking he had run into a secret anti-aircraft weapon, Meiers tensed and waited for a German on the ground to push a button and blow him up. But the balls merely kept pace with him for a while and then disappeared.

That was more than a month ago, one of the first times Allied fighters encountered what they now call "foo-fighters."* In addition to the wingtip balls, pilots have reported two other types. One is a group of three similar balls which fly in front of their planes, the other a group of about fifteen which appear some distance away and flicker on and off. Apparently controlled by radio, the foo-fighters keep

*The name comes from the "Smokey Stover" comic strip.

formation with the planes, even when they dive, climb, or take violent evasive action. "But they don't explode or attack us," Meiers said last week. "They just seem to follow us like will-o'-the-wisps."

Probably related to the silvery balls seen by daylight pilots (NEWSWEEK, Dec. 25, 1944), the foo-fighters so far apparently baffle intelligence officers. Possibly they are the results of a new anti-radar device which the Germans have developed. On the other hand, they may be the exhaust trails of a smaller model of the radio-controlled Messerschmitt-163, a rocket-propelled flying wing.

Foo-Fighter

If it was not a hoax or an optical illusion, it was certainly the most puzzling secret weapon that Allied fighters have yet encountered. Last week U.S. night fighter pilots based in France told a strange story of balls of fire which for more than a month have been following their planes at night over Germany.* No one seemed to know what, if anything, the fireballs were supposed to accomplish. Pilots, guessing that it was a new psychological weapon, named it the "foo-fighter."

Their descriptions' of the apparition varied, but they agreed that the mysterious flares stuck close to their planes and appeared to follow them at high speed for miles. One pilot said that a foo-fighter, appearing as red balls off his wing tips, stuck with him until he dove at 360 miles an hour; then the balls zoomed up into the sky.

Skeptical scientists, baffled by the whole affair, were inclined to dismiss the fireballs as an illusion, perhaps an afterimage of light which remained in the pilots' eyes after they had been dazzled by flak bursts.

But front-line correspondents and armchair experts had a Buck Rogers field day. They solemnly guessed: 1) that the balls of fire were radio-controlled (an obvious absurdity, since they could not be synchronized with a plane's movements by remote control); 2) that they were created by "electrical induction of some sort"; 3) that they were attracted to a plane by magnetism.

The correspondents further guessed that foo-fighters were intended: 1) to dazzle pilots; 2) to serve as aiming points for antiaircraft gunners; 3) to interfere with a plane's radar; 4) to cut a plane's ignition, thus stop its engine in midair.

Some scientists suggested another possibility: that the fireballs were nothing more than St. Elmo's Fire, a reddish, brush-like discharge of atmospheric electricity which has often been seen near the tips of church steeples, ships' masts and yardarms. It often appears at a plane's wing tips.

* Last month pilots reported that they had seen mysterious floating silvery balls, apparently another "secret weapon," in daylight flights over Germany.

TIME, JANUARY 15   71

On the left is part of an article in *Newsweek*, 15 January 1945, and, right, an article from *Time* of the same date, relating to the mysterious 'foo-fighters' encountered by Allied and Axis aircrews in Europe and other theatres of operation around the world during the Second World War.

3. GHOST ROCKETS

In the summer of 1946 an extraordinary wave of sightings of what became known as 'ghost rockets' proliferated in Denmark, Finland, Norway and Sweden, followed by reports from Portugal, Morocco, Italy, Greece and India.[1] There were also sporadic reports from other countries, including the United States.

So called because they often appeared like rocket-shaped craft with fiery trails, the ghost rockets (or 'spook bombs') sometimes performed fantastic manoeuvres, crossing the sky at tremendous velocity, diving and climbing, though at other times proceeding in a leisurely manner. An early 1947 US War Department intelligence review, classified Secret at the time, summarizes the observations:

> The two most common descriptions of the missiles were 'a ball of fire with a tail' and 'a shiny cigar-shaped object'. The reported direction of flight covered all points of the compass, with a northerly direction being slightly predominant. Variations in altitude ranged from treetop height to 160,000 feet, the higher altitudes almost exclusively being reported from Finland. Speeds reported were from 65 mph to 'lightning fast', with the majority described as having great or very great speed. The missiles generally have been described in horizontal flight; a few have been reported as diving into the ground or into lakes, or exploding in the air. In no case have fragments been found other than bits of material described as 'non-metallic slag' . . .
>
> In September and October, flying objects were reported over widely separate points in Europe and Africa, including Belgium, Greece, Italy, Morocco, and Austria. In the main, these reports have not been confirmed . . .[2]

According to a memorandum for Commanding General Carl ('Tooey') Spaatz, US Army Air Forces, dated 19 July 1946, classified secret, the first sighting was reported to have occurred over Finland on 13 May. A 'rocket' was observed travelling at supersonic speed in a south-westerly direction over Helsinki at an altitude of 1,000 feet, emitting a magnesium-like light and a trail of smoke.

An overwhelming majority of reports came from Sweden. The memorandum, written by Major General George C. McDonald, Assistant Chief, US Air Staff, for Intelligence, lists numerous reports of what are sometimes referred to as 'V-bombs'. The prevailing explanation was that the objects were rockets based on captured German V-weapons (the V-1 pulse-jet flying bomb and the V-2 (actually called the A-4) rocket).

Approximately ten apparently patternless V-bomb sightings have been reported between 23 May and 8 June, the missiles travelling from northeast to southwest over southern Sweden. These missiles were reported as being cigar-shaped, about the size of a small airplane. They were flying at an altitude of 100 to 1,000 meters and were accompanied by a continuous ball of fire with intermittent flashes of fire about every ten seconds. Swedish astronomers dismiss the meteor theory but the Swedish Army is at a loss to account for them . . .

The memorandum cites a State Department cable of 12 July 1946:

On Tuesday afternoon, 9 July, a member of the Legation saw a rocket-like missile. It seemed to be falling rapidly toward the Earth and no sound of explosion was heard. On the same afternoon another landed on the beach near Stockholm. No damage was caused . . . military authorities are now studying fragments. According to a local scientist, the first inspection indicated that the fragments contained an organic substance which looked like carbide . . .

If the missiles are of Russian origin, as believed generally . . . their purpose might be of a political nature to intimidate the Swedes in connection with Russian pressure on Sweden for current loan negotiations or possibly to offset the supposed increase in US military prestige in Sweden . . . Due to the lack of conclusive evidence and the variety of reports, it is difficult at this time to reach any definite conclusion as to the origin of these reported missiles.[3]

General McDonald speculated that the Russians may have been launching rockets from sites in Estonia or Latvia, and that it was conceivable they intended to establish an area similar to Peenemünde, the German missile complex on the Baltic Sea where the V-weapons were tested – and later used against Britain in the Second World War – some of which had come down in Sweden.

Although the Americans were well ahead in the race to acquire German V-weapon technology, as a result of the defection of Wernher von Braun and most of his top associates to the US-held western zone of Germany in June 1945, the Russians eventually succeeded in recruiting a number of

German scientists and technicians, and set up a rocket research institute in Bleichenrode, not far from the original A-4 rocket underground production centre in Mittelwerke. Helmut Gröttrup, a top physicist and a leading expert on the V-2's flight-control system, headed a team of hundreds, whose main job was to produce a full set of drawings for the V-2 and restart production.

'As flightworthy V-2 missiles started rolling off the restored production line in 1946,' reports aerospace journalist Anatoly Zak, 'the Soviet government made a secret decision, signed by Josef Stalin on May 13, to transfer all ballistic missile work, along with the German rocket experts, to Russia by year's end.' The production team was transferred in October 1946, and the launch site was established at Kapustin Yar, near the border with Kazakhstan, in August 1947.[4] Further evidence will be adduced later to prove that Russia could not have been responsible for the ghost rockets of 1946.

On 18 July 1946, two British intelligence officers were sent to Stockholm to liaise with their counterparts in the Swedish Government. One was from the Air Ministry (Squadron Leader Heath) and the other (Major Malone) from MI10(a), a branch of the Directorate of Military Intelligence which, in part, specialized in ordnance and rocketry. The Swedes stressed the need for maximum secrecy over the meetings.[5] They seemed particularly anxious to prevent the Americans knowing of their liaison with the British. 'I have been asked by the Swedish Air Staff to take all possible measures to prevent the Americans finding out about Swedish full co-operation with us in investigating mysterious missiles,' a telegram from the British air attaché in Stockholm reveals.[6]

The V-weapons hypothesis continued to hold sway in the intelligence community. A top-secret memorandum to President Truman, dated 1 August 1946 and sent on behalf of General Hoyt S. Vandenberg, USAAF, Director of Central Intelligence, mentions that the Swedish and Norwegian Governments had imposed a news blackout with respect to the subject, and adds that from the information then available, the 'missiles' were an advanced type of V-1 flying bomb, deliberately launched by the Soviets to intimidate Sweden, Norway, Britain and the United States with a display of superior weaponry.[7]

In the United States, a ghost rocket was seen on 1 August by Captain Jack Puckett, a flying safety officer based at the headquarters of Tactical Air Command, 300th Base Unit, Langley Field, Virginia. Puckett was making a scheduled flight from Langley Field to MacDill Field, Tampa, Florida, when the incident occurred:

At approximately 6 p.m., while flying a C-47 at 4000 feet northeast of
Tampa, I observed what I thought to be a shooting star to the southeast
over the Atlantic Ocean. My co-pilot, Lt. Henry F. Glass and my
engineer both observed this object at the same time.

This object continued toward us on a collision course at our exact
altitude. At about 1000 yards it veered to cross our path. We observed
it to be a long, cylindrical shape approximately twice the size of a B-
29, with luminous portholes.

Puckett stated that the object seemed to be rocket propelled, trailing a
stream of 'fire' about one-half its own length. The sighting lasted between
two-and-a-half and three minutes.[8]

On 11 August, three of the missiles were said to have exploded in
central Sweden. Another passed directly over Stockholm and crashed north
of the city. First reports from army investigators indicated that they had
found nothing. A Swedish Air Force lieutenant estimated the missile's body
length at about 20 metres (65 feet), 'shaped like a cigar, with a green
foremost projecting part and white sides. He said it moved at exceptionally
low altitude with terrific speed.'[9]

On an undisclosed date during this period, a Swedish astronomer
studying some clouds through binoculars suddenly caught sight of a
luminous, fast-moving 'projectile'.

I first believed it to be an airplane, but soon I noticed it was travelling
much too fast for that, and within ten seconds I got a full view of the
projectile. I managed to get a clear view of the bomb's body and
estimate that it was at least 90 feet long. The body was torpedo-shaped
and shining like metal. No sound could be heard, although the bomb
was only two kilometres away. At the explosion, a terrific light flashed
up that for a moment completely blinded me. No fire, smoke or sparks
were discernible.[10]

This report, sent to the Swedish General Staff, leaves no doubt that
many of these objects were 'projectiles' of some sort, but whose? And why?
Indeed, a three-page Top Secret report from the US Naval Attaché in Paris,
dated 13 August, is confidently headed: 'Report on Guided Missiles sent
from Soviet Controlled Territories over Scandinavian Territories'. The
evaluation is quite specific:

A good number of these projectiles are of the V-1 type in the form of
a torpedo with two small wings (of a spread of from 2.50 to three
meters) and a system of jet propulsion (which allows the escape every
two seconds of a jet of flame of about thirty meters often stated to be

of a blue-green color. One witness states that the anterior portion
shines like fire which is undoubtedly the opening of the pulse-reactor
shutters) ... there exists undoubtedly one or more other types of
machines characterized by:

A supersonic speed (a non-official evaluation of the headquarters
of the Finnish Air Force places this at 2800 kilometers per hour) ...
Although certain descriptions bring to mind the V-2 (trailings, whist-
lings, meteor appearance), one report mentions 'an engine resembling
a huge cigar'. There is no reason to believe a complete identification
(assimilation complete) with the classic German V-2 ...

In conclusion it would now seem possible to state that Sweden
and Finland have been flown over by jet-propelled projectiles whose
general itineraries are fairly well known and whose range must clearly
surpass those of the classic V-1 or V-2 ...[11]

COLLISION COURSE

On 13 August 1946, newspapers in Stockholm reported an aerial collision
with one of the missiles. The following is extracted from the *Washington
Post*:

Three fliers were killed when a Swedish military reconnaissance plane
collided head-on with a rocket bomb yesterday [12 August]. The
newspaper *Aftonbladet* said the reconnaissance plane crashed near
Vaggeryd in southern Sweden. Shortly after the plane's pilot spotted
the bomb, it said, radio contact was broken and the listening post
'heard a crash', the newspaper, quoting investigators, reported. The
report, published by other afternoon papers, was not confirmed.[12]

There were conflicting accounts of what happened. According to one
newspaper, the aircraft – a twin-engined Saab B18 bomber on a navigation
exercise flight – was seen circling by several witnesses over Valdshult at
1,000 metres for 15 minutes (later refuted – it was another plane), before
crashing almost vertically to the ground. No radio transmissions were
received from the plane, apparently.[13] A commission to investigate the
accident arrived the next day.

The Valdshult accident remains listed in the Royal Swedish Air Force
statistics as unexplained. Sweden's leading UFO research group, AFU, have
studied the official files. Major C.F. Westrell, an explosives expert, was
emphatic that no explosion took place in the air. Another member of the
commission stated that the pilot, Sergeant Segerhorn, had no previous

experience in this particular aircraft type in 'blind instrument flying' (which the pilot had apparently been engaged in at the time).[14]

The Saab company built 243 B18s, of which ten were involved in fatal accidents in 1946 alone: up to and including the crash on 12 August, thirty-four crew members had been killed. Although the Swedish Air Force attributed the main cause of these accidents to 'new aircraft types and insufficient training',[15] I am mindful of the fact that many such accidents have been reported during waves of UFO sightings – as we shall learn.

Government authorities prepared a nationwide 'rocket-hunting' programme and alerted all military units, air bases and radar stations to be on the lookout for the cigar-shaped 'ghost bombs'.[16]

On the same day as the B18 crash, a couple boating on a lake in central Sweden were nearly hit by a 'diving bomb' which burst into many parts and disappeared beneath the water. And near Göteborg, a group of boy scouts saw a 'flying missile turn 35 degrees and then return to its original course'.[17]

Two days later, on 14 August, the two-man crew of a B18 reported a close encounter with one of the missiles. The following is translated from the first part of an official report to the Air Defence Department, Stockholm, by Lieutenant 'I':

I was the pilot, on a navigational training flight with a B18A, at an altitude of 100 m, on the route F1 [Swedish Air Force base at Västerås] – Malingsbo (18 km NW of Skinnskatteberg) – Krylbo – F1. Sergeant M. was the [back-seat] signaller/observer [and wireless operator].

On the route Malingsbo–Krylbo we noticed, after about 2 minutes, an aircraft-shaped object, on the left front, about 60 degrees, on a south-easterly course, slightly above the horizon. I estimated the altitude over terrain of the object to be about 250 m. My own altitude was about 200 m above the ground. The distance to the object was about 2000 m. Weather conditions were as follows: cloud altitude, about 800 m; amount of clouds, 6–8/10; horizontal visibility, 30–40 km.

With the latest newspaper reports, regarding overflights of Swedish territory by the above-mentioned missiles, on my mind, I immediately became suspicious. Furthermore I could not identify the object as any Swedish aeroplane. Therefore, I decided to keep eye contact with the object and attempt to overtake it at a suitable opportunity. After about 10 seconds (I had to look down at the instruments to switch over to maximum cruising speed) the object was gone.

I suspected it had disappeared under the horizon, therefore I reduced our own cruising altitude. It appeared that both the object and I had come over a relatively low countryside, and we had both reduced the cruising altitude thus maintaining a constant altitude above the ground.

After about 20 seconds my [back-seat] observer Sergeant M. discovered the object again, 30 degrees to our right. We had, meanwhile, kept our own course all the time. Immediately, I made a [right] turn ending up on a parallel course with the object, and switched to maximum speed.

The shortest distance between us was about 1000 m. It immediately appeared that I would not be able to keep pace with the object, whose speed I estimated to be at least 600–700 km/h. After about 2 minutes the object had vanished in a south-easterly direction. A storm with heavy rain and a cloud height of 100–300 m lay straight ahead of the object's course, and the object disappeared into it.

The object kept a constant cruising altitude of 250 m. Thus (on the whole) it followed the topography of the ground. Speed was considerably higher than the speed of a plane ... at least 600–700 km/h. Our own speed [at the time] 380 km/h. Appearance of the object: reminding me of the fuselage of a B18. No wings, [tail-fin] or protruding parts visible at observation distance. Colour, dark. The observation was made at 10:02 ...

No smoke or exhaust was observed. At the time of the sighting, Lieutenant I. was the head of a B18 division at the F1 wing. He later became head of the Air Force's experimental station, working on flight tests of new Swedish aircraft and missiles. In telephone interviews in 1986 with leading researcher Clas Svahn, the pilot confirmed the accuracy of his report and added that he had been summoned to Stockholm by the Air Director to give an oral statement.

'What I saw could have been a disc seen from the side, or a cigar,' the pilot explained to Svahn. 'It was close enough for me to be able to judge whether it was a conventional aircraft or not. The object was torpedo-shaped. It was pointed both at the front end and at the stern – like a big and fat cigar [see plate section]. There were no contours or nuances of colour. It was dark grayish.'[18]

The following extracts from a lengthy top-secret intelligence report by the US Naval Attaché in Stockholm on 16 August (p. 50) reveal the increasing frustration in military circles:

To date no U.S. military or naval personnel in Sweden have seen any fragments, photographs, radar tracks, points of impact, or other evidence of any kind to prove that guided missiles have actually been seen over Swedish territory . . .

Although sightings of brilliant light phenomena over Stockholm on 11 August created a great furore in the Swedish press and considerable concern among the Swedish public, the Swedish Air Force has not called back its officers from their summer leave, and the Swedish aircraft warning net has not been mobilized to spot reported missiles. Considering the fact that hundreds of reports from all over the country have described cigar-shaped missiles with fiery tails at altitudes low enough for interception by Swedish jet-propelled aircraft, this apparent unconcern . . . is peculiar.[19]

FURTHER CENSORSHIP

On the same date, a Top Secret US War Department message reveals that the Americans were aware of the presence in Stockholm of the British intelligence officers Heath and Malone, though they seem to have accepted that the purpose of the visit was not specifically connected with the ghost rockets. However, the officers 'were told to investigate reports of missiles as an additional duty. They were able to discover nothing except what had already been published in the press.'[20]

By 22 August, another top-secret cable referred to Heath and Malone as 'guided missile experts sent to Sweden by Air Ministry . . . Intelligence Section Air Ministry reports that a news leak has occurred regarding request of Sweden for radar equipment and also the sending of guided missile technicians to Sweden . . . Further that although Swedes had requested radar installation and technicians they have now withdrawn request and Air Ministry will send no personnel to Sweden on subject . . .'[21]

In fact, both Britain and America sent experts. Lieutenant General James H. Doolittle, a USAAF expert with specialized knowledge of long-distance bombing techniques, arrived in Stockholm together with David Sarnoff, an intelligence specialist in aerial warfare. The two men were consulted by Colonel C.R. Kempf, Chief of the Swedish Defence Staff. Sarnoff was later quoted as saying that the objects reported were neither mythological nor meteorological but were 'real missiles'.[22]

By this time, further censorship had been imposed – in Norway. On 31 August 1946, the London *Daily Telegraph* reported that:

The discussion of the flight of rockets over Scandinavia has been dropped in the Norwegian newspapers since Wednesday. On that day the Norwegian General Staff issued a memorandum to the press asking it not to make any mention of the appearance of rockets over Norwegian territory but to pass on all reports to the Intelligence Department of the High Command.

Military security and political nervousness appear to be responsible, in equal proportions, for this measure. In Sweden the ban is limited to any mention of where the rockets have been seen to land or explode.

Censorship was justified. Firstly, it was an established practice during the V-1 and V-2 bombardments of the London area in the Second World War not to reveal publicly where the missiles had fallen, so that the enemy would remain in ignorance of the degree of accuracy of the targeting. Secondly, the ghost rockets were causing considerable public concern, if not panic, and because the authorities had failed to come up with a plausible explanation for the missiles, they needed to play down the situation.

MILITARY AND SCIENTIFIC INTELLIGENCE

The notion that the Soviets were responsible continued to prevail. In a top-secret memorandum to President Truman on 22 August, for instance, General Vandenberg, Director of Central Intelligence, reported that the Soviets had reactivated Peenemünde, and that the ghost-rocket reports most probably could be attributed to test flights.[23]

On 23 August it was reported that British radar experts, having returned from Sweden, had 'submitted secret reports to the British Government on the origin of the rockets'.[24] One of the scientists to examine the reports was Professor R.V. Jones, Director of Intelligence on Britain's Air Staff at the time, as well as scientific adviser to Section IV of MI6, the Secret Intelligence Service. He was ideally qualified, having also been in charge of intelligence against the V-1 and V-2 missiles.

Jones was understandably dismissive of a Soviet origin. 'The Russians were supposedly cruising their flying bombs at more than twice the range that the Germans had achieved,' he wrote, 'and it was unlikely that they were so advanced technologically as to achieve a substantially greater reliability at 200 miles than the Germans had reached at 100 miles.'[25]

The Americans continued to suspect that they were 'out of the loop' as far as British and Swedish intelligence assessments were concerned. A top-secret communiqué on 1 October from the US Military Attaché in London to Washington (p. 51) reveals that 'Military and Naval Attaché Sweden as well as some MA [military attaché] Staff feel British may not have given us all available information on reported rockets over Scandinavia . . .'[26]

On 10 October, the Swedish military authorities announced that their four-month investigation had failed to ascertain the origin or nature of the ghost rockets. A special communiqué declared that 80 per cent of 1,000 reports could be attributed to 'celestial phenomena'. The V-type weapon theory was dismissed.[27] 'But,' added the communiqué, 'in some cases clear, unambiguous observations have been made which cannot be explained as natural phenomena, Swedish aircraft, or imagination on the part of the observer. Echo, radio and other equipment registered readings, but gave no clue as to the nature of the objects.' Fragments found at crash sites turned out to be 'ordinary slag'.[28]

In February 1947, a Top Secret message from the US Naval Attaché in London to the Chief of Naval Intelligence reported that the British Air Ministry had been given 'bits of metal' by the Swedish Air Force 'which had been subjected to high temperatures, and which the Swedes thought might possibly have been part of a guided missile'. However, tests revealed that 'they in themselves did not afford sufficient evidence to show they were part of a guided missile'.[29]

The pieces had been analyzed at the Royal Aircraft Establishment, Farnborough, and although scientists initially reported that one of the fragments contained over 98 per cent of an unknown element, Professor R.V. Jones pointed out that the material had not been tested for carbon. 'Carbon would not have shown up in any of the standard tests, but one had only to look at the material,' claimed Jones, 'to see that it was a lump of coke.'[30]

Had any anomalous elements or materials been found in the fragments, however, such a discovery would immediately have been shrouded in layers of secrecy, protected by a cover story – the sort of cover story provided by Professor Jones, for instance.

*

Sightings of the 'ghost rockets' continued to be reported, though sporadically. By the autumn of 1947, it is probable that a few sightings – in Scandinavia and the Soviet Union at least – related to Soviet activity, since the Russians really were test-launching V-2 rockets then (from Kapustin Yar) and, later, an improved version called the G-1 (also designated G-10), with a longer range than the V-2.[31] The Soviets also did many flight tests of V-1-type pulse-jets.

Is there a remote possibility that the Russians *were* actually responsible for the ghost rockets? Bill Gunston, one of the world's leading experts, thinks not. 'In my opinion,' he told me, 'the Russians were the principal pioneers of rockets used as a means of boosting the flight performance of aircraft. On the other hand, at the end of the Second World War they were (like everyone else) light years behind Von Braun and his A-4 and A-10 programmes. I know of no major Russian programme involving test launches of rocket vehicles in the years immediately following 1945, apart from German-made A-4s and Russian derivatives, all of which had prominent tails but no wings.'[32]

Furthermore, a ghost rocket was encountered in the United States two years after the Scandinavian wave. In the early hours of 25 July 1948, Captain Clarence Chiles and his co-pilot John Whitted, flying an Eastern Airlines DC-3 over Alabama, were buzzed by an object on a collision course. 'It flashed down toward us and we veered to the left,' said Chiles, 'and passed us about 700 feet to our right and above us. Then, as if the pilot had seen us and wanted to avoid us, it pulled up with a tremendous burst of flame from the rear and zoomed into the clouds, its prop wash or jet wash rocking our DC-3.'

The pilots described the object as 'a wingless aircraft, 100 feet long, cigar-shaped and about twice the diameter of a B-29 with no protruding surfaces ... From the side of the craft came an intense, fairly dark blue glow that ran the entire length of the fuselage.' Windows or openings appeared along its side (see p. 52). Air Force intelligence investigators found that the only other aircraft in the vicinity was a C-47 transport.[33]

Whatever their origin, there is no doubt that, in military intelligence circles at least, alarm bells were ringing.

In 1947, Professor Paul Santorini, Greece's leading physicist, was supplied by the Greek Army with a team of engineers to investigate what were believed to be Russian missiles flying over Greece.[34] Santorini, who studied with Albert Einstein at Zurich University, had developed the first proximity fuze to explode the Hiroshima atomic bomb at a predetermined height, and designed a guidance system which was later used on US Nike missiles.[35] In 1967, three years after retiring, he gave a lecture to the Greek Astronautical Society, broadcast on Athens Radio, during which he guardedly disclosed the results of the Greek investigation into the ghost rockets: 'We soon established they were not missiles. But before we could do any more, the Army, after conferring with foreign officials, ordered the investigations stopped. Foreign scientists flew to Greece for secret talks with me.' Among the foreign personnel who conferred with the physicist were Pentagon and other unnamed American scientists.

A 'world blanket of secrecy' surrounded the UFO question, Santorini declared, because, among other reasons, the authorities were unwilling to admit the existence of a force against which we had no possibility of defence . . .[36]

REFERENCES

1. Gross, Loren E., 'Ghost Rockets of 1946', *The Encyclopedia of UFOs* (ed. Ronald D. Story), New English Library, London, 1980, pp. 147–9.
2. ' "Ghost Rockets" over Scandinavia', *Intelligence Review*, No. 47, Intelligence Division, War Department General Staff, Washington, DC, 9 January 1947. *The Ghost Rocket File*, edited by Jan Aldrich, Fund for UFO Research, PO Box 277, Mount Rainier, MD 20712, 2000.
3. *The Ghost Rocket File.*
4. Zak, Anatoly, 'The Rest of the Rocket Scientists', *Air & Space*, Smithsonian, Vol. 18, No. 3, August/September 2003, pp. 69–71.
5. The National Archives, FO371/56988, Memo from C.B. Jerram (Stockholm) to Foreign Office, 13 July 1946.
6. The National Archives, FO371/56951, Memo from a Mr Henderson (Stockholm) to Foreign Office, 27 July 1946.
7. *The Ghost Rocket File.*
8. Report submitted to the National Investigations Committee on Aerial Phenomena (NICAP), published in *The UFO Evidence*, edited by Richard C. Hall, Barnes & Noble Books, New York, 1997, p. 25.
9. 'Swedish Army Investigating Rocket Mystery', *Washington Post*, 12 August 1946.
10. 'Swedes Use Radar in Fight on Missiles', *New York Times*, 13 August 1946.
11. Intelligence Report, Top Secret, Office of Chief of Naval Operations, prepared by Lt. Cdr. A.A. Rocheleau, forwarded by Capt. R.H. Hillenkoetter [who, promoted to rear admiral, became CIA director the following year], 13 August 1946.
12. 'Plane Hits Rocket, Three Swedes Killed', *Washington Post*, 14 August 1946.
13. *Jönköpings-Posten*, 12 August 1946.
14. Final investigation report, 13 October 1946, Swedish Air Staff archives.
15. *Morgon Tidningen*, 14 August 1946.
16. 'Sweden Declares War on Rockets', *News-Journal*, Mansfield, Ohio, 14 August 1946.
17. 'Two Swedes escape a "Ghost Rocket" ', *New York Times*, 14 August 1946.
18. *AFU Newsletter*, Issue 44, September 2002, Archives for UFO Research Foundation, PO Box 11207, S-600 11 Norrköping, Sweden.
19. Intelligence Report, Top Secret, forwarded by Captain William D. Wright, US Naval Attaché, Stockholm, 16 August 1946.

20. War Department Classified Message Center, Top Secret TOT [time of transmission] Priority, from the Military Attaché, London, to General Spaatz and others, 16 August 1946. *The Ghost Rocket File.*

21. US War Department, Classified Message Center, Top Secret TOT Priority, 22 August 1946. *The Ghost Rocket File.*

22. Flammonde, Paris, *UFO Exist!*, G.P. Putnam's Sons, New York, 1976, pp. 127–34.

23. *The Ghost Rocket File.*

24. *New York Times*, 23 August 1946.

25. Jones, Professor R.V., 'The Natural Philosophy of Flying Saucers', *Physics Bulletin*, Vol. 19, July 1968, pp. 225–30.

26. War Department Classified Message Center, Top Secret TOT, from the US Military Attaché London to War Department, Washington, for Generals Chamberlin, Spaatz and Norstad. *The Ghost Rocket File.*

27. 'Swedish Inquiry Fails To Solve Rocket Case', *New York Times*, 11 October 1946.

28. 'Swedish Report on "Rockets"', *Daily Telegraph*, London, 11 October 1946.

29. Top Secret message from Tully Shelley, US Naval Attaché, American Embassy, London, to the Chief of Naval Intelligence.

30. Jones, Professor R.V., op. cit.

31. Zak, op. cit., p. 71.

32. Email, 3 March 2006.

33. Arnold, Kenneth and Palmer, Ray, *The Coming of the Saucers*, Amherst Press, Wisconsin, 1952, pp. 90–1.

34. *Sydney Sun*, 25 February 1967.

35. Fowler, Raymond E., *UFOs: Interplanetary Visitors*, Exposition Press, Jericho, New York, 1974, p. 106.

36. *Sydney Sun*, 25 February 1967.

WAR DEPARTMENT
CLASSIFIED MESSAGE CENTER
INCOMING CLASSIFIED MESSAGE

URGENT

TOP SECRET PIE

PARAPHRASE NOT REQUIRED. HANDLE AS TOP SECRET
CORRESPONDENCE PER PARAS 51(1) and 60(a) AR 380-5

TOP SECRET

From: USMA Stockholm, Sweden

To: War Department for MILID

Nr: 1042   16 July 1946

Swedish Army Staff studying 300 to 400 rocket
incidents Ref your WAR 94001 of 12 July. They advise:
6 phenomena have been observed to explode in the air, up to
50 points of impact observed. No evidence of radio control
and Army Staff believes phenomena not radio controlled.
Defense Research Institute studying fragments but key
personnel on leave and report being delayed therefore. No
large fragments yet found and small fragments appear to be
nonferrous. Afton Bladet states Russians have established
research base with Staff of German scientists on Dago
Island off Estonia. (Staff checking basis of this report)
Staff has rather tenuous hypothesis to support this as
follows:

Two circular rocket courses both with radius of
approximately 300 kilometers and centres respectively in
the 56-57 N latitude, and 19-20 E longitude quadrangle
and the 61-62 N latitude, 21-22 E longitude quadrangle with
rockets launched from Dago clockwise on both courses. This
theory accounts for only portion of incidents. Staff has
not yet processed all reports. Some highly placed officials
believe phenomena are Russian rocket experiments either
purely for research or for War of Nerves. Staff very
nervous about release of info to United States and United
Kingdom for fear Russians will cry "West bloc". This office
urges greatest protection this information. Detailed report
by next pouch also later followup on ultimate findings.

ACTION: Gen Chamberlin
INFO : Gen Spaats, Gen Norstad, Gen Aurand

CM IN 3219   (16 Jul 46)   DTG 160900Z   tl

GEN. McDONALD

TOP SECRET

GEN. EVEREST

M05547

COPY NO. 22

EXACT COPY OF THIS MESSAGE IS FORBIDDEN

A Top Secret UF War Department message (16 July 1946) relating to the 2,000-plus
sightings of mysterious 'ghost rockets' and 'spook bombs', which appeared over
Scandinavia – Sweden in particular – and other countries in 1946.
(The National Archives, Washington)

Stockholm Says Missiles Make Arc to North Russia

Newspaper Quotes Londoner as Stating Projectiles Remind Him of Buzz Bombs

Stockholm, Sweden, Aug. 13 (U.P). Three fliers were killed when a Swedish military reconnaissance plane collided head-on with a rocket bomb yesterday, Stockholm newspapers reported today.

The newspaper Aftonbladet said the reconnaissance plane crashed near Vaggeryd in southern Sweden. Shortly after the plane's pilot spotted the bomb, it said, radio contact was broken and the listening post "heard a crash," the newspaper, quoting investigators, reported.

The report, published by other afternoon newspapers, was not confirmed.

Report Changes of Course

Meanwhile, government authorities prepared a nation-wide hunt for rockets. Air bases, radar stations and all military units were alerted for immediate action.

A well informed source said the bombs seen recently apparently were radio-controlled. Witnesses have reported seeing the bombs change course.

This source said the Swedish defense staff has established that the rockets made a wide semicircle over southern Sweden, proceeding over northern Finland toward the Kola peninsula of Russia.

The second rocket bomb in two nights streaked over Stockholm like a meteor early yesterday, unconfirmed press reports said today.

Englishman Quoted

Descriptions of several eyewitnesses coincided with details of the first bomb. The newspaper Morgentidningen quoted an English visitor as saying "It looked just like the flying bombs I saw in London."

Other reports said bombs, "small and going very fast," passed over southern and central Sweden.

Although the press and public complained bitterly about the "ghost bombs," military and government officials remained silent. But the newspaper Dagens Nyheter said editorially that the "ghost rockets" were a summer for "earthly phenomenon" and that "these ghostly disturbances must be regarded as a preliminary exercise of the most unwelcome kind."

Headline (vertical): The Washington Post — WASHINGTON, WEDNESDAY, AUGUST 14, 1946 — **Plane Hits Rocket, Three Swedes Killed**

Lead story (14 August 1946) relating to a reported aerial collision with one of the ghost rockets. *(The Washington Post)*

ISSUED BY THE INTELLIGENCE DIVISION
OFFICE OF CHIEF OF NAVAL OPERATIONS
NAVY DEPARTMENT

INTELLIGENCE REPORT

Monograph Index Guide No: _____

From: U. S. Naval Attache _____ at Stockholm, Sweden Date 16 August 1946.

Reference (a) M.A. Stockholm's Top Secret Report R334-46 of 13 August 1946.

Source: Swedish Defense Staff, Chief Defense Staff Intelligence,
Swedish Army Staff, Asst. British RAF Attache, Evaluation _____

Subject SWEDEN   Guided missiles   Rocket sightings over Sweden

TOP SECRET

No tangible evidence to date as to nature or origin of
rockets reported over Sweden, although Swedish Defense
Staff insists that they are rockets. Swedish press and
public aroused, but Swedish Air Force officers still on
summer leave, aircraft warning net not mobilised, and no
attempts made to intercept missiles with jet fighters;
improbable that rockets, if any, are Russian or British,
but possible that they are Swedish. Swedish Defense Staff
evasive and their communiques contradictory and confusing.
Sweden may be experimenting with rockets, but is conceal-
ing the fact and encouraging the belief that rockets of
foreign origin are being launched over Sweden, with
civilian observers reporting jet fighters, contrails, and
meteors as rockets.

Encls: (A) Copy of M.A. Stkm Top Secret Report R334-46 of 13 August 1946.
        (B) Translation of Miscellaneous Swedish Newspaper Articles.

1. This report is an attempt to correlate various reports on the recently
reported sightings of light phenomena or rockets over Sweden and, in the
absence of any tangible evidence, to formulate a hypothesis as to their nature
and origin.

2. To date no U.S. military or naval personnel in Sweden have seen any fragments, photographs, radar tracks, points of impact, or other evidence of any
kind to prove that guided missiles have actually been seen over Swedish
territory.

3. On 12 August the reporting officer asked three Swedish Air Force officers
what they thought of the reported sightings. They answered that they believed
definitely that these were rockets. On 13 August the reporting officer and the
Assistant U.S. Military Attache were permitted to talk to three Swedish Air
Force officers from the Defense Staff, who stated in answer to direct questions
that while they had no definite evidence to back their belief, they believed
that the reported phenomena were rockets. This may therefore be accepted as
the official Swedish military expression as to the nature of the reported
phenomena.

                       Comnaveu; London

Distribution By Originator_____

Part of a Top Secret US Naval Intelligence report (16 August 1946) expressing
bewilderment and confusion about the ghost rockets.
(The National Archives, Washington)

WAR DEPARTMENT
CLASSIFIED MESSAGE CENTER
INCOMING CLASSIFIED MESSAGE

TOP SECRET TOT

PARAPHRASE NOT REQUIRED. HANDLE AS TOP SECRET CORRESPONDENCE
PER PARAS 511 and 60a, AR 380-5.

From: USMA, London, England egd Bisnoll

To   :   War Department for MILID personal for Chamberlin

Nr :   71085   1 October 1946

Military Attache report 3658-46 of 25 September
on route by mail raises 6 points under comments on cover
sheet. Military and Naval Attache Sweden as well as some of
FA Staff London feel British may not have given us all
available information on reported rockets over Scandivavia.
My understanding is that Intelligence Division is securing
everything available to the British through British Staff
Mission (See our Radio number 70872 of 6 August and your
WARX 96774 of 7 August). If British data on 6 points
raised on cover sheet has not been made available in
Washington do you desire effort made here to secure this
information?

End

Note: 70872 is CM-IN-1391 (7 Aug) General Chamberlin

ACTION: General Chamberlin

INFO : General Spaatz
         General Norstad

CM-IN-193 (1 oct 46)   DTG: 011310Z   jjf

GEN. EVEREST   TOP SECRET
                                                    23
GEN. McDONALD   COPY NO. 6184
     THE MAKING OF AN EXACT COPY OF THIS MESSAGE IS FORBIDDEN

A Top Secret US War Department message (1 October 1946) addressing American
concerns that the British may not have given them 'all available information on
reported rockets'. *(The National Archives, Washington)*

EXHAUST, 30-50 ft.   OPENINGS

90-100 ft. MACHINE
GLOWING "PORTS"   BLUE GLOW

The 'ghost rocket' encountered by an Eastern Airlines DC-3 at 02:45 on 25 July 1948,
near Montgomery, Alabama. 'Whatever it was,' reported Captain Clarence Chiles,
'it flashed down toward us and we veered to the left and passed us about 700 feet to
our right and above us.' *(Sketch from* The UFO Evidence, *edited by Richard H. Hall,
Barnes & Noble, New York, 1964)*

4. CONFLICT

Following the Second World War, the United States needed to adapt what had been code-named the Manhattan Engineering District Project into a stable peacetime operation, producing and maintaining a nuclear-weapons stockpile for the nation. Part of J. Robert Oppenheimer's answer to this problem was to create 'Z Division' in July 1945,[1] named after Jerrold R. Zacharias, a physics professor at the Massachusetts Institute of Technology (MIT), who led the division from its inception until October 1945 at Los Alamos Scientific Laboratory, New Mexico.

'The primary mission of the new group was to improve the ordnance design of the Fat Man [A-bomb] model,' Rebecca Ullrich, Sandia Laboratories' corporate historian, explained to me in 2005. 'Overall, it took on the ordnance engineering activities related to atomic weapon design . . . Z was organized into several groups by topic area.' One such group was Z-12 – the Manual Preparation Group – formed in September 1947.[2] By that time, Z Division had been ensconced in what was then known as Sandia Base, Albuquerque, New Mexico.

Z Division comprised twelve groups (although thirteen are listed for 1948), some with sub-groups. For example, Z-1 ('Experimental System') had Z-1A ('Airborne Testing') and sub-groups B and C. Jon 'Andy' Kissner, a former Republican State Representative for Las Cruces, New Mexico (1997–2000), who also worked with a space systems division at a major US defence contractor, has done a great deal of research into this matter.[3] He believes that a division of Z attached to 'Project Y' – the Los Alamos Scientific Laboratory, which later became the Los Alamos National Laboratory – was associated with the problem of unidentified aerial objects, beginning in the summer or early autumn of 1947.

Dr Zacharias's first task at MIT in the war years had been to develop a radar system 'capable of detecting distant objects'. He also helped develop other sophisticated radar systems, including the British 'Oboe' blind-bombing system. In 1951 he served as associate director of Project Charles, established to make recommendations on the air defence of the North American continent, and in 1952 he directed a Lincoln Laboratory study that recommended setting up a chain of distant early-warning (DEW) radars stretched across the Arctic to detect approaching missiles.[4] Project Charles was renamed Project Lincoln that year, and Zacharias chaired the project's 'Summer Study Group', which included MIT and CIA scientists who had become so alarmed about air defence problems associated with UFOs that they took their concerns directly to the National Security Council.[5]

Beginning in the Second World War, many committees – official and unofficial – were set up to study unidentified aerial craft. The Army's Interplanetary Phenomenon Unit (IPU) of the Scientific and Technical Branch, Counterintelligence Directorate, was established in 1947 (or, reportedly, in 1945, by General Douglas MacArthur) and disbanded in the 1950s. In a letter to researcher William Steinman, Lieutenant Colonel Lance Cornine explained that:

> The 'unit' was formed as an in-house project purely as an interest item for the Assistant Chief of Staff for Intelligence. It was never a 'unit' in the military sense, nor was it ever formally organized or reportable, it had no investigative function, mission or authority, and may not even have had any formal records at all. It is only through institutional memory that any recollection exists of this unit.[6]

Colonel Anthony Gallo Jr, Director of Counterintelligence, informed me that 'the aforementioned Army unit was disestablished during the late 1950's and never reactivated. All records pertaining to this unit were turned over to the US Air Force Office of Special Investigations in conjunction with operation "BLUEBOOK".'[7] Such records, if they survive, have yet to be released. Officially titled Project Blue Book, this was the third and final official US Air Force investigation into aerial phenomena (1952–69).

The failed attempts to shoot down unidentified aircraft in Los Angeles (1942), Detroit and Colorado (1945), as well as the extraordinary proliferation of sightings of possibly hostile 'missiles' and other craft in 1946 and early 1947, renewed the determination by US military authorities to bring down one or more craft for scientific and technical intelligence evaluation. (I do not know if the craft allegedly recovered at San Antonio, New Mexico, in August 1945, was shot down.) Since the burgeoning nuclear weapons programme most probably had led to the increase of what appeared to be a strategic reconnaissance by forces whose motives were unknown, it would be of vital importance to protect the facilities at Los Alamos, Sandia and elsewhere (also, of course, to counter any potential Soviet threat).

Such a plan would need to be Top Secret, as well as highly compart-

mented. The nuclear programme, with its multiple levels of 'compartmentalization', would provide the perfect cover. 'Compartmentalization of
knowledge,' wrote General Leslie Groves, military leader in charge of the
Manhattan Project, 'was the very heart of security. My rule was simple . . .
each man should know everything he needed to know to do his job, and
nothing else.'[8]

In later years, extremely sensitive secrets were designated 'Sensitive
Compartmented Information' (SCI), or 'Extremely Sensitive Information'
(ESI), though other systems exist. For example, 'Very Restricted Knowledge'
(VRK), established by the National Security Agency in 1974, limits access
to uniquely sensitive communications intelligence (COMINT) activities and
programmes. According to William M. Arkin, VRK normally contains even
further restrictions, categorized by number (such as VRK-7).[9]

A T-Force, Andy Kissner explains, was 'a specialized, often inter-service
US military unit assigned a mission to take, hold and defend a specialized
enemy facility or specific piece of enemy equipment possessing high
scientific or technical value, as defined by the OSRD [Office of Scientific
Research & Development] and the JCS [Joint Chiefs of Staff] during
WWII.'[10] T-Forces – which had secured Hitler's most secret aerospace
laboratories – were drawn from agents of the Office of Strategic Services
(OSS), which later became the CIA.

'Our technical "collection" capabilities for foreign-manufactured items
have been very highly classified since the end of WWII,' Kissner told me.
'"Paperclip" and other foreign hardware collections (missiles, aircraft,
tanks, electronic gear, etc.) and the methods used to secure these systems
for analysis are equally highly classified. Flying discs were another "foreign"
technology that we collected, I believe. The T-Forces operated under the
authority of the Research and Development Board of the Joint Chiefs of
Staff, OSRD and the Executive Office of the President.'

Kissner also informed me that, based on his information regarding the
Roswell incident, 'a T-Force was assigned the responsibility to collect a
flying disc (or discs) and clean up the crash sites, under orders from the
OSRD . . .'[11]

'PECULIAR PHENOMENA' DEFLECT V-2 ROCKET

On 15 May 1947, 'peculiar phenomena' were blamed by Lieutenant Colonel
Harold R. Turner, commanding officer at White Sands Proving Ground
(WSPG), New Mexico, for the erratic test flight of a V-2 (A-4) rocket.[12] As

the rocket climbed to an intermediate altitude of 40 miles, Kissner learned that radar technicians assigned to US Army Ordnance watched in amazement as another target instantaneously appeared right next to the missile.[13] The V-2 veered off course and crashed to earth two minutes later, 40 degrees off the normal flight path. Pending a formal report from the ground search crew, Turner said there were no clues to the cause of the missile's behaviour.[14]

This incident, says Kissner, 'began an episode that would evolve over the next half-century into the most highly classified military and scientific research and development project in world history – more highly classified than the Manhattan Engineering District project that detonated its first nuclear experiment at Trinity Site ... Not surprisingly, this project would require use of some of the same Atomic Energy Commission laboratories.' He continues:

> Whatever had mysteriously appeared and vanished after observing a V-2 in flight and affecting its trajectory at a highly classified missile range became an immediate priority within a small closed circle. It involved highly ranked general staff officers and civilian scientists assigned to the Office of Scientific Research and Development and the Joint Research and Development Board of the Joint Chiefs of Staff, under whose authority White Sands Proving Ground was established and operated. Both of these national weapons research and development organizations were headed by one key man – Dr Vannevar Bush.

Citing published material, Kissner reports that initial speculation centred on the object being a long-range Russian reconnaissance aircraft or drone launched from Mexico, though the 'peculiar phenomenon' had not been detected before the V-2 launch.

> Recorders attached to an array of tracking radars assessing the rocket's performance, and film from a battery of high-speed ground cameras were reviewed. German scientists, including Wernher von Braun, brought to Fort Bliss (El Paso, Texas) to support the V-2 programme at WSPG by US Army Ordnance, Enemy Equipment Intelligence Section, at the encouragement of Dr Bush, had witnessed the launch, as had scientists working with the Naval Research Laboratory including Dr James Van Allen of the Applied Physics Laboratory of Johns Hopkins University. The Germans ... were also at a loss to explain the phenomenon.

Others brought to WSPG to review the evidence included Brigadier General Robert M. Montague, an anti-aircraft/guided missile specialist, and

Major General John Homer, commanding the Army's Anti-aircraft Artillery and Guided Missile Center at Fort Bliss.

The Army Air Forces at Alamogordo Field were placed on heightened alert for unknown airborne intruders. Lieutenant Colonel Turner and General Montague requested a more rapid deployment of the Gapa (ground-to-air pilotless aircraft), operated under the auspices of the Technical Branch of Air Materiel Command, headed by General Nathan F. Twining, with a programme site at Wendover Field, Utah.[15] According to Wernher von Braun, more than one hundred Gapas were built before the project was cancelled in 1949. All were two-stage missiles with solid-propellant boosters.[16]

RETALIATION

Andy Kissner believes that the incident on 15 May led later to several discs being shot down – and an unprecedented wave of aircraft crashes, attributed to retaliation. The first post-war attack on the unknown flying objects is said to have occurred on 29 May 1947. At 16:00, a V-2 launch had been aborted at WSPG. At 17:30, a US Navy Curtiss SB2C Helldiver crashed at Las Cruces Airport, 25 air miles west of the launch site, due to failure of its landing gear. At around 18:00, a second plane flown by a student pilot overturned as it attempted to land at the same airport. At 19:15, at least one surface-to-air missile with a 674-pound high-explosive warhead was fired at one or more radar targets hovering to the south-west of WSPG Launch Row. Kissner claims:

> At approximately 7:20 pm, at an altitude above 60,000 feet, the proximity fuze on the warhead detonated – ten miles north and slightly west of Mt. Franklin. This explosion, witnessed by General Homer and reported by Hanson Baldwin in the *New York Times* the following day, occurred more than 10 minutes before a second explosion at least 30 miles further south. Gen. Homer dispatched troops to look for missile wreckage and investigate the first crash site 10–15 miles northwest of Ft. Bliss, towards WSPG.
>
> The surface-to-air missile's target, possibly crippled by the explosion, continued to fly in airspace north of Ft. Bliss, eventually impacting within one mile of the then-new Buena Vista airport south of downtown Juarez, Mexico, at 7:32 pm . . . A 'blinding flash of light' followed by a tremendous pressure wave [and] by the appearance of a mushroom cloud excited local rumours that an atomic bomb had exploded . . . The

ground shock generated by the explosion was felt 35 miles northwest of the impact crater.

'Whatever the object had been was not apparent,' Kissner explains. 'It was totally vaporized by the explosion. Small shreds of "burned gray metal fused with molten sand and rock" were found around the 50 ft x 50 ft x 24 ft crater. There was no V-2 rocket body at the bottom of the hole, nor anything else. Two Mexican pilots who landed their plane shortly before the object detonated reported seeing a flash of light that temporarily blinded them, followed by a deafening explosion.'

Military police stationed at Fort Bliss and other US Army personnel from WSPG rushed across the border into Mexico in an attempt to secure the downed object. They were met at the crater by Mexican troops and summarily evicted. Mexico's general in command of the Juarez garrison, Enrique Diaz Gonzalez, placed Juarez off-limits to US Army personnel for several weeks after the incident. It was never learned what the security detail dispatched by General Homer found at the site of the first explosion, on the west side of the Franklin Mountains east of Anthony, New Mexico – 12 minutes before the explosion in Mexico.

An effective cover story was immediately provided to the Press that another V-2 launched from White Sands had gone astray, experienced a total gyroscopic failure, flew 180 degrees off course and crashed in Mexico.

Together with neighbours, the editor of *Las Cruces Sun News* observed the rocket as it climbed high, then turned to the south. 'At that instant, as the rocket, its exhaust resembling another bright star, drifted past two first-magnitude stars and the Moon, we realized something was wrong,' he said. Kissner points out that it was too light at the time for even first-magnitude stars to be visible, thus these must have been discs, he believes. As for the 'V-2' rocket, the newspaper editor surmised that it was a modified version, due to the extended length of its burn time.[17] He was right.

'Up until about 1999,' Kissner told me, 'the Army maintained that what crashed at the Juarez airport was a V-2. In 1999, they changed the story and now say that a Hermes A-1 impacted at the airport. No explanation yet however about the explosion that left a "mushroom-shaped" cloud witnessed and reported by a pilot, or of the crater left by the explosion, or of the clock that stopped in the El Paso sheriff's department.'[18]

Based on the German *Wasserfall*, the A-1 was basically a one-third-size model of the V-2. It was designed to knock out planes at high altitude and could fly up to 15 miles at 1,850 mph. Five A-1 missiles were launched from White Sands between May 1950 and April 1951, according to Wernher von Braun and others. He provides no information about earlier flights.[19] Citing hundreds of newspaper articles, Kissner reports on the alarming escalation of aircraft crashes at this time:

> From research conducted to date, over sixty US Army and Navy aircraft – B-29s, B-17s, Corsairs, P-80s, P-84s, AT-6s, P-51s, C-47s, C-54s, F-7s – were lost over this two-month period. A hundred and twenty airmen were killed and seventy-four others injured in these incidents – gleaned from four local and one national newspaper. The vast majority of these accidents occurred over the continental US. Special military missions and alerts, coupled with unusually high levels of domestic air patrolling, consumed the US military's aviation and jet fuel stockpile, reported to be less than one-third of the required inventory level by mid-July 1947.

As well as military aircraft, civilian planes came to grief in increasing numbers. A review of accidents reported within a period of a few days is sobering:

May 29
— US Navy Curtiss SB2C Helldiver crashes on take-off from Las Cruces.
— Trainer overturns on landing at the same airfield.
— United Airlines DC-4 fails to gain altitude on take-off from La Guardia Field, New York, killing thirty-eight. 'Several gleaming things, like metal' were seen falling away from the plane.
— US Army C-54 crashes near Tokyo, killing forty-two.
— USAAF B-29 bomber fails to gain altitude at Ladd Field, Alaska, killing three.
— Two Dutch army planes collide in mid-air at Tilburg, killing twelve.
— Icelandic Airways DC-3 crashes into a mountain in Iceland, killing twenty-five.
— French government Junkers Ju-52 transport plane crashes into a mountain in southern Algeria, killing three.

May 30–31
— Eastern Airlines DC-4 turns over on its back and plummets into the ground near Port Deposit, Maryland, killing fifty-three – the worst commercial airline disaster in US history by that date.
— Royal Air Force (UK) B-24 Liberator explodes inexplicably while sitting on the runway, injuring four.
— China Air Transport DC-3 makes forced landing following fire in wing.

— DC-4 operated by the Office of Naval Research collides in mid-air in New
Jersey with a Piper Cub that was diving vertically, killing two.
— An aircraft mechanic is killed when the light plane he is flying is unable to
maintain altitude and crashes in Hemet, California.
— US Army 'twin-engine training bomber' with four on board 'disappears'
on a flight between Shreveport, Louisiana, and San Antonio, Texas.

On 6 June, the US Army Transport Command grounded all C-54
planes (the military version of the DC-4). 'A spokesman for the Army Air
Forces discussed the two largest US commercial air disasters in history
involving DC-4s over the past week, but didn't discuss the other air
accidents, now totalling over forty, involving almost every type of airplane
in major military and general aviation service.'

As crashes continued, the *New York Times* reported on the need to
recruit more personnel into the anti-aircraft artillery, and that the new
threat 'of planes and the *long range robot* looms over every battlefield.'[20]
(The 'long-range robot', emphasized by Kissner, almost certainly was a
cover term for the unknown flying objects.) And in an appearance before
the US Congress House Appropriations Committee on 13 June, Jerome C.
Hunsaker, chairman of the National Advisory Committee for Aeronautics,
demanded a huge increase in his budget request in order to maintain air
superiority. 'Much of the testimony at the hearings was so secret that it was
stricken from the public record,' reported a newspaper.[21]

On 13 June, a Pennsylvania Central DC-4 crashed into a ridge near
Leesburg, Virginia, killing fifty people.[22] Later that day, a B-29 based at
Davis-Monthan Field, near Tucson, went missing, and two-and-a-half
hours later slammed into Hawks Mountain near Springfield, Vermont,
killing twelve crew members. On 15 June, an Army C-47 transport plane
crash-landed at Godman Field, Kentucky, but all crew members escaped
with injuries.[23] Twenty of the crew members were part of an intelligence
group headed by Major General W.G. Wyman.[24] Deeply concerned by the
frequent aviation disasters, President Truman appointed a special board of
inquiry, headed by the Chairman of the Civil Aeronautics Board, with Dr
Jerome C. Hunsaker as his aide.[25] (See p. 64.)

In Atlantic City, New Jersey, on 16 June, a Navy fighter pilot forced to
make an emergency landing on a suburban highway managed to escape
just before his plane – loaded with ammunition – caught fire and
exploded.[26] The crashes continued – as did the sightings of 'flying discs'.

On 24 June 1947, pilot Kenneth Arnold observed nine crescent-shaped
objects near Mount Rainier, Washington. The report made news around
the world. Flying at the time in his CallAir single-engine plane, Arnold

had been looking for the wreckage of a lost C-46 Marine transport which had gone down in the mountains a few months before. The Navy had offered a $5,000 reward for the discovery of the aircraft and the bodies of the thirty-two Marines on board.

The wreckage was eventually recovered from the Tacoma Glacier, some 9,500 feet up on Mt Rainier, by a Search and Rescue Squadron from McChord Field. Arnold, who worked with Idaho Search and Rescue at the time, learned from the head of the McChord squadron that when their team eventually reached the crash site, the fuselage section remained fairly intact, with all the luggage and parachutes still on board. 'He said there was no blood, no bones, and there were no bodies,' Arnold told reporter Bob Pratt. 'He said it looked like mountain lions carried off the bodies ... they finally ended up saying the terrain was too treacherous to bring the bodies down and so they didn't bring them down, [and] that apparently was the official explanation. However, they had funerals for the people who perished in that crash [and] there were thirty-two coffins there and no bodies in them ... and they never paid the reward.'[27]

'FALLING SILVER OBJECTS'

On 27 June, a witness driving to El Paso from Albuquerque at San Antonio, New Mexico, 15 miles west of White Sands Proving Ground (WSPG), reported a 'falling silver object', which she described as 'just as bright and shining as it could be. If it had been any closer it would have blinded us ... It left a short white trail. I just supposed they were firing something at White Sands Proving Ground.' Officials denied there had been any rocket launches since 12 June. Earlier on 27 June, a witness observed a 'shiny disc' about 40 feet across over Mt Franklin, Texas.[28]

On receiving additional reports of 'falling objects' near the base, Lieutenant Colonel Harold Turner, commanding officer at WSPG, ordered search parties 'in attempts to locate the objects or secure additional information'.[29]

By 5 July, flying discs had been reported over thirty-one states – particularly in the El Paso, Las Cruces and Carrizozo region of southern New Mexico and west Texas.

On 7 July 1947, reports came from Wisconsin, the first of which involved a 'saucer' that travelled at a speed of 6,000 miles per hour, according to a flying instructor and student pilot who had just taken off from Eikhorn. The second observation, in Eagle, of a saucer that travelled at an estimated 9,000 mph, was reported by Captain R.J. Southey, a USAAF wing supply officer, and his passenger.[30] On the same day, the *New York Times* reported that, 'A P-80 jet fighter at Muroc Army Air Field in California and six fast regular fighters at Portland, Oregon, stood ready to take off on an instant's notice should any flying saucers be sighted in those areas.'

At 09:20 the following day, at Muroc, Lieutenant J.C. McHenry and three others saw two objects, spherical in shape, flying at 300 mph at 8,000 feet. Earlier the same day, two military engineers reported a metallic disc 'diving and oscillating' above the base. Curiously, no planes were sent aloft to intercept these intruders, despite the order issued only days earlier.[31]

Perhaps the military was reluctant to further engage the intruders at this stage. As it transpired, two discs had already crash-landed in New Mexico – in late June – leading to the extraordinary series of events that have become known collectively as 'the Roswell incident'.

REFERENCES

1. *Sandia History Program & Corporate Archives*, Sandia National Laboratories. www.sandia.gov/recordsmgmt/zdiv.html

2. Letter, 5 July 2005.

3. Kissner, J. Andrew, *Peculiar Phenomenon: Early United States Efforts to Collect and Analyze Flying Discs.* (Currently unpublished.)

4. Ramsey, Norman F., 'Biographical Memoirs of Jerrold R. Zacharias'. http://stills.nap.edu/html/biomems/jzacharias.html

5. Hall, Michael David and Connors, Wendy Ann, *Captain Edward J. Ruppelt: Summer of the Saucers – 1952*, Rose Press International, Albuquerque, NM, 2000, pp. 117–18, 202.

6. Steinman, William S. and Stevens, Wendelle C., *UFO Crash at Aztec: A Well Kept Secret*, UFO Photo Archives, PO Box 17206, Tucson, AZ 85710, 1987, p. 55.

7. Letter from Colonel Anthony Gallo Jr, Colonel, General Staff, Director of Counterintelligence, Department of the Army, Washington, DC, 12 March 1987.

8. Weisgall, J.M., *Operation Crossroads: The Atomic Tests at Bikini Atoll*, Naval Institute Press, Annapolis, Maryland, 1994, p. 84.

9. Arkin, William M., *Code Names: Deciphering US Military Plans, Programs, and Operations in the 9/11 World*, Steerforth Press, Hanover, NH 03755, 2005, p. 548.

10. Kissner, op. cit.

11. Letter, 4 June 2005.

12. 'V-2 Goes Astray', *Las Cruces Sun News*, 16 May 1947.

13. Kissner, op. cit.

14. *Las Cruces Sun News*, 16 May 1947.

15. Kissner, op. cit.

16. Von Braun, Wernher and Ordway III, Frederick I., *History of Rocketry & Space Travel*, Nelson, London, 1966, p. 144.

17. *Las Cruces Sun News*, 1 June 1947.

18. Email, 3 October 2005.

19. Von Braun, op. cit., p. 126.

20. Baldwin, Hanson W., 'Few Men Assigned to Anti-Aircraft', *New York Times*, 7 June 1947.

21. 'Aerial Weapons Research Funds Urged to Keep Air Superiority', *Las Cruces Sun News*, 14 June 1947.

22. *New York Times*, 15 June 1947.

23. *Arizona Republic*, 16 June 1947.

24. *El Paso Times*, 16 June 1947.

25. *Arizona Republic*, 16 June 1947.

26. *New York Times*, 18 June 1947, p. 10.

27. Pratt, Bob, 'Conversations with Major Donald Keyhoe'. www.bobpratt.org/keyhoe.html

28. 'More El Pasoans Report Seeing "Flying Discs" In Southwest', *El Paso Times*, 29 June 1947.

29. 'Now – "Falling Objects"', *El Paso Times*, 28 June 1947.

30. Kissner, op. cit.

31. 'Report on Flying Saucers', a USAAF report (Secret) for the Commanding General, 32nd AAF Base Unit, Bolling Field, Washington, DC, by John D. Schindler Jr, AAF-CAP [Civil Air Patrol] Liaison Officer, 7 July 1947.

Round-the-World Series of Plane Wrecks Kills 180

BY ASSOCIATED PRESS

A world-wide series of disasters in recent days has taken 180 lives more than a third of the 428 killed in major commercial airline accidents so far this year.

At least 26 other persons were injured, some critically, and three fliers were missing.

Investigators and witnesses reported the apparent causes of the crackups were varied.

83 Die in One Crash

The worst tragedy and biggest plane disaster in the history of the United States was the crash of an Eastern Airlines DC-4 Friday near Port Deposit, Md., with the loss of 53 lives. The cause still was in doubt but some witnesses told investigators they saw the tail section of the big plane come off before it plunged in flames.

Less than 24 hours earlier, the second biggest crash in the nation's aviation history occurred when a United Air Lines plane crashed in New York state. Federal investigators saw a sudden shift in wind took place as the plane was attaining air speed. A flight instructor and his student were killed Saturday when their light plane crashed after it and a Navy DC-4 collided near Red Bank, N. J. The Navy plane returned to its base and none of its passengers was injured.

Army Wreck Kills 40

Near Tokyo, an Army transport crashed in the mountains Thursday killing 40. The American craft struck a 900-foot ridge as it was approaching Tachikawa for a landing.

... a possible cause for the crackup of an Icelandic Airways plane which struck a mountain in northern Iceland on Thursday, June 26. Twelve persons were killed in the collision of a Netherlands and an Argentine plane...

Other crackups included: Three were missing and nine escaped when an Army B-29 crashed on a takeoff at Fairbanks, Alaska Thursday. Twelve were injured at Bogota, Columbia, when a Colombian airforce transport crash-landed Friday after striking a buzzard. A Royal Air Force liberator bomber flew up on an airport runway Friday at Litchfield, England, injuring four civilians.

Domestic Travel Low

Three French government fliers were killed Thursday when their Junkers transport plane crashed in a mountain range 650 miles south of Algiers.

Domestic plane travel at La Guardia Field, New York dropped below peak capacity Saturday. Although some airline representatives said unofficially the recent air crashes might be the cause, the majority said the condition was normal in the middle of a weekend holiday.

Aviation Inquiry Ordered

WASHINGTON, June 15—(INS) President Truman acting to end the wave of death-dealing airline disasters across the nation— appointed a special board of inquiry today to make a sweeping investigation of American air safety.

Mr. Truman designated James M. Landis, Civil Aeronautics Board chairman, head of the new national board, and Dr. Jerome C. Hunsaker, chairman of the National Advisory Committee for Aeronautics, as his aid.

He named Brig. Gen. Milton W. Arnold, vice president of the operations and engineering of the Air Transport Association; Theodore P. Wright, civil aeronautics administrator, and H. B. Cox, a flying member of the Air Line Pilots Association, to serve on the board.

MR. TRUMAN said he was "deeply concerned" about air safety "especially in view of the recent accidents to aircraft of our certified domestic air carriers."

The President acted less than 48 hours after the nation was shocked by the crash of a DC-4 Capital air liner in the Blue Ridge mountains, with a death toll of 50.

Other crashes within the past 15 days killed 43 at New York's La Guardia Field and 53 near Perryville, Md. The total for major plane crashes within the period, including that in the Blue Ridge, stood at 244 lives.

Mr. Truman, in a letter to each member-designate of the new board, declared "the development of our air transportation system has repeatedly been recognized as

(Continued On Page 8, Col. 4)

Army Plane Burns; 20 Escape Death

FORT KNOX, Ky., June 15—(UP)—An army C-47 transport plane crashed and burned in a landing at Godman Field here today, but all of the approximately 20 persons on board escaped without serious injury.

The two-engined transport, army version of the commercial DC-3 air liner, bounced and crumpled upon the runway as it came down for a...

A front-page article from the *Las Cruces Sun News*, New Mexico (1 June 1947) and part of an article in the *New York Times* (16 June 1947) reporting President Truman's deep concern about the unprecedented wave of military and civilian air disasters then proliferating. There is evidence that many of these incidents were related to UFO phenomena.

Now--'Falling Objects'

New Mexicans Add To Mystery Reports

Mysterious falling objects reported near Tularosa and Engle N.M. Friday had not been located or identified late Friday night. There were no rockets fired from the White Sands Proving Ground Friday.

There was much conjecture as to whether the falling objects had any relation to the mysterious flying discs which had been variously reported seen recently from Oregon to Oklahoma.

Lt. Col. Harold R. Turner commanding officer at White Sands said that he had received reports that a track walker said he had seen a falling object near Engle N. M. and an Army captain flying his own plane reported seeing an object falling from the skies near Tularosa.

Search parties were sent out from White Sands in attempts to locate the objects or secure additional information.

At Silver City Dr. R F. Sensenbaugher, a dentist said that while traveling along the Tyrone Road Wednesday he saw a luminous disc sail out of the northern sky. According to Associated Press dispatches Dr Sensenbaugher was

(Continued on Page 6, Col.. 7)

with his wife and her sister Mrs. C. B. Munroe when the disc appeared for a few seconds before disappearing over the southern horizon.

He said it appeared to be about half the size of a full moon very brilliant, far-distant and not moving at a very high rate of speed. He told his story after reading reports of similar objects in Washington and Oklahoma.

According to the United Press an Oklahoma City flier Byron Savage refused to budge from his story of having seen the sailing saucers- just like residents of Oregon and Washington had seen them. But when Tinker Army Air Field jet plane experts were asked about them the reply was:

"Oh Applesaucers!"

Col. Frederick Bell though skeptical added that he would like to meet the man who's flying the disc-like objects.

Savage said even his wife scoffed at his story but he felt better after reading the papers. They reported led that an excited man telephoned the Daily Oklahoman city desk Thursday night to report he saw one of the saucers flying overhead from northeast to southwest.

Assistant City Editor Ed Hunter said the caller was so excited he hung up without giving his name or address. One cynical jet pilot at Tinker said maybe the caller had been seeing headlines instead.

A few days before the recovery of one or more discs in New Mexico, several observers reported disc-like objects 'falling' or 'sailing' out of the sky. Search parties were dispatched from the White Sands Proving Ground. Had a disc or discs been shot down? This article appeared in the *El Paso Times*, Texas, 28 June 1947.

Military Planes Hunt Sky Discs With Cameras in Vain on Coast

By The Associated Press.

SAN FRANCISCO, July 6—Military aircraft hunted the skies over Pacific Coast states today for sight of the mysterious "flying saucers" that for twelve days have puzzled the entire country. Early reports of results were negative.

Five P-51's of the Oregon National Guard cruised over the Cascade Mountains of Washington — the area where the strange objects first were reported sighted. A sixth circled over Portland, in constant radio contact with the other five. All carried photographic equipment.

Col. G. R. Dodson, commanding, described their flight as a "routine patrol," but said they had been instructed to watch for the flying discs.

At Manhattan Beach, Calif., A. W. McKelvey took a Mustang fighter plane up above Van Nuys. For two hours he cruised at 35,000 feet.

"I didn't see a thing," he said when he landed.

Gen. Carl Spaatz, commandant of the Army Air Forces was in the Pacific Northwest. He denied knowing anything about the flying discs or of plans to use AAF planes to look for them.

"I've been out of touch with things for four or five days," he said. Then he went to Medford, Ore., on a fishing trip.

A P-80 jet fighter at Muroc Army Air Field in California and six fast regular fighters at Portland, Ore., stood ready to take off on an instant's notice should any flying saucers be sighted in those areas. Some of the planes carried photographic equipment.

First sighted on June 25 and greeted generally with scornful laughs, the objects have been reported every day since by observers in thirty-three states. Airline pilots said they had seen the discs, larger than aircraft, flying in "loose formation" at high speed.

A cautious attitude marked both official and scientific comments,

Part of an article in the *New York Times* (7 July 1947).

5. ROSWELL

On the evening of 2 July 1947, several witnesses observed a fast-moving, saucer-shaped object, heading north-west over the town of Roswell, New Mexico. One of the witnesses, Dan Wilmot, decided to report it to the local newspaper on 8 July – only minutes before the intelligence office at Roswell Army Air Field issued a press release stating that they had come into possession of a 'flying disk', making headline news on that day.[1]

Thus began the 'Roswell Incident', which has been the subject of numerous books, articles, documentaries, and even a feature film starring Martin Sheen. From the outset, Roswell has also been the subject of an intensive counter-intelligence campaign, using every conceivable trick of 'tradecraft', by fair means or foul, such as threatening and discrediting witnesses and fabricating counter-evidence. In addition to summarizing the case here, I am including some important new information that has come to light in recent years.

Approximately the same time as the Roswell sightings, an unusual aerial vehicle crashed during a violent storm on the J.B. Foster Ranch, south-east of Corona and about 75 miles north-west of Roswell. Early the next morning, ranch manager William 'Mac' Brazel discovered a large amount of unusual debris scattered over a wide area. A few days later he drove into Roswell and alerted Sheriff George Wilcox, who in turn contacted the Roswell Army Air Field, home of the elite 509th Bomb Group, the world's first atomic-bomb unit.

Major Jesse Marcel, the bomb group's intelligence officer, together with Captain Sheridan Cavett, a Counter Intelligence Corps officer, accompanied Mac Brazel to the site, where a quantity of wreckage was discovered. Marcel testified that he found an area measuring about three-quarters of a mile long by 200 to 300 feet wide, strewn with a large amount of lightweight, strong material. 'I'd never seen anything like that, and I still don't know what it was,' Marcel told journalist Bob Pratt in 1979. 'I lit a cigarette lighter to some of this stuff [as a test], and it didn't burn.' There were also 'small, solid members that you could not bend or break, but it didn't look like metal. It looked more like wood. They varied in size . . . None of them were very long.' The largest of these was about 3 feet long, but weightless. 'You couldn't even tell you had it in your hands – just like you handle balsa wood.' Marcel also described having seen unusual 'hieroglyphics' on some of the pieces, as well as parchment-like material which, again, did not burn.[2]

Dr Jesse Marcel Jr (Major Marcel's son), who also handled some of the wreckage, described 'a thick, foil-like metallic gray substance; a brittle, brownish-black plastic-like material, like Bakelite [and] fragments of what appeared to be I-beams. On the inner surface of the I-beam, there appeared to be a type of writing [of] a purple-violet hue [with] figures composed of curved, geometric shapes . . .'[3]

The US Air Force has explained the materials as fragments from the balloon trains used in Project Mogul, a top-secret effort to develop a means for monitoring Soviet nuclear weapons, whose operations were conducted from Alamogordo Army Air Field, New Mexico, in June and July 1947. Indeed, in the foreword to the USAF's second report on the Roswell case, Air Force Historian Richard P. Hallion writes that Project Mogul 'provides the explanation for the "Roswell Incident."'[4] Although balloons and their accompanying instruments may account for some of the debris recovered, they manifestly do not explain the Roswell incident in its entirety.

Dr Jesse Marcel Jr is a former State Surgeon of Montana and served as a colonel with the Montana Air National Guard, flying helicopters. He is also a certified air-crash investigator. When I met him in 2004, I asked about the Air Force explanation. 'The foil that they brought in had a paper backing,' he said. 'The material I saw did not. The symbols on the Mogul pieces were stuck on with Scotch tape fixed to balsa wood. Again, that's not what we saw. Even though I was 12 years old, the memory is so fixed in my mind. No-one has explained satisfactorily what I saw.'[5]

Jesse Marcel Sr described how later he tried unsuccessfully to bend or dent a piece of extremely light and thin metal about 2 feet long and a foot wide. 'We even tried making a dent in it with a 16-lb sledge hammer. And there was still no dent in it . . . It was possible to flex this stuff back and forth, even to wrinkle it, but you could not put a crease in it that would stay . . . I would almost have to describe it as a metal with plastic properties.'[6]

The area near Corona was sealed off by the military, and a wide search was initiated to recover the remaining debris. An official press statement was released at Roswell Army Air Field, authorized by Colonel William H. Blanchard, Commander of the 509th Bomb Group.

'On July 8th, I got a call from Colonel Blanchard; he told me to report to his office,' Walter Haut, the base press officer in 1947, told me. 'At that time he gave me the basic facts that he wanted put into the news release ... that we had in our possession a flying saucer. A rancher had brought parts of it in to the Sheriff's office, and the material was flown to Roger Ramey, Commanding General of the Eighth Air Force at that time.'[7]

Major Marcel was ordered to load the debris on a B-29 (one of several aircraft involved in transporting the materials from Roswell AAF) and fly it to Wright Field in Dayton, Ohio. On arrival at an intermediate stop at Fort Worth AAF, Texas, headquarters of the Eighth Air Force, Major General Ramey took charge. He ordered Marcel and others on the plane not to talk to reporters.

A second press release was issued to the effect that the wreckage was nothing more than the remains of a weather balloon and its attached tinfoil target – which were prominently displayed at the press conference. Meanwhile, the real wreckage arrived at Wright Field under armed guard; Marcel returned to Roswell, and Brazel was held incommunicado by the military for nearly a week while the crash site was stripped of every scrap of debris.[8]

Andy Kissner points out that Brazel 'could never understand why the Army Air Forces stated that he had found the wreckage two or three weeks before he reported it, when in fact he had found it two days before reporting it. The simple answer is that Colonel Turner, only seven days before, had publicly said that two flying discs were seen about to crash by White Sands Proving Ground personnel, and the White Sands Proving Ground sent out search parties to find them.'[9]

Andy revealed to me that a friend of his who worked in the Navy for the Atomic Energy Commission told him that in the mid to late sixties, following a verbal briefing, he was taken on a field trip to the Manzano nuclear-weapons repository at Kirtland Air Force Base, where he was shown what was described to him as the 'Roswell flying disc'. 'He saw obvious exit holes on the top which he said appeared to be from anti-aircraft shells.'[10]

A news leak via press wire from Albuquerque describing the recovery of the 'flying disc' was interrupted, and the radio station in question, and another one, were warned not to continue the broadcast: 'ATTENTION ALBUQUERQUE: CEASE TRANSMISSION. REPEAT. CEASE TRANSMISSION. NATIONAL SECURITY ITEM. DO NOT TRANSMIT. STAND BY . . .'[11]

SCIENTIFIC AND TECHNICAL EVALUATION

Brigadier General Arthur E. Exon was assigned (in the rank of Lieutenant Colonel) to Air Materiel Command HQ at Wright Field (later merged with Patterson Field into Wright-Patterson Air Force Base), and became commander of the base in 1964. He has confirmed that the peculiar fragments from New Mexico were secretly flown to Wright Field, and that laboratory chiefs established a special unit to study them. Various tests were carried out, including 'chemical analysis, stress tests, compression tests, flexing,' he said. 'The metal and material was unknown to anyone I talked to. Whatever they found, I never heard what the results were.'

Exon surmised that some remnants were still stored at Wright-Patterson AFB, most probably at the Foreign Technology Division (now the National Air Intelligence Center).[12]

In the early 1990s, I had learned from a well-placed source that even some recovered fabric was subjected to a process of analysis known as 'reverse engineering', in an endeavour to discover the composition of unknown materials contained therein. This was confirmed for me some years later by another source. And then, in 1995, came *The Day After Roswell* by Lieutenant Colonel Philip J. Corso, an intelligence officer who served on President Dwight D. Eisenhower's National Security Council staff and who headed the Army staff's Research and Development Foreign Technology desk at the Pentagon. He claimed that from 1961 to 1963 he was steward of an Army project directed by Lieutenant General Arthur Trudeau, which 'seeded' examples of alien technology at American companies such as IBM, Hughes Aircraft, Bell Labs and Dow Corning – without their knowledge of where the technology originated. In his book, Corso alleged that the materials – including devices – found aboard the Roswell craft were precursors for today's integrated circuit chips, fibre optics, lasers and super-tenacity fibres.[13]

According to information supplied to science journalist Andreas von Rétyi by a qualified and credible source, the National Aeronautics and Space Administration (NASA) is in possession of physical evidence relating to Roswell. In 1974 'Dr Cris' (pseudonym), a Polish biophysicist and engineer contracted to NASA, was a member of an international team, including British, French and Italian scientists, which was given some odd metallic- and plastic-like material to analyse. The material reportedly originated in the Soviet Union or another potentially hostile foreign power. Precise details were not given to the team, Dr Cris told von Rétyi, but the team's task over the ensuing months was to research this foreign material to further NASA's knowledge.

The outer part of the metallic material was very smooth and shiny, whereas the areas where the material had fractured were matt. The team was allowed to use only tiny samples taken from the separately tagged material. Under analysis with an electron microscope, small pyramid structures in the nanometre range (i.e. one thousand-millionth, or 10^{-9} metre), showing a kind of 'super-reflectivity', were revealed. The metallurgical experts found alloys that could only have been made in conditions of weightlessness.

Because the materials appeared to have been made in the early 1950s or even earlier, the scientists became suspicious of their origin. 'The main thing,' explained Dr Cris, 'is that these "foamed" metals – material like Kevlar – had not existed at that time, and Kapton was unknown. The metal foil had been produced in a similar way to today's "glass-metal"; a production procedure unknown at that time.' The melting point of the metals was above 2,000°C, and it remained unaffected by tests using helium-neon and ruby lasers. Furthermore, the foil seemed to possess a 'memory', as do current memory-metals, but to a factor of 10^3 or better.[14] In 1977, Dr Cris and his colleagues were shown even more interesting materials by NASA, as described later in this chapter.

ALIEN BODIES

A confusing aspect of the Roswell incident is that, apart from Corona, many witnesses claim that there were *three* crash sites, at two of which alien bodies were recovered. Discrepancies between the various descriptions of the bodies also compound the confusion.

General Exon recalled that when flying over the area a year or two after the incident, he saw two distinct crash sites between Corona and Roswell, which were 'probably part of the same accident'. He believed that one site consisted mostly of debris, while at the other was, 'the main body of the spacecraft ... where they did say there were bodies [and] they were all found dead, apparently, outside the craft itself...'[15] Some witnesses to the actual recovery operation, however, claim that there were survivors. Among the various military personnel summoned from Roswell AAF to a crash site was Technical Sergeant Ernest R. Robbins, whose important story only surfaced in the late 1990s and remains little known.

Robbins's wife recalls the night in July 1947 when her husband received a call to go to the base. She would not see or hear from him for eighteen hours. 'We had been to a dinner party at the NCO [non-commissioned officers] club on the base, and didn't get home until 10:30 or 11,' Anne Robbins told reporter Carlton Stowers in 2003. 'We'd already gone to bed but weren't yet asleep when everything outside lit up like it was daylight. It was like that for what seemed like several minutes, and we both assumed it was probably helicopters from the base with searchlights on.' Shortly afterwards, a phone call came, ordering Sergeant Robbins to report to the base.

'I just assumed that there had been a plane crash somewhere nearby. But I couldn't figure why my husband, a sheet-metal man who repaired planes, was called in.'

Sergeant Robbins did not return until the following evening, his uniform wrinkled and damp. 'I asked him what had happened to him, why he was so wet, and he told me he'd had to go through the decontamination tank at the base. I asked, "In your clothes?" and he said, "They were what I was wearing when I was out there."'

Still assuming that her husband had been called to the site of a plane crash, she questioned him further. '"Well, I guess you might as well know; it's going to be in the papers," he replied. "A [saucer] crashed outside of Roswell." I told him he was crazy. I don't remember him being particularly shocked or very emotional about it. In fact, he seemed cool as a cucumber. He just made it clear to me that he wasn't going to talk about it.'

The following morning Anne Robbins continued to press her husband for details. Asked about the shape of the craft, he explained that it looked like two saucers put together, on the top layers of which were oblong-shaped windows all the way around. He said he had not looked inside.

'I asked him if there was anybody on it. He said, "I can tell you this much: there were three people. One was dead and two were still alive. I can't tell you anything more."' (Mrs Robbins says that of the two live beings, one was near death and the other very much alive.)

Several days later, Sergeant Robbins finally agreed to drive his wife out to what was probably the main crash site. (The area is not specified, but some researchers believe it to be 15–20 miles closer to Roswell than Corona.) By then, all the debris had been cleared away and there were no signs of military personnel. 'He didn't say much of anything,' said Anne Robbins, 'until we got to a place where there was this big burned spot, a perfect circle so black that it was shiny. No normal fire could have made something like that.' It was as if the sand had been melted and turned into a sheet of black glass. 'This,' said Robbins, 'is where I was for eighteen hours.'

On the drive home, Mrs Robbins asked what had become of the spaceship and the people who were on it. 'I can't tell you that; don't ask me any more,' he replied. It was many years before the matter was raised again, this time by the couple's son. Robbins repeated what he had told his wife, but at the insistence of his son for more details, drew a sketch of one of the beings, depicting a 'pear-shaped head with large black eyes'. Their skin 'was brown and they had no nose, no mouth'.

The last time Ernest mentioned the incident was a few years before he died in 2000. After a TV re-enactment of the Roswell case, Mrs Robbins asked him if it was a hoax. 'All he said was, "It's the truth. It did land." "Well, if it did, where is it?" He again said he couldn't tell me that.'[16]

A witness reported to have been on the scene of a crashed spacecraft was Grady L. 'Barney' Barnett, a civil engineer with the US Soil Conservation Service on military assignment at the time, working from Magdalena at the Plains of San Agustin, some 175 miles west-north-west of Roswell. Barnett revealed his experience – which occurred on an unspecified date in the summer of 1947 – to several people, including William Leed III and his friends LaVerne and Jean Maltais (see affidavit, p. 90).

According to Alice Knight, a relative of Barnett's wife, Barney told her that the incident occurred 'near Datil', some 190 miles west-north-west of Roswell,[17] but research by leading investigator Stanton T. Friedman, a retired nuclear physicist, places the location some 20 miles to the southwest, near Horse Springs. If the descriptions of the alien bodies by Barnett and Ernest Robbins, for example, were accurately reported, and if both witnesses were telling the truth, the hypothesis of two separate crash sites, in addition to the debris field in Corona, remains tenable.

AT ROSWELL ARMY AIR FIELD

Ruben Anaya and his brother Pete worked as civilians at the Roswell base during the time of the incident. In an interview with Tim Shawcross, a British TV director and producer, Ruben described receiving a phone call from Senator Joseph Montoya, Lieutenant Governor of New Mexico, whom he knew, ordering a car to collect him at the base. 'Many times Senator Montoya used to come to Roswell,' explained Pete, 'and we went to pick him up because we were the only ones who had the [security clearance] to go in the base.'

'You got to hurry up and bring Pete with you,' said Montoya, sounding very excited. On the way, Ruben picked up two more friends. 'So I took them over there to pick up Lieutenant Governor Montoya,' Ruben related. 'He was at the hangar, so the MPs [Military Police] just led us over there. I didn't park close to the hangar, I parked about half a block away and I said, what the hell's going on? And when they went over there I moved a little closer and that's when the hangar door was open, the Senator came out and he said, "Let's get the hell out of here!" and he was even praying . . . I said, "What's the problem?" and then the nurse came out running [and] says, "I can't believe it! I can't believe one is moving!" So naturally I wanted to see what was moving.

'There were two bodies covered with a white sheet but they were too small to be a man's body . . . and then one was uncovered, he was moving. I said, what the hell's going on? And I asked the nurse, "Who are they?" She said, "They are not from this world" and that was it, you know. And then [Montoya] got back in the car; he was so scared he sat between the two guys in the back.' Pete Anaya confirms most details reported by his brother. '[Governor Montoya] said he'd seen two little men with the big heads – one was alive,' he told Shawcross. 'He was so scared when he came out but then they didn't allow me or Ruben or nobody to go in there. There were a lot of officers, MPs, but I didn't like to get close to it. Then the nurse came out 'cos I knew the nurse at the Officers' Club and I went to ask her if they'd let us go in. She said, "Pete, you don't wanna see that" and then I didn't see her no more.'

Mrs Anaya remembered when her husband Pete returned home from the base, together with his brother and the Senator (they were all on friendly terms). 'He came in pretty excited and told me that the Senator was out here in the car and he wanted me to see him and talk to him . . . So I came out and the Senator was shaking and scared like and he told me, "You know what? I have seen something I have never seen before" . . .' According to Ruben, Montoya was in such a state that he drank about two-thirds of a bottle of Jim Beam bourbon.[18]

Initial autopsies of the alien bodies were carried out at Roswell Army Air Field. Glenn Dennis, a Roswell mortician for the Ballard Funeral Home, contracted to provide mortuary services for the base, has provided compelling and consistent testimony regarding his involvement in the dramatic events he was caught up in at the time (see pp. 91–3). The Air Force had called Dennis, wanting to know how best to preserve, without embalming, hypothetical dead bodies in the desert while being transported to the base. 'Back in those days,' said Dennis, 'we didn't have an air-conditioned hearse, or a pathologist in Roswell. I told him I would go to Sunset Creamery or Clardy's Dairy [and] buy all the dry ice I could, and pack them in it.'[19]

It seems the Air Field immediately took up Dennis's recommendation. Telling new evidence has been provided for me by Rogene Cordes (née Corn), who lived in Roswell on the Hub Corn Ranch at the time. On 4 or 5 of July, she went to get some ice to pack the drinks in for a family picnic. 'But there was no ice anywhere,' she explained to me. 'I often took blocks of ice to our ranch for our big freezers, so I had a lot of sources. The Clardy's Dairy family lived across the street from my grandmother, but they were closed for the holidays so I tried the train station. They informed me that the Air Force base had cleaned them out. The story that I had always heard was that Glenn had suggested dry ice to preserve bodies.'[20]

Further to the information in Dennis's affidavit relating to the alien autopsy, the nurse also told Dennis that the 'suction cups' on the four fingers only became apparent when a severed hand was turned over with long forceps. She also said that the eyes were very large, 'and sunken so far back in you couldn't tell what they looked like. If the bodies had lain out for sometime, their eyes probably ruptured, but she said the bone structure showed they were large.'[21]

Many years later, Dennis made some sketches based on his recollection of those given to him by the nurse (see plate section). Dennis once 'revealed' the name of the nurse to a researcher as 'Naomi Maria Selff'. I asked him if this was indeed the real name. 'I do not confirm nor do I deny any information concerning the nurse and the Roswell UFO crash,' he replied.[22] Later he said he had given out a false name to a researcher as a test, to see if he would keep his mouth shut. The researcher failed the test.

The US Air Force, faced with mounting criticism that it had failed to address the issue of alien bodies in its initial reports on the Roswell incident, conducted another investigation, culminating in *The Roswell Report: Case Closed*. No records could be found for a Naomi Maria Selff. No such person had ever served at Roswell AAF Station Hospital, and a search through the National Archives and Record Administration failed to find a record of anyone by that name having ever served in any branch of the US Armed Forces. Furthermore, records 'did not indicate a sudden or overseas transfer of a nurse or any other person.'[23] But the investigation did yield some pertinent information.

'Even though the name of the nurse is incorrect,' states the USAF report, 'it appears that a nurse assigned to the Roswell AAF Station Hospital in 1947 may have been the basis for the claims. Eileen M. Fanton was the only nurse of the five assigned to Roswell AAF in July 1947, whose personal circumstances and physical attributes not only resembled those of the missing nurse, but appeared to be nearly an exact match.' The report goes on to list the similarities, based on information provided by Glenn Dennis to Stanton T. Friedman and Karl T. Pflock:

> 1st Lt. Eileen M. Fanton was assigned to the Roswell Army Air Field Station Hospital from December 26, 1946 until September 4, 1947 . . . In [Pflock's] account, the missing nurse is described as single, 'real cute, like a small Audrey Hepburn, with short black hair, dark eyes and olive skin.' Lieutenant Fanton was single in 1947, 5' 1" tall, weighed 100 pounds, had black hair, dark eyes, and was of Italian descent . . .
>
> [Dennis] also recalled that the 'missing nurse' was a lieutenant, was a general nurse at the hospital, and had sent him some correspondence at a later date which stated she was in London, England with a New York, NY APO number (military overseas mailing address) as the return address. Records revealed that Fanton was a First Lieutenant (promoted from Second Lieutenant in June 1947), and she was classified as a 'nurse, general duty'. Records also indicated that of the five nurses assigned to the Roswell AAF Station Hospital in July 1947, she was the only one that later served a tour of duty in England. Furthermore, she was assigned to the 7510th USAF Hospital, APO 240, New York, NY, where she served from June 1952 until April 1955. The 7510th USAF Hospital . . . 45 miles north of London at Wimpole Park, Cambridge.
>
> An additional similarity between Fanton and the 'missing nurse' is that her personnel record indicated that she quickly departed Roswell AAF and it is probable that the hospital staff would not have provided information concerning her departure. Fanton's unannounced depart- ure from Roswell AAF, on September 4, 1947 was to be admitted to Brooke General Hospital, Ft. Sam, Houston, Texas, for a medical condition . . .

'Therefore,' concludes the Air Force report, 'if someone other than a family member contacted the Station Hospital at Roswell AAF and inquired about Fanton, as Dennis stated he did, the staff was simply protecting her privacy as a patient. The staff was not participating in a sinister "cover-up" of information as alleged by UFO theorists.'[24] Though the Air Force report states that Fanton was the nurse who 'may have been the basis for the claims', I find Glenn Dennis's claims more credible than those of the US Air Force, given its long history of provable deception and egregious public 'perception management' regarding the UFO problem.

AT FORT RILEY

Earlier I cited testimony from Lieutenant Colonel Philip J. Corso relating to the US Army Intelligence project to 'seed' alien materials recovered near Roswell into American companies. Corso also claimed to have seen alien bodies at Fort Riley, Kansas, where he was serving as an intelligence officer in the rank of major. The incident reportedly occurred on the evening of 6 July 1947.

Master Sergeant Bill Brown, who was supposed to be guarding the old veterinary building – 'off-limits' that night – alerted Corso to something unbelievable contained in a crate, one of many delivered that day from Fort Bliss, Texas. While Brown stood guard outside, Corso went inside, and with the aid of a flashlight soon located a crate that looked as though it had previously been opened, and prized off the lid. What he saw sickened him. Inside a thick glass container, floating submerged in a thick light blue liquid, was what Corso initially took to be a dead child:

It was a four-foot human-shaped figure with arms, bizarre-looking four-fingered hands – I didn't see a thumb – thin legs and feet, and an oversized incandescent lightbulb-shaped head ... I know I must have cringed at first, but then I had the urge to pull off the top of the liquid container and touch the pale gray skin. But I couldn't tell whether it was skin because it looked like a very thin one-piece head-to-toe fabric covering the creature's flesh.

Its eyeballs must have been rolled back in its head because I couldn't see any pupils or iris or anything that resembled a human eye. But the eye sockets themselves were oversized and almond shaped and pointed down to its tiny nose, which didn't really protrude from the skull. It was more like the tiny nose of a baby that never grew as the child grew, and it was mostly nostril.

The creature's skull was overgrown to the point where all its facial features – such as they were – were arranged absolutely frontally, occupying a small circle on the lower part of the head. The protruding ears of a human were nonexistent, its cheeks had no definition, and there were no eyebrows or any indications of facial hair. The creature had only a tiny slit for a mouth and it was completely closed, resembling more of a crease or indentation between the nose and the bottom of the chinless skull than a fully functioning orifice ... I could see no damage to the creature's body and no indication that it had been involved in any accident. There was no blood, its limbs seemed intact, and I could find no lacerations on the skin or through the gray fabric.

I looked through the crate encasing the container of liquid for any paperwork or shipping invoice or anything that would describe the nature or origin of this thing. What I found was an intriguing Army Intelligence document describing the creature as an inhabitant of a craft that had crash-landed in Roswell, New Mexico, earlier that week and a routing manifest for this creature to the log-in officer at the Air Materiel Command at Wright Field and from him to the Walter Reed Army Hospital morgue's pathology section where, I supposed, the creature would be autopsied and stored . . .[25]

In his book *Roswell*, Karl T. Pflock, a former Deputy Assistant Secretary of Defense and CIA officer, is totally disparaging in his assessment of Corso's claims. 'As I read *The Day After Roswell*, I did not know whether to laugh or to cry,' he writes. 'Corso provided absolutely nothing to back up his claims about crashed saucers and alien technologies.'[26] Corso may not have provided any physical evidence to support his claims, but his testimony is nonetheless compelling. However, I do agree with Pflock that there are errors in the book (some compounded by co-writer William J. Birnes, on his own admission). Furthermore, Corso told a friend of mine that he much regretted not properly checking the manuscript before publication. Of crucial importance, for example, was the fact that the Army Foreign Technology office *waited* until American companies were beginning to make inroads on the relevant technologies before handing over the alien materials.

Corso was held in high regard by those who knew him. 'The colonel had a great deal of credibility and expertise, not only as a military officer but also in the fields of intelligence and national security,' wrote Senator Strom Thurmond in his foreword to Corso's book. 'A veteran of World War II and Korea, Corso also spent four years working at the National Security Council. In short, he was very familiar with issues that concerned me and my colleagues on the Senate Armed Services Committee, and he very quickly became a valued source of bountiful information that was insightful and, most important, accurate.'[27]

It is also important to point out here that Corso's military records for that period (see p. 94) show that from February 1954 to June 1956 he served on the Intelligence Staff of the National Security Council's Operations Coordinating Board, later known as 'Special Group 5412', then 'Special Group 5412/2'. This was the group that, under various names (starting with the Psychological Operations Group during the late 1940s) and across several presidential administrations, planned, coordinated, approved and evaluated the most sensitive covert, paramilitary and clandestine operations ever mounted by the United States – including, I assume, those relating to the alien problem. Thus, during the mid-fifties, there was little or nothing in the way of US covert operations to which Corso might not have been exposed.

TESTIMONY OF A BIOPHYSICIST

Earlier I cited the testimony of the Polish biophysicist and engineer 'Dr Cris', who in 1974, with a small team of scientists on contract to NASA, analysed some extraordinary materials. In April 1977, the team met again at NASA's Jet Propulsion Laboratory (JPL) at the California Institute of Technology in Pasadena, California, when a certain NASA physicist held a semi-official party to celebrate his voluntary departure from the agency. At this party, the official informed his guests that they might be interested in seeing some special 'equipment', and after expressing some concerns as to whether or not he should do so, led them to a restricted area in one of the buildings on the JPL facility. There, three floors below ground level, the five scientists entered a secure room, protected by a heavy door with two seals. About 8–10 metres in length and over 4 metres wide, the room seemed to serve principally to exhibit certain items.

'The first thing we saw was two small, shiny Plexiglas containers,' Dr Cris related to science writer Andreas von Rétyi. 'In one of the two was a hip bone, a bit broken at the bottom. It looked like a child's hip bone, but the form was different.' The structure, shape and colour were somewhat different – that is, the bone was not typical yellowish-white but light greyish-white, the cavity for the bone marrow was smaller, and the structures where the muscles would have been attached were formed differently, reported Dr Cris.

> In the second container we saw the fragment of a skull; maybe one-third or forty percent of it. The segment included the eye socket and part of the right half of the skull. This head was about as big as that of an elderly child. It looked human-like, but derived neither from a child nor from an ape. The colour was different from that of the hip bone – it appeared lighter. I don't know if some parts of the bone had been damaged by fire; in any case, the colour was not the same ... part of the skull protecting the brain was much thinner than a human's skull. There was even a short, small explanation: *From the first and*

second incidents in New Mexico. We took our American friend aside
and asked him what this meant. 'That's highly secret,' he replied. 'We
are not really allowed to talk about that.'

In addition to these exhibits, three of the scientists were surprised to
recognize the materials from which they had analysed samples in 1974.
'These objects were about half a year in our laboratory,' said Dr Cris. 'The
material was probably presented to us to test us; to what extent we would
agree, or even find out new things about it. These samples [evidently] had
been investigated umpteen times by several teams of scientists in order to
gain further insight.' Dr Cris learned later that in 1947 'there had been
altogether at least two spaceships, with at least three crew, that crashed'.

It was reported that one member of the second crew had survived. I
don't know anything specific about his fate. The first three beings were
totally charred, whereas the other two corpses were mostly preserved;
for example, the skull, skin and bones. There were also parts of
clothing found. As I learned from biologists, their blood is similar to
ours [but] shows a totally different reaction toward oxygen; so inside
the spaceship they must breathe a mixture of helium and oxygen, since
nitrogen, for whatever reasons, is really not good for them.

Andreas von Rétyi attests to the credibility of the biophysicist. 'In
lengthy personal conversations with Dr Cris, I have been able to convince
myself of his great knowledge and insights,' he assured me. 'Besides, he is
unquestionably in a position where he doesn't need to draw attention to
himself by making up such a story.'[28]

Dr Cris's comments on the 'totally different reaction toward oxygen'
are reportedly endorsed by none other than General George C. Marshall,
US Army Chief of Staff in the Second World War and Secretary of State
from 1947 to 1949. In 1951 Dr Rolf Alexander (whose fields included
biochemistry) spoke to General Marshall, following sightings of UFOs at
Mexico City Airport as newsmen awaited the arrival of the great general
(Chapter 11). Marshall revealed not only that alien craft and their occupants
had been recovered, but also that contact with the men in the craft had
been established. On three occasions, he said, there had been landings that
had proved disastrous for the occupants. On each of these occasions,
'breathing the heavily oxygenated atmosphere of this Earth had literally
incinerated the visitors from within and had burned them to a crisp.'[29]

TESTIMONY OF DR WERNHER VON BRAUN

Clark C. McClelland is a retired aerospace engineer who worked for more than three decades on numerous projects at NASA's launch facilities at the Cape Canaveral/Kennedy Space Center. On many occasions he spoke to scientists assigned to the Army Ballistics Missile Agency, in particular Dr Wernher von Braun, who from 1945 to 1950 was adviser to the US Army's V-2 test firings at the White Sands Proving Grounds in New Mexico. During a break one evening at a meeting of the Manned Flight Awareness programme near the Cape, McClelland asked Dr von Braun if he knew anything about the Roswell incident, knowing that he had been employed at White Sands at the time. Von Braun raised an eyebrow, lit a cigarette, and revealed the following:

> Dr von Braun explained how he and [certain of] his associates had been taken to the crash site after most of the military were pulled back. They did a quick analysis of what they found. He told me the craft did not appear to be made of metal as we know metal on Earth. He said it seemed to be created from something biological, like skin. I was lost as to what he indicated, other than thinking perhaps the craft was 'alive'.
>
> The recovered bodies were temporarily being kept in a nearby medical tent. They were small, very frail and had large heads. Their eyes were large. Their skin was greyish and reptilian in texture. He said it looked similar to the skin texture of rattlesnakes he'd seen several times at White Sands. His inspection of the debris had even him puzzled: very thin, aluminum coloured, like silvery chewing-gum wrappers. Very light and extremely strong. The interior of the craft was nearly bare of equipment, as if the creatures and craft were part of a single unit.

He trusted me to hear such astonishing events because I vowed not to report it,' McClelland explains. 'I never broke that vow. Since he is deceased, and the incident happened over fifty years ago, I am now disclosing what I heard.'[30]

Clark McLelland seems to have a good professional reputation, at least, though some researchers doubt his reliability. However, evidence for von Braun's probable involvement in the Roswell recovery has been provided by a scientist, Dr Robert I. Sarbacher (see p. 133).

(see p. 133)

*

Fred Whiting, who served on Capitol Hill from 1977 to 1983 as a press secretary and special assistant to two congressmen, has provided a timeline of events relating to Roswell, from July to September 1947, from which I cite the following from the month of July (my comments in brackets):

July 7 13:55 – Gen. Curtis LeMay [Deputy Chief of the Air Staff for Research and Development] and Gen. Hoyt S. Vandenberg [Deputy Commander-in-Chief of the Air Staff] meet at the Pentagon 're: flying discs'.

July 8 Gen. Nathan F. Twining, Commander, USAAF Air Materiel Command, makes an unannounced visit to Kirtland Army Air Field, near Albuquerque. Referring to press accounts about 'flying discs', Twining says 'the mysterious objects are definitely not the result of experiments by the air forces'.

July 9 10:30 – President Truman meets with Senator Carl Hatch of New Mexico.

10:35 – Lt. Gen. James Doolittle [who had been at the forefront of investigations into the 'ghost rockets'] and deputy Army Air Forces chief Gen. Hoyt Vandenberg [involved in the same investigations] meet with Stuart Symington, Secretary of War for Air.

11.58 – Vandenberg calls the President's office.

12:50 – Vandenberg and Symington meet with Joint Chiefs.

14:30 – Vandenberg and Symington meet again.

Army Air Forces intelligence [requirements] chief Brig. Gen. George Schulgen requests FBI cooperation in solving the flying-disc problem.

The War Department tells the FBI that the discs do not belong to the Army or Navy.

July 10 Aborted V-2 launch at White Sands. Gen. Twining stops at White Sands before returning to Wright Field.

10:30 – Maj. Gen. Leslie Groves, head of the Armed Forces Special Weapons Project, and Gen. Robert Montague, commander of the Army Guided Missile School, meet with Vandenberg and LeMay.

12:15 – Doolittle and Vandenberg meet with President Truman.

14:40 – Secretary of War Robert Patterson meets with Groves and Montague.

An FBI memo dated July 10 reveals that Army Air Forces intelligence had asked the FBI for their cooperation in collecting flying-disc data.[31]

CONGRESSIONAL INQUIRY

In March 1993, in response to constituent information requests, US Congressman Steven Schiff (First Congressional District, New Mexico) initiated inquiries into the Roswell incident. Schiff had a background in law, and had served as a pilot with the rank of lieutenant colonel in the New Mexico Air National Guard. He began the inquiries with a letter to Defense Secretary Les Aspin, requesting a written report and a full briefing by Pentagon officials on the nature of the Roswell debris and an explanation for the government's actions. There was no response.

A second request resulted in a reply from the Defense Department's Congressional liaison office, referring Schiff to the National Archives, on the grounds that all Air Force records from Project Blue Book were stored there. However, no files on Roswell could be found in Blue Book records.

'I thought that the response I got was not routine – to be just referred to another agency without even an offer of assistance,' said Schiff during an interview with Lawrence Moore and myself for a British documentary in 1994. 'That simple bit of courtesy is something frankly I would have expected from a government agency.'[32]

In October 1993 Schiff took up the matter with the Comptroller General, Charles Bowsher, head of the General Accounting Office (GAO), the investigative arm of Congress. Within a few days, Schiff's office received a call from the GAO investigator (a specialist in military and intelligence matters) who had been assigned to the case. Difficulties ensued at the outset. Colonel Larry Shockley, Director of Plans and Operations in the Secretary of Defense's Congressional liaison office, warned the GAO investigator, 'You've got no business getting into that.'[33]

In May 1994 I received an official request from Congressman Schiff, whom I had met earlier that year in his Congressional office, to assist him with his inquiry.[34] (See p. 98.) In September 1994 – to pre-empt the GAO's findings, made available to Schiff's office in July 1995 – the Air Force issued a twenty-three-page *Report of Air Force Research Regarding the 'Roswell Incident'*. The report concluded that a Project Mogul balloon array and instrument package were most probably responsible for the 'tales' of a crashed flying saucer. This report was later incorporated into *The Roswell Report: Fact versus Fiction in the New Mexico Desert* (referenced earlier).

It needs to be mentioned here that although the former report was issued by the USAF's Public Affairs Media Relations Division, its author was Colonel Richard L. Weaver, Director, Security and Special Program

Oversight, of the Office of Special Investigations – an agency whose work involves counter-intelligence operations and deception, including 'perception management', and which has a long record of deep involvement in the UFO problem.

In late July 1995 the GAO delivered its report to Congressman Steve Schiff's office. The press release from that office, encapsulating the GAO's findings, appears on p. 97. Sadly, Steven Schiff died in office in the spring of 1998, after a sudden and virulent bout of skin cancer.

'When critically examined,' the Air Force's final report in 1997 concluded, 'the claims that the US Army Air Forces recovered a flying saucer and alien crew in 1947, were found to be a compilation of many verifiable events. For the most part, the descriptions collected by UFO theorists were of actual operations and tests carried out by the US Air Force in the 1950s.'[35]

The 'aliens', the report explains, were either injured airmen involved in crashes, or anthropomorphic dummy-drop tests, part of an Air Force project to find a way of parachuting pilots safely from high altitudes. The dummy drops, however, began in 1953 – six years after the Roswell incident. Interestingly, Lieutenant Colonel Raymond A. Madson, project officer for the tests from 1956 to 1960, states that during his tour of duty at Wright-Patterson Air Force Base he heard rumours that there was 'a very secure building' where alien bodies were kept. 'I didn't pay a lot of attention,' he said, 'because the climate at that time was you didn't ask questions.'[36]

No cover-up? Obviously there was. And for very sound reasons.

'You have to understand what was happening in this country at the time, things that had never happened before in the history of man,' explained Brigadier General Thomas J. DuBose in the final interview he gave on the Roswell affair. 'We had just gone through a world war. We had seen the firebombing of great cities, atomic bombs, destruction on an unprecedented scale. Then came this flying saucer business. It was just too much for the public to have to deal with . . .'[37]

REFERENCES

1. 'RAAF Captures Flying Saucer on Ranch in Roswell Region', *Roswell Daily Record*, 8 July 1947.
2. Interview with Jesse A. Marcel Sr by Bob Pratt, 8 December 1979, published in *Roswell in Perspective*, by Karl T. Pflock, The Fund for UFO Research, PO Box 277, Mount Rainier, Maryland 20712, 1994, pp. 119–26.

3. Affidavit by Jesse A. Marcel MD, 6 May 1991, *The Roswell Events*, compiled by Fred Whiting, The Fund for UFO Research, 1993, reproduced in both books by Pflock.

4. *The Roswell Report: Fact versus Fiction in the New Mexico Desert*, Headquarters United States Air Force, US Government Printing Office, 1995.

5. Personal interview, Helena, Montana, 10 May 2004.

6. Berlitz, Charles and Moore, William, *The Roswell Incident*, Granada, London, 1980, pp. 68–9.

7. Personal interview, Roswell, 1 June 1993.

8. Moore, William L., *Crashed UFOs: Evidence in the Search for Proof*, William L. Moore Publications and Research, 4219 W. Olive Street, Suite 247, Burbank, California 91505, 1985, p. 46.

9. Kissner, J. Andrew, *Peculiar Phenomenon: Early United States Efforts to Collect and Analyze Flying Discs*.

10. Interview, Phoenix, 25 September 2005.

11. Moore, op. cit.

12. Randle, Kevin D. and Schmitt, Donald R., *UFO Crash at Roswell*, Avon Books, New York, 1991, pp. 108–11.

13. Corso, Col. Philip J. with Birnes, William J., *The Day After Roswell*, Pocket Books, New York, 1997.

14. Von Rétyi, Andreas, *Das Alien Imperium: UFO-Geheimnisse der USA*, Langen Müller, Munich, 1995. Extracts translated by Dorothee Walter.

15. Randle, Kevin and Schmitt, Donald, *The Truth About the UFO Crash at Roswell*, M. Evans and Company, New York, 1994, pp. 62–3.

16. Stowers, Carlton, 'Contact: A half century later, witnesses insist little green – or maybe brown – men crashed in New Mexico', *Dallas Observer*, 3 April 2003.

17. Affidavit by Alice Knight, 9 July 1991, *The Roswell Events*.

18. Shawcross, Tim, *The Roswell File*, Bloomsbury, London, 1997, pp. 41–5.

19. Dennis, Glenn, 'The Roswell Mortician' (ed. William J. Birnes), *UFO Magazine*, PO Box 4252, Sunland, CA 91041–4252, Vol. 13, No. 8, December 1998, p. 36.

20. Personal interview, Charleston, South Carolina, 30 October 2004, and letter, 26 August 2005.

21. Dennis, op. cit., p. 39.

22. Fax, 11 June 1996.

23. McAndrew, Captain James, *The Roswell Report: Case Closed*, Headquarters United States Air Force, Washington, DC, US Government Printing Office, 1997, p. 81.

24. Ibid., pp. 82–3.

25. Corso and Birnes, op. cit., pp. 30–3.

26. Pflock, Karl T., *Roswell: Inconvenient Facts and the Will to Believe*, Prometheus Books, Amherst, New York, 2001, p. 204.

27. Corso, op. cit., p. x. (Senator Thurmond's foreword was removed from the second edition of the book.)
28. Von Rétyi, op. cit., and letters, August/September 1995.
29. *Flying Saucer Review*, Vol. 2, No. 1, 1956, p. 2.
30. www.stargate-chronicles.com
31. Whiting, Fred, *The Roswell Events*, The Fund for UFO Research, PO Box 277, Mount Rainier, MD 20712, pp. 9–14.
32. *Network First: UFO*, Central Productions for Central Television, 10 January 1995.
33. Fred Whiting, interviewed on *Network First: UFO*.
34. Letter, 24 May 1994.
35. McAndrew, op. cit., p. 123.
36. Choate, Trish, 'Alien report debunked by retired Cibola County Army officer', *Independent*, Gallup, NM, 3 July 1997.
37. Cox, op. cit.

Additional books on the Roswell incident include *Crash at Corona* by Stanton T. Friedman and Don Berliner (Paragon House, New York, 1992) and *Beyond Roswell* by Michael Hesemann and Philip Mantle (Michael O'Mara, London, 1997).

RAAF Captures Flying Saucer On Ranch in Roswell Region

ROSWELL, NEW MEXICO, TUESDAY, JULY 8, 1947.

No Details of Flying Disk Are Revealed

Roswell Hardware Man and Wife Report Disk Seen

The intelligence office of the 509th Bombardment group at Roswell Army Air Field announced at noon today, that the field has come into possession of a flying saucer.

According to information released by the department, over authority of Maj. J. A. Marcel, intelligence officer, the disk was recovered on a ranch in the Roswell vicinity, after an unidentified rancher had notified Sheriff Geo. Wilcox, here, that he had found the instrument on his premises.

Major Marcel and a detail from his department went to the ranch and recovered the disk, it was stated.

After the intelligence office here had inspected the instrument it was flown to "higher headquarters."

The intelligence office stated that no details of the saucer's construction or its appearance had been revealed.

Part of the lead story in the *Roswell Daily Record* (8 July 1947). By the following day the US Army Air Forces had announced that the wreckage was not that of a flying saucer, but of a weather balloon.

A map from *The Roswell Report: Case Closed* (Headquarters US Air Force, 1997) depicting the various sites relating to the Roswell incident. *(US Air Force)*

AFFIDAVIT

(1) My name is Thomas Jefferson DuBose.

(2) My address is: ███████████████████████████

(3) I retired from the U.S. Air Force in 1959 with the rank of Brigadier General.

(4) In July 1947, I was stationed at Fort Worth Army Air Field [later Carswell Air Force Base] in Fort Worth, Texas. I served as Chief of Staff to Major General Roger Ramey, Commander, Eighth Air Force. I had the rank of Colonel.

(5) In early July, I received a phone call from Maj. Gen. Clements McMullen, Deputy Commander, Strategic Air Command. He asked what we knew about the object which had been recovered outside Roswell, New Mexico, as reported by the press. I called Col. William Blanchard, Commander of the Roswell Army Air Field and directed him to send the material in a sealed container to me at Fort Worth. I so informed Gen. McMullen.

(6) After the plane from Roswell arrived with the material, I asked the Base Commander, Col. Al Clark, to take possession of the material and to personally transport it in a B-26 to Gen. McMullen in Washington, D.C. I notified Gen. McMullen, and he told me he would send the material by personal courier on his plane to Benjamin Chidlaw, Commanding General of the Air Materiel Command at Wright Field [later Wright Patterson AFB]. The entire operation was conducted under the strictest secrecy.

(7) The material shown in the photographs taken in Maj. Gen. Ramey's office was a weather balloon. The weather balloon explanation for the material was a cover story to divert the attention of the press.

(8) I have not been paid or given anything of value to make this statement, which is the truth to the best of my recollection.

_____
(Signature)

_____
(Date)   9/16/91

Signature witnessed by:

_____
(Name)

Notary Public, State of Florida
My Commission Expires Dec. 2, 1991
Bonded Thru Troy Fain - Insurance Inc.

Notary Public
State of Florida
County of Orange

Affidavit by Brigadier General Thomas J. DuBose confirming that 'the weather balloon explanation for the material was a cover story to divert the attention of the press'.

(The Fund for UFO Research, Inc.)

AFFIDAVIT

(1) My name is L. W. Maltais.

(2) My address is: ██████████████████████

(3) I am retired.

(4) I met Grady L. "Barney" Barnett in 1943 when I was serving in the U.S. Army, and he was employed by the state of New Mexico as a civil engineer. We had a father-son relationship.

(5) Around 1950, Mr. Barnett told me that several years before, during a field trip in New Mexico, he discovered a crashed disc-shaped craft with the bodies of strange beings on the ground. He was absolutely convinced that the craft was from outer space.

(6) The beings he described were similar--but not identical--to humans. They were 3 1/2 to 4 feet tall; slim and hairless, with large pear-shaped heads. They had four fingers on each hand. They were dressed in tight-fitting, metallic suits. All of them were dead.

(7) Mr. Barnett said that at the same time as his discovery, he was joined by four or five people on an archeology dig.

(8) Shortly afterward, military personnel arrived and escorted them from the area. They told him to keep quiet about the incident, that it was in the national interest for them to get out of there.

(9) Mr. Barnett was a man of great personal integrity who would never tell a lie.

(10) I have not been paid or given anything of value to make this statement. It is the truth to the best of my recollection.

L. W. Maltais
(Signature)

23 APRIL 1991
(Date)

Signature witnessed by:

_____
(Name)

Subscribed and sworn to before me this 23rd day of April, 1991.

Arlyce Bruun

Arlyce R. Bruun
NOTARY PUBLIC-MINNESOTA
BELTRAMI COUNTY
My Commission Expires SEPT. 25, 1991

Affidavit by LaVerne Maltais. (*The Fund for UFO Research, Inc.*)

AFFIDAVIT

(1) My name is Glenn Dennis.

(2) My address is: ███████████████████████████████

(3) I am ( ) employed as: _____ ( ) retired.

(4) In July 1947, I was a mortician, working for the Ballard Funeral Home in Roswell, which had a contract to provide mortuary services for the Roswell Army Air Field. One afternoon, around 1:15 or 1:30, I received a call from the base mortuary officer who asked what was the smallest size hermetically sealed casket that we had in stock. He said, "We need to know this in case something comes up in the future." He asked how long it would take to get one, and I assured him I could get one for him the following day. He said he would call back if they needed one.

(5) About 45 minutes to an hour later, he called back and asked me to describe the preparation for bodies that had been lying out on the desert for a period of time. Before I could answer, he said he specifically wanted to know what effect the preparation procedures would have on the body's chemical compounds, blood and tissues. I explained that our chemicals were mainly strong solutions of formaldehyde and water, and that the procedure would probably alter the body's chemical composition. I offered to come out to the base to assist with any problem he might have, but he reiterated that the information was for future use. I suggested that if he had such a situation that I would try to freeze the body in dry ice for storage and transportation.

(6) Approximately a hour or an hour and 15 minutes later, I got a call to transport a serviceman who had a laceration on his head and perhaps a fractured nose. I gave him first aid and drove him out to the base. I got there around 5:00 PM.

(7) Although I was a civilian, I usually had free access on the base because they knew me. I drove the ambulance around to the back of the base infirmary and parked it next to another ambulance. The door was open and inside I saw some wreckage. There were several pieces which looked like the bottom of a canoe, about three feet in length. It resembled stainless steel with a purple hue, as if it had been exposed to high temperature. There was some strange-looking writing on the material resembling Egyptian hieroglyphics. Also, there were two MPs present.

(8) I checked the airman in and went to the staff lounge to have a Coke. I intended to look for a nurse, a 2nd Lieutenant, who had been commissioned about three months earlier right out of college. She was 23 years of age at the time (I was 22). I saw her coming out of one of the examining rooms with a cloth over her mouth. She said, "My gosh, get out of here or you're going to be in a lot of trouble." She went into another door where a Captain stood. He asked me who I was and what I was doing here. I told him, and he instructed me to stay there. I said, "It looks like you've got a crash; would you like me to get ready?" He told me to stay right there. Then two MPs came up and began to escort me out of the infirmary. They said they had orders to follow me out to the funeral home.

Affidavit by Glenn Dennis. *(The Fund for UFO Research, Inc.)*

(9)   We got about 10 or 15 feet when I heard a voice say, "We're not through
with that SOB. Bring him back."   There was another Captain, a redhead with
the meanest-looking eyes I had ever seen, who said, "You did not see anything,
there was no crash here, and if you say anything you could get into a lot of
trouble."   I said, "Hey look mister, I'm a civilian and you can't do a damn
thing to me." He said, "Yes we can; somebody will be picking your bones out
of the sand." There was a black Sergeant with a pad in his hand who said, "He
would make good dog food for our dogs."   The Captain said, "Get the SOB out."
The MPs followed me back to the funeral home.

(10)   The next day, I tried to call the nurse to see what was going on. About
11:00 AM, she called the funeral home and said, "I need to talk to you." We
agreed to meet at the officers club. She was very upset. She said, "Before I
talk to you, you have to give me a sacred oath that you will never mention my
name, because I could get into a lot of trouble."   I agreed.

(11)   She said she had gone to get supplies in a room where two doctors were
performing a preliminary autopsy. The doctors said they needed her to take
notes during the procedure. She said she had never smelled anything so
horrible in her life, and the sight was the most gruesome she had ever seen.
She said, "This was something no one has ever seen." As she spoke, I was
concerned that she might go into shock.

(12)   She drew me a diagram of the bodies, including an arm with a hand that
had only four fingers; the doctors noted that on the end of the fingers were
little pads resembling suction cups. She said the head was disproportionately
large for the body; the eyes were deeply set; the skulls were flexible; the
nose was concave with only two orifices; the mouth was a fine slit, and the
doctors said there was heavy cartilage instead of teeth. The ears were only
small orifices with flaps. They had no hair, and the skin was black--perhaps
due to exposure in the sun. She gave me the drawings.

(13)   There were three bodies; two were very mangled and dismembered, as if
destroyed by predators; one was fairly intact. They were three-and-a-half to
four feet tall. She told me the doctors said: "This isn't anything we've ever
seen before; there's nothing in the medical textbooks like this." She said
she and the doctors became ill. They had to turn off the air conditioning and
were afraid the smell would go through the hospital. They had to move the
operation to an airplane hangar.

(14)   I drove her back to the officers' barracks. The next day I called the
hospital to see how she was, and they said she wasn't available. I tried to
get her for several days, and finally got one of the nurses who said the
Lieutenant had been transferred out with some other personnel. About 10 days
to two weeks later, I got a letter from her with an APO number. She indicated
we could discuss the incident by letter in the future. I wrote back to her
and about two weeks later the letter came back marked "Return To Sender--
DECEASED."   Later, one of the nurses at the base said the rumor was that she
and five other nurses had been on a training mission and had been killed in a
plane crash.

(15)   Sheriff George Wilcox and my father were very close friends. The
Sheriff went to my folks' house the morning after the events at the base and
said to my father, "I don't know what kind of trouble Glenn's in, but you tell

your son that he doesn't know anything and hasn't seen anything at the base."
He added, "They want you and your wife's name, and they want your and your
children's addresses." My father immediately drove to the funeral home and
asked me what kind of trouble I was in. He related the conversation with
Sheriff Wilcox, and so I told him about the events of the previous day. He is
the only person to whom I have told this story until recently.

(16) I had filed away the sketches the nurse gave me that day. Recently, at
the request of a researcher, I tried to locate my personal files at the
funeral home, but they had all been destroyed.

(17) I have not been paid or given anything of value to make this statement,
which is the truth to the best of my recollection.

_____
(Signature)

_8 - 7 - 91_____
(Date)

Signature witnessed by:

_____
(Name)   WALTER G. HAUT

Timothy Good

Military records showing that from February 1954 to June 1956, Lt. Col. Philip J. Corso served on the Intelligence Staff of the National Security Council's Operations Coordination Board, later known as the 'Special Group 5412', then 'Special Group 5412/2', which planned, coordinated, approved and evaluated the most sensitive covert, paramilitary and clandestine operations ever mounted by the United States.

(US Army Archives)

CENTRAL INTELLIGENCE GROUP
2430 E Street, N. W.
Washington 25, D. C.

19 SEP 1947

MEMORANDUM FOR THE MILITARY ASSESSMENT OF THE JOINT INTELLIGENCE
COMMITTEE

SUBJECT: Examination of Unidentified Disc-like Aircraft near Military
Installations in the State of New Mexico: A Preliminary Report

1.   Pursuant to the recent world events and domestic security
problems within the Atomic Energy Commission, the intelligence reports
of so-called "Flying Saucers" and the intrusion of unknown aircraft over
the most secret defense installations, a classified intelligence project
is warranted. The National Security Act of 1947 established a Central
Intelligence Agency under the National Security Council. When the
Director of Central Intelligence assumes his official responsibilities,
the National Intelligence Authority is abolished the files pertaining to
unidentified aircraft sightings, intelligence personnel and funds of the
Central Intelligence Group will be transferred to the Agency.

2.   The recovery of unidentified planform aircraft in the state of
New Mexico on 6 July 1947, ten miles northwest of Oscura Peak, and a debris
field 75 miles northwest of the Army's 509th Atomic Bomb Group, Roswell
Army Air Field, is confirmed. A subsequent capture of another similar craft
30 miles east of the Army's Alamogordo Army Air Field on 5 July 1947, has
convinced the Army Air Forces S-2, Army G-2 and Navy ONI, that the craft
and wreckage are not of US manufacture.

3.   Until a clear directive from the President is issued, there can
be no co-ordinated scientific examination of the objects in question.
Currently, the core material is being secured at the Naval Research
Laboratory hanger facilities at the White Sands Proving Ground, the Sandia
Base facilities (Armed Forces Special Weapons Project), Alamogordo AAF and
the Aero Medical Research facilities at Randolph Field, Texas.

4.   The research scientists at the Air Forces Research and Development Center, Wright Field, are utilising their test facilities and a new
biological laboratory in an on-going study program. The offices of the
JRDB, FBI and the State Department are assisting the Joint Intelligence
Committee in acquiring any intelligence from MI5 and MI6 on possible Soviet
long-range reconnaissance aircraft/missile research and development tests.

/S/

R. H. HILLENKOETTER
Rear   Admiral, USN
Director of   Central Intelligence

TOP SECRET/EYES ONLY

An unauthenticated Top Secret/Eyes Only memorandum from Rear Admiral Roscoe
Hillenkoetter, Director of Central Intelligence, relating to unidentified discs recovered
by the military in New Mexico in July 1947. The handwritten note seems to read 'Joint
Chiefs concern'. (Timothy Cooper)

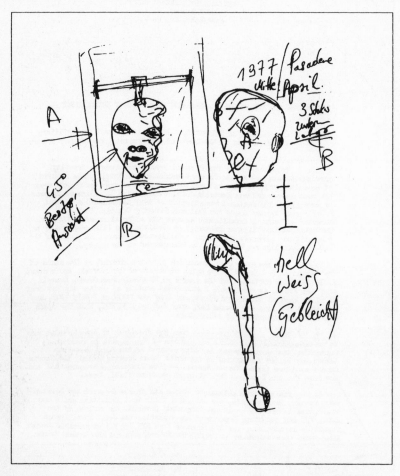

Sketches by a Polish biophysicist of the skeletal remains of an alien recovered from 'one of the two incidents in New Mexico'. Dr Cris examined these, and other materials which he had previously examined in 1974, together with a small international team of scientists, at NASA's Jet Propulsion Laboratory (JPL), Pasadena, California, in April 1977.

(Andreas von Rétyi)

08/02/95   16:36   ☎   ☐002/003

News Release

U.S. CONGRESSMAN
Steve Schiff   FIRST CONGRESSIONAL DISTRICT
NEW MEXICO

WASHINGTON OFFICE: 2404 Rayburn Building • Washington, D.C. 20515 • (202) 225–6316 • FAX (202) 225–4975
DISTRICT OFFICE: 625 Silver Ave., S.W., Suite 140 • Albuquerque, NM 87102 • (505) 766–2538 • FAX (505) 766–1674

Immediate Release   J. Barry Bitzer
July 28th, 1995   (202) 225-2245

Schiff Receives, Releases Roswell Report
(missing documents leave unanswered questions)

Washington: Congressman Steve Schiff today released the General
Accounting Office (GAO) report detailing results of a records
audit related to events surrounding a crash in 1947, near
Roswell, New Mexico, and the military response.

The 20 page report is the result of constituent information
requests to Congressman Schiff and the difficulty he had getting
answers from the Department of Defense in the now 48-year-old
controversy.

Schiff said important documents, which may have shed more light
on what happened at Roswell, are missing. "The GAO report states
that the outgoing messages from Roswell Army Air Field (RAAF) for
this period of time were destroyed without proper authority."
Schiff pointed out that these messages would have shown how
military officials in Roswell were explaining to their superiors
exactly what happened.

"It is my understanding that these outgoing messages were
permanent records, which should never have been destroyed. The
GAO could not identify who destroyed the messages, or why." But

-more-

Part of a news release from Congressman Steve Schiff's office relating to the investigation
into the Roswell incident by the General Accounting Office. 'The GAO report states that
the outgoing messages from Roswell Army Air Field for this period of time were
destroyed without proper authority,' declared Schiff. *(US Congress)*

STEVEN SCHIFF
FIRST DISTRICT, NEW MEXICO

COMMITTEES:
SCIENCE, SPACE, AND TECHNOLOGY
JUDICIARY
STANDARDS OF OFFICIAL CONDUCT
GOVERNMENT OPERATIONS
SUBCOMMITTEE ON HUMAN RESOURCES AND
INTERGOVERNMENTAL RELATIONS
RANKING MEMBER
REPUBLICAN RESEARCH COMMITTEE
TASK FORCE ON CRIME
CHAIRMAN

Congress of the United States
House of Representatives
Washington, DC 20515-3101

May 24, 1994

PLEASE REPLY TO:

☐ WASHINGTON OFFICE:
    1009 LONGWORTH BUILDING
    WASHINGTON, DC 20515-3101
    (202) 225-6316

☐ DISTRICT OFFICE:
    625 SILVER AVENUE, SW
    SUITE 140
    SILVER SQUARE
    ALBUQUERQUE, NM 87102
    (505) 766-2538

Timothy C. Good

Dear Timothy:

It was an honor to meet you last February and I look forward to viewing your documentary when it arrives. I would also like to acknowledge and sincerely thank you for your expression of support for my request to the General Accounting Office regarding the "Roswell Incident."

My intention in this effort has been variously reported, but I want you to know that I am intent on finding the military and government files on this incident with the purpose of releasing the information in the files to the public.

Many people who have contacted me have asked if there is any way in which they could be of help in my effort. I would appreciate copies of any correspondence directed to government departments or agencies specifically regarding the Roswell Incident, along with the department or agency reply.

If you or someone with whom you are acquainted has such correspondence, I would request that you send copies of it to my District Office in Albuquerque, the address of which is listed above.

Further, I would be grateful to learn of other Members of Congress who are now, or, who before me, pursued this same issue with government agencies.

Again, I appreciate your support in this effort, and I will keep you informed on the progress of my inquiry. If you have additional information, or questions, please do not hesitate to contact me. I will always be pleased to hear from you.

Sincerely,

Sten Schiff

Steven Schiff

SS:md

6. A STATE OF SIEGE

On 8 July, the day that the Roswell recovery made headline news, a US Army Air Forces C-54 transport on a flight from Bermuda to Florida simply 'disappeared' in the Atlantic, according to Air Transport Command, its crew presumed lost at sea, since two seat cushions and debris were seen.[1] This is not to insinuate that the accident was related to Roswell. However, as the following examples by Andy Kissner show, aircraft accidents coincidentally continued on a wide scale that month:

July 13
— Twenty killed and fifteen injured when a DC-3 crashes into a swamp in Florida, after its two engines stopped in quick succession.
— An American Airlines DC-4 en route to Shannon, Ireland, lands in Newfoundland after two of its four engines 'went dead'.
— A Navy Corsair crashes and explodes in Harbourton, New Jersey, killing the pilot.
— An Army Reserve pilot killed in his trainer.

July 14
— Two USAAF aircraft collide in mid-air near Frankfurt, Germany.

July 20
— Eight UK Royal Navy crew members killed in a series of three accidents involving two Firefly planes (which had interlocked with each other) and two Seafire planes (landing on the aircraft carrier HMS *Theseus*).

July 21
— Seventeen killed when an Argentine transport plane, unable to stop on the runway, runs into a crowd.
— Two US Marine Corps aircraft interlock in mid-air above El Toro Airfield, California, killing one.
— Two Fifth Air Force pilots killed when their planes collide near Tokyo.[2]

On 15 July 1947, a P-80 Shooting Star, similar to the jet fighter placed on stand-by at Muroc Field, California (mentioned in the previous chapter), landed in New Mexico on a remote stretch of Highway 380, 25 miles south-west of the Corona flying-disc crash site, at Carrizozo, a small community close to the north-east corner of White Sands. 'The P-80 waited at Carrizozo,' reports Kissner. 'Its mission, although secret to this day, was to provide air cover for the recovery operation. This was necessary in the event that another flying disc appeared and attempted to impede elements of the recovery T-Force. Perhaps a disc would attempt to retrieve the bodies of the crashed disc's dead crew members.'

> The fighter was based at March Field, California. Using aircraft based at a distance from the site of a possible engagement is a further security precaution ... The P-80 sat next to Highway 380, and was refuelled by a US Army tank truck driven from Fort Bliss ... The cover story was that the fighter 'ran low on fuel' in a rainstorm. Over four days at least two C-47 transports, another 'Army transport' and the P-80 all used either the Carrizozo airport runway (a dirt strip) or Highway 380 as a makeshift landing strip.
>
> On the afternoon of 18 July, Capt. Floyd G. Soule brought his fighter back onto the centre of the road and applied power ... As he passed stall speed and accelerated to 120 mph and pulled back on the stick, the plane lifted off the roadway to an altitude of 100 feet but gained no more altitude [and] the fighter veered violently to the right, nose down.[3] An eyewitness reported that the airplane was flying very fast, and without any observable or explainable cause simply rolled over.
>
> The P-80, out of control, flew directly into the Monte Vista gas station [on] State Route 54 and Highway 380. The airplane and the gas station exploded in a fireball simultaneously, killing Capt. Soule instantly. It also killed Joe Drake, 25, of Carrizozo, and injured four others.[4]

Many sightseers had lined the highway to watch the take-off. Although a newspaper reported that the P-80 'barely cleared the ground', one of Kissner's sources said it reached about 100 feet before crashing (see above). I should mention here that in September 1947, four major P-80 accidents were attributed to loss of lateral control owing to inadequate hydraulic pressure reaching the power-boosted ailerons, and this was suspected as the cause of five other crashes. Three of the first twenty-nine fatal P-80/F-80 accidents were caused by loss of control.[5]

Kissner was the first to associate this tragedy with the recovery operation of a flying disc. 'This is not surprising that an association wasn't made,' he says, 'since it was only reported in a few [local] newspapers.'

In September 1994, in the official US Air Force Study related to the 'Roswell Incident', the Air Force reports no aircraft accidents as having occurred in or near the crash site at the same time . . . In addition, the Air Force reported losing [only] five aircraft in New Mexico during July 1947. With the exception of the P-80, which is mentioned to have crashed somewhere in New Mexico, *the Air Force reports four other aircraft losses during July that I wasn't able to find in any published news source from 1947.*[6]

On 1 August 1947, an AAF B-25 Mitchell twin-engined bomber crashed near Kelso, Washington, killing the pilots, Captain William Davidson and Lieutenant Frank Brown, both intelligence officers from the Fourth Air Force Headquarters at Hamilton Field, California. Two others parachuted to safety. Davidson and Brown were returning from Tacoma, Washington, where they had interviewed pilots Kenneth Arnold and Captain Edward Smith, both witnesses to UFO sightings earlier that summer. Arnold and Smith had become embroiled in the complex and sinister Maury Island incident of 21 June when, according to witnesses in a boat, including the captain, Harold Dahl, six flying objects were seen circling above Puget Sound, one spewing 'slag', of which some fell on the boat.

Arnold and Smith had introduced the officers to Fred Crisman, a mysterious character with a background in counter-intelligence (including 'black operations' for the CIA) who had investigated (and 'contaminated') the case. At the end of the meeting, Crisman gave the officers a heavy box containing large chunks of the recovered fragments, which were later loaded on the B-25 at McChord Field. Arnold noted that the materials were rather different from the aluminium-type metals that he and Smith had been shown previously by Crisman.

Arnold and Smith had run into many weird and disturbing experiences during their investigations into the Maury Island case. Was the B-25 crash in any way related to its cargo, they wondered? According to a survivor, an AAF passenger, one of the engines had caught fire nearly twenty minutes after take-off. When the emergency fire-fighting system failed to work, the pilots ordered the others to bail out. For some reason, the pilots never followed. 'It was never completely explained by the military why [the pilots] did not notify anyone by radio signifying their distress nor why they hadn't parachuted also,' wrote Arnold. 'According to the [passenger] a good ten minutes had elapsed between the time he was shoved out of the B-25 until the fire reached serious proportions . . .'[7]

On 3 August 1947, a Navy carrier plane crashed near Fort Hancock,

Texas. Shortly before the accident, the pilot radioed Biggs Army Air Field and warned them that he was 'running out of gas and about to crash'. An ambulance sent to recover the pilot went out of control and ran head-on into a truck,' Kissner reports. 'The episode was reported as a car accident, not one involving a crashed military aircraft.'[8]

On a flight between Tokyo, Kwajalein Island and Honolulu on 16 August, a B-17 bomber carrying US Ambassador George C. Atcheson, the chief US political adviser to the Japan Occupation Forces, and nine others crashed in shark-infested waters 65 miles west of Honolulu after the plane 'ran out of gas'. Three crew members were rescued but the others were never found.[9]

'Running out of gas' seems to have occurred rather too many times. Pilots seldom fail to check the required amount of fuel for any given flight. Another common cause of accidents at this time was engine failure. Probably many of these instances have a conventional explanation, but I am mindful of the fact that since the Second World War, unknown aircraft have been responsible for triggering engine failure (Chapter 1). The inability of planes to gain altitude on take-off is similarly hard to rationalize in all cases. 'The idea that an airplane at 100 per cent power can't get off the ground is very difficult to understand,' says Kissner.

> The only way an airplane doesn't gain altitude at take-off is if it can't build relative air speed . . . is overweight, has experienced a condition known as density altitude (a function of heavy weight, high temperature and high altitude), or if something's holding it down. Its corollary in the air is 'failure to maintain altitude'. Again, this is very rare . . .

'There was a real threat to the national security of the United States in the summer of 1947,' says Kissner, 'but few were aware of it. It wasn't the USSR, Eastern Europe, the Soviet Union or the Chinese revolution, and it wasn't the Koreans; nor was it the design, control or use of the atomic bomb. It was a totally new technology with new weapons that were more capable than anything on Earth. And it was a new technology that our best scientists didn't understand . . .'[10]

EVENTS IN THE USSR

Sergei P. Korolyev was one of the USSR's leading rocket scientists, and his impressive achievements had earned him the high honour of a state funeral in 1966.[11] According to Valery P. Burdakov, a professor of engineering sciences and fellow of the Russian Academy of Sciences, in July 1947 (some accounts say 1948) Korolyev was invited to the Ministry of State Security (MGB – later KGB) headquarters in Moscow, where he was informed by the MGB chief that the invitation was at the behest of Josef Stalin. Together with a team of translators, Korolyev was taken to a special apartment and given many foreign documents dealing with flying saucers, including some relating to the Roswell incident, and told he had three days to come up with an opinion.

Three days later Korolyev was summoned to a meeting with Stalin, who asked him whether these mysterious objects posed a threat to the state. Korolyev replied that the objects did not appear to be weapons of a potential enemy, but that the phenomenon was real nonetheless. According to Korolyev, Stalin also consulted other leading scientists, who came up with the same conclusion.[12]

On an unspecified date in 1947, anti-aircraft guns of the Soviet Army's Transcaucasian Military District fired on a cigar-shaped object which had entered Soviet airspace from the Turkish border. Even though the object's altitude was below 4,000 metres and the guns were capable of reaching a target at up to 12,000 metres, the cigar merely accelerated and flew away across the mountains. Embarrassed because border guards and military monitoring services had earlier also missed the target, the Border District command ordered the monitors not to disclose the fact that the object had reached a speed of up to 2,000 km/h.[13]

US INTELLIGENCE REQUIREMENTS

In late September 1947, Lieutenant General Nathan F. Twining, commanding general of Air Materiel Command (AMC), sent a three-page secret letter to Brigadier General George Schulgen, intelligence chief of the Army Air Forces, confirming that 'the phenomenon reported is something real and not visionary or fictitious', and that 'there are objects probably approximating the shape of a disc, of such appreciable size as to appear to be as large as man-made aircraft' (see p. 113).

Although Twining referred to 'the lack of physical evidence in the shape of recovered crash exhibits which would undeniably prove the existence of these objects' in his report, he was well aware of such, since debris from at least one of the crashed discs in New Mexico had been flown to AMC Headquarters. Assuming that access to crashed-disc data would have been on a 'need to know' basis, it would hardly have been appropriate to let those on the other end of the data-collection line know why such data were needed.

On 1 October 1947, the USAAF became the US Air Force (USAF). That month, an Air Intelligence Requirements Division (AIRD) 'Draft of Collection Memorandum', classified Secret and prepared for the signature of General Schulgen, listed the 'current intelligence requirements in the field of Flying Saucer type aircraft', and included much of Twining's AMC data on the phenomena.

'An alleged "Flying Saucer" type aircraft or object in flight ... has been reported by many observers from widely scattered places, such as the United States, Alaska, Canada, Hungary, the Island of Guam, and Japan,' the memo begins. 'This object has been reported by many competent observers, including USAF rated officers.' The remainder of the memo lists the technical data required to establish the origin of the saucers – assumed to be either German or Russian.[14]

THE MANTELL CASE

On 7 January 1948, a flight of four Air National Guard F-51 Mustang aircraft, led by Captain Thomas Mantell, flying from Marietta, Georgia, to Standiford Field, Kentucky, was requested by the control tower at Godman Air Force Base, Kentucky, to investigate an unidentified airborne craft in the vicinity of Godman. An official summary describes the incident:

> Three of the ships started to climb toward the object. Pilot Hendricks in NG336 continued on and landed at 1501C [Central Time] at Standiford Field ... Pilots Hammond, NG737 & Clements NG800, climbed to 22,000 feet with Mantell in NG3869 then continued on to their original destination because of lack of oxygen arriving there 1540C. Mantell continued climbing toward object. Standiford operations advised Wright Field Service Center at 1750E [Eastern Time] that NG3869 pilot Mantell crashed 2 miles southwest of Franklin, Kentucky at approximately 1645C. Accident fatal to pilot, major damage to aircraft.[15]

The official explanation? Mantell had simply been chasing the planet Venus (!) – later changed to a Skyhook balloon – and had lost consciousness as a result of oxygen starvation. However, a 1948 secret/top-secret joint Air Force and Navy intelligence analysis of UFO incidents states: 'While it is presumed that this pilot suffered anoxia, resulting in his crash, his last message to the tower was, "It appears to be metallic object ... of tremendous size ... directly ahead and slightly above ... I am trying to close for a better look." [16] (See plate.)

There are some conflicting accounts of the crash. Mrs Joe Phillips had heard the plane, engine apparently in trouble, flying over her farmhouse near Franklin. Almost immediately there was a loud explosion and she saw the disintegrating plane hit the ground about 200 yards from her house. However, school student Barbara Mayes said that she saw the plane explode while high in mid-air. [17]

Little-known information on the Mantell case has been acquired by John Timmerman, a leading researcher who learned some interesting details from Edward Hertzberg, former chief physical anthropologist for the US Air Force at the Aerospace Medical Laboratory. Hertzberg had spoken to Carl O. Horst, a high-ranking engineer who had been sent to Godman Field to investigate the crash. As Mantell closed in on the object, Horst said, the Mustang disintegrated.

'The top-secret Skyhook balloon allegation is baloney,' Hertzberg told Timmerman. 'It was a UFO which whirled vertically to high altitude after sitting over the landing strip for a long time, and which was seen by hundreds of Godman Field employees before the Mantell flight wanted to land on the runway. The UFO ... was considered to have sat there at about 400 feet (or maybe even lower).' [18]

Leonard Stringfield, the former US Air Force intelligence officer whose aerial encounter with unknown objects is cited in Chapter 1 (and who collaborated with the USAF in UFO investigations in the mid-1950s), learned more:

> I have heard a number of exotic stories about the Mantell incident, but one stands out that comes from a reliable source [who] related that he had talked with Mantell's wingman, who witnessed the incident. The pilot stated that Mantell pursued the UFO because he was the only pilot equipped with an adequate oxygen mask [and] also related that he saw a burst of 'what appeared to be tracers' fired from the UFO, which hit the P-51 and caused it to disintegrate in the air! Since the Mantell case, all other military encounters ending in disaster have been hidden from the public. [19]

TOP SECRET USAF ANALYSES

In August 1948, the USAF Air Technical Intelligence Center (ATIC), earlier the T-2 division of Twining's Air Materiel Command, decided to make what intelligence jargon refers to as an 'Estimate of the Situation'. Captain Edward Ruppelt was one of the few to see the lengthy Top Secret document, dated 5 August 1948. He confirmed that ATIC concluded that the UFOs were interplanetary in origin. General Hoyt S. Vandenberg, then Chief of Staff, rejected this conclusion for lack of proof, even after a group from ATIC visited his office at the Pentagon in an attempt to persuade him to change his mind. Some months later, Vandenberg ordered the document to be burned.[20] (See p. 114.)

'The general said it would cause a stampede,' Ruppelt told Major Donald Keyhoe, an early author and authority on the subject with intelligence sources in the Pentagon. 'How could we convince the public the aliens weren't hostile when we didn't know it ourselves?'[21]

In 1985 a document that had been classified Top Secret, entitled *Analysis of Flying Object Incidents in the US*, was declassified and released in response to a Freedom of Information Act request. Dated 10 December 1948, this appears to be a watered-down version of the earlier 'Estimate of the Situation', in that it merely concluded that 'some type of flying objects have been observed, although their identification and origin are not discernible'.[22]

Another Top Secret report from 1948, declassified in 1997, is much more revealing:

'For some time we have been concerned by the recurring reports on flying saucers,' begins a US Air Forces in Europe (USAFE) memorandum (see p. 115). 'They periodically continue to crop up; during the last week, one was reported hovering over Neubiberg Air Base [Germany] for about thirty minutes. They have been reported by so many sources and from such a variety of places that we are convinced that they cannot be disregarded and must be explained on some basis which is perhaps slightly beyond the scope of our present intelligence thinking.'

When officers of this Directorate recently visited the Swedish Air Intelligence Service, this question was put to the Swedes. Their answer was that some reliable and fully technically qualified people have reached the conclusion that 'these phenomena are obviously the result of a high technical skill which cannot be credited to any presently known culture on Earth'. They are therefore assuming that these objects originate from some previously unknown or unidentified technology, possibly outside the Earth.

One of these objects was observed by a Swedish technical expert near his home on the edge of a lake. The object crashed or landed in the lake and he carefully noted its azimuth from his point of observation. Swedish intelligence was sufficiently confident in his observation that a naval salvage team was sent to the lake. Operations were underway during the visit of USAFE officers. Divers had discovered a previously uncharted crater on the floor of the lake. No further information is available, but we have been promised knowledge of the results. In their opinion, the observation was reliable, and they believe that the depression on the floor of the lake, which did not appear on current Hydrographic charts, was in fact caused by a flying saucer.

'Although accepting this theory of the origin of these objects poses a whole new group of questions and puts much of our thinking in a changed light,' concluded the memo, 'we are inclined not to discredit entirely this somewhat spectacular theory, meantime keeping an open mind on the subject . . .'[23]

CONTINUING SIGHTINGS AT SENSITIVE FACILITIES

Sightings at some of the United States' most sensitive installations, such as the Los Alamos Atomic Energy Commission's facility, increased. A US Air Force Intelligence report in May 1949 (pp. 116) reveals the extent of concern at that time.

At the instigation of Major General Charles P. Cabell, Director of Air Force Intelligence, and Air Force Scientific Advisory Board Chairman Dr Theodore von Kármán,[24] secret meetings were held at Los Alamos National Laboratory on 16 February 1949. Among the scientists and military officials present were the nuclear physicist Dr Edward Teller and Dr Lincoln LaPaz, a New Mexico University astronomer who himself had had a sighting in December 1948. LaPaz (who held a Top Secret clearance) ruled out conventional fireballs or meteorites and left the conference in no doubt that the phenomena were inexplicable.[25]

At Killeen Base, a highly sensitive nuclear-weapons storage site inside Camp Hood, central Texas, intrusions by unknown aerial objects were observed by security guards on 6 March 1949.[26] 'Unusual Lights' were reported at the site (the 'Q' Area) on many occasions later that month, one involving eight lights that flew over units of the Fourth Army's 2nd Armored Division.

On 24 April 1949, near Arrey, New Mexico, west of the White Sands Proving Ground, Charles B. Moore and a crew of four enlisted men tracking a weather balloon observed an unknown flying object flying high above it at an estimated altitude of 56 miles and a speed of 7 miles per second. Moore trained a 25-power theodolite on the object, revealing it to be roughly 40 feet wide and 100 feet long. The object dropped swiftly from an elevation of 210 degrees to 25 degrees, and passed in front of a mountain range before accelerating vertically and disappearing. 'With good reason this sighting convinced many influential persons that UFOs were real and extraterrestrial,' say researchers Brad Sparks and Jerome Clark, who point out that when news of the sighting leaked out, agents of the Air Force Office of Special Investigations (AFOSI) 'went into a frenzy to try to hunt down the source of the leak'. He turned out to be Commander Robert B. McLaughlin, chief of the Navy's guided missile programme at White Sands at the time, and responsible for the team headed by Moore.[27,28]

A month later, McLaughlin himself had a sighting at White Sands. Following the launch of a rocket, he and two other officers were looking skywards when they noticed a white, slow-moving object of some kind. It passed over the onlookers at a leisurely pace, and then put on a prodigious burst of speed and disappeared behind some hills. In the following month, two small discs were observed from five observation posts as they appeared alongside an Army rocket following its launch. One object then shot through the wake of the rocket and appeared to be 'racing' with the other one before they both accelerated vertically and disappeared.[29] McLaughlin had not been present on this latter occasion, but in 1950 he stated: 'Many times I have seen flying discs following and overtaking missiles in flight at the experimental base at White Sands, where, as is known, the first American atom bomb was tried out.'[30]

From 27 to 28 April, Dr Joseph Kaplan of the Air Force Scientific Advisory Board (SAB) visited Kirtland Air Force Base's Office of Special Investigations (AFOSI), as well as the AEC's Sandia Base and Los Alamos, under orders from Dr von Kármán. A secret memo states that the purpose of the visit was to review reports of 'unidentified aerial phenomena that have been observed in this area during the last five months'.[31] That very night, various security patrols located south-east of Killeen Base reported nine separate sightings of slow-moving lights of varying colours.

The following week, the Fourth Army's 2nd Armored Division planned an operation to deal with the phenomena. On 5 May, personnel from the

Fourth Army, Office of Naval Intelligence (ONI), AFOSI, Army Counter Intelligence Corps (CIC), the Armed Forces Special Weapons Project (AFSWP), together with the FBI, met at Camp Hood for urgent discussions. Twenty-four-hour observation posts, including special cameras and other instruments, were eventually agreed.

The Army tried to take control of the project, reluctant to share much of their data with the other agencies. Each day, the commander of the 'Artillery Training Force' (in reality the security-classified UFO patrol) received fresh orders, which were passed on to the observation posts. The operation lasted until August 1949, during which the phenomena persisted – one involving an object estimated to be 30–70 feet in diameter.[32]

On 14 September, Air Force Chief of Staff General Vandenberg ordered the new commander of Air Materiel Command (AMC), Lieutenant General Benjamin W. Chidlaw, to evaluate the New Mexico sightings (and others) with a view to getting better instrumented data. A special meeting was held at Los Alamos a month later, attended by some top physicists – including Dr Teller, Dr George Gamow and mathematician Stanislav Ulam – and delegates from AFOSI, AFSWP, the Atomic Energy Security Service and other Los Alamos personnel. AMC was represented by Major Frederick C. Oder, who was later to become involved with UFO investigations at the CIA. The group agreed that the phenomena were real, and the project was approved in December by General Chidlaw and the Research and Development Board.[33]

Sometime in 1949, on a plateau near Camp Hood, an even more extraordinary event is said to have occurred. Investigator John Timmerman interviewed an Army man who had served in the 2nd Armored Division. One of the tasks that he and many others were given was 'division guard', which involved being taken out to a plateau and standing guard over the apparently vacant, fenced-off area. 'Why they sent us to guard a plateau was beyond me, at the time,' said the witness. About a month later, around 01:00, very bright and silent lights in the sky approached the plateau and then descended. 'All of a sudden, the end of the plateau opened up and we could see light coming out of the inside. And these other bright lights just came down inside the plateau. And the door closed.'[34] Is it possible that that the plateau – which may well have been used as a top-secret nuclear-weapons storage facility – was also being used as an alien base?

In *Unearthly Disclosure* I reveal information relating to the alien presence given to me in Washington, DC, by a US Army Intelligence veteran, a respected author and reporter who, from 1986 to 1989, had meetings with a high-ranking Air Force intelligence source who had worked at the Pentagon in the USAF Air Staff and Joint Staff. My source learned that following the Second World War, aliens had begun to establish bases in Australia, the Caribbean, the Pacific Ocean, the Soviet Union and the United States. In the US, these bases reportedly were located in Alaska, New Mexico and West Virginia. Camp Hood (Texas) was not mentioned – though I was told that the American bases were guarded by elements of the Army. 'The aliens are there doing their own thing,' declared the source. 'We're there to keep them secure.'

I also learned that a number of alien craft had crashed and had been recovered, together with bodies, by the military. Regarding New Mexico, the base was said to be sited in the vicinity of the nuclear-weapons storage area in the Manzano Mountains, close to Kirtland AFB. On an undisclosed date, two creatures who had survived a crash, or crashes, were killed by an Air Force policeman outside Kirtland, provoking a phenomenal response by the creatures' colleagues, who demonstrated the ease with which they could control local weather. Communications were established. The aliens insisted on the return of the two corpses and, I was told, contact with the US military, represented by an Air Force major, was initiated at an undisclosed location in the south-west desert.[35]

All this seems outlandish, of course. But I have good reasons for believing the information to be essentially reliable. Another Washington reporter has independently learned about an alien base in the Manzano area, as well as the establishment of communications there (to be discussed in the final chapter). And regarding control of local weather, a similar demonstration was witnessed in 1978 by a friend of mine, the well-known Brazilian meteorologist Rubens Villela, who has worked for the CIA and NASA.[36]

According to a number of sources, the most important case involving the recovery of an alien craft took place outside the little town of Aztec, New Mexico, in March 1948. As we shall learn in the next chapter, a great deal of technical and other intelligence resulted from this recovery, intelligence which gave the Americans a giant leap forward in technology and weaponry unparalleled in human history.

REFERENCES

1. *New York Times*, 9 July 1947.
2. Kissner, J. Andrew, *Peculiar Phenomenon: Early United States Efforts to Collect and Analyze Flying Discs.* (Currently unpublished).

3. Ibid.

4. 'Tragedy Hits Carrizozo Last Friday', *Lincoln County News and Carrizozo Outlook*, 25 July 1947.

5. Werrell, Kenneth P., 'Those Were the Days: Flying Safety during the Transition to Jets, 1944–1953', *Air Power History*, Air Force Historical Foundation, Vol. 52, No. 4, Winter 2005, p. 41.

6. Kissner, op. cit.

7. Arnold, Kenneth and Palmer, Ray, *The Coming of the Saucers*, published by the authors, 1952. Those interested in this case, and in Crisman's extraordinary background – including his arrest in Dallas as one of the three 'tramps' following the assassination of President Kennedy – should read *Maury Island UFO: The Crisman Conspiracy*, by Kenn Thomas, IllumiNet Press, PO Box 2808, Lilburn, GA 30048, 1999.

8. *El Paso Times*, 4 August 1947.

9. *Las Cruces Sun News*, 18 August 1947.

10. Kissner, op. cit.

11. Von Braun, Wernher and Ordway III, Frederick I., *History of Rocketry & Space Travel*, Nelson, London, 1966, p. 140.

12. Interview with Professor V. Burdakov, published in *Rabochaya Tribuna*, 13 August 1991. Further information can be found in *The Soviet UFO Files* by Paul Stonehill, Bramley Books, Godalming, Surrey, GU7 1XW, UK (1998).

13. Dremin, Alexander, 'Soviet Army fought UFOs', *Pravda*, Moscow, 23 January 2004.

14. Draft of collection memorandum (Secret) prepared for the signature of Brigadier General George F. Schulgen, Chief, Air Intelligence Requirements Division of the Assistant Chief of Staff of the Air Force for Intelligence, 30 October 1947.

15. 'Report of Aircraft Accident', signed by Major Armand E. Matthews, Wright Field Service Center, Dayton, Ohio, 9 January 1948.

16. *Analysis of Flying Object Incidents in the U.S.*, (Secret/Top Secret), Air Intelligence Division Study No. 203, Directorate of Intelligence and Office of Naval Intelligence, Washington, DC, 10 December 1948, Appendix (Secret), p. 12.

17. *Franklin Favorite*, 8 January 1948.

18. Scott, Irena, *Ohio UFOs (and many others)*, Vol. 1, Greyden Press, Columbus, Ohio, 1997, p. 73.

19. Stringfield, Leonard, *Situation Red: The UFO Siege!*, Doubleday, New York, 1977, p. 137.

20. Ruppelt, Edward J., *The Report on Unidentified Flying Objects*, Doubleday, New York, 1956, pp. 41, 45.

21. Keyhoe, Major Donald E., *Aliens from Space: The Real Story of Unidentified Flying Objects*, Panther Books, St Albans, UK, 1975, p. 27.

22. *Analysis of Flying Object Incidents in the U.S.*, Summary and Conclusions, (Top Secret), 10 December 1948, p. 2.

23. USAFE Item 14, TT 1524, (Top Secret), 4 November 1948 (declassified in 1997).

24. 'History of Air Technical Intelligence Center, 1 January–30 June 1952', publication T55–7568, ATIC, Wright-Patterson AFB, Dayton, OH, 1952, p. 3.

25. 'Report of Trip to Los Alamos, New Mexico, 16 February 1949', by Commander Richard S. Mandelkorn, US Navy, Research and Development Division, Sandia Base, Albuquerque, 18 February 1949.

26. Hall, Michael David and Connors, Wendy Ann, *Captain Edward J. Ruppelt: Summer of the Saucers – 1952*, Rose Press International, Albuquerque, NM, 2000, pp. 4–5.

27. Ibid., p. 19.

28. Sparks, Brad and Clark Jerome, 'The Southwestern Lights, Part III', *International UFO Reporter*, Vol. 10, No. 5, September/October 1985, p. 9.

29. Heard, Gerald, *The Riddle of the Flying Saucers: Is Another World Watching?* Carroll & Nicholson, London, 1950, pp. 40–2.

30. *True* magazine, March 1950.

31. Memorandum (Secret) from Lt. Col. Doyle Rees, USAF, District Commander, 17th District Office of Special Investigations, Kirtland AFB, Albuquerque, to the Director of Special Investigations, Office of the Inspector General USAF, Washington 25, DC, 12 May 1949.

32. Sparks and Clark, op. cit., pp. 10–12.

33. Ibid., p. 16.

34. Swords, Michael D., 'Timmermania: A step too far into the Timmerman Files?' *International UFO Reporter*, Winter 2002–2003, p. 9.

35. Good, Timothy, *Unearthly Disclosure: Conflicting Interests in the Control of Extraterrestrial Intelligence*, Century, London, 2000, pp. 254–7.

36. Ibid., pp. 23, 84.

'The phenomenon reported is something real and not visionary or fictitious.' Part of a three-page memorandum (previously classified Secret) from Lieutenant General Nathan F. Twining to the Commanding General, Army Air Forces, 23 September 1947. *(The National Archives, Washington)*

CONFIDENTIAL

319.1   Air Intelligence Division Stud

25 Sept 1950

FROM: Dept of the Air Force Hqs U.S. Air Force

TO: See below

Ltr
SUBJECT: Destruction of Air Intelligence Report Number 100-203-79

    1. It is requested that action be taken to destroy all copies of
Top Secret Air Intelligence Report Number 100-203-79, subject, "Analysis
of Flying Object Incidents in the U.S.," dtd 10 Dec 1948.

The order to destroy copies of a Top Secret US Air Force Intelligence report which
concluded that UFOs were interplanetary in origin. The order came from General
Hoyt S. Vandenberg, then USAF Chief of Staff. 'The general said it would cause a
stampede,' revealed Captain Edward Ruppelt, who later headed Project Blue Book.
(The National Archives, Washington)

REPRODUCED AT THE NATIONAL ARCHIVES

DECLASSIFIED
Authority NND 913055
By V.C. NARA Date 7/24/97

2-5317.

TOP SECRET

| USAFE 14 | TT 1524 | TOP SECRET | 4 Nov 1948 |

From OI OB

For some time we have been concerned by the recurring reports on flying saucers. They periodically continue to cop up; during the last week, one was observed hovering over Neubiberg Air Base for about thirty minutes. They have been reported by so many sources and from such a variety of places that we are convinced that they cannot be disregarded and must be explained on some basis which is perhaps slightly beyond the scope of our present intelligence thinking.

When officers of this Directorate recently visited the Swedish Air Intelligence Service. This question was put to the Swedes. Their answer was that some reliable and fully technically qualified people have reached the conclusion that "these phenomena are obviously the result of a high technical skill which cannot be credited to any presently known culture on earth." They are therefore assuming that these objects originate from some previously unknown or unidentified technology, possibly outside the earth.

One of these objects was observed by a Swedish technical expert near his home on the edge of a lake. The object crashed or landed in the lake and he carefully noted its azimuth from his point of observation. Swedish intelligence was sufficiently confident in his observation that a naval salvage team was sent to the lake. Operations were underway during the visit of USAFE officers. Divers had discovered a previously uncharted crater on the floor of the lake. No further information is available, but we have been promised knowledge of the results. In their opinion, the observation was reliable, and they believe that the depression on the floor of the lake, which did not appear on current Hydrographic charts, was in fact caused by a flying saucer.

Although accepting this theory of the origin of these objects poses a whole new group of questions and puts much of our thinking in a changed light, we are inclined not to discredit entirely this somewhat spectacular theory, meantime keeping an open mind on the subject. What are your reactions?

T O P   S E C R E T

(END OF USAFE ITEM 14)

A previously Top Secret US Air Forces Europe (USAFE) report. 'These phenomena are obviously the result of a high technical skill which cannot be credited to any presently known culture on Earth', the Swedish Air Intelligence Service told their American counterparts in 1948. *(The National Archives, Washington)*

DEPART~~MENT~~ ~~AIR~~ FORCE

HEADQUARTERS UNITED STATES AIR FORCE
WASHINGTON

THE INSPECTOR GENERAL USAF
17th DISTRICT OFFICE OF SPECIAL INVESTIGATIONS
KIRTLAND AIR FORCE BASE, NEW MEXICO

DR/MSN/web
12 May 1949

File No : 24-8

SUBJECT: UNKNOWN (Aerial Phenomena)

TO: Director of Special Investigations
Office of The Inspector General USAF
Washington 25, D. C.

1. Reference is made to TWX from this district, OSI 4-26-C, dated
27 April 1949, pertaining to file number 24-8 of this district.

2. On 27 and 28 April 1949, Dr Joseph Kaplan, University of California, Member of the Scientific Advisory Board, USAF, visited this
district office and other Governmental and military installations in
the area. The purpose of this visit was to review the reports of investigation and the circumstances surrounding the unidentified aerial
phenomena that have been observed in this area during the last five
months and to thereby make recommendations as to the advisability of
making a scientific investigation of these occurrences. The investigation of Dr. Kaplan was conducted under orders transmitted to him by
Dr Theodore Von Karman, Secretary of the Scientific Advisory Board,
USAF.

3. Dr Joseph Kaplan, accompanied by Lt Col Doyle Rees and Captain
Melvin E. Neef, of this office, and Dr Lincoln LaPaz, Institute of Meteor-
ities, University of New Mexico, visited Sandia Base, New Mexico, and
Los Alamos, New Mexico.

4. Present at the conference at Sandia Base on the morning of 27
April 1949 were:

  Lt Col Herbert L. Crisler, Armed Forces Special Weapons Project
  Lt Col Fredrick J. Clark, Armed Forces Special Weapons Project
  Mr. Matthew J. Doyle, Armed Forces Special Weapons Project
  Comdr R. K. Mandelkorn, Armed Forces Special Weapons Project
  Dr Joseph Kaplan
  Dr Lincoln LaPaz
  Lt Col Doyle Rees
  Captain Melvin E. Neef

UND 34509 7-25-85
BY WCLN Date

8-50422

Part of a US Air Force Intelligence report relating to the multiple intrusions by
unknown flying craft at the top-secret nuclear weapons laboratories at Los Alamos and
Sandia, New Mexico, in 1949. *(The National Archives, Washington)*

7. AZTEC

It was the famous and respected columnist Frank Scully who first alerted the world to sensational stories of recovered flying saucers and alien beings. In his bestselling book *Behind the Flying Saucers*, published in 1950,[1] Scully claimed that up to that time there had been four such recoveries (though, curiously, the Roswell events are not mentioned in his book!).

While it is true that two of Scully's informants had shady backgrounds, and that some of the facts provided to him had – intentionally or not – been distorted, there is abundant evidence that the stories are not without substance. One point invariably overlooked by his debunkers is that 'Dr Gee', his principal source of information, did not exist. Scully turned down an offer by Warner Brothers of $75,000 for film rights, providing he obtained a clearance from his source. 'But Dr Gee is a composite character of eight men who have given me pieces of this story,' he explained to Warners' lawyers. 'I can't give you a clearance on a character I invented for convenience to simplify the telling of the story.'[2] One of Scully's sources is believed to have been Dr Carl A. Heiland, a leading scientist in the field of geophysics and magnetism, who died in 1956.[3]

Later, I shall present some important new evidence from Scott and Suzanne Ramsey, who have spent years investigating the case, but for the benefit of those who may not be familiar with the story, it is essential to begin with the information provided by Frank Scully and others.

According to Scully's informants, an alien disc came down near Farmington, in the vicinity of Aztec, New Mexico, in 1948. About 100 feet in diameter, its exterior was composed of a very light metal resembling aluminium, but so durable that no amount of heat (up to 10,000° F was applied) or diamond-tipped drilling had the slightest effect. The disc apparently incorporated large rings of metal which revolved around a central, stabilized cabin, using an unfamiliar gear ratio. There were no rivets, bolts, screws or signs of welding. Investigators were eventually able to gain entry, Scully was told, because of a fracture in one of the portholes, which they enlarged, revealing a double knob inside the cabin which when pushed (with a long pole) caused a hidden 'door' to open.

Sixteen small humanoids, ranging in height from 36 to 42 inches, were found dead inside the cabin, their bodies charred to a dark brown colour. Scully learned that the craft was undamaged, having landed under its own propulsion. Eventually it was dismantled, the investigators having discovered that it was manufactured in segments which fitted in grooves and were pinned together around the base. The complete cabin section, measuring 18 feet in diameter, was lifted out of the base of the saucer, around which was a gear that fitted a gear on the cabin. These segments, together with the bodies, were then transported to Wright Field (later Wright-Patterson Air Force Base).[4]

Another fairy tale about crashed flying saucers and little men? I believe not. In addition to the pioneering research by William S. Steinman,[5] in particular, and Leonard Stringfield, there is also the lengthy testimony provided to Dr Berthold Schwarz by a former military intelligence officer, to which I devoted five pages in *Above Top Secret* and its successor. The officer claimed to have been taken to a top-secret base in Arizona in the 1970s, where he was shown a recovered alien craft and parts of another craft – the latter being the one which had crashed near Aztec.

The officer examined five humanoid alien bodies – three males and two females. At variance with the information supplied to Scully, none was charred; they were all very pale. Though no genitals were evident, the sex had been determined during autopsy. They averaged about three-and-a-half feet or so in height, with large, hairless heads, large tear-shaped eyes, and vestigial noses and ears. The teeth were smooth, flat and very small. On one of the female bodies, suture marks were clearly apparent. 'My friend [another intelligence officer] said there had been an autopsy, and that from a study of her brain it was estimated that she was 200 years old [estimated by] the count of the ridges on the brain,' the officer told Dr Schwarz.

Apparently, the craft had been tracked on radar as it came down to Earth, and the location had been pinpointed by triangulation. 'When [the military] got out there,' said the officer, 'they found a small hole. Evidently a meteorite had hit this craft, causing rapid decompression, and the people died from that.'[6] This explanation presupposes that the visitors' spacecraft was not designed to withstand, or repel, meteorites. Given their highly advanced technology, I find this unconvincing.

In connection with what Scully learned about the craft being manufactured in segments, retired Rear Admiral Sumner Shapiro, a former Director of Naval Intelligence (with a background in engineering), reportedly revealed some interesting information during a meeting with former NASA-

contracted engineer Bob Oechsler. The meeting, in 1989, had been instigated by Admiral Bobby Ray Inman, former Director of Naval Intelligence,
Director of the National Security Agency and Deputy Director of the CIA.

'One of the things [he revealed] that was fascinating was the discovery
of how they had the interlocking components of the craft,' Oechsler told
me. 'The whole thing comes apart in pieces, and apparently when it's
locked together it's like one of those Oriental puzzles: you can't get it apart
unless you know the precise places to push, and everything has to be done
in a specific sequence . . .'[7]

Recent research by Scott Ramsey and his wife Suzanne has yielded
crucial new evidence about the Aztec incident. The crash occurred early on
the morning of 25 March 1948. At around 05:00, Ramsey has learned, a
large brush fire on a mesa off Hart Canyon Road – unrelated to the crash
– was reported by oilfield workers in the vicinity, who alerted the El Paso
Gas Company and the local police officer. Ramsey interviewed two key
witnesses not long before they passed away. One, Doug Nolan, a nineteen-
year-old worker at the time of the incident, was travelling in a truck with
his boss, Bill Ferguson, when they were called on the radio to come out
and attend to the Hart Canyon brush fire.[8] Upon arriving at the fire site,
Nolan told Ramsey, the other fire workers alerted them to a very large
metallic disc resting on a mesa. On approaching closer, they could see no
seams, rivets, bolts or weld marks. Nolan and Ferguson climbed on top of
the craft and could see two bodies slumped over what appeared to be a
control console.

Another witness, Ken Farley, fresh out of the military, was in the
vicinity at the time when a friend in Cedar Hill told him about a lot of
commotion going on in Hart Canyon Road, attributed to a downed aircraft.
Farley told Ramsey that the two drove out to the crash site and walked out
to the western side of where the disc lay. There they joined a group of
oilfield workers and two law-enforcement officers, one from Aztec and the
other from Cuba, New Mexico. The disc appeared undamaged, Farley said,
and was 'perfectly smooth on the outside, with no seams or markings
except for around the middle of the craft'. The military, plus others
(presumably scientific and technical intelligence specialists), arrived on the
scene later in the afternoon. Farley claimed that the witnesses were
'threatened with their lives' and sworn to secrecy.

Another witness interviewed by Scott Ramsey is Fred Reed, who had
served with the Office of Strategic Services (OSS), predecessor to the CIA.
Reed said that he and his group had been sent out to the area to make it
look as though nothing had happened. 'They were ordered to collect any

foreign items they found, bury them eighteen inches deep, and to "soft landscape" any areas where heavy equipment tracks were visible,' reports Ramsey. Reed also noted 'a newly-cut road and an out-of-place, large concrete pad in the freshly altered and silty soil'. The concrete pad was recovered in the 1980s and has been undergoing a number of tests, the results of which will be published in due course.

Ramsey has protected the identity of yet another witness, stationed at Walker Field (formerly Roswell AAF). Although not present at the site, this witness read daily intelligence reports on the progress of the clean-up operation. 'He explained to me that everything was very compartmentalized during the recovery operation,' says Ramsey. 'He did see black and white photos of the "extremely large craft" . . . He told me that the work force at the site consisted of some 200 persons during the two-week recovery.'[9]

It is believed that the 767th Aircraft Control and Warning System radar unit, based at Air Force Station P-8 next to El Vado Dam, tracked the craft to Aztec. At the time, three top-secret radar sites were located in a triangle in New Mexico to protect the nuclear sites at Kirtland, Los Alamos and Sandia. These sites, Ramsey learned, had been requisitioned by the Atomic Energy Commission. In addition to the temporary one at El Vado Dam (set up in 1946–7), the others were sited at the Continental Divide (Gonzalez), and at Moriarty. These were probably the most powerful radar sets in the world at that time, requiring elaborate safety precautions.[10]

According to an FBI report, an Air Force investigator learned that 'the saucers were found in New Mexico due to the fact that the Government had a very high-powered radar set-up in that area and it is believed the radar interferes with the controlling mechanism of the saucers.'[11]

Glenn Pace, who had lived in the Farmington area, worked as a technical photographer at the nuclear test site in Nevada from 1961 to 1964, assigned to Otto Krause, a German physicist who came to the US after the Second World War. Pace claims that Krause – a project physicist for some of the nuclear tests – confirmed that he knew of two saucers which had crashed at that time, one near Roswell and another in Aztec. Pace told investigator Glenn Campbell: 'He said they were both brought to White Sands and put in a hangar there. The aliens he never saw. He talked to people that had seen the bodies and evidently one [from the Roswell incident] supposedly lived, and they [eventually] took him out to Area 51.'[12]

Area 51 – also known as 'Dreamland', 'The Ranch', etcetera – occupies Groom Dry Lake, adjacent to the Nevada Test Site, and is where top-secret aircraft such as the Lockheed U-2 and F-117A 'Stealth' and other highly advanced planes have been tested since the early 1950s. In *Alien Liaison* I described various reports – some spurious – relating to sightings of both alien craft and bodies in that vicinity, including the area known as S-4 (allegedly the Alien Technology Center) at Papoose Dry Lake.

'Otto said it took them a long time to get into the [Aztec] thing and figure out how it worked,' Pace told Campbell. 'That was what was the classified part of the UFO – the mechanism that powered it. That was more classified than the atomic bomb . . .'[13]

When I interviewed Pace in 1995, I asked if he knew anything more about the Aztec incident. It is claimed, for instance, that a story appeared in the local newspaper (the *Hustler* – later the *Farmington Daily Times*), though many people have denied it. Pace insists such a story did appear. 'We used to go riding with a horse,' he told me. 'What came out in the paper about the crash at Aztec was [that it happened] right out in a canyon where we had ridden. And the next day it came out in the newspaper that this was all a big hoax, that nothing had crashed. And then, when I worked with Otto at the test site, I'd called my mom to go to the *Daily Times* and get me a copy of that paper for that issue, because I wanted to show it to Otto. And she went there, and the issue didn't exist – it conveniently disappeared . . .'[14]

As Scott Ramsey explained to me in 2006, 'All copies of the *Hustler* are missing due to the fact that they were a small newspaper, and this was before the days of microfiche. When Lincoln O'Brien purchased the paper and consolidated it with the *Daily Times*, he did not see the value of keeping the old copies. However, with that said, Mr O'Brien also kept secret files on all UFO activities that went on in the area: we got his personal files after his death . . .'[15]

Otto Krause confirmed many of the details as reported to Scully, for example, that all the occupants were deceased and that, with the exception of a very small hole in one of the portholes, the craft itself was 'pretty much intact'. 'The one at Aztec is the one they gained the technology from,' Pace was told.[16]

Interviewed years later by researcher William Moore, Mrs Frank Scully maintained that the basic story behind her husband's book was factual. She also referred to a revealing comment made to her and her husband in 1953 by Captain Edward Ruppelt, the intelligence officer who had recently retired as head of the Air Force's Project Blue Book. 'Confidentially,' said Ruppelt, 'of all the books that have been published on flying saucers, your book was the one that gave us the most headaches because it was the closest to the truth . . .'[17]

REFERENCES

1. Scully, Frank, *Behind the Flying Saucers*, Henry Holt, New York, 1950.

2. Scully, Frank, *In Armour Bright*, Chilton Books, Philadelphia, 1963, pp. 198–9.

3. Evans, Chris B., *Alien Conspiracy: Unravelling the UFO/Alien Mystery*, Alarm Clock Publishing, PO Box 1389, Ceredo, WV 25507, 2003, pp. 94–5.

4. *Behind the Flying Saucers*, pp. 128–37.

5. Steinman, William S. and Stevens, Wendelle C., *UFO Crash at Aztec: A Well Kept Secret*, UFO Photo Archives, PO Box 17206, Tucson, AZ 85710, 1987.

6. Schwarz, Berthold Eric, MD, *UFO Dynamics: Psychiatric and Psychic Dimensions of the UFO Syndrome*, Book II, Rainbow Books, PO Box 1069, Moore Haven, Florida 33471, 1983, pp. 536–45. See also *Above Top Secret* and *Beyond Top Secret*.

7. Good, Timothy, *Alien Liaison: The Ultimate Secret*, Century, London, 1991, pp. 194–5.

8. *Aztec 1948: Government Cover-up – or Con?* Documentary written, directed and produced by Paul Kimball, Redstar Films Ltd., 2004, www.aztec1948.com

9. Ramsey, Scott, 'Aztec Crash/Retrieval Story Revisited', *MUFON UFO Journal*, No. 436, August 2004, pp. 3–7.

10. *Aztec 1948*, plus additional information supplied by Andy Kissner.

11. Memorandum from Guy Hottel [Special Agent], to Director, FBI, 22 March 1950.

12. *The Groom Lake Desert Rat*, PO Box 448, Rachel, NV 89001, Issue 23, 17 March 1995, pp. 1–5.

13. Ibid.

14. Telephone interview, 17 May 1995.

15. Email, 13 March 2006.

16. *The Groom Lake Desert Rat*, op. cit.

17. Berlitz, Charles, and Moore, William, *The Roswell Incident*, Granada, London, 1980, p. 51.

CONFIDENTIAL

HEADQUARTERS FIFTH ARMY
INTELLIGENCE DIVISION
OFFICE OF AC of S, G-2

6 October 1950
(Date)

Chicago 15, Illinois
(Place)

SUBJECT: Purchase Offer of Flying Saucer Photographs

Summary of Information:

1. The Fifth Army Regional Office in Denver, Colorado, reported
the following information: On 30 September the Regional Office
received a call from CID, Denver, reporting that an ======
Melwyn Hotel, Denver, said that when he was at the Edelweiss Bar a
man named ===== offered him $1500 for photographs he had taken of a
flying saucer. ======= said he photographed this saucer which
had crashed near Aztec, New Mexico. '======= said that "army
officials" had attempted to take the photographs of the crashed
saucer away from him but that he had given them another roll of film.
He said that '----- in some way had found out about the photographs
and offered him $1500 for the photographs.

2. On 2 October ======= was interviewed at the Fifth Army
Regional Office in Denver. He then denied any knowledge of the
flying saucer episode. The Regional Office commented that in spite
of his denials his manner indicated that he had some knowledge of the
incident or may have taken pictures of it. His appearance did not
give the impression of one who was either mentally unbalanced or was
seeking attention. He stuck persistently to his story of being drunk
when he made the call to CID.

3. ======= said that ===== was from "The Baltimore Sun."

	Evaluation	
	-of source	-of information
X	Reliable	
	Credible	
	Questionable	
	Undetermined	
	Unknown	X

Previous Distribution:

Distribution:
AC of S, G-2, Wash
FBI, Chgo
OSI   OSI
PCRM 62
1947

CONFIDENTIAL

A US Army Intelligence report relating to the crashed disc recovered near Aztec,
New Mexico, in March 1948. *(The National Archives, Washington)*

PART TWO

1950–9

8. MAJIC

Is it possible to trace the reaction of the US Government's military and intelligence community to these momentous events, apart from the officially released documentation? In 1984 some documents of spurious provenance were leaked to Hollywood TV producer Jaime Shandera on a roll of 35mm film. Even though these documents are fabrications, in my opinion they have yielded vitally important clues.

The documents are an alleged preliminary briefing paper prepared for President-elect Dwight D. Eisenhower in November 1952 by Rear Admiral Roscoe Hillenkoetter, the former CIA director, and a September 1947 memo from President Truman to Secretary of Defense James Forrestal, supposedly authorizing 'Operation Majestic Twelve'. Classified 'TOP SECRET/MAJIC/EYES ONLY', the briefing paper summarized what the Majestic-12 committee had learned about the UFO problem up to 1952, including details about the Roswell recovery.

In early 1987 I received a copy of the documents from an American source, and these were published for the first time in my book *Above Top Secret* later that year. Among the reasons for my conviction that the papers are bogus is the fact that the signature on the Truman memo was 'lifted' from a document that was known to be authentic. And General Eisenhower, as Army Chief of Staff in 1947, would almost certainly have been given the essential details about Roswell at the time. However, I believe that those who fabricated the papers had inside knowledge, since there is good evidence that a committee by that name (Majestic-12) – or similar – did exist, and the briefing paper's list of the original committee includes many of those who it is believed were involved, as described in this chapter and earlier. They were:

— **Dr Lloyd Berkner** – a scientist who was executive secretary of the Joint Research and Development Board in 1946 (under Dr Vannevar Bush) and later a member of the CIA's 'Robertson Panel', a scientific advisory panel on UFOs requested by the White House and sponsored by the CIA in 1953.

— **Dr Detlev Bronk** – an internationally known physiologist and biophysicist who was chairman of the National Research Council and member of the Medical Advisory Board of the Atomic Energy Commission.

— **Dr Vannevar Bush** – recognized as one of America's leading scientists, he organized the Office of Scientific Research and Development, which led to the Manhattan Project. After the war he became head of the Joint Research and Development Board – and head of a small group investigating the 'flying saucers'.

— **James S. Forrestal** – Secretary of Defense in July 1947, he set up the initial Air Force Project Saucer, which became Project Sign in September. A mental breakdown led to his resignation in March 1949, and he committed suicide at Bethesda Naval Hospital in May 1949. The 'MJ-12 briefing paper' names General Walter Bedell Smith, then CIA director, as his successor.

— **Gordon Gray** – Secretary of the Army in 1949, he was appointed special assistant to President Truman on National Security Affairs and in 1951 directed the CIA's Psychological Strategy Board. He became adviser on national security matters to President Eisenhower, and was chairman of the highly secret '54/12 Group' or 'Special Group' (referred to in Chapter 5 in connection with Lieutenant Colonel Philip Corso).

— **Rear Admiral Roscoe Hillenkoetter** – the first director of the CIA (1947–50), Hillenkoetter was involved in investigations into the 'ghost rockets' (Chapter 3) and was the first intelligence chief to make public his conviction that UFOs are real, and that 'through official secrecy and ridicule, many citizens are led to believe the unknown flying objects are nonsense'.

— **Dr Jerome C. Hunsaker** – headed the Department of Mechanical and Aeronautical Engineering at the Massachusetts Institute of Technology, and was chairman of the National Advisory Committee for Aeronautics. As noted earlier, Hunsaker pressed the Congress for huge budget increases during the flying disc/aircraft accident crisis.

— **Dr Donald Menzel** – Professor of Astrophysics at Harvard College (1939–71) and involved in several military projects relating to the tracking of guided missiles, Menzel is chiefly remembered for his dismissive statements and books on UFOs, *all* of which, he insisted, could be explained in mundane terms. Stanton Friedman, a retired nuclear physicist and leading authority on the UFO phenomenon, discovered that Menzel had been a top-class expert in code-breaking (holding a Top Secret Ultra security clearance), had a lengthy association with the National Security Agency, and had been a consultant to several presidents on national security affairs. Moreover, he was well connected with several other members of the MJ-12 group – especially Dr Bush.[1]

— **Brigadier General Robert Montague** – as an expert on anti-aircraft missiles, he was among those who investigated the first intrusions at White Sands (described earlier). He became base commander at the Atomic Energy Commission installation at Sandia Base, Albuquerque, New Mexico (July 1947–February 1951).

— **Rear Admiral Sydney Souers** – first Director of Central Intelligence (January–June 1946), he became executive secretary of the National Security Council in September 1947.

— **Lieutenant General Nathan F. Twining** – as noted earlier, Twining was commanding general of Air Materiel Command, which in 1947 confirmed the reality of the flying discs.

— **General Hoyt Vandenberg** – second Director of Central Intelligence (June 1946–May 1947), he had been involved in the 'ghost rocket' investigations and attended meetings with President Truman and others to assess the Roswell situation.

In UFO research, confusion surrounds the code names MAJESTIC, MAGIC and MAJIC. In the Second World War, 'Operation Majestic' had been an alternate plan for the invasion of the southernmost Japanese home island of Kyushu (averted by the atomic bomb). It was rejected in favour of 'Olympic', though elements of Majestic were incorporated into deception plans such as 'Pastel'.[2] In an August 1946 top-secret message – contained, coincidentally, in the War Department 'ghost rockets' file – the Olympic code word is referenced as having been cancelled and substituted with Majestic in August 1945. The questioner asks if restrictions still applied to Majestic.[3] Both code words had been declassified by the Joint Chiefs of Staff (JCS) in October 1945, came the response.[4]

According to another top-secret report, however, the Majestic code name was reinstated in October 1952 as a 'Joint Outline Emergency War Logistic Plan MAJESTIC', drawn up by the JCS in the event of war with the Soviets.[5] Currently, there is 'Blue MAJIC', the Air Force Space Command's Blue Force Microsatellite Areawide Joint Information and Communication Systems.

Although code names may be cancelled and later reused, it seems improbable that Majestic – per se – would have been used in connection with a briefing paper for Eisenhower on the alien contingency, especially within two months of Plan Majestic.

The code word MAGIC was used early in the Second World War. As relations between the United States and Japan continued to deteriorate, by August 1940 American cryptographers had solved the Japanese Foreign Ministry's top-secret codes. Magic entailed 'the interception, decryption, and translation on a current basis of secret Japanese worldwide diplomatic messages'.[6] Subsequently, Magic was replaced by the code names 'Red', and then 'Purple'.

Kevin Randle and Donald Schmitt cite General Exon's reference to a group he dubbed 'The Unholy Thirteen' – not knowing the actual name of the group – which was established following the Roswell incident. 'One thing that Exon made clear,' state Randle and Schmitt, 'was that no elected officials, outside the President, were ever included as a member of the top echelon.'[7]

In late 1950 the Canadian Government established its first secret committee to investigate aerial phenomena, code-named Project Magnet and headed by Wilbert Smith as engineer-in-charge. In a three-page top-secret 1950 Canadian Government memorandum, senior radio engineer Wilbert B. Smith stated as follows:

a. The matter is the most highly classified subject in the United States Government, rating higher even than the H-bomb.
b. Flying saucers exist.
c. Their modus operandi is unknown but concentrated effort is being made by a small group headed by Doctor Vannevar Bush.
d. The entire matter is considered by the United States authorities to be of tremendous significance . . .[8]

Dr Bush's background in coordinating top-secret research projects and his concern (shared with General Groves) with the compartmentalization of classified information, would have made him the ideal choice to head a special committee following (or perhaps preceding) the Roswell incident.

Wilbert Smith had obtained his information from Dr Robert I. Sarbacher, an American scientist and consultant to the Research and Development Board. In a letter to researcher William Steinman, Sarbacher lists names of several of those involved, following the recoveries of alien craft and bodies (see p. 134). In his meeting with Sarbacher in September 1950, Wilbert Smith learned more (see following chapter) and, according to his son, eventually gained access to inspect the bodies of the deceased. I asked James Smith if he could provide me with some details. 'Nothing further available,' he replied. 'He was under the Official Secrets Act and gave me no further details.'[9]

In a recorded conversation with nuclear physicist Stanton T. Friedman, Sarbacher confirmed that British-born scientist Dr Eric A. Walker had attended all the meetings dealing with the recovery of craft and bodies.[10] Dr Walker was a Harvard graduate whose posts included executive secretary of the Research and Development Board, chairman of the National Science

Foundation's Committee for Engineering, chairman of the Institute for Defense Analyses and President of Pennsylvania State University. In a recorded telephone conversation in 1987 with William Steinman, Dr Walker also confirmed that he had attended meetings at Wright-Patterson Air Force Base (around 1949–50) concerning the military recovery of flying saucers and bodies of occupants.

'Did you ever hear of the MJ-12 group?' asked Steinman.

'Yes, I know of MJ-12. I have known of them for forty years,' replied Walker. 'You are delving into an area that you can do absolutely nothing about . . . Why don't you just leave it alone and drop it?'[11]

As reported in *Above Top Secret*, I corresponded at some length with Admiral Stansfield Turner, Director of the CIA (DCI) from 1977 to 1981, and asked him several times if he was aware of a Majestic-12 group. This was the only question he refrained from responding to.[12] However, Admiral Bobby Ray Inman, Deputy Director of the CIA (DDCI) from 1981 to 1982, who had been director of Naval Intelligence as well as of the National Security Agency, indirectly acknowledged the existence of 'MJ-12' during a brief meeting with investigator Bob Oechsler in Maryland in May 1988, at a ground-breaking ceremony for the National Security Agency's new supercomputer facility for the Institute for Defense Analyses, of which Inman was a former director.[13]

Andy Kissner believes that the acronyms MAJIC and MJ-12 could have been formed from Manhattan [Engineering District] Joint [Chiefs of Staff] Integrated Command, [Project Y, Division Z, Group] 12.[14] I asked Rebecca Ullrich, Sandia Laboratories' historian, if any of these acronyms had surfaced in the archives. 'We have no records pertaining to any entities called MJ-12, MAJIC-12, or MAJESTIC 12,' she replied.[15] Another possibility (suggested by Dr Robert M. Wood) is that MAJIC was formed from Military Assessment of the Joint Intelligence Committee.

Whatever its precise code name, it remains abundantly clear, despite the lack of official recognition, that a highly secret committee (perhaps one of several) was established in 1947 to deal with the greatest secret on Earth – a secret which remains classified to this day.

REFERENCES

1. Friedman, Stanton T., *Top Secret/Majic*, Marlowe, New York, 1996, pp. 28–33.
2. McCombs, Don and Worth, Fred. L., *World War II Superfacts*, Warner Books, 1983, p. 434.

3. War Department message (Top Secret) from the office of the Commander-in-Chief, Air Force, Pacific, 7 August 1946.

4. War Department message (Restricted), 8 August 1946.

5. 'Report by the Joint Logistics Plans Committee to the Joint Chiefs of Staff on Joint Logistic Plan for "Majestic"' (Top Secret Security Information), from the Chief of Naval Operations to various US Navy commanders-in-chief and commanders, 2 October 1952.

6. Loureiro, Pedro, 'The Imperial Japanese Navy and Espionage: The Itaru Tachibana Case', *International Journal of Intelligence and Counterintelligence*, Vol. 3, No. 1, Spring 1989, p. 106.

7. Randle, Kevin D., and Schmitt, Donald R., *UFO Crash at Roswell*, Avon, New York, 1991, pp. 231–4.

8. Memorandum to the Controller of Telecommunications (Top Secret), from W.B. Smith, Senior Radio Engineer, Department of Transport, Ottawa, 21 November 1950.

9. Letter, September 2005.

10. *The Wilbert Smith Archives* (CD), edited by Grant Cameron. www.presidentialufo.com/smith.htm

11. Transcript of William Steinman's telephone interview with Dr Eric Walker, 30 August 1987, published in *UFOs, MJ-12 and the Government: A Report on Government Involvement in UFO Crash Retrievals*, by Grant Cameron and T. Scott Crain Jr, Mutual UFO Network, PO Box 369, Morrison, CO 80465–0369, 1991, pp. 8–10.

12. Good, Timothy, *Above Top Secret: The Worldwide UFO Cover-up*, Sidgwick & Jackson, London, 1987, p. 359.

13. Good, Timothy, *Alien Liaison: The Ultimate Secret*, Century, London, 1991, p. 187.

14. Kissner, J. Andrew, *Peculiar Phenomenon: Early United States Efforts to Collect and Analyze Flying Discs*.

15. Email, 16 September 2005.

LONG BEACH

Press-Telegram

Dedicated to Interests of Greater Long Beach and South Coast Region

PRESS-TELEGRAM PHONE 699-88   LONG BEACH, CALIF., WEDNESDAY, FEBRUARY 25, 1942   16 Pages—Two Sections   HOME EDITION—FIVE CENTS

GUNS BOMBARD SKY AS STRANGE PLANES
BLACK OUT SOUTHLAND IN FIRST 'RAID'

Headlines from the *Long Beach Press-Telegram* of 25 February 1942 describing the five-hour air alarm earlier that morning.

No Bombs Fell, No Aircraft Downed, Report From Army

BULLETIN

SAN FRANCISCO, Feb. 25 —(A. P.) No bombs were dropped and no planes were shot down during the antiaircraft firing in the Los Angeles area early today, the Western Defense Command announced.

A photograph showing searchlight beams converging on one of the fifteen aerial intruders seen over Culver City, Los Angeles. The blobs of light are probably bursts of anti-aircraft rounds. (Image enhanced by Steven Lacey.)
(Los Angeles Times)

A Lancaster Mk III (PA474), of the type involved in a number of UFO encounters during the Second World War.
(Timothy Good)

A Thunderbolt P-47D similar to the type flown by Free French Air Force pilot Jean Kisling, when he attempted to shoot down a UFO above Mount Clemens Army Air Base near Detroit in July 1945. *(Republic Aviation)*

Jean Kisling at Oscoda (later Wurtsmith AFB), a sub-base for Mount Clemens, in 1944. *(Jean Kisling)*

In August 1945, a C-46 Commando was en route to Tokyo via Iwo Jima when three unknown objects closed with the plane, causing the port engine to stall and the plane to lose altitude. *(US Air Force)*

Artwork depicting a Saab B18 of the Royal Swedish Air Force and one of the 'ghost rockets' it encountered on the morning of 14 August 1946.
(© Johan Andersson)

ca 15 m

Above. The first American-adapted V-2 at White Sands, New Mexico, shown during engine check-out.
(US Army)

Right. A contemporary news report of the UFO interference encountered during the tests in May 1947.
(Las Cruces Sun News)

'Peculiar Phenomena' Is Blamed as V-2 Rocket Goes Astray

The German V-2 rocket, launched at White Sands Proving Ground, Thursday afternoon, landed only six miles east of Alamogordo, at the town of Indian Springs.

"Peculiar phenomena" was blamed by Lt. Col. Harold R. Turner, commanding officer of White Sands, for the erratic test flight.

The rocket carrying a warhead installed by the Naval Research Laboratory, was spotted at its landing about 55 miles from the launching site where it was fired at 4:00 p. m. A crew was sent out immediately to recover rocket body and warhead.

Fuel was cut off at the blockhouse after the V-2 climbed to 80 miles at a top speed of 4700 feet per second. Total flight time was five minutes and 30 seconds.

A quantity of rye seed was placed in the rocket to determine the effect of cosmic rays on its germination. Heavy camera equipment also was carried in rocket and warhead.

Dr Wernher von Braun, designer of the V-2 rocket and advisor to the US Army V-2 test firings at White Sands. He also examined the craft and alien bodies discovered near Roswell.

Lieutenant Colonel Philip Corso *(left)*, who stewarded the Roswell artefacts in a reverse-engineering project instigated by Lieutenant General Arthur Trudeau *(right)*.
(Collection of Philip Corso Jr.)

Below. Congressman Steven Schiff, whose request to see official records pertaining to the Roswell incident revealed that they had been destroyed without proper authority.
(Timothy Good)

Jon 'Andy' Kissner. His pioneering research reveals that attacks on the UFOs by the US military in the 1940s led to a worldwide wave of crashes of military and civilian aircraft.
(Timothy Good)

Roswell Army Air Field, home of the 509th Bombardment Group, the world's first unit equipped to carry nuclear weapons, where one or two alien craft plus bodies were first taken after crashes in New Mexico in July 1947. *(Timothy Good)*

Above. A B-25 Mitchell bomber, of the type used to fly some or all of the debris found by Mac Brazel to Fort Worth, Texas. *(Timothy Good)*

Major General Clements McMullen, who ordered the containment strategy to cover up the Roswell incident.
(US Air Force)

1st Lieutenant Eileen M. Fanton, the nurse said to have attended the autopsy of one of the alien beings at Roswell Army Air Field.
(US Air Force)

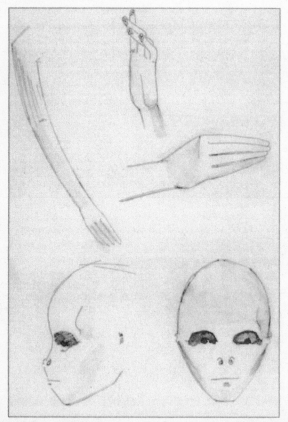

Artwork by Glenn Dennis based on drawings by the nurse who attended one of the alien autopsies. The fingertips appeared to have suction cups and the eyes were sunken so far back – from exposure to the desert – that it was difficult to tell what they looked like.
(Glenn Dennis)

P-51 Mustangs of the California Air National Guard, of the type Captain Thomas Mantell was flying when he was killed intercepting a UFO in January 1948. An intelligence report (*below*) confirms that his last radio message was, 'It appears to be metallic object . . . of tremendous size . . . directly ahead and slightly above . . . I am trying to close for a better look.'
(Via Philip Jarrett)

~~SECRET~~

k. On 7 January 1948, a National Guard pilot was killed while attempting to chase an unidentified object up to 30,000 feet. While it is presumed that this pilot suffered anoxia, resulting in his crash, his last message to the tower was, "it appears to be metallic object....of tremendous size....directly ahead and slightly above....I am trying to close for a better look."

Part of a US Air Force Intelligence summary referencing the incident, confirming Mantell's last radio message to Godman AFB control tower. *(US Air Force)*

Captain Thomas F. Mantell, who was killed while intercepting a UFO near Franklin, Kentucky, on 7 January 1948. *(US Air Force)*

Frederick C. Durant III, a Naval aviator, test pilot and instructor, who later became an expert on missiles, rockets and UFOs. He is shown here as an ensign, serving with Squadron VN15 in 1942. *(US Navy)*

General Hoyt Vandenberg, second Director of Central Intelligence. When a Top Secret report concluded that UFOs were interplanetary, he ordered it to be burned. *(US Air Force)*

Wilbert B. Smith, who headed the Canadian Government's first Top Secret investigations into UFOs. *(Van's Studio, Ottawa)*

Royal Air Force Flight-Lieutenant Stan Hubbard, who observed a disc of about 100 feet in diameter over the experimental aircraft test centre at Farnborough, Hampshire, in August 1950. *(Stan Hubbard / UFO Magazine – UK)*

One of four photographs taken through a telescope by George Adamski in California, 5 March 1951, showing a 'mothership' releasing smaller 'scout' craft. *(George Adamski Foundation)*

UFO photographed by a US Marine Air Group pilot over the northeast China Sea during the Korean War. The object came close to the aircraft before shooting off at over 1,000 mph. It had a very bright top, which 'burned' into the film emulsion, and a bronze coloured base. *(W. Gordon Allen)*

from another planet. Scully claimed that the preliminary studies of
one saucer which fell into the hands of the United States Government
indicated that they operated on some hitherto unknown magnetic
principles. It appeared to me that our own work in geo-magnetics
might well be the linkage between our technology and the technology
by which the saucers are designed and operated. If it is assumed that
our geo-magnetic investigations are in the right direction, the theory
of operation of the saucers becomes quite straightforward, with all
observed features explained qualitatively and quantitatively.

I made discreet enquiries through the Canadian Embassy
staff in Washington who were able to obtain for me the following
information:

a. The matter is the most highly classified subject in the United
   States Government, rating higher even than the H-bomb.

b. Flying saucers exist.

c. Their modus operandi is unknown but concentrated effort is being
   made by a small group headed by Doctor Vannevar Bush.

d. The entire matter is considered by the United States authorities
   to be of tremendous significance.

An extract from a previously Top Secret memorandum to the Controller of
Telecommunications from Wilbert Smith, Senior Radio Engineer with the Canadian
Government's Department of Transport, 21 November 1950. This information was
revealed to Smith by Dr Robert I. Sarbacher, an American consultant to the Joint
Research and Development Board. *(Department of Transport, Canada)*

A Top Secret memorandum relating to the information acquired by Wilbert Smith
from Dr Sarbacher. *(Department of Transport, Canada)*

TOP SECRET

Mr. Edwards should write to the Dept of National Defence Ottawa

requesting that clearance may be obtained for Mr. W. B. Smith to visit

the appropriate Service in the United States to discuss the use of
terrestrial magnetic forces in relation to ... aerodynamic problems
associated with saucer shaped objects .

In the covering request, the Department of Transport should relate in as
much detail as possible the objects of this study and also detail the
work which has been carried out in the geophysical field in Canada.

Information unofficial- obtained from Dr. Robert I Sarbacher , dean of
the Graduate school, Georgia University.

WASHINGTON INSTITUTE OF TECHNOLOGY

OCEANOGRAPHIC AND PHYSICAL SCIENCES

DR. ROBERT I. SARBACHER
PRESIDENT AND CHAIRMAN OF BOARD

November 29, 1983

*Answer
from Dr. Sarbacher
Received 12-5-83
Wm Steinman*

Mr. William Steinman
15043 Rosalita Drive
La Mirada, California 90638

Dear Mr. Steinman:

I am sorry I have taken so long in answering your letters.
However, I have moved my office and have had to make a
number of extended trips.

To answer your last question in your letter of October 14,
1983, there is no particular reason I feel I shouldn't or
couldn't answer any or all of your questions. I am delighted to answer all of them to the best of my ability.

You listed some of your questions in your letter of
September 12th. I will attempt to answer them as you had
listed them.

    1.   Relating to my own experience regarding re-
covered flying saucers, I had no association with any
of the people involved in the recovery and have no knowledge regarding the dates of the recoveries. If I had I
would send it to you.

    2.   Regarding verification that persons you list
were involved, I can only say this:

        John von Neuman was definitely involved. Dr.
Vannever Bush was definitely involved, and I think Dr.
Robert Oppenheimer also.

        My association with the Research and Develop-
ment Board under Doctor Compton during the Eisenhower
administration was rather limited so that although I had
been invited to participate in several discussions associated withthe reported recoveries, I could not personally
attend the meetings. I am sure thatthey would have asked
Dr. von Braun, and the others that you listed were probably
asked and may or may not have attended. This is all I know
for sure.

500 BRAZILIAN AVENUE   PALM BEACH, FLORIDA 33480   305-833-1116

The first page of a letter to researcher William Steinman from Dr Robert Sarbacher
confirming the recovery of alien craft and bodies. *(William Steinman)*

9. NAVAL INTELLIGENCE

On 7 October 1975, two months after Robert Suffern witnessed a landed UFO and its occupant at Bracebridge, Ontario, he and his wife were visited by three officials who arrived in an Ontario Provincial Police car, by prearranged appointment. The three men, in full uniform, bore impressive credentials from the Canadian Forces in Ottawa, the US Air Force, the Pentagon and the US Office of Naval Intelligence.

The officials showed Suffern a number of gun-camera photographs and other data on UFOs, and implied that the United States and Canadian governments had known all about the alien issue since 1943, supposedly as a result of a US Navy experiment involving radar invisibility – the legendary 'Philadelphia Experiment' when the USS *Eldridge* (DE-173) is alleged to have inadvertently teleported from Philadelphia to Norfolk, Virginia. Suffern was informed that contact with aliens was established as a direct result of that incident, and the officials said they had been cooperating with the aliens ever since then. To Suffern's astonishment, the officials knew the precise time of the UFO landing he witnessed, which had not been revealed to anyone.[1]

KOREA

In September 1950, during the Korean War, three US Navy fighter-bombers, each with a crew of pilot and radar gunner, had taken off from an aircraft carrier to attack an enemy convoy. At about 07:00, at 10,000 feet, the radar gunner in one of the planes was startled by 'two large circular shadows coming along the ground' at a high rate of speed. 'When I saw the shadows,' he said, 'I looked up and saw the objects which were causing them.'

> They were huge. I knew that as soon as I looked at my radar screen. They were also going at a good clip – about 1,000 or 1,200 mph. My radar display indicated one and a half miles between the objects and our planes when the objects suddenly seemed to halt, back up and

begin a 'jittering', or 'fibrillating' motion. My first reaction, of course, was to shoot. I readied my guns, which automatically readied the gun cameras ... however, the radar went haywire. The screen 'bloomed' and became very bright. I tried to reduce the brightness ... but this had no effect. I realized my radar had been jammed and was useless. I then called my carrier ... I said the code name twice, and my receiver was out – blocked by a strange buzzing noise. I tried two other frequencies, but couldn't get through. Each time I switched frequencies the band was clear for a moment, then the buzzing began.

While this was going on the objects were still jittering out there ahead of us, maintaining our speed. About the time that I gave up trying to radio the carrier the things began manoeuvring around our planes, circling above and below ... I had never seen anything like them before, and I learned after we reached our carrier that the other men in that flight were of the same opinion. They were huge ... Before my radar set was put out of commission, I used the indicated range plus points of reference on the canopy to determine their size. They were at least 600 or possibly 700 feet in diameter.

The objects had a 'silvered mirror' appearance, with a reddish glow surrounding them. They were shaped somewhat like a coolie's hat, with oblong ports from which emanated a copper-green coloured light which gradually shifted to pale pastel-coloured lights and back to the copper-green again. Above the ports was a shimmering red ring which encircled the top portion ... In the middle of the underside was a circular area, coal black and non-reflective ...

When the objects seemingly had finished their 'inspection' of the Navy planes, they took off in the same direction from which they had come, and disappeared at a high rate of speed.

The above account was related by the witness in person to Jim and Coral Lorenzen, who had held Air Force or defence-related jobs and founded the Aerial Phenomena Research Organization (APRO). Asked by Jim if any other peculiarities had been noted, the witness said that he and all the men in that flight had noticed a 'feeling of warmth' in the planes, and also what he described as 'a high-frequency' vibration.

'The six men were questioned individually and then in a group by combat intelligence,' wrote Coral. 'They were thoroughly tested for radiation, as was their aircraft. The men never knew the results of the Geiger-counter tests, but they did learn that the instrument dials on their [planes] had become extremely luminous and all the gun-camera film had been fogged or exposed, although none of the crews had used either guns or cameras.'[2]

CLOSE ENCOUNTER NEAR NEWFOUNDLAND

Graham Bethune, a US Naval Reserve pilot who qualified in over 100 different types of aircraft, was a 'VIP Transport Plane Commander' and held a Top-Secret clearance. Following a high-level Defense Department meeting in Washington, DC, in February 1951, Bethune, then a lieutenant, was one of two officers sent to Keflavik, Iceland, on a classified mission to meet Icelandic Government and other officials who had requested the United States to provide troops to protect them from a possible Soviet invasion. The Icelanders had expressed particular concern about sightings of unusual aircraft, which the Americans had told them were 'possibly experimental Russian bombers'. 'Our mission,' said Bethune, 'was to work out the logistics for flying in troops and supporting them.'

Asked by Bethune to describe the unidentified aircraft being observed over Iceland, a senior official from the Lockheed Aircraft Corporation replied that 'they were very large, circular, with many lights, at times a fiery ring around the perimeter, made no noise and could move out of sight instantly'. Bethune explained that his team was from the Naval Air Test Center at Patuxent River, Maryland, where secret aircraft were tested, and that he was unaware of any such aircraft.

On 10 February at 00:55, Bethune was co-piloting a four-engine Douglas R5D (DC-4 version) Navy transport on its return flight from Keflavik to Naval Air Station Argentia, Newfoundland, when he and his crew caught sight of 'what gave the appearance of approaching a distant city at night'. Bethune was in the left seat at the time, getting a route check in order to qualify as plane commander. Another crew, as well as thirty-one passengers, were on board.[3]

'While flying in the left seat at 10,000 feet on a true course of 230 degrees at a position of 49-50 North 50-03 West, I observed a glow of light below the horizon about 1,000 to 1,500 feet above the water,' Bethune's statement to Naval Intelligence begins. 'Its bearing was about 2 o'clock ... I called it to the attention of Lieutenant Kingdon in the right hand seat ... We both observed its course and motion for about 4 or 5 minutes before calling it to the attention of the other crew members ... '

> Suddenly its angle of attack changed, its altitude and size increased as though its speed was in excess of 1,000 miles per hour. It closed in so fast that the first feeling was we would collide in mid air. At this time its angle changed and the colour changed. It then [appeared] definitely circular and reddish orange on its perimeter. It reversed its course and

tripled its speed until it was last seen disappearing over the horizon. Because of our altitude and misleading distance over water it is almost impossible to estimate its size, distance and speed. A rough estimate would be at least 300 feet in diameter, over 1,000 miles per hour in speed, and approached to within 5 miles of the aircraft.[4]

Bethune had disengaged the autopilot, anticipating that he might have to dive to avoid the disc. Before disappearing, it appeared to be pacing the plane. 'At this time we could see its shape, a dome and the coronal discharge around the perimeter.

'When I began to reset the autopilot I noticed the magnetic compass oscillating back and forth . . . the two ADFs (auto direction finder) needles were oscillating radically, pointing toward the UFO. Our remote compass was also oscillating. The autopilot hydraulically-operated directional gyro and the vacuum-operated directional gyro were both stable.'

Bethune went aft to check the cabin. 'I noticed the passengers on the right side watching the craft, and Commander M., a Navy medical officer (psychiatrist), was back at the galley . . . When I asked him if he saw what we saw, he replied: "Yes, it was a flying saucer. I did not look at it because I do not believe in them." '

'When we landed at Argentia, Newfoundland, we were met by USAF Capt. Paulsen who was to interrogate us. His questions indicated we were not the first to have an encounter in the general area . . .'[5]

During the two-hour debriefing, the pilots tried to obtain some information about the flying discs. 'What's behind all this?' asked Bethune. 'Up to now, I believed the Air Force. You people say there aren't any flying saucers. After a scare like that we've got a right to know.'

'I'm sorry,' replied Paulsen, 'I can't answer any questions.'

The completed intelligence reports were 'flashed' to four commanders, with an information copy to the Director of Naval Intelligence. At the Naval Air Test Center, pilots and crew members were interrogated, and made out individual reports as requested by Naval Intelligence.[6]

A few months later, Bethune learned that Gander airfield radar had tracked the object at a speed in excess of 1,800 mph.[7] He was to learn more.

In May 1951 Bethune was visited at his home, unannounced, by an officer from Naval Intelligence, explaining that he wished to discuss the 'encounter' with a flying saucer. As in the 1975 Ontario case, Bethune was shown photographs of UFOs:

He had a binder holding photographs of UFOs interspersed with what seemed to be printed material. As he listened to my story, he was writing on a note pad and thumbing through the binder. Occasionally he would stop at a photograph and show it to me, asking if it looked like my UFO ... One photograph seemed a good representation of the UFO we had encountered, and it was noted as being 30 feet in diameter ... I told him it was much too small. So he went to another picture that was marked as having a diameter of 100 feet, and asked, 'Did this look like what you saw?' (It did not.)

As I went through the details of my encounter, he listened with keen attention. I recall telling him that the colour of the lights on the rim of the object could best be compared to the colour of the electrical discharge of the commutator on an automobile generator when seen in the dark.

I asked where these reports ended up. He replied that they would first go to a committee of twelve men who would screen them for 'national security impact'. If it was found to have such impact, it would never be sent elsewhere. Cases where no such impact was found by this committee were sent to the Air Force or Navy offices handling ordinary UFO cases ...

When he was getting ready to leave, he pulled out a magazine and opened it to a page where an article began. He said something like, 'I think you'll find this interesting'. Then he gave me the magazine, and left ... It was *Pageant* magazine for October 1950, and it contained an article called 'Flying Saucers' written by Frank Scully.

Coincidentally, although he didn't know it at the time, Bethune had met one of Scully's principal informers at Big Springs, Texas, in 1949, after landing in a PBM-5A Mariner amphibian. Parked beside him was a war surplus private plane and its pilot, who said he was carrying a magnetic anomaly detector (MAD) for oil exploration (a device developed by the Navy during the Second World War for detecting submarines). Shortly, the owner of the plane and equipment arrived and Bethune was introduced – to Silas Newton.[8]

GIANT USOS NEAR THE IRANIAN COAST

As is the case with UFOs, numerous accounts of USOs – unidentified submarine or submersible objects – have been reported for centuries. The following is abbreviated from a report by Commander J.R. Bodler, US Naval Reserve, published in a Navy journal early in 1952. Unfortunately, no actual date is given for the occurrence.

'My vessel had passed through the Strait of Hormuz, bound for India,' wrote Commander Bodler. 'The night was bright and clear. The Third Mate called me to the bridge, saying he had observed something I ought to see. About four points on the port bow, toward the coast of Iran, there was a luminous band which seemed to pulsate ... binoculars showed that the luminous area was definitely below the horizon, in the water, and drawing nearer to the vessel.'

At a distance of about a mile from the ship, it was apparent that the disturbance was roughly circular in shape, about 1,000 to 1,500 feet in diameter. The pulsations could now be seen to be caused by a revolving motion of the entire pattern about a rather ill-defined centre; with streaks of light like the beams of searchlights, radiating outward from the centre and revolving (in a counter-clockwise direction) like the spokes of a gigantic wheel.

For several minutes the vessel occupied the approximate centre of the phenomenon. Slightly curved bands of light crossed the bow, passed rapidly down the port side from bow to stern, and up from aft, forward. The luminosity was sufficient to make portions of the vessel's upper works quite visible ... the effect was weird in the extreme; with the vessel seeming to occupy the centre of a huge pinwheel whose 'spokes' consisted of phosphorescent luminance revolving rapidly about the vessel as a hub.

The central 'hub' of the phenomenon drew gradually to starboard, and passed aft; becoming more and more distant ... While it was still in sight, several miles astern, and appearing, by this time, as a pulsating bank of light, a repetition of the same manifestation appeared on the starboard bow ... slightly smaller in area than the first, and a trifle less brilliant. Its centre passed slowly aft on the starboard side, with the pattern of revolving, luminous 'spokes' clearly defined.

It was my impression that the actual illumination was caused by the natural phosphorescence in the water, periodically stimulated by waves of energy. The shape of the 'pinwheel', the well-defined 'spokes', the revolution about the centre, all preclude the possibility of this phenomenon being caused by schools of fish, porpoises, or similar cause.

About half an hour later, a third such 'manifestation' was observed, much closer to the vessel than the others; but this one, noted Commander Bodler, was much smaller and less brilliant, with a diameter not over 800 to 1,000 feet.[9]

In his book on USOs, *Invisible Residents*, Ivan T. Sanderson, a former British Royal Navy intelligence officer, cites this and many other remarkably similar cases. The theory of luminescent plankton being responsible for the phenomenon was mulled over at length, though both Sanderson and an associate, Dr Wallace Minto, rejected the hypothesis.[10]

According to a navigator who flew many strategic reconnaissance missions for the Navy during the late 1940s and early 1950s, unidentified craft were the subject of frequent investigations. 'Back in those days,' the source told researchers William Jones and Dr Irena Scott, 'we were frequently assigned to fly to various locations around the world to help indigenous personnel conduct UFO investigations. Many of these missions were to South America. There was a lot going on there, apparently.'

'They would fly into the country, pick up a team of investigators and then fly them into the region where the report or reports were to be taken,' Scott and Jones explained.

In effect, it seemed that his team acted as 'truck drivers' for groups of indigenous military personnel who did not have access to their own aircraft. The final reports were flown back with them to Turkey [Adana] and then sent back to the Pentagon (apparently not to Project Blue Book) in Washington, DC, through Oslo, Norway. When asked why they were sent via this [unusual] route, he replied, 'For diplomatic purposes'. They were classified 'Secret' before being forwarded. His group did no analysis of the reports they collected, and no information about what they were used for ever came back to them.[11]

'Possible connections of Submarine contacts with flying discs' is the subject of a US Air Force Intelligence (AFOIN) memo to the Air Technical Intelligence Center (ATIC), dated 24 April 1952 and classified secret. The memo, from AFOIN-X(SG) – a 'special group' dealing with the subject, referred to later – is addressed to Colonel Frank Dunn, then commander of the ATIC. It begins: 'Attached are nine (9) reports of submarine contacts, ONI [Office of Naval Intelligence] serials listed below . . .' The serial numbers, however, are replaced with nine sets of asterisks, and the remainder of the memo is blanked out, apart from a note stating that the memo is filed under 'ONI Reports & Navy Publications' (see p. 145). My efforts to acquire further details via Navy sources in Washington have so far drawn a blank. The submarine force remains true to its reputation as 'the silent service'. Indeed, US Naval Intelligence has released suspiciously few UFO/USO reports, under terms of the Freedom of Information Act, compared to the other armed services.

MULTIPLE CRAFT OBSERVED NEAR HAWAII

One night late in May 1952, formations of strange aircraft were observed from a Canadian 'pocket ship' warship, HMCS *Iroquois*, en route from Pearl Harbor, Hawaii, to Guam, and thence (in June) to serve in the Korean War. The following report is by Commander George R. McFarlane, Royal Canadian Navy (retired), who was Officer of the Watch at the time:

> At about 0100, I saw a single white light on the port bow at about 30 degrees elevation at a visual range of about a mile. It moved from right to left at a rapid rate. It had a halo around it due to the [thin] mist. I assumed it to be a low-flying aircraft. It did not appear on the Sperry navigational radar. The air defence radar was not in service . . . I thought it unusual to see a low-flying aircraft, which at this time was about 100 miles from Hawaii. There were no scheduled military aircraft listed on the operational schedule for this area. A short time later another light appeared from the same direction passing at high speed. It was not picked up on the navigational radar either, which was not surprising as the radar detection lobe covers the surface but not the sky . . .
>
> At about 0200 I saw the first of many strange lights in the sky. The vast majority were in formation; usually quarter line [half of a 'V' formation] and all appeared on the port side. Many were going in groups of three, some in groups of five or six. They appeared and disappeared instantly at the same speed a computer screen operates.
>
> They moved from time to time and the numbers changed frequently. At one time I counted more than thirty. I recall discussing the possible identity of these lighted objects with the signalman on watch with me. He thought they were very strange. Suddenly one of these objects appeared at close range on our port bow at a low elevation. It was disc-shaped and consisted of a very bright light with black windows running around the whole side which was visible to us. It maintained perfect station on us for at least fifteen minutes.
>
> I scanned the object with binoculars attempting to see into it but saw nothing. I counted the windows and recall there were about two dozen. They were very large and close together and completely black. Although the body of the object glowed very brightly it did not prevent me from looking directly at it. The object appeared more oval in shape than round. And then suddenly it was gone. There was no sound made at any time.
>
> There were still some objects visible far off on the port side. They also had disappeared by 0300. It was at this time that I realized that I

hadn't informed the captain nor anyone else. I did not debrief any of
the watch who were at other stations. It was conduct so unlike my
usual practice that I was left quite disturbed . . . The problem then was
what to enter in the ship's log! I decided to state that many meteorites
had been sighted during the watch . . .[12]

McFarlane made a sensible decision regarding the log entry. As confirmed later, when naval officers make factual reports relating to observations
of UFOs or USOs, the logbook entries are almost invariably altered or deleted
altogether (presumably after the reports have been forwarded elsewhere).
Such a policy seems to have been adopted by a number of the world's navies
since the early 1950s, implying a degree of international collaboration among
heads of naval intelligence to deal with the problem – a problem that was
to become increasingly pervasive.

REFERENCES

1. Berlitz, Charles and Moore, William, *The Philadelphia Experiment: Project
   Invisibility*, Souvenir, London, 1990, pp. 173–7. Bob Beckwith, a retired US Navy
   and Office of Strategic Services intelligence officer, whom I met in 2005, contends
   that the actual ship involved in the experiment was not the USS *Eldridge* (DE-
   173) but USS *Martha's Vineyard* (IX-97), an experimental minesweeper
   commanded by William W. Boyton, USNR; nor was the ship 'teleported' from
   Philadelphia to Norfolk, Virginia, but supposedly moved back two weeks in time
   (!) to Newport, Rhode Island. See *LTT: Levitation, Teleportation & Time Travel* by
   Robert W. Beckwith, Beckwith Electric Co. Inc., 6190 118th Avenue North, Largo,
   FL 33773-3724, published in 2002.

2. Lorenzen, Coral E., *Flying Saucers: The Startling Evidence of the Invasion from
   Outer Space*, Signet, New York, 1966, pp. 30–2.

3. Bethune, Cdr. Graham, *UFO in the North Atlantic: February 10, 1951*, privately
   published, 1991.

4. Memorandum report (Confidential) taken from Lt. Graham E. Bethune, US Naval
   Reserve, Fleet Logistic Air Wing, Air Transport Squadron One, US Naval Air
   Station, Patuxent River, MD, for Commanding Officer, 10 February 1951.

5. Bethune, op. cit.

6. Keyhoe, Maj. Donald E., *Flying Saucers: Top Secret*, G.P. Putnam's Sons, New
   York, 1960, pp. 19–20.

7. *UFO Investigator*, National Investigations Committee on Aerial Phenomena
   (NICAP), October 1970, p. 3.

8. Bethune, op. cit.

9. Bodler, Cdr. J.R., 'Unexplained Phenomenon in the Sea', *U.S. Naval Institute Proceedings*, January 1952; reprinted in *Fate* magazine, September 1952.

10. Sanderson, Ivan T., *Invisible Residents*, World Publishing, Cleveland, OH 44102, 1971, pp. 96–114.

11. Jones, William and Scott, Dr Irena, 'US Navy Support of UFO Research'. Mid-Ohio Research Associates (MORA), PO Box 162, Dublin, OH 43017.

12. McLeod, Gavin, 'Canadian Naval Officer has Close Encounter in Hawaiian Waters', *UFOBC Quarterly*, Vol. 3, No. 2, Spring 1998, pp. 18–19. www.ufobc.org

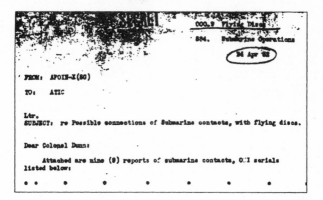

An April 1952 report from a US Air Force Intelligence specialist UFO study
group – AFOIN-X(SG) – to Air Technical Intelligence Center, relating to nine
encounters with unknown objects reported by US Navy submarines to the Office
of Naval Intelligence (ONI). The nine reports have yet to be released.
(*The National Archives, Washington*)

A sketch by L. Schultz based on a report by a US Navy radar operator serving on an
aircraft carrier near the Philippines in 1957. 'The entire top of the radar screen whited
out,' said the officer. 'Within seconds, the radio commentary from all the [accompanying]
four destroyers described a large, cylindrical metal object, located immediately above
our carrier. When I joined the over 3,000 men from five ships who were out on deck,
I was able to see a dark gray, cigar-shaped object, over 4,000 feet long and about
350 feet in diameter. The carrier captain refused to launch any jets to investigate . . .'
(*The Communion Letter*, Vol. 1, No. 2, 1989: PO Box 1975, Boulder, Colorado
80306-1975. © 1989, Wilson and Neff, Inc.)

10. FIGHTER COMMAND

The fact that they can hover and accelerate away from the Earth's gravity again and even revolve around a V-2 in America (as reported by their head scientist) shows they are far ahead of us. If they really come over in a big way that might settle the capitalist-communist war. If the human race wishes to survive they may have to band together.

Thus, in 1950, wrote Admiral of the Fleet Earl Mountbatten of Burma, Supreme Allied Commander, Southeast Asia, during the Second World War, and later Chief of the Defence Staff.[1] Mountbatten showed a keen interest in the subject, having had a sighting in the Pacific during the war, as I learned from Air Marshal Sir Peter Horsley. Moreover, as reported in *Above Top Secret*, an unknown flying machine complete with occupant is said to have landed at his estate near Romsey in Hampshire in February 1955, witnessed by one of his workmen. After investigating the landing site and interrogating the witness, Mountbatten wrote in a signed statement that the workman 'did not give me the impression of being the sort of man who would be subject to hallucinations, or would in any way invent such a story'.[2]

Mountbatten is also believed to have disclosed some fascinating information to the respected American journalist Dorothy Kilgallen. 'I can report today on a story which is positively spooky, not to mention chilling,' she cabled from London in May 1955. 'British scientists and airmen, after examining the wreckage of one mysterious flying ship, are convinced these strange aerial objects are not optical illusions or Soviet inventions, but are flying saucers which originate on another planet.' Her syndicated report continues:

> The source of my information is a British official of Cabinet rank who prefers to remain anonymous. 'We believe, on the basis of our inquiry thus far, that the saucers were staffed by small men – probably less than four feet tall. It's frightening, but there is no denying the flying saucers come from another planet.'

This official quoted scientists as saying a flying ship of this type could not possibly have been constructed on Earth. The British Government, I learned, is withholding an official report on the 'flying saucer' examination at this time, possibly because it does not wish to frighten the public . . .[3]

The late Gordon Creighton, former diplomat, intelligence officer and long-time editor of *Flying Saucer Review*, told me that the crash was alleged to have occurred during the Second World War, and that the story was related to Kilgallen during a cocktail party given by Lord Mountbatten. No further details are available to me. The crash may relate to one of the several that are reported to have occurred during the war, as discussed in Chapter 1.

THE FLYING SAUCER WORKING PARTY

In June 1950 a report on what was described as 'Britain's first flying saucer' appeared in national newspapers. During an exercise from the Royal Air Force (RAF) station at Tangmere, Sussex, the pilot of a Gloster Meteor twin-jet fighter had reported an encounter with a 'shining, revolving disc-like' object that shot past the jet at high altitude. Intelligence officers debriefed the pilot and a report was sent to Fighter Command.[4]

One paper asserted that the disc had been tracked on radar, but an Air Ministry spokesman said this could not be confirmed, adding that there was no evidence that what was seen 'was anything more than natural or meteorological phenomena'. The paper claimed that 'a curtain of secrecy' had been drawn over the subject.[5]

That summer, 1950, a top-secret meeting was held at the Air Ministry's Metropole Building in London to discuss the 'flying saucers'. Chaired by the Deputy Director of Intelligence, Hugh Young, attendees included representatives of MI10 (a military intelligence branch which had been involved in the 'ghost rocket' investigations four years earlier) and various scientific and technical intelligence specialists, such as Wing Commander Myles Formby. The chairman explained that Sir Henry Tizard, Chief Scientific Adviser at the Ministry of Defence, 'felt that reports of flying saucers should not be dismissed without some investigation' and he had agreed that a small Directorate of Scientific Intelligence/Joint Technical Intelligence Committee 'working party' should be set up to investigate future reports. It was agreed that the membership of the working party should comprise representatives of various technical and scientific intelligence branches of the Air Ministry, the Admiralty (Royal Navy) and the War Office.[6]

RAF Fighter Command was advised that all future reports of aerial phenomena were to be directed to the Flying Saucer Working Party (FSWP). Over an eight-month period, the FSWP studied numerous reports and liaised with its counterparts in the US and other countries. The US Air Force's Project Grudge team, as well as the CIA, were consulted.[7] Grudge's negative conclusions undoubtedly contributed to the scepticism evinced by some FSWP members: the astronomer Dr J. Allen Hynek, a consultant to the CIA and the US Air Force, had concluded that 70 per cent of sightings could be explained, the remainder either lacking sufficient evidence 'or the evidence offered suggested no explanation, though some of these might conceivably be astronomical'.[8]

In my opinion, the FSWP team would not have been granted access to the US Government's most sensitive secrets relating to the subject. Air Marshal Sir Peter Horsley, who had been given carte blanche to study any UFO reports and interview pilots when serving as equerry to HRH Prince Philip and HM the Queen in the 1950s, learned from Air Marshal Sir Thomas Pike, Air Officer Commanding-in-Chief, Fighter Command, that the Americans were 'extremely sensitive' about the subject. Sir Peter was also informed by Group Captain Bird-Wilson of the British Defence Staff in Washington that the American authorities were not prepared to 'give information about any conclusions which they might have reached'.[9]

Sir Peter, whose later posts included Assistant Chief of Air Staff (Operations) and Deputy Commander-in-Chief of Strike Command, told me that although he held very high security clearances – including those relating to nuclear weaponry – when he liaised with the Americans, his requests for more information were always politely turned down.[10]

In its final report, classified Secret/Discreet, the FSWP reviewed its investigations, including reports by RAF pilots. The most interesting of these took place at the experimental aircraft test centre at the Royal Aircraft Establishment, Farnborough, Hampshire, in August 1950, reported by Flight Lieutenant (later Wing Commander) Stan Hubbard and others:

> F/Lt. Hubbard, an experienced pilot, said that at 1127 on 14th August, 1950, he and two other officers on the airfield heard a subdued humming noise, like a model Diesel motor, which caused them to search the sky overhead ... The other two officers saw nothing, but F/Lt. Hubbard, who alone was wearing sun-glasses, states that he saw, almost directly overhead at first sighting, an object which he describes

as a flat disc, light pearl grey in colour, about 50 feet in diameter at an estimated height of 5,000 feet. He stated that he kept it under observation for 30 seconds, during which period it travelled, at a speed estimated at 800–1,000 mph, on a heading of 100°, executing a series of S-turns, oscillating so that light reflection came from different segments as it moved.

The second incident occurred during preparations for the annual Farnborough Air Display:

F/Lt. Hubbard was also concerned in the other incident, when, at 1609 on 5th September, 1950, he was standing on the watch-tower with five other officers, looking south in anticipation of the display by the Hawker 1081. The sky was about 3/8 obscured, with a strato-cumulus cloud base at 4,000 feet. At about the same moment, they all saw, at an estimated range of 10–15 miles, an object which they described as being a flat disc, light pearl grey in colour, and 'about the size of a shirt button.' They all observed it to follow a rectangular flight path, consisting in succession of a 'falling leaf,' horizontal flight 'very fast,' an upward 'falling leaf,' another horizontal stretch, and so on; finally it dived to the horizon at great speed. The pattern was estimated to be executed somewhere over the Guildford-Farnham area.

F/Lt. Hubbard was satisfied that the objects he saw on the two occasions were identical; the other observers agreed that the second object fitted the description they had been given of the first.

'We have no doubt that all these officers did in fact see a flying object of some sort,' concluded the FSWP. 'We cannot, however, regard the evidence of identification of this object, which was only seen at very long range, with the earlier one as of any value whatever [and] find it impossible to believe that an unconventional aircraft, manoeuvring for some time over a populous area, could have failed to attract the attention of other observers. We conclude that the officers in fact saw some quite normal aircraft, manoeuvring at extreme visual range, and were led by the previous report to believe it to be something abnormal . . .'[11]

Hubbard remained unaware of these conclusions until he read the report after its declassification fifty years later. His comments on the report and amendments to it are significant. The following is abbreviated from his communications in 2001 with investigators David Clarke and Andy Roberts:

. . . The sound emanating from this strange object [14 August 1950] increased markedly as it got closer, to a heavy, dominant humming with an associated subdued crackling/hissing sound, which reminded me strongly of the ambient noise inside a large active electrical power generating station ... The exterior was almost entirely featureless except that the periphery was edged by a band of a darker colour with indistinct markings of some sort, which kept changing appearance, but from which emanated strange bluish flickering points of light ... I also got the impression that either the main body or the peripheral rim was rotating ... and most remarkably there was a concurrent smell of ozone, that normally is associated with heavy electrical discharges ...

Whereas the FSWP stated that Hubbard had estimated the craft's altitude at 5,000 feet, Hubbard recalled that it was probably between 700 and 1,000 feet, and he guessed its diameter at about 100 feet – not 50 feet as officially reported. As the saucer disappeared into the distance, he recalls hearing screaming and shouting coming from the nearby flight dispatch office, and that a terrified dispatcher came out and asked him if he had seen 'that awful thing'. During an interrogation by RAF scientific intelligence personnel shortly afterwards, Hubbard asked whether they had spoken to the dispatcher. They refused to answer. Asked what he thought about the craft and its origin, Hubbard replied that in his opinion 'it was not something that had been designed and built on this Earth'. From the effect it had on the team, this was clearly the wrong answer.[12]

Regarding the second event on 5 September 1950, Hubbard added that pandemonium prevailed, with people shouting for cameras and binoculars (none were forthcoming). Among the other five witnesses was Wing Commander Frank Jolliffe, who was interviewed in 'mufti' (plain clothes) by Wing Commander Myles Formby, who had come down to Farnborough with other scientific intelligence officers. Formby told Jolliffe that the department 'had never had a more reliable and authentic sighting'. So much for the official conclusions, which were dismissed by Jolliffe as 'ludicrous', leading him to believe that 'the Working Party was following a high-level cover-up directive'. Indeed they were – and one instigated by the Americans.

Hubbard's interview on this occasion was shorter as, interestingly, the team had to catch a plane to Brazil to conduct other investigations. 'We were not given their names and we were strictly warned not to ask questions of them, nor make enquiries elsewhere in the Ministry,' he told Clarke and Roberts. 'We were also warned not to discuss the subject later, even amongst ourselves in private ... I find it quite strange that so much information that we thought critically relevant at the time was not only not included but misrepresented and taken completely out of context, resulting in flawed conclusions.'[13]

Significantly, when the FSWP presented their final report to the Air

Ministry, Dr H. Marshall Chadwell of the CIA's Office of Scientific
Intelligence (OSI) was in attendance. In the Top Secret minutes of the last
meeting, G. Turney (of the Directorate of Scientific Intelligence) stated that
'following the lead given by the Americans on this subject, the Report
should, he thought, have as little publicity as possible and outside circulation should be confined to one copy to Sir Henry Tizard'.[14]

The Working Party was disbanded in June 1951. 'This is the report on
"Flying Saucers" for which you asked,' wrote Dr Bertie Blount in a letter to
Sir Henry accompanying a copy of the report. 'I hope that it will serve its
purpose . . .'[15]

EXERCISE MAINBRACE

During a major NATO operation (Exercise Mainbrace) in September 1952,
sightings were reported by observers from several countries, including those
from the Royal Air Force (RAF) and Royal Navy. At the height of the
Mainbrace operations, unknown aerial targets were tracked by radar at a
number of RAF stations, including Langton, Lincolnshire (reported by
Frank Redfern, father of author Nick), Neatishead, Norfolk, and Ventnor,
Isle of Wight.

At a secret underground radar station located near RAF Sandwich
(possibly RAF Ash) in Kent, Senior Aircraftman William Maguire reported
to Nick Redfern that a huge, unidentified object had been tracked on radar
high over the English Channel. 'This thing just sat there and I recall that I
logged it on my sheets of paper for eighteen minutes,' Maguire told
Redfern. 'Eventually it split into three and zoomed off at some phenomenal
speed. One went north, one headed over to France and the other disappeared in the Eastern Balkans region . . . I wasn't on the height finder but I
remember the mechanics said that it was higher than anything we knew
about . . . afterwards we were told not to talk about it.'[16]

On 19 September 1952, at RAF Topcliffe, Yorkshire, two RAF officers
and three aircrew observed a silver flying disc as it followed a Meteor jet at
about 10,000 feet. 'As the Meteor turned to start its landing run the object
appeared to be following it,' said Flight Lieutenant John Kilburn. 'But after
a few seconds it stopped its descent and hung in the air, rotating as if on
its own axis. Then it accelerated at an incredible speed to the west, turned
south-east and then disappeared.' Witnesses all agreed that the object was
solid, appearing to be the size of a Vampire jet at a similar height.[17]

Captain Ruppelt relates that the Topcliffe incident was one of a number in 1952 (including another report by an RAF pilot during Mainbrace) 'that caused the RAF to officially recognize the UFO'.[18] During his tenure at Blue Book, he says, 'two RAF intelligence officers who were in the US on a classified mission brought six single-spaced typed pages of questions they and their friends wanted answered.'[19] And no wonder. By this time, the Royal Air Force must have begun to realize that they had been sold short on the 'facts' provided to them by the Americans in 1950–51.

On the afternoon of 21 October 1952, Flight Lieutenant Michael Swiney and his student pilot, Royal Navy Lieutenant David Crofts, had taken off from RAF Little Rissington, Gloucestershire, in a Meteor T.7 twin-jet trainer for a high-level navigation exercise at 35,000 feet. Not long after they broke out of cloud in the climb at around 13,000 to 14,000 feet, Swiney got a shock. 'I was rather horrified to see, framed in the front windscreen of the Meteor, three circular white objects.'

Crofts, in the back seat, had not seen the objects. 'Is your oxygen connected?' asked Swiney. 'Mick,' replied Crofts, 'we've just done the 30,000-foot check, and you checked that your oxygen was alright, and I told you that mine was OK. What's the problem?'

'Well, take a look straight ahead.' Crofts did so, and spotted three very bright dots.

'My immediate reaction,' said Swiney, 'was three people coming down in parachutes – and they're right in front of the aircraft. So I took the controls to turn the aeroplane away from what I perceived to be a dangerous situation.'

'As we went towards them,' Crofts continued, 'they of course got closer, in that instead of being all in the small direct-vision window, they were now above the windshield and either side of the windshield.'

'They moved across us,' explained Swiney. 'They were perfectly circular, but looking up at them as we continued on in the climb, they lost their circular shape and took on more or less a flat plate shape.'

Crofts suggested going after the objects to find out what they were.

'No,' retorted Swiney. 'Something like that happened [in] America and the pilots were never seen again, and the aeroplane was, I believe, vaporized.'

Swiney called the base, reported 'three unidentified objects' and requested assistance. 'I have to admit – and I don't mind admitting it – that I was somewhat frightened by what I was witnessing. These objects were then to the starboard side and had remained there. During the period of looking at them and looking away, to see if by chance there was some other explanation, when one looked back, they were nowhere to be seen – as quickly as that.'

On returning to Little Rissington, the pilots were immediately separated. 'I was told to go to my room and that I was not to go to the Mess for tea, and that all my meals would be brought to me in my cabin,' reported Crofts. 'I wasn't to talk to anyone at all until I had gone back to the Wing Commander's office the following morning at nine o'clock.' The pilots were interviewed separately by intelligence officers from the Air Ministry. 'The man that interviewed me was in plain clothes – he told me that the objects had been picked up on radar . . .'[20]

Two Meteor F.8 fighters on twenty-four-hour Quick Reaction Alert (QRA) at RAF Tangmere, Sussex, had apparently been scrambled to chase the unknown targets, but were unable to make a contact. According to Terry Barefoot, who had worked as a switchboard operator in the underground nerve centre of RAF Southern Sector at Rudloe Manor, Wiltshire (known then as RAF Box), 'three objects had entered our airspace going at a fantastic speed, approximately 3,000 mph', which led to an order to scramble an entire squadron in an unsuccessful attempt to intercept them.[21]

Britain's Government Communications Headquarters (GCHQ), the Signals Intelligence (SIGINT) centre based at Cheltenham, is the equivalent of America's National Security Agency (NSA). Investigator Robin Cole learned from a source that radio communications between the Meteor T.7 and Little Rissington had been intercepted by GCHQ, and it thus became the first UFO case to be linked with the top-secret listening base.[22] From my own sources, I have learned that GCHQ continues to this day to share communications on the UFO problem with the NSA.

On 3 November 1953 at 10:00, Flight Lieutenant Terry S. Johnson and his navigator, Flying Officer Geoffrey Smythe, based at RAF West Malling, were flying a Vampire NF.10 night-fighter jet at 30,000 feet when Johnson suddenly spotted a bright circular object dead ahead, about a mile away, 'glowing with greater intensity around its periphery than at the centre. After about 10 seconds it moved to our right, at very high speed. It did not appear on Geoff's radar screen at any time.'

On landing at West Malling, the men were questioned by Squadron Commander Furze, who reported the sighting to the station commander, Group Captain P. Hamley – who took a special interest, having sighted 'foo-fighters' in the Second World War. 'We were called up to the Air Ministry to give a full account to the Duke of Edinburgh's equerry [Air Marshal Sir Peter Horsley]. We were told that Prince Philip [a qualified pilot] was interested in flying saucers.'[23]

An incident similar to that reported by Swiney and Crofts occurred on the afternoon of 14 October 1954. Flight Lieutenant James Salandin of No.

604 County of Middlesex Squadron, Royal Auxiliary Air Force, was flying at 16,000 feet in a Meteor F.8 from RAF North Weald, Essex, when three discs headed towards him on a collision course.

'When they got to within a certain distance,' he told me, 'two of them went off to my port side and the third object came straight towards me and closed to within a few hundred yards, almost filling the windscreen, then it went off towards my port side. I tried to turn round to follow, but it had gone. It was saucer-shaped with a bun on top and a bun underneath, and was silvery and metallic. There were no portholes, flames, or anything.'

'Jimmy' Salandin's one regret is that there was insufficient time for him to trigger the gun-camera button.[24]

British author Harold T. Wilkins was among the first to associate UFOs with the proliferation of aircraft disasters in the 1950s. He cites a number of these in one of his books, and quotes a statement by the British Under-Secretary of State for Air that as many as 507 RAF jets crashed in 1952–4, with great loss of life (112).[25] Most of these accidents were probably subsequently explained in conventional terms, though unexplained accidents were not uncommon during this period. On 5 February 1952, for instance, Lieutenant-Commander Malcolm Orr-Ewing, a test pilot, was killed when his Supermarine Attacker FB.1 suddenly pitched rapidly nose-down at low altitude and crashed vertically in the Test Valley, Hampshire. No cause could be determined from the wreckage. Bizarrely, the accident happened exactly a year (almost to the minute) after another fatal Attacker crash.[26]

Compared with the US, there seem to have been far fewer aircraft accidents and disappearances associated with UFOs in the UK. The most I have gleaned thus far, from a former Ministry of Defence scientist, is that during the 1950s a Meteor night-fighter sent to intercept a UFO simply 'disappeared'. I doubt that it was an isolated incident.

We tend to ascribe to alien visitors either benevolent or hostile motives – seldom both. In this regard, I can do no better than to quote Air Chief Marshal Lord Dowding, Commander-in-Chief, RAF Fighter Command, during the Battle of Britain:

> I think that we must resist the tendency to assume that they all come from the same planet, or that they are actuated by similar motives. It might be that visitors from one planet wished to help us in our evolution from the basis of a higher level to which they had attained. Another planet might send an expedition to ascertain what have been these terrible explosions which they have observed, and to prevent us from discommoding other people beside ourselves by the new toys with which we are so light-heartedly playing.

Other visitors might have come bent solely on scientific discovery and might regard us with the dispassionate aloofness with which we might regard insects found beneath an upturned stone . . . [27]

REFERENCES

1. Ziegler, Philip, *Mountbatten: The Official Biography*, Collins, London, 1985, p. 494.
2. Good, Timothy, *Above Top Secret: The Worldwide UFO Cover-up*, Sidgwick & Jackson, London, 1987; Morrow, New York, 1988. See also *Beyond Top Secret: The Worldwide UFO Security Threat*, Sidgwick & Jackson/Pan Macmillan, London, 1996/1997.
3. *Los Angeles Examiner*, 23 May 1955.
4. Daily Herald, London, 7 June 1950.
5. *Daily Mail*, 7 June 1950.
6. The National Archives, DEFE 41/74, Minutes, DSI/JTIC, 1950–51 (Secret/Top Secret).
7. Clarke, David and Roberts, Andy, *Out of the Shadows: UFOs, The Establishment and The Official Cover Up*, Piatkus, London, 2002, pp. 77–80.
8. 'Unidentified Flying Objects', Directorate of Scientific Intelligence and Joint Technical Intelligence Committee, Report No. 7, June 1951 (Secret/Discreet), The National Archives, DEFE 44/119.
9. Horsley, Peter, *Sounds From Another Room*, Leo Cooper, London, 1997, pp. 173–4.
10. Personal interview, Broughton, Hampshire, 16 May 2000.
11. 'Unidentified Flying Objects'.
12. Clarke and Roberts, op. cit., pp. 87–9.
13. Ibid., pp. 90–3.
14. The National Archives, DEFE 41/75, Minutes, DSI/JTIC 11th Joint Meeting, 19 June 1951 (Top Secret).
15. The National Archives, DEFE 44/1, letter from B.K. Blount to Sir Henry Tizard, 26 June 1951.
16. Redfern, Nick, 'UFOs on Radar – Remarkable New Data!', *UFO Magazine* (UK), January/February 2000, pp. 9–12.
17. *Sunday Dispatch*, London, 21 September 1952.
18. Ruppelt, Edward J., *The Report on Unidentified Flying Objects*, Doubleday, New York, 1956, p. 196.
19. Ibid., p. 130.
20. *The British UFO Files*, a documentary by David Howard and Madoc Roberts, produced by Rik Hall. A Barkingmad Production for Channel Five, 2004.

21. Clarke, David and Roberts, Andy, 'The Little Rissington Incident', *UFO Magazine* (UK), February 2003, pp. 6–7.

22. Cole, Robin D., *GCHQ and the UFO Cover-up*, privately published, 1997. Available from the author at The Flat, Sheldon, Battledown Approach, Cheltenham, GL52 6RA, UK.

23. Williams, Justin, 'The West Malling Incident', *Kent Messenger*, 19 April 1996.

24. Personal interview, London, 10 October 1985.

25. Wilkins, Harold T., *Flying Saucers Uncensored*, Arco, London, 1956, p. 137.

26. Burnet, Charles, 'Supermarine Superpriority', *Aeroplane*, Vol. 27, No. 4, March 1999, p. 77.

27. *Sunday Dispatch*, London, 11 July 1954.

<u>TOP SECRET</u>

WING COMMANDER FORMBY suggested that No.2 should
read: "To examine from now on the evidence on which
reports of British origin of phenomena attributed to
'Flying Saucers' are based".

He also suggested a new No.4. as follows:
"To keep in touch with American occurrences and
evaluation of such."

After discussion it was agreed to amend the Terms
of Reference accordingly.

WING COMMANDER FORMBY said that, as requested, he
had informed Headquarters, Fighter Command, of the
existence of this Working Party.

Minutes from meetings of Britain's 'Flying Saucer Working Party', from 1950 *(above)*
and 1951. *(The National Archives, London)*

8.   <u>UNINDENTIFIED FLYING OBJECTS</u>

The JOINT MEETING had before them a Report by the "Flying
Saucers" Working Party.

MR. TURNEY said that he thought that the document should be
regarded as a final report by the Working Party and in view of
the conclusions reached, suggested that it should now be dissolved.

DSI/JTIC Report No.7.

<u>TOP SECRET</u>

He went on to say, that following the lead given by the
Americans on this subject, the Report should he thought, have
as little publicity as possible and outside circulation should
be confined to one copy to Sir Henry Tizard.

The JOINT MEETING:

    (i)   Approved the Report.

    (ii) Agreed that the "Flying Saucers"
        Working Party should be dissolved
        forthwith, and

    (iii) Invited the Chairman to forward
        a copy of the Report to
        Sir Henry Tizard.

11. UPSURGE

A remarkable sighting from the early 1950s was reported to investigators Dr Irena Scott and Pete Hartinger by a decorated war hero (unidentified) who had served with the US Army in the Pacific theatre in the Second World War. The incident took place in daytime at the Columbus, Ohio, Army Depot, later known as the Defense Construction and Supply Center (DCSC).

'He was standing on the dock of one of the warehouses with two other men,' Scott reports, 'when he saw an object swoop down over the warehouses. It came in so low that he thought it had come out of a hangar at the nearby Curtiss-Wright aircraft manufacturing plant. He remembers telling the others that this object must be ours, because it was flying so close to the ground.'

> The object was circular, but had two fins on the rear. He believed it was 500–700 feet in altitude ... He could not estimate its actual size. He just recalls viewing the underneath part of it and not the top. He has never seen an aircraft that resembled it. It flew slowly down the main street of DCSC and then turned east and flew away. There was a vapour trail behind it. He does not recall a noise ...
>
> Soon after this, he believes it was the next day, one of the buildings that had been unsecured became highly secured. The windows were blocked, and no one was allowed in. Part of the outside area was roped off ... He thinks (or heard a rumour) that the object may have buzzed DCSC because of reported UFO artefacts in storage in there.[1]

Scott cites several reports from witnesses who caught glimpses of a disc-type craft stored under wraps at DCSC. Unfortunately no date is given for the above incident.

On 8 March 1950, four F-51 Mustang fighters were scrambled from Wright-Patterson Air Force Base in Dayton, Ohio, to intercept a UFO visible from and tracked by the base – home of the Air Technical Intelligence Center. Two of the pilots reported a contact with the intruder, described as huge, circular and metallic, but the planes were forced to turn

back due to bad weather.[2] It is reasonable to suppose that these discs were
checking on a craft known to have been stored at Wright-Patterson AFB.

Intrusions above nuclear installations continued to be reported, as the
following Army Intelligence memo from Major U.G. Carlan in August 1950
reveals:

> Since 30 July 1950 objects, round in form, have been sighted over the
> Hanford AEC plant. These objects reportedly were above 15,000 feet
> in altitude. Air Force jets attempted interception with negative results.
> All units including the anti-aircraft battalion, radar units, Air Force
> fighter squadrons, and the Federal Bureau of Investigation have been
> alerted for further observation . . .

UFO RETALIATION

Attacks on unidentified aerial vehicles by military forces increased dramatically in the 1950s. In his book on 'advanced aerial devices' reported during
the Korean War (1950–3), Dr Richard F. Haines, a former NASA contract
research scientist, cites the following remarkable case, which occurred one
night in the early spring of 1951.

Francis P. Wall, Private First Class, was serving in the 25th Division,
27th Regiment, 2nd Battalion, 'Easy' Company, in the 'Iron Triangle' near
Chorwon, South Korea, when an unusual orange glowing object was
observed during an artillery attack. 'It could get into the centre of an
airburst of [our] artillery and yet remain unharmed,' Wall told investigator
John Timmerman in 1987. 'But then this object approached us. And it
turned a blue-green brilliant light.'

> It's hard to distinguish the size of it; there's no way to compare it. It
> pulsated [though] it wasn't regular. I asked for and received permission
> from Lieutenant Evans, our company commander at that time, to fire
> upon this object, which I did with an M-1 rifle with armour-piercing
> rounds. And I did hit it. It must have been metallic because you could
> hear when the projectile slammed into it.
>
> The object went wild. The light was going on and off, and it went
> off completely once, briefly. And it was moving erratically from side to
> side, as though it might crash to the ground. We opened up with
> everything we had and after that nothing would affect it – that one
> shot got it . . . Then [it made] a sound – we had heard no sound
> previous to this – like diesel locomotives revving up. And then, we

were attacked, I guess you would call it. In any event, we were swept by some form of a ray that was emitted in pulses, in waves that you could see only when it was aiming directly at you, like a searchlight sweeps around and the segments of light you would see coming at you.

Now you could feel a burning, tingling sensation all over your body, as though something were penetrating you. So the company commander hauled us into our bunkers. We didn't know what was going to happen. We were scared. These are underground dugouts where you have peep-holes to look out to fire on the enemy. We're peeping at this thing. It hovered over us for a while, lit up the whole area with its light, then I saw it shoot off at a 45 degree angle; it's that quick, it was there and was gone.

It was as though that was the end of it. But three days later the entire company of men had to be evacuated by ambulance. They had to cut roads in there and haul them out; they were too weak to walk. And they had dysentery, and then subsequently, when the doctors did see them, they had an extremely high white blood cell count which the doctors could not account for. In the military, especially the Army, each day you file a report – a company report. Now, we had a confab about that. Do we file it in the report or not? And the consensus was 'no', because they'd lock every one of us up, and think we were crazy.

Following the incident, Wall suffered from severe headaches, dysentery and nausea, and loss of appetite. 'We didn't know what it was. And I still don't know what it was. But I do know that since that time I have periods of disorientation, memory loss, and I dropped from 180 pounds to 138 pounds after I got back to this country. And I've had great difficulty keeping my weight up . . .'[3]

GENERAL MARSHALL'S REVELATIONS

One morning during the summer of 1951, news reporters, photographers and film cameramen gathered at Mexico City Airport to meet General George C. Marshall, US Army Chief of Staff in the Second World War and Secretary of State from 1947 to 1949. Suddenly, someone looked up and shouted. Three saucers could be seen hovering at about 5,000 feet over the airport. Immediately, cameras went into action and many photographs as well as movie films were taken. Several hundred people poured out of the waiting areas and had a good view of the saucers before they shot out of sight.

Newspapers broke the story the following day – but no pictures appeared. The photographs and film, explained reporters, had been confiscated by the American and Mexican authorities, but pending studies they would be released for publication. (They have yet to appear.) As reported in Chapter 5, Dr Rolf Alexander discussed the subject with General Marshall at this time, and during the meeting the general confirmed that alien craft and humanoid bodies had been recovered; that on three occasions the humanoids had been burned to a crisp owing to their different reaction to oxygen, and that contact had been established. In addition, said Dr Alexander, Marshall revealed that 'the visitors were completely friendly – their hovering over defence establishments and airports being taken to mean, "We could blow you all to bits at our leisure if we had any evil intent" . . . He said they were undoubtedly trying to work out a method of remaining alive in our atmosphere before landing and establishing friendly communications, and that the United States authorities were completely convinced that Earth had nothing to fear from them [and] that the USAF had been ordered to take no action against their craft.'[4]

Marshall was either unaware of the facts or being economical with the truth. American authorities – at least, those with 'need to know' – were well aware that some of the crafts' occupants appeared to be hostile, and that the USAF (and Army) *had* been ordered to take action, with often disastrous consequences.

Why, Alexander wanted to know, had such emphasis been imposed on denying the existence of extraterrestrial craft and censoring reports? General Marshall responded that 'the US wanted its people to concentrate on the real menace – Communism – and not be distracted by the visitors from space'. He added that the famous Orson Welles pre-war broadcast of H.G. Wells's story *The War of the Worlds* had 'demonstrated what reaction might be expected were the true facts generally known: a welter of hysterical nonsense, and a complete disorientation from the tasks in hand'. Rumours and speculation, he said, would create an atmosphere that the propagandists of the Kremlin would be certain to exploit.[5]

INTERCEPTIONS OVER GERMANY

L. Gordon Cooper, the former jet pilot and astronaut, was assigned to Neubiberg Air Force Base, Germany, with the 525th Fighter Bomber Squadron, US Air Forces Europe, in 1951, when he saw his first UFO. At the time, the new Soviet MiG-15 jets often penetrated the German border, easily outpacing the F-84 Thunderjets. Although the USAF planes were not supposed to be armed, both sides went aloft with charged guns, Cooper reports, and one US jet had been shot down by a MiG. Only when the Air Force received the swept-wing F-86 Sabre did the MiGs meet their match.

One day, the alarm sounded. 'My squadron mates and I dashed from the ready room and· scrambled skyward in our F-86s to intercept the bogies,' reported Cooper, then a second lieutenant. 'We reached our maximum ceiling of around 45,000 feet, and they were still way above us, and travelling much faster: I could see that they weren't balloons or MiGs or like *any* aircraft I had seen before. They were metallic silver and saucer-shaped. We couldn't get close enough to form any idea of their size; they were just too high.'

For the next two or three days the saucers passed over the base daily. Sometimes they appeared in groups of four, other times as many as sixteen. They could outmanoeuvre and outflank us seemingly at will. They moved at varying speeds – sometimes very fast, sometimes slow – and other times they would come to a *dead stop* as we zoomed past underneath them.· We had no idea whether they were looking at us or what they were doing. They came over the base at regular intervals all day long, generally heading east to west over central Europe ... Since the UFOs were too high and too fast for us to intercept, we eventually stopped going up after them.[6]

PANDEMONIUM IN THE PENTAGON

Major General Charles P. Cabell, who became Director of the Joint Staff for the Joint Chiefs of Staff and later served as Deputy Director of the CIA, was Director of Air Force Intelligence in September 1951, and had become increasingly concerned about the proliferation of reports. 'Before I came into Air Intelligence, the "Flying Saucer" reports had begun to flow in,' he wrote in his autobiography. 'They were completely mystifying and, at times, became very numerous and wide-spread.'

A near mass-hysteria developed from time to time. For those of us in Air Intelligence who were officially responsible for the evaluation of reports, they caused a vast amount of work and puzzlement ... it was not until December, 1969 [following a study which led to the closure of Project Blue Book] that the Air Force felt justified in ruling out any substance of a harmful nature in the mass of reports ...[7]

In September 1951 a top-secret meeting was held at the Pentagon to discuss the UFO situation. It was presided over by General Cabell and his entire staff, plus Lieutenant Jerry Cummings, who had taken over the administration of Project Grudge in June 1951, as well as a special representative from Republic Aviation Corporation. The civilian was 'supposedly representing a group of top US industrialists and scientists who thought there should be a lot more sensible answers coming from the Air Force regarding the UFOs', reported Captain Edward J. Ruppelt, who later headed Project Blue Book. Many expressed scepticism about the negative findings of Project Grudge, and a state of confusion and embarrassment prevailed regarding, among other matters, the procedure for processing reports.[8]

In his private papers, Ruppelt reveals some remarkable information he learned from Lieutenant Cummings. Cabell had asked Cummings to give a resumé of what had been taking place on the project over the past year and a half.

Cummings began by explaining that 'every report was taken as a huge joke', and that at the personal direction of Colonel Harold Watson, everything was done 'to degrade the quality of the reports; and how the only analysis consisted of [James] Rodgers trying to think up new and original explanations that hadn't been sent to Washington before'.

Cabell was livid. 'I want an open mind, in fact, I *order* an open mind,' he began. 'Anyone that doesn't keep an open mind can get out, now. As long as there is any element of doubt, the Project will continue.'

Cabell asked about the results of the investigations of several good sightings, but a telephone check to Air Technical Intelligence Center 'showed they had been lost – no-one ever could find them'.

'Why do I have to stir up the action?' Cabell responded. 'Anyone can see that we do not have a satisfactory answer to the saucer question.' He demanded action: the project should be reorganized and all directives reissued 'because it was obvious that they were not being followed'.

At this point, according to Cummings, General Cabell looked at his staff of colonels for about forty-five seconds and then said, 'I've been lied to, and lied to, and lied to, and lied to. I want it to stop. I want the answer to the saucers, and I want a good answer.'

Citing the Mantell case, Cabell said that he had 'never heard such a collection of contradictory and indefinite statements' and that he had 'a great deal of doubt in his mind that the saucers were all "hoaxes, hallucinations or the misrepresentation of known objects"'. He took a swing at the Grudge Report by saying it was 'the most poorly written, inconclusive, piece of unscientific tripe' that he'd ever seen.[9]

Project Grudge, which had superseded Project Sign (sometimes called Project Saucer), the Air Force's first official investigation, was soon reorganized as the 'New Grudge', with Ruppelt at the helm. In March 1952, the code name was changed to Project Blue Book. In his personal papers, Ruppelt reveals how he was taught to deal with public relations:

'I was never told not to give the straight story but I was told to "play down" the straight story. Stay off the 20 percent unknown [cases] and tell how we solved the ones we did. I was to answer only direct questions and volunteer nothing on sightings that weren't publicly known . . .'[10]

AFRICA AND KOREA

'Recently, two fiery disks were sighted over the uranium mines located in the southern part of the Belgian Congo in the Elisabethville district,' begins an Austrian newspaper article in March 1952, translated by the CIA. 'Suddenly,' the report continues, 'both disks hovered in one spot and then took off in a unique zigzag flight to the northeast. A penetrating hissing and buzzing sound was audible to the onlookers below. The whole performance lasted from 10 to 12 minutes.'

A Belgian Air Force fighter piloted by a Commandant Pierre, stationed at Elisabethville airfield, was sent in pursuit:

On his first approach he came within about 120 meters of one of the disks. According to his estimates, the 'saucer' had a diameter of from 12 to 15 meters and was discus-shaped. The inner core remained absolutely still, and a knob coming out from the centre and several small openings could be seen. The outer rim was completely veiled in fire and must have had an enormous speed of rotation. The colour of the metal was similar to that of aluminium.

The disks travelled in a precise and light manner, both vertically and horizontally. Changes in elevation from 800 to 1,000 meters could be accomplished in a few seconds; the disks often shot to within 20 meters of the tree tops . . . Pierre had to give up pursuit after 15 minutes since both disks, with a loud whistling sound which he heard despite the noise of his own plane, disappeared in a straight line toward Lake Tanganyika. He estimated their speed at about 1,500 kilometres per hour.[11]

The presence of the discs over the uranium mines is further evidence of the special interest shown by those controlling the flying machines in all things related to our nuclear developments.

That same month, British Wing Commander J. Baldwin, a Second World War fighter ace, was on a meteorological reconnaissance flight over Korea when his jet failed to come out of a cloud. Around the same time, a US Navy aircraft carrier in Korean waters had sighted a strange aerial craft. Baldwin's colleagues, flying with him, failed to discover what had happened.[12] Aircraft disappearing in proximity to UFOs were to increase with alarming frequency.

INCREASING US AIR FORCE SIGHTINGS

On 1 May 1952, five discs in formation were spotted by a USAF major a few miles from George AFB, Victorville, California. 'They were sharply outlined against the mountains and appeared large enough so that the major could see their shape,' reported then Lieutenant Edward Ruppelt, in a section that was cut from his book. 'Suddenly they all pulled up in a tight "V" formation, made an almost 90-degree turn and zoomed over the mountains.'

> The major told me that he was pretty excited so he drove right back to the base and went to see the intelligence officer [who] was already in his office listening to a report from a group of airmen who had seen a UFO from the base firing range. They had also seen five disk-shaped UFOs flying in formation . . .
>
> I plotted out the lines of sight and computed the UFOs' speed and size. Unfortunately when I got it plotted, the angles between the lines of sight were such that triangulation would be only a rough estimate at the best. The UFOs were travelling somewhere between 900 and 1,200 miles an hour and were from 1,000 to 1,200 feet in diameter.

The sighting was the first of a series of nine sightings at the base in a three-week period.[13]

On the same day, a giant B-36 Peacemaker bomber (which could deliver nuclear weapons) was approached to a close distance by two flying discs over Davis-Monthan AFB, near Tucson, Arizona. One witness was Major Pestalozzi, an Air Intelligence officer who investigated UFO reports routinely, and who had filed a lengthy report for Blue Book, including not only his own observation but those of the B-36 crew and other USAF personnel at different locations around the base. The following is excerpted from a letter sent to Major Hector Quintanilla, a head of Project Blue Book, by Dr James McDonald, former senior atmospheric physicist at the University of Arizona:

[Maj. Pestalozzi] actually saw the two UFOs overtake the west-bound B-36, and he held them under observation as the aircraft passed overhead [at 20,000 feet] until the objects departed ... he estimated the total time of observation at perhaps 3 minutes ... all of the crew, save the pilot, were able to get back to the starboard blister to see the UFO before it left ... The UFO near the aircraft was at a level distinctly lower than the mid-section of the fuselage ... [Pestalozzi] mentioned to me that the B-36 crew was a bit shaken by this experience. He pointed out to me that, after the UFO departed, the B-36 radioed Davis-Monthan control tower and demanded permission to land immediately. It was just after they landed that Operations called him over to interrogate the crew ... [14]

The discs were estimated by the crew to have had a diameter of 20–25 feet and a depth of 10–12 feet.

Twelve unidentified objects, flying in three groups in tight formation at an estimated speed of between 1,500 and 2,000 mph, and emitting a 'definite soft, intermittent hum', appeared over Randolph AFB, Texas, at around 21:27 on 25 May 1952.[15] Meanwhile, on the same date, but in Korea (26 May), ground radar alerted the crew of an F-94 Starfire jet to 'an unidentified object on its tail'. The USAF report continues:

The interceptor aircraft turned into the unknown and locked on with its radar at 7,000 yards and started to close. Both the pilot and the R.O. [Radar Operator] observed a brilliant white light straight ahead. The unidentified [object] performed a steady climbing turn and accelerated at a tremendous speed drawing away from the F-94 which now had cut in its after-burner. The pilot was unable to close and the R.O. lost the object at 2600 yards after 15 seconds of contact ... [16]

A huge upsurge of sightings around the world in June 1952, culminating in July – particularly over the United States – caused alarm in military and government circles. 'Air Force intelligence men say they are continually astounded by the number of trained scientists who believe they are interplanetary in origin,' reported Robert Moskin in *Look* magazine. 'Lieutenant Ruppelt says he has talked with hundreds of scientists and heard many such theories. He adds, "We can deal with these things if they are from Russia. If they are from Mars, I don't know what we will do." '[17]

All these events were leading up to what the American authorities feared the most – a mass appearance over a major city. And it turned out to be the nation's capital.

REFERENCES

1. Scott, Irena, *Ohio UFOs (and many others)*, Greyden Press, Columbus, Ohio, 1997, p. 53.
2. Hall, Richard H. (ed.), *The UFO Evidence*, National Investigations Committee on Aerial Phenomena (NICAP), 1964, p. 84.
3. Haines, Richard F., *Advanced Aerial Devices Reported During the Korean War*, LDA Press, PO Box 880, Los Altos, CA 94023-0880, 1990, pp. 28–30, citing Report 6601, UFO Information Research Center, 1966, pp. 18–27.
4. *Flying Saucer Review*, Vol. 2, No. 1, 1956, p. 2.
5. Ibid.
6. Cooper, Gordon with Henderson, Bruce, *Leap of Faith: An Astronaut's Journey into the Unknown*, HarperCollins, New York, 2000, pp. 80–1.
7. Cabell, General Charles P., *A Man of Intelligence: Memoirs of War, Peace, and the CIA*, Impavide, Colorado Springs, CO 80919, 1997, p. 246.
8. Ruppelt, Edward J., *The Report on Unidentified Flying Objects*, Doubleday, New York, 1956, p. 93.
9. Hall, Michael David and Connors, Wendy, *Captain Edward J. Ruppelt – Summer of the Saucers – 1952*, Rose Press International, Albuquerque, NM, 2000, pp. 58–9.
10. Ibid., p. 67.
11. Sitte, Franz, 'Flying Saucers over Belgian Congo Uranium Mines', *Die Presse*, Vienna, 29 March 1952, translated and produced as a report by the CIA.
12. Watkins, Harold T., *Flying Saucers on the Moon*, Peter Owen, London, 1954, p. 288.
13. Hall and Connors, pp. 100–102.
14. Ibid., pp. 97–8.
15. Air Intelligence Information Report by Capt. Marvin Thompson, Wing Intelligence Officer, Randolph AFB, Texas, to Chief, Air Technical Intelligence Center, 28 May 1952.
16. USAF, Project 10073 Record Card, Project Blue Book Files.
17. Moskin, Robert, 'Hunt For The Flying Saucer', *Look*, 1 July 1952, pp. 37–41.

10 March 1950

Dr. Robley D. Evans
Massachusetts Institute of Technology
Cambridge, Massachusetts.

Dear Dr. Evans:

Inclosed you will find a Memorandum Report on the Psychological Analysis of Reports of Unidentified Aerial Objects, which was prepared by one of our psychologists at the Aero Medical Laboratory at Wright Field. As you will note, this report is almost a year old and was originally classified "confidential". However, the classification has recently been changed to "restricted", therefore, this report is for your information only.

I have also received information that a new report is in the process of being published and will be classified "top secret". I regret to say that I do not know what this latest report contains, however, I will attempt to get a copy as soon as it is published.

It has recently been rumored that one of these so-called flying saucers crashed in Mexico; however, the details are somewhat bizarre at this moment. When you have finished with the inclosed report, will you please return it to this office.

With best regards.

Sincerely,

ROBERT H. BLOUNT
Lt. Colonel, USAF (MC)
Chief, Medical Research Division
Office of the Surgeon General

1 Incl:
Subj Report
MC REXD-694-18 D
28 apr 49

RESTRICTED

A 1950 letter from Robert H. Blount, Chief, Medical Research Division, Office of the Surgeon General to Dr Robley D. Evans, Professor of Physics, MIT, relating to a crashed flying saucer in Mexico. (*The National Archives, Washington*)

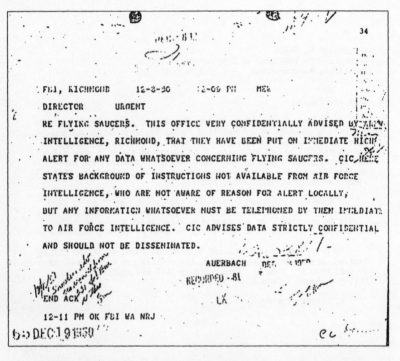

FBI, RICHMOND   12-8-50   :8-09 PM   MEL

DIRECTOR   URGENT

RE FLYING SAUCERS. THIS OFFICE VERY CONFIDENTIALLY ADVISED BY ARMY
INTELLIGENCE, RICHMOND, THAT THEY HAVE BEEN PUT ON IMMEDIATE HIGH
ALERT FOR ANY DATA WHATSOEVER CONCERNING FLYING SAUCERS. CIC HERE
STATES BACKGROUND OF INSTRUCTIONS NOT AVAILABLE FROM AIR FORCE
INTELLIGENCE, WHO ARE NOT AWARE OF REASON FOR ALERT LOCALLY,
BUT ANY INFORMATION WHATSOEVER MUST BE TELEPHONED BY THEM IMMEDIATE
TO AIR FORCE INTELLIGENCE. CIC ADVISES DATA STRICTLY CONFIDENTIAL
AND SHOULD NOT BE DISSEMINATED.

                                          AUERBACH

END ACK

12-11 PM OK FBI WA NRJ

An FBI message relating to an 'immediate high alert for any data whatsoever concerning flying saucers', December 1950. (*The National Archives, Washington*)

12. WASHINGTON WATERSHED

On 1 July 1952, at 07:25 Eastern Standard Time, two F-94 Starfire fighters were scrambled to intercept what witnesses on the ground described as a bright silver 'cigar-shaped object about six times as long as it was wide' travelling south-west across Boston. At the same time, a USAF captain at Bedford, 15 miles north-west of Boston, saw both the jets and a 'silvery cigar-shaped craft' travelling south.[1] It appeared to be about 100 feet long, and flew at the speed of a jet but 'hung' in mid-air on two occasions.[2] At 08:40, Fort Monmouth, New Jersey, radar confirmed two UFOs directly above its secret Army laboratories. Visual sightings of two shiny objects were made – and of another object, at 09:15. The objects were last seen heading towards Washington, DC. Shortly afterwards, over 500 people saw a strange object hovering north-north-west of the city, including a physics professor from George Washington University who said that during the eight minutes it was in sight, the object steadily came so low that downtown buildings were obscured from his view.[3]

On the evening of 14 July, six glowing discs, about 100 feet in diameter and flying in echelon formation, approached a Pan American Airways DC-4 at 'a fantastic speed' a mile below the airliner, in the vicinity of Langley Air Force Base, Virginia. After slowing down abruptly, the discs 'flipped up on edge', then accelerated away. Two other discs then appeared underneath the airliner and joined the others. Finally they all climbed to high altitude at an estimated speed of 200 miles per minute.[4] On landing at Miami, pilots William B. Nash and W.H. Fortenberry were interviewed by agents of the Air Force Office of Special Investigations (AFOSI), and a classified cable describing these events was distributed to Army and Naval Intelligence, as well as to the Armed Forces Security Agency (forerunner of the National Security Agency), the Joint Chiefs of Staff and the CIA.[5]

THE 'MERRY-GO-ROUND'

'No flying saucer report in the history of the UFO ever won more world acclaim than the Washington National Sightings,' wrote Captain Ruppelt, in a chapter of his book entitled *The Washington Merry-Go-Round*. These extraordinary intrusions – some over the restricted air space above the Capitol Building and the White House – generated headlines around the world. Here follows a brief but comprehensive summary by reporter Bob Pratt:

> Between 2 am July 18 and 5 am July 29, UFOs were seen and/or tracked on radar over the Washington, DC area at least 17 times, with some of the witnesses being military personnel or airline pilots. The UFOs were tracked on radar eight times with as many as 10 to 12 objects being detected at a time.
>
> Jet fighters were scrambled at least twice from bases in nearby Delaware and New Jersey. The incidents attracted considerable publicity, and at 4 pm on July 29 – just eleven hours after 8 to 12 UFOs were tracked by radar – the Pentagon staged a large Washington press conference to debunk the flood of UFO reports. Major General Roger M. Ramey participated in the conference, as did Major General John A. Samford, the chief of Air Force Intelligence. Ramey and Samford were referred to as the Air Force's top two saucer experts.[6]

The events on 26 July led President Truman to summon assistance from the Air Force in dealing with growing public concern. At the overcrowded press conference (the largest by the USAF since the Second World War), the sightings were casually explained as mostly having been caused by a 'temperature inversion', i.e., when a layer of warm air lies adjacent to a cooler layer, producing optical distortions in the atmosphere. However, asked by a reporter if some highly secret new American weapon could be causing the reports, Samford replied, perhaps ambiguously, 'We have nothing that has no mass and unlimited power!'[7]

At a meeting of the National Security Council on 28 July, President Truman asked General Walter Bedell Smith, Director of Central Intelligence, to set the Agency to work on the problem. This led to a project called the Special Study Group, located in the CIA's Physics and Electronics division of the Office of Scientific Intelligence (OSI). Frederick C. Durant III, a CIA specialist in chemistry and rocketry (and UFOs), began gathering information at the Pentagon.[8]

In addition to causing solid radar returns that directed the jet interceptors to specific targets, the 'temperature inversion' caused coincidental
electrical interference on several nights at a television reception centre,
severely affecting local stations. The source of the interference, it was
reported, must have originated 'between the station and the receiving set'.[9]

In London, Prime Minister Sir Winston Churchill expressed his con-
cern about the Washington events. In a minute to the Secretary of State for
Air and Lord Cherwell (Frederick A. Lindemann, Churchill's scientific
adviser), he wrote: 'What does all this stuff about flying saucers amount to?
What can it mean? What is the truth?'[10] A reply came back from the Air
Ministry that unidentified flying objects had been 'the subject of a full
Intelligence study in 1951' (by the Flying Saucer Working Party) and that
'all the incidents reported could be explained'.[11]

One of the pilots who chased the saucers, Lieutenant Colonel Charles
H. Cook – who had worked for Blue Book – occasionally discussed
the incident with his family. He had been disturbed by the fact that the
government failed to brief pilots on UFOs: they thought they were going
after Russian planes invading US airspace. When the other pilots arrived at
the target area, he explained to Cathy Johnson, 'It wasn't what they were
told it was.' Cook, who died in 1973, had been Cathy's first husband's
father. She says that on the day of his funeral in Cooperstown, New York,
in 1973, 'people who identified themselves as being from the CIA taped off
his house for four hours and didn't let anyone in. They ended up taking
[most] of his files, [many] of them concerning UFOs, that he kept in a
locked cabinet'.[12]

According to Major Donald E. Keyhoe, during the period UFOs were
being tracked in the Washington area, 'gigantic' objects were tracked
orbiting Earth. 'Two of them came down between Washington and Baltimore and hovered at around 79,000 feet,' Keyhoe revealed to Bob Pratt.

> I talked with one of the pilots who was in the jet squadron that was
> trying to get up near (one of) these things. And he told me, 'I have
> never been more terrified in my life. Just to look at that thing you
> could tell that you would be crazy to go up there and try and shoot at
> it. Thank God we couldn't get up that close.' Later on he had a friend
> (who told me), 'Yeah, I was there and I was scared too. I don't know
> any of the pilots that were involved who weren't scared just seeing
> these damned, huge things like that . . .'[13]

ATTEMPTS TO SHOOT DOWN SAUCERS

In a telegram to President Truman, Robert L. Farnsworth, President of the American Rocket Society, urged the nation's top defence officials to restrain the armed forces from shooting at 'flying saucers'. Farnsworth said there were unconfirmed rumours that the armed forces had been ordered to shoot at any unidentified objects in the sky, but he believed that hostile action might alienate mankind from 'beings of far superior powers'. Should these objects be extraterrestrial, he said, 'such action might result in the gravest consequence; friendly contact should be sought as long as possible.'[14] As we have learned, there had indeed been attempts to shoot down such craft – and many more were to follow.

During his tenure as chief of the Aerial Phenomena Section at the Air Technical Intelligence Center, working with Project Blue Book, Captain Ruppelt learned that one morning in the summer of 1952 a radarscope near a certain USAF base picked up an unknown target that approached at 700 mph and then slowed to a point north-east of the airfield. Two F-86 Sabre jets were scrambled, but at first were unable to locate the target. The second pilot then spotted what he took to be a balloon, but a closer view showed it to be saucer-shaped – 'like a doughnut without a hole'. He began pursuing the object and got as close as 500 yards, when it began to accelerate. When it was at a range of 1,000 yards (the machine gun rounds usually converge at 1,300 yards) he began firing at the target, but it pulled up into a climb and disappeared in seconds.

Ruppelt was shown this report by an intelligence officer, who said he had been ordered to burn all copies, but had saved one.[15]

While involved with Canada's Project Second Storey – the Canadian Government's second official UFO study project – Wilbert Smith confirmed that a number of fragments from UFOs had been recovered and analysed by his research group, including one that had been shot from a disc near Washington in July 1952. Smith, who held a top-secret clearance and liaised with his American counterparts at the time, was informed that the disc, which was about 2 feet in diameter, was glowing:

A glowing chunk flew off, and the pilot saw it glowing all the way to the ground. He radioed his report, and a ground party hurried to the scene. The thing was still glowing when they found it an hour or so later. The entire piece weighed about a pound. The segment that was loaned to me was about one third of that ... There was iron rust

– the thing was in reality a matrix of magnesium orthosilicate. The matrix had great numbers – thousands – of 15-micron spheres scattered through it.

Asked if he had returned the piece to the US Air Force when he had completed his analysis, he replied, 'Not the Air Force. Much higher than that.' 'The Central Intelligence Agency?' asked his interviewers. 'I'm sorry, gentlemen, but I don't care to go beyond that point,' he replied, but added: 'I can say to you that it went to the hands of a highly classified group.'[16]

A SENSATIONAL DISCLOSURE

In the aftermath of the Washington sightings, sensational developments were announced by the columnist Robert Allen in September 1952. 'The Air Force has a breathtaking report on "flying saucers",' he began. 'Noted scientists and Air Force experts express the belief that some of the mysterious flying objects are genuine and that they originate from "sources outside of this planet". That is, these devices are interplanetary aircraft of some kind . . .

'Russia is profoundly mystified and worried by "flying saucers" and strongly suspects they are a new US weapon. The Kremlin has four different investigations underway . . .'

The Air Force study is based on more than 1,800 sightings in the past five years. One important point stressed in the report is that the most authoritative and detailed sightings come from atomic plants and military bases and research centers. These highly significant sightings number around 20 per cent of the total reported. Following is a list of the locations of the most important of these sightings:

New Mexico – Los Alamos and White Sands atomic plant and testing grounds, Albuquerque, and the Holloman, Kirtland and Walker air bases.
California – Muroc, Travis, Hamilton, George, Edwards, Sacramento, and Mint Canyon airfields.
Tennessee – Oak Ridge atomic plant, Knoxville and Dickson AFB.
Arizona – Williams, Davis-Monthan, and Luke AFBs.
Illinois – Scott [AFB] and O'Hare [airport].
New Hampshire – Grenier AFB.
New York – Mitchell AFB.

Mississippi – Air bases at Jackson, Keesler and Biloxi.
Michigan – Selfridge AFB.
Massachusetts – Westover AFB.
Nebraska – Offutt AFB.
North Carolina – Chapel Hill and Pope AFBs.
South Carolina – Spartanburg and at Greenville AFBs.
Texas – Kelly, Randolph and AFBs Carswell and San Marcos.
Washington State – Mount Rainier, Mount Jefferson and McChord
   AFBs.
Oklahoma – Tinker and Norman AFBs.
South Dakota – Air base at Rapid City.
Ohio – Air Force research center at Dayton, and Lockbourne
   AFB.

'The sensational study is the work of the Air Technical Intelligence Center [ATIC], Wright-Patterson Air Force Base, Dayton, Ohio,' continued Allen. 'A number of scientists are devoting their full time there analysing reports. Their objectives are so secret the Air Force will not permit publication of their names. In fact, no one connected with the project or the report would allow his name to be used. However, Air Force authorities are considering publishing certain portions of the report. Chiefly deterring them is fear [that] the sensational nature of the findings may cause undue public alarm. These findings were described by a high Air Force official as "fantastic but true" . . .'[17]

It is possible that some of those who leaked details of this report to Robert Allen included members of a small US Air Force Intelligence (AFOIN) 'special group', designated AFOIN-X(SG), to which I alluded in Chapter 9. Headed by a Colonel Kieling, the group included Dr Stefan T. Possony, a USAF civil service intelligence specialist, as 'acting chief', and Lieutenant Colonel F. Sterling, military 'chief' of the project. It was, explains Professor Michael Swords of Western Michigan University, 'a flexible study group to take on *ad hoc* tasks of special interest or timeliness, which did not necessarily fit into well-worn institutional structures of the Directorate.'[18]

Following the Washington sightings, several teams of CIA and USAF specialists travelled abroad to liaise with their foreign counterparts regarding the crisis. In this connection, Jean Kisling, the French pilot who fired at a UFO over Selfridge Field, Michigan, in 1945 (Chapter 2), told me of an interesting experience he had during this period, when he was flying for Air France on the New York–Paris route. 'One day, when the crew arrived at Idlewild airport,' he began, 'we were told that the regular schedule had been changed. The chief of security at the airport asked me to accompany him to his office. I was warned not to disclose the information he was about to reveal to me.'

He explained that this would now be a 'special security' VIP flight to take a delegation of about twenty or thirty military officers from the Pentagon to Paris on a classified mission. Our Super Constellation plane had been parked away from the terminal – with a military guard.

We had a double, or 'heavy', crew on board. When I took my rest period during the flight across the Atlantic, I chatted to an elderly man with a beard. We got to talking about UFOs, so I related the Selfridge episode to him. He revealed that he was a UFO specialist and that a very important unit in the Pentagon dealt exclusively with the subject. He said that a flying saucer had crashed at El Paso, Texas, some time previously, and that 'small people' – not from Earth – had been recovered. I asked him why all this was kept secret. He replied that everyone would panic.

When we arrived at Orly airport in Paris, there were special procedures. We had to park a long way from the terminal, and were escorted from the plane by a military or police guard. This group of specialists, I understood, was en route to somewhere in East Europe . . .[19]

A Secret CIA memorandum dated 24 September 1952, from Dr H. Marshall Chadwell, Assistant Director, Scientific Intelligence, to General Walter Bedell Smith, Director of Central Intelligence, reveals the extent of concern in the Agency during this critical period. Chadwell, incidentally, had been involved with Britain's Flying Saucer Working Party. In addition to its concerns about the phenomenon per se, he rightly emphasized the military dangers inherent in 'false alerts' arising from failure to distinguish UFOs from incoming Soviet aircraft or missiles.

CIA director Walter Smith took up Chadwell's recommendation. 'It is my view that this situation has possible implications for our national security which transcend the interests of a single service,' he wrote in an undated 1952 Secret memorandum to the Executive Secretary of the National Security Council (p. 181). 'A broader, coordinated effort should be initiated to develop a firm scientific understanding of the several phenomena which apparently are involved in these reports, and to assure ourselves that the incidents will not hamper our present efforts in the Cold War or confuse our early warning system in case of an attack.'

The destruction or disappearance of military aircraft during interceptions of UFOs continued apace. As General Benjamin Chidlaw, former
commanding general of Air (later Aerospace) Defense Command, told
Robert C. Gardner (ex-USAF) in 1953: 'We have stacks of reports of flying
saucers. We take them seriously, when you consider we have lost many
men and planes trying to intercept them.' Leonard Stringfield, the former
Air Force intelligence officer, was told by a reliable source in the 1950s that
the 'Air Force was losing about a plane a day to the UFOs . . .'[20]

*

Stringfield was reliably informed. According to US Defense Department
figures, from 1952 until the end of October 1956, there were 18,662 major
accidents of military aircraft, broken down as follows:

	Air Force	Navy
1952	2,274	2,086
1953	2,075	2,325
1954	1,873	1,911
1955	1,664	1,566
1956	1,530	1,358

Of this astonishing total, most involved fast new jets (such as those
scrambled in UFO interceptions), of which 56.2 per cent were found to be
caused by pilot error; 8.1 per cent by ground-crew or other personnel
failure; 23.4 per cent by failure of parts and equipment in the aircraft; 2.8
per cent by various 'unsafe conditions', and – tellingly – 9.5 per cent
(1,773) were due to 'unknown factors'.[21]

REFERENCES

1. Ruppelt, Edward J., *The Report on Unidentified Flying Objects*, Doubleday, New
   York, 1956, pp. 150–1.
2. Spot Intelligence Report by Lt. Col. Robert S. Jones, DO#1 Westover AFB, MA, 3
   July 1952, Project Blue Book files, cited by Loren E. Gross in *UFOs: A History,
   1952: June–July 20th*, privately published by the author, Fremont, California, 1986,
   p. 36.
3. Ruppelt, op. cit., pp. 150–2.
4. Keyhoe, Major Donald E., *Flying Saucers from Outer Space*, Henry Holt, New
   York, 1953, pp. 124–6.
5. Classified message, Headquarters USAF, AFOIN-2A3, 16 July 1952.

6. Pratt, Bob, 'Conversations with Major Donald Keyhoe'. www.bobpratt.org/keyhoe.html
7. Hall, Michael David, and Connors, Wendy, *Captain Edward J. Ruppelt – Summer of Saucers – 1952*, Rose Press International, Albuquerque, NM, 2000, p. 280.
8. Ibid., p. 149.
9. *Cumberland* (Maryland) *Times*, 23 July 1952.
10. Prime Minister's Personal Minute to the Secretary of State for Air and Lord Cherwell, 28 July 1952, The National Archives, PREM 11/855.
11. Memo to the Prime Minister from the Secretary of State for Air, Air Ministry, Whitehall, 9 August 1952, The National Archives, PREM 11/855.
12. Scott, Irena, *Ohio UFOs (and many others)*, Greyden Press, Columbus, OH, 1997, p, 189.
13. Pratt, op. cit.
14. *Los Angeles Times*, 30 July 1952.
15. Ruppelt, op. cit., pp. 1–5.
16. Edwards, Frank, *Flying Saucers – Serious Business*, Lyle Stuart, New York, 1966, pp. 87–8.
17. Berkeley, California, *Gazette*, 26 September 1952.
18. Hall and Connors, op. cit., pp. 158–9.
19. Personal interviews, Paris, 12 December 2000/16 November 2004.
20. Stringfield, Leonard H., *Situation Red, The UFO Siege*, Doubleday, New York, 1977, p. 138.
21. Supplied by Dr Olavo Fontes in a letter to Richard H. Hall, 15 March 1958.

July 29, 1952

U. S. PROBES MYSTERY

'Scores' of Saucers Tracked by Radar

WASHINGTON (INS)—The government radar station at Washington National Airport today recorded "scores" of unidentified objects traveling at speeds of 90 to 120 miles an hour and the air force sought a new way to solve the 1952 "flying saucer" mystery.

Civil aeronautics officials said the radar sightings lasted three and a half hours and that as many as 12 objects showed on the screen simultaneously.

But because no visual confirmation could be obtained, jet fighters. on a 24-hour "flying saucer" alert, were not sent aloft to investigate.

The Air Force disclosed it turned to a new type camera when 600-mile-an-hour jet planes were unable to catch up with the strange objects sighted in eastern skies in recent days.

Jet Pilots Alerted

Jet pilots have been told to "shoot down" the fantastic objects "if they ignore orders to land" but so far no plane has come within shooting distance.

The CAA said that one commercial pilot today was routed directly over the spot where an unidentified object showed up on the radar screen but that he sighted nothing.

Today's unidentified objects were reported moving "from northwest to southeast, at a 60-degree angle from the prevailing wind"—indicating they were not windborne unless there were unrecorded air currents.

The incident marked the third time mysterious objects have shown up on the airport radarscope. However, on the two previous occasions, pilots and some Washington area residents reported sighting flashing lights and fast moving discs.

An Air Force spokesman said a new-type camera may be able to bring the mystery to an end. He said the camera photographs "luminous phenomenon." It uses the principle employed by astronomers in determining the composition of stars.

Meanwhile, as new reports continued to pour into the Pentagon of more sightings of mysterious objects the Air Force summoned several "saucer" specialists from Dayton, O., for a conference today.

Flooded by Reports

The Air Force said it is receiving new reports of "flying saucers" at the rate of 100 a month.

The Air Force contended that its intensive investigation of more than 1,000 "saucer" reports has convinced it that they are not being sent over the United States by an enemy.

The Air Force added that its investigation indicated also that they are not being controlled by "a reasoning body."

An article in an unknown newspaper relating to the UFO sightings over Washington, DC, in July 1952.

MEMORANDUM TO: The Executive Secretary
                National Security Council

SUBJECT: Unidentified Flying Objects (Flying Saucers)

1. The Central Intelligence Agency has reviewed the current situation concerning unidentified flying objects which have caused extensive speculation in the press and have been the subject of concern to Government organizations. The Air Force, within the limitations of manpower which could be devoted to the subject, has thus far carried the full responsibility for investigating and analyzing individual reports of sightings. Since 1947, approximately 2000 official reports of sightings have been received and, of these, about 20% are as yet unexplained.

2. It is my view that this situation has possible implications for our national security which transcend the interests of a single service. A broader, coordinated effort should be initiated to develop a firm scientific understanding of the several phenomena which apparently are involved in these reports, and to assure ourselves that the incidents will not hamper our present efforts in the Cold War or confuse our early warning system in case of an attack.

3. I therefore recommend that this Agency and the agencies of the Department of Defense be directed to formulate and carry out a program of intelligence and research activities required to solve the problem of instant positive identification of unidentified flying objects. A draft of an appropriate directive is attached.

                                    Walter B. Smith
                                    Director

Enclosure

Declassified by _____
date _____

'Since 1947, approximately 2,000 official reports of sightings have been received and, of these, about 20% are as yet unexplained . . . A broader, coordinated effort should be initiated to develop a firm scientific understanding of the several phenomena which apparently are involved in these reports . . .' General Walter B. Smith, Director of Central Intelligence, to the Executive Secretary of the National Security Council in 1952, previously classified Secret. *(Central Intelligence Agency)*

13. INIMICAL FORCES

It was around 22:00 on 11 February 1953. At the Naval Auxiliary Air Station, Edenton, North Carolina, Marine First Lieutenant Edward Balocco, recently returned from a tour of duty in the Korean War (gaining the Distinguished Flying Cross), stood on 'dirty duty' as the only pilot on 'intercept-ready status'. Suddenly, the alert whistle sounded. Balocco ran to his F9F Panther jet. 'Unknown bogey at two three zero,' the tower advised him, 'Get in the air, now!' Minutes later Balocco was airborne, heading north to Virginia Beach while being vectored to the unknown target by the 2nd Marine Aircraft Wing at Cherry Point. His orders were to 'run black' – without navigation lights.

By the time Lieutenant Balocco had been vectored to the target by Norfolk Naval Air Station, the 'bogey' had disappeared off Norfolk radar. After searching the area for about fifteen minutes, he radioed Norfolk to tell them he was heading back to base as fuel was getting low. Proceeding south at 20,000 feet, he suddenly noticed a bright light below him on his port side. The light appeared to be on or near the surface of the ocean. He paid little heed to it and continued flying south, turning on his navigation lights so he could be seen by other pilots. Glancing back up to the horizon, he was astonished to see that the light had risen to his altitude, and now hovered approximately 2,000 feet away.

The pilot headed his jet directly at the light. Closing in, he could now see that it was disc-shaped, with red blinking lights on its hull.[1]

'I guess it was my Korean combat experience, but my reaction was to squeeze the trigger on my control stick to blast this "enemy",' Balocco told Fred Blechman, a fellow Marine pilot, in 2005. Nothing happened. The guns were empty. 'With full throttle, I got to about 350 feet from the UFO when my entire cockpit was bathed in a strong, blue-white light,' he recalled. 'Everything seemed to be motionless.' As he glanced at his gloved hand he was shocked to discover that he could see right through the glove and the flesh to the bones of his hand.

'It was like an X-ray. For what I think was several seconds there was no sound – not even the sound of my engine. Suddenly, there was a flash,

183

and the UFO broke away at incredible speed, as sound and motion returned.'[2]

Balocco radioed Cherry Point tower, giving them the bearing, heading and estimated speed of the object. He tried unsuccessfully to pursue it again. Another Marine pilot who had been scrambled in a Panther, Captain Thomas Riggs, also reported sighting the object, which he observed moving swiftly down the North Carolina coast at low altitude.

On landing at Edenton, Balocco learned that the Marine Corps would be sending a plane to take him to Cherry Point for debriefing. Here he was led to a conference room and interrogated by Marine and Navy officers. A few hours later he was allowed to leave, having been ordered by a Marine colonel to 'say absolutely nothing' about the incident.[3]

Edward Hertzberg (cited earlier in connection with the Mantell incident) served as the US Air Force's chief physical anthropologist at the Aerospace Medical Research Laboratory, Wright-Patterson AFB, from 1946 to 1972. During this period, an instructor on F-84 jets (probably the F-84G Thunderjet) based at Keesler Air Force Base, Texas, told him of an extraordinary encounter, also involving the projection of light into a cockpit. Hertzberg related to investigator John Timmerman that on this particular occasion (on an unspecified date following the Korean War, which ended mid-1953), the instructor and his student pilot were flying east back to Keesler across north Texas near midnight, at around 20,000 feet, when a light appeared. They flew towards this light, and as they neared it, it suddenly shot past them – now clearly appearing as a craft – and went to the rear of the F-84.

'The instructor did a vertical bank, and went right back following the vehicle,' said Hertzberg. 'They flew straight toward that vehicle and once again, as they neared it, this thing went by them at a tremendous clip.'

> ... it was [an] elliptically shaped object, with a bright glow, and he said they were close enough that he thought he could distinguish the lines between various plates that made up the vehicle. He said there were windows, but [they] were not lighted. He could not see into the craft. It had a dome on top ... and he flew straight toward this thing. He said all of a sudden it just went right by him again, going in the opposite direction ... whereupon he simply pulled into a vertical bank once again and started back the other way ... they had this little dog fight between him and the saucer for maybe ten to fifteen minutes.
>
> On one occasion, as the vehicle had just passed him and he had gone into a vertical bank, suddenly a light came on; a brilliant pencil of light that came on from that vehicle and shone directly into his

cockpit ... He said he saw the shadows of his knees on the floor of his cockpit. He thought to himself, 'This is no place for me'. So, while he was in his vertical bank, he simply kicked the [left] rudder hard and dived [then] levelled out and headed back toward Keesler.

The debriefing lasted two hours. Next morning, the Pentagon called the instructor, saying that the report of his 'combat with a flying saucer' had been received, but that they wanted him to relate the experience once more.[4]

THE DURANT REPORT

By the end of 1952 the UFO problem had become so worrying that the CIA's Office of Scientific Intelligence (OSI) convened a panel of scientists, and meetings were held at the Pentagon from 14 to 17 January 1953. Members of the Scientific Advisory Panel included Dr H.P. Robertson as chairman, whose field was physics and weapons systems; Dr Luis Alvarez (physics and radar); Dr Lloyd V. Berkner (geophysics); Dr Samuel Goudsmit (atomic structure and statistical problems), and Dr Thornton Page (astronomy and astrophysics). The associate members were the OSI's Frederick C. Durant III (missiles and rockets), and Dr J. Allen Hynek (astronomy).

Numerous high-ranking military, scientific and technical intelligence specialists attended the meetings as interviewees, including Captain Edward Ruppelt and Major Dewey Fournet, Air Force Intelligence Monitor of the UFO Project. After twelve hours of meetings, during which the panel was shown movie films of UFOs, case histories of sightings, statistics, and so on, it was concluded that 'reasonable explanations could be suggested for most sightings [and that] by deduction and scientific method it could be induced (given additional data) that other cases might be explained in a similar manner'. In other words, a regurgitation of Project Grudge's tendentiously negative findings.

The panel also concluded unanimously that 'there was no evidence of a direct threat to national security' and that the 'absence of any "hardware" ... lends a "will-of-the-wisp" nature to the [Air Technical Intelligence Center] problem' and that 'no evidence of hostile act or danger exists'. No evidence was found either, they said, 'that any of the unexplained objects sighted could be extraterrestrial in origin' – though it was conceded that Major Fournet 'showed how he had eliminated each of the known and probable causes of sightings leaving him "extra-terrestrial" as the only one remaining in many cases'.

The CIA panel expressed concerns regarding dangers resulting from misidentification of 'actual enemy artifacts'; 'Overloading of emergency reporting channels with "false" information' and the 'Subjectivity of public to mass hysteria and greater vulnerability to possible enemy psychological warfare'. Another of the panel's recommendations was that a policy of debunking UFO reports should be instigated: 'The "debunking" aim would result in reduction in public interest in "flying saucers" ... This education could be accomplished by mass media such [as] television, motion pictures, and popular articles. Basis of such education would be actual case histories which had been puzzling at first but later explained.' Documentary films and cartoons (Walt Disney Inc. being recommended for the latter) were proposed, and 'it was believed that business clubs, high schools, colleges and television stations would all be pleased to cooperate in the showing of documentary type motion pictures if prepared in an interesting manner'.

Another recommendation was that civilian UFO groups should be watched 'because of their potentially great influence on mass thinking if widespread sightings should occur. The apparent irresponsibility and the possible use of such groups for subversive purposes should be kept in mind.'

The panel concluded that 'the continued emphasis on the reporting of these phenomena does, in these parlous times, result in a threat to the orderly functioning of the protective organs of the body politic', and recommended that 'the national security agencies take immediate steps to strip the Unidentified Flying Objects of the special status they have been given and the aura of mystery they have unfortunately acquired ... We suggest that these aims may be achieved by an integrated program designed to reassure the public of the total lack of evidence of inimical forces behind the phenomena ...'[5]

Put into context with fears then prevalent about a possible impending nuclear war with the USSR, for example, the CIA had little alternative in making such recommendations. Though the panel stated that 'there was no evidence of a direct threat to national security' and that 'no evidence of hostile act or danger exists', evidence to the contrary is abundant. As to the alleged absence of any 'hardware', such evidence would be restricted to those with a need to know.

An Air Force Intelligence colonel present at the meetings complained afterwards that the CIA merely wanted to bury the subject. 'We had over a hundred of the strongest verified reports,' he explained to Major Donald Keyhoe. 'The agents bypassed the best ones. The scientists saw just fifteen cases, and the CIA men tried to pick holes in them. Fournet had sightings by top military and airline pilots – even scientists ... I know those CIA agents were only following orders, but once or twice I nearly blew up.'[6]

Dr J. Allen Hynek, one of the panel's consultants on astronomy, claimed many years later that although he was an associate member of the panel, he had not been invited to participate in all the sessions. 'I was dissatisfied even then with what seemed to me a most cursory examination of the data,' he complained.[7] Yet Hynek offered his full cooperation with the debunking programme, as the report shows. And no wonder. According to my information, in addition to being a consultant to Blue Book (and other related projects[8]) he had been assigned for many years as a consultant to the Office of Scientific Intelligence. Furthermore, he was well aware of recovered alien vehicles and bodies, I learned from two sources, and had even shown some photographs of these to a person known to me.

Dr David R. Saunders, who resigned in disgust as a member of the University of Colorado UFO Committee set up by the Air Force in the late sixties to debunk the subject, believed that the Robertson Panel Report, as released, was a cover story, 'conceived and executed for the dual purposes of confusing foreign intelligence and reassuring the cadre of our own establishment. There is ample precedent for the use of such double and triple layers of security ...'[9]

Though listed as an 'associate' on the panel, Frederick C. Durant, as a CIA-appointed officer, was secretary to the panel and dealt directly with the membership, and thus the Robertson Panel Report is commonly known as the Durant Report. 'Actually,' he pointed out to me, 'none of the members of the panel wanted their names openly associated with UFOs or the CIA, because their involvement was security classified.'[10]

In October 2004 I had the pleasure of spending a day in the company of this charming and cultured gentleman. Now nearly ninety, his mental acuity remains undiminished. He greeted me warmly, chiding me jokingly about my interest in 'flying saucers'. Since my interest in unidentified flying objects is matched by an even longer interest in the identified variety, I spent the first few hours happily discussing his career as a former Navy test pilot as well as a missiles and rockets expert.

Long retired from the US Naval Reserve (with the rank of commander), Durant's memory is impressive: he named every single aircraft he had flown, such as the F4F-3 Wildcat ('a great plane'), the F6F Hellcat and the F4U Corsair ('that was my favourite – great acceleration on take-off'). He had also served as Flight Deck Officer as well as a pilot on the USS *Sable* aircraft carrier. Following a period at the Naval Air Rocket Test Station, Dover, New Jersey, he was transferred in 1951 as a Naval officer attached to the CIA's Office of Scientific Intelligence (OSI). 'I've been fully debriefed now,' he explained. 'It was a fairly open assignment.'

Durant's memories suddenly became vague, however, when we finally got round to the dreaded UFO subject. I first asked if he could shed any light on the 'ghost rocket' sightings of 1946. As an expert on guided missiles and rockets, I assumed he must have drawn some conclusions, since the ghost rockets are alluded to in Navy and CIA documents. 'I have no residual knowledge of this,' he replied, somewhat hesitantly, though he did imply that the rockets were neither German nor Russian in origin.

I asked about the hitherto Top Secret 1950 Canadian Government memorandum, which states that, 'The matter is the most highly classified subject in the United States Government, rating higher even than the H-bomb,' and that a small group, headed by Dr Vannevar Bush, had been set up to deal with the problem.

'It's overblown, that sort of writing,' Durant retorted. 'I never ran into anything like that – I wasn't in Intelligence then. It's certainly sensational but, honestly, I cannot connect threads to it with anything I came across . . . I only casually met Vannevar Bush.'

Finally, I wanted Fred Durant's opinion on the statement by former CIA director Rear Admiral Roscoe Hillenkoetter in 1960 that 'through official secrecy and ridicule, many citizens are led to believe the unknown flying objects are nonsense'. 'I think that's true,' he replied, 'but only because too many "high-ups" have been laughed at – it's the "giggle factor" – or, they're excited about a project, go and investigate it, and it turns out to be a hoax . . . Simply, Timothy, if anything had been startling, I would have known, eventually. You can't keep a secret in Washington . . .'[11]

THE 4602ND AIR INTELLIGENCE SERVICE SQUADRON

The 4602nd Air Intelligence Service Squadron (AISS) comprised specialists trained for field collection and investigation of matters pertinent to air-intelligence interest in the so-called Zone of Interior (ZI) – unidentified flying objects ('UFOBs') in particular – according to Air Force Regulation (AFR) 200–2 (see p. 203). The squadron, set up in the late 1940s and based at Peterson Air Force Base, Colorado, adjacent to Air Defense Command HQ, was highly mobile: flights were attached to air-defence divisions with detachments in each of the defence forces.[12]

Researchers Brian Skow and Terry Endres cite further clarification of the Squadron's capabilities, contained in AFR 24–4 (January 1953). Members of 4602nd were trained in 'general intelligence procedures, written and spoken foreign languages, technical intelligence investigation, photography and photo interpretation, and such activities as may be necessary for the accomplishment of the mission'. The unit also had the capacity to conduct operations in remote areas of all climates and terrains and, as Skow and Fndres point out, its liaison programme guaranteed cooperation from all military branches, and from many government agencies and civilian organi-i:ations at state and local levels.[13]

All information on UFOB sightings was to be promptly reported, with electrical reports multiple-addressed to commanders of Air Defense Command and Air Technical Intelligence Center (ATIC), and to the Director of Intelligence at Air Force HQ. In some cases reports were forwarded to the CIA and the National Security Agency (NSA), although there is no mention of this in AFR 200–2, such information being restricted to those with a need to know. Under 'Release of Facts', the regulation order states that:

> Headquarters USAF will release summaries of evaluated data which will inform the public on this subject. In response to local inquiries, it is permissible to inform news media representatives on UFOBs when the object is positively identified as a familiar object ... For those objects which are not explainable, only the fact that ATIC will analyze the data is worthy of release, due to the many unknowns involved.[14]

FURTHER DISAPPEARANCES

One evening in June 1953, an F-94C Starfire interceptor of the Air National Guard was scrambled to intercept a UFO at Otis Air Force Base, Cape Cod, Massachusetts. The following is extracted from a written report by retired Master Sergeant Clarence O. Dargie, who had been stationed at Otis at the time of the incident:

'Just after dark an F-94C with classified electronic gear on board took off in a westerly direction,' Dargie told investigator Raymond E. Fowler. 'The crew consisted of the pilot, Captain Suggs, and the radar officer [R/O], Lt. [Robert] Barkhoff. According to the pilot's testimony, shortly after breaking ground – at an altitude of 1,500 feet over the Base Rifle Range – the engine quit functioning and the entire electrical system failed. As the aircraft's nose dropped towards the ground at an ever-increasing angle, the pilot stop-cocked the throttle and yelled to the R/O to bail out.'

The normal bail-out sequence in this particular type of aircraft calls for the R/O to jettison the canopy by pulling a lever which activates explosive bolts, then pulling a second handle which ejects him from the aircraft by means of an explosive device under the seat. The pilot, upon hearing the second explosion, which tells him that the R/O is clear of the aircraft, is then free to eject. In this case, however, the pilot ejected immediately after the R/O jettisoned the canopy because the aircraft had now descended to about 600 feet at a steep angle and was about 3 seconds from impact.

The parachute opened and acted as an airbrake to slow the pilot down and stopped his forward motion just as his feet hit the ground. He landed in the backyard of a house near the base, and the first indication that the owner had that there was something amiss was when he heard Captain Suggs calling out to his R/O, 'Bob, where are you?'

The R/O could not be found and the pilot had a difficult time convincing the owner that his aircraft had crashed because the man had been sitting near an open-screened window and had heard nothing. The crippled plane should have crashed near where Suggs landed but it wasn't there. This caused one of the most extensive and intensive searches I have ever seen ... The Cape was literally combed, both on foot and from the air for three months without turning up a thing.

'In view of the fact that the pilot stop-cocked the throttle and the pilot was descending at a steep angle only 600 feet from the ground when the pilot ejected, we can discount the possibility that the aircraft crashed in water,' Dargie continued.

The aircraft had a full fuel supply aboard and if it did not explode in flames on impact, it would have left a large fuel slick on the surface ... This whole event took place in a well-populated area at the height of the tourist season. If it did crash in that area, it would have created a detonation heard for miles; yet, no explosion was heard ... As I recall, the canopy was found on the rifle range, which would indicate that whatever happened took place in close proximity to the airfield proper.

What caused the complete and simultaneous failure of all engine and electrical systems? ... the pilot swears that, without warning, the cockpit lights, navigation lights, instruments, radio and engine simply went dead ... Some of the circumstances involved in this case were classified and I have had to frame my story around them. Jets of this nature were dispatched to intercept aerial objects that failed to respond to radar identification. It was on just this type of mission that this aircraft vanished.[15]

Reporter Bob Pratt obtained a copy of the accident investigation report from Norton AFB. 'They claim the plane was up at 8,000 feet, had been up there 20 minutes, caught fire, and they both bailed out and the plane and the man in the back seat simply disappeared into the sea. And they refused to release to me the testimony of the pilot ... claiming it would impugn his reputation.'[16]

On an undisclosed date, possibly in 1953, radar at an Air Force base in Florida picked up a 'blip' as a UFO circled over the airbase. Three interceptors were scrambled to intercept.[17] Leonard Stringfield reports:

As the jets climbed skyward the UFO continued its circling manoeuvre; then it levelled off, heading toward them. Trying to avoid a collision, the jets spread out. Then the UFO accelerated to a higher elevation, leaving the interceptors under it. Suddenly and inexplicably the jets vanished from the scope. Said Keyhoe: 'It was as though the UFO swallowed up the jets. Then the UFO made a turn and streaked off the scope. The radar had over a 200-mile range, but there was no trace of the three jets or the UFO.'[18]

In conversation with Bob Pratt in 1978, Donald Keyhoe said he had heard of the case via two Air Force colonels and had interviewed two witnesses separately: no inconsistencies were found in their accounts.[19]

Stringfield cites an alarming case revealed to him by an assistant crew chief who had been attached to the 64th Fighter Intercept Squadron at Ernest Harmon AFB, Newfoundland. The source, who held a high security clearance, said that in the summer of 1953, two F-94 Starfire jets were scrambled when an uncorrelated target was picked up on base radar. One jet's engine had stalled in a 'hot start' and went off on to an apron beside the runway. 'The second jet got off OK,' said the source, 'and in a minute it was up in the clouds ... we heard the pilot radio that he had visual confirmation of the UFO and then he said it had locked in on his short-range radar. He gave his speed and altitude and then said he was going into a steep climb to give chase.

'That was the last we heard. No Mayday, no nothing. The next thing I knew was the jet going straight down in a dive. It crashed into a mountain.' A special detachment sent to the crash site had to dig to 40 feet to retrieve the remains. The case was hushed up and the base put on red alert, Stringfield learned.[20]

THE GREAT LAKES TRIANGLE

On the afternoon of 27 August 1953, John W. Wilson, the pilot of an F-86 Sabre jet flying over southern Lake Michigan, made a fragmentary distress call from 15,000 feet. He was cut off in mid-sentence. A newspaper report the next day stated that search crews found no trace of the plane or pilot, in spite of the fact that Lieutenant Garrett, flying another F-86 about 500 feet behind Wilson's plane, witnessed the tragedy. 'I heard Wilson call base saying there was an emergency and indicating he would bail out,' said Garrett. 'But almost as he spoke the plane flew apart. No parachute was seen and I believe Wilson never got out of his seat.'[21]

This is one of several cases I include in this book that are cited in *The Great Lakes Triangle* by Jay Gourley,[22] an aviator turned journalist who has made a special study of mysterious accidents and disappearances of planes and ships in the Great Lakes area.

On the afternoon of 23 November 1953, an F-89C Scorpion jet of the 433rd Fighter Interceptor Squadron (FIS), based at Truax AFB, Wisconsin, crashed into a marsh beside Lake Wingra, in the suburbs of Madison. The pilot, Captain Glen E. Collins, and his observer, First Lieutenant John W. Schmidt, were killed. Scores of people witnessed the crash. 'Several witnesses said a saucer flew near the plane, just before it dived into a swamp,' broadcaster Frank Edwards told Major Keyhoe.[23]

At around 18:15 on the same date, an Air Defense Command ground-controlled intercept (GCI) controller was alerted by the presence of an unidentified and unscheduled target on his radarscope in the vicinity of Soo Locks, Michigan. Another F-89C – #51–5853A, also from the 433rd FIS[24] – was scrambled from Kinross AFB, piloted by Lieutenant Felix Moncla Jr and his observer, Lieutenant R.R. Wilson, in the rear seat.

As he vectored the F-89 to the target, the GCI controller noted that the unidentified air traffic changed course as the plane approached at over 500 mph. Nine minutes went by. Gradually the F-89 closed the gap, and the controller advised the men that the target should now be in sight. Suddenly the two 'blips' on the GCI radarscope merged into one, as if they had collided. For a moment a single blip remained on the scope, but then it disappeared. Marking the position, the controller flashed an emergency message to Search and Rescue. Possibly Moncla and Wilson had baled out in time – possibly not.

After an all-night air/sea rescue search, not a trace of wreckage or the missing men was found. 'The plane was followed by radar until it merged

with an object 70 miles off Keweenaw Point in upper Michigan,' an Air
Force press release stated tersely.[25,26]

Just before noon on 1 July 1954, an unknown aerial object was tracked
over New York State by Griffiss AFB radar. An F-94 Starfire jet was
scrambled and the pilot climbed steeply towards the target, guided by his
radar observer in the back seat. 'When a gleaming disc-shaped machine
became visible he started to close in,' reports Keyhoe.

> Abruptly a furnace-like heat filled the cockpit. Gasping for breath,
> the pilot jettisoned the canopy. Through a blur of heat waves he
> saw the radar observer bail out. Stunned, without even thinking, he
> ejected himself from the plane. The cool air and the jerk of his open-
> ing parachute aroused him. He was horrified to see the jet diving
> toward the heart of a town. The F-94, screaming down into Walesville,
> NY, smashed through a building and burst into flames. Plunging on,
> the fiery wreckage careened into a car.

Four died in the disaster – a man and his wife and their two infant
children. Five other Walesville residents were injured, two of them
seriously. 'Soon after the pilot came down, at the edge of town, a reporter
appeared on the scene,' Keyhoe continues. 'Still half dazed, the pilot told
him about the strange heat. Before he could tell the whole story, an Air
Force car arrived. The pilot and radar observer were hurried back to Griffiss
AFB. Interviews were prohibited, and when the Walesville reporter's story
of the sudden heat was published the Air Force quickly denied it. There
was no mystery, headquarters told the press, merely engine trouble.'

In 1968 Keyhoe learned from a USAF officer that the F-94 pilot had
reported a separate effect apart from the heat. 'Something made his mind
black out,' said the officer. 'He couldn't even remember bailing out. He did
recall the sudden heat and he saw the radar observer eject himself. But
everything was blank from then on until his parachute opened ... [The
radar observer] was stunned too, but he didn't black out. Of course, he got
out sooner than the pilot.'[27] In *The Great Lakes Triangle*, Jay Gourley
reports a number of instances where pilots or passengers, or both, have
suffered a similar loss of memory.

Questioned by Gourley about the Walesville disaster, the distinguished
author Dr Jacques Vallée (who gives the date as 2 July 1954) said that
Lieutenant William E. Atkins had been the pilot, and Henry Coudon the
radar observer. After bailing out, Atkins had landed near Westmoreland,
New York, and Coudon near Cary Corner, New York.[28]

Jay Gourley cites a statistical analysis of aircraft disasters in this area by a National Transportation Safety Board statistician, who found that the Great Lakes accounted for more of these strange accidents than even the Bermuda Triangle. On 23 August 1954, for example, the pilot of a Royal Canadian Air Force (RCAF) twin-jet CF-100 interceptor baled out near the north shore of Lake Ontario, explaining later that the aircraft became impossible to control. 'Publicly, the Canadian Defence Headquarters refuses to reveal the cause of the accident,' writes Gourley. 'The official cause is classified secret. I have seen this secret file. It says the scientists who studied the case *could not determine* what caused the jet to become unmanageable.'[29]

On 27 September 1960 a Royal Canadian Air Force CF-100 Canuck twin-jet interceptor (#18469) took off on a routine mission, followed by another CF-100, trailing the lead plane by just a few miles. Over Lake Ontario, conditions were good, with light cirrus clouds and excellent visibility. However, as 18469 entered the cirrus, it vanished instantly.

'The airborne eyewitness's account might raise questions about attentiveness,' reports aviator Jay Gourley, 'except that a clear white contrail (or vapour trail) remained for some time. It ended, but not in the normal way. The contrail was not changing altitude into warmer or drier air [and] didn't end in an explosion ... It simply ended as though both engines had simultaneously flamed out. [But] why didn't the pilot simply explain his problem over the radio, then bail out?'

Gourley has seen some of the classified documents pertaining to this event. The case is unexplained, and both the interceptor and its crew of two were never found.[30] Although no unidentified objects were reported in the vicinity (within the Great Lakes Triangle), the similarity of this case to the many other aircraft disappearances involving UFOs warrants its inclusion here.

FURTHER AERIAL EVENTS

At midnight on 19 October 1953, an American Airlines DC-6 en route to Washington, DC, was buzzed by an unknown object over Conowingo Dam, north of Baltimore, Maryland. The object appeared to be heading towards the airliner on a collision course, so Captain J.L. Kidd threw the plane into a dive as the UFO streaked overhead and disappeared. Several passengers were thrown into the aisle, and Captain Kidd radioed to Washington Airport for ambulances and doctors. The UFO was estimated to be as large as the DC-6 (length 100 feet, span 117 feet). No other aircraft within a 100-mile area were near the airliner.[31]

Harold T. Wilkins cites a series of strange accidents to commercial aircraft taking off or landing at Newark, New Jersey, in 1953. 'So serious was the loss of life that public protests forced the authorities to close this airport,' he writes. 'All that was said was that "for some reason unknown the planes went out of control and suddenly crashed". It is odd that "running out of fuel" was the reason advanced for crashes and force-landings of British and American jets in England and West Germany on January 11, 1954, and December 16, 1953.' He also pointed out that in 1954 the Royal Danish Air Force grounded all its Thunderjets and Sabre jets after numerous disasters.[32]

Clarence L. 'Kelly' Johnson was one of the greatest aeronautical engineers of all time, and oversaw the development of many of the Lockheed Aircraft Corporation's famous aircraft, such as the F-94 Starfire and U-2 spyplane. At around 17:00 on 16 December 1953, Johnson and his wife were at their ranch near Agoura, California, when a dark elliptical shape appeared in the sky. Initially stationary, it then began to move, accelerating away in a shallow climb. It seemed to be very large and distant.

Coincidentally, at 16:58, the test crew of a newly built Navy Airborne Early Warning (AEW) four-engine Lockheed WV-2 aircraft, flying in the vicinity at 16,000 feet, spotted an unknown object. In the cockpit were Rudy Thoren and Roy Winner, assisted by Joseph F. Ware Jr – all highly experienced test pilots – as well as Charlie Crugan, a veteran company pilot, and Lockheed's chief aerodynamicist, Philip A. Colman. One could not wish for better qualified witnesses.

'Thoren turned the WV-2 a bit to the right to head toward the object,' reports UFO investigator Joel Carpenter. 'It appeared to be a very large aircraft of some type, but as it remained stationary and unchanged in shape over at least a five-minute period (note how this corresponds to Johnson's observation of a stationary object), they became more and more intrigued. Thoren finally diverted from his course [and] flew toward it at about 225 mph for some time without appearing to gain on it at all ... Within a few moments it appeared to head west directly away from them at high speed, remaining dark and solid-looking the entire time as it dwindled to a tiny dot.'

'I should state that for at least five years I have definitely believed in the possibility that flying saucers exist,' Kelly Johnson declared in a report sent to Air Technical Intelligence Center. 'Having seen this particular object on December 16th, I am now more firmly convinced than ever that such devices exist, and I have some highly technical converts in this belief as of that date ...'[33]

REFERENCES

1. Iahn, Tim, 'The Iahn Interceptor Files', *UFO Magazine* (US), Vol. 14, No. 2, February 1999, pp. 44–7.

2. Blechman, Fred, 'True Tales From the Fred Baron: Seeing UFOs!' *Airport Journals*, Centennial, Colorado, May 2005.

3. Iahn, op. cit.

4. Scott, Irena, *Ohio UFOs (and many others)*, Greyden Press, Columbus, Ohio, 1997, pp. 98–9.

5. Durant, F.C., 'Report of Meetings of Scientific Advisory Panel on Unidentified Flying Objects Convened by Office of Scientific Intelligence, CIA' (Secret/Security Information), January 14–18, 1953.

6. Keyhoe, Major Donald E., *Aliens from Space: The Real Story of Unidentified Flying Objects*, Panther Books, St Albans, 1975, p. 86.

7. Slate, B. Ann and Druffel, Ann, 'UFOs and the CIA Cover-Up, *UFO Report*, Vol. 2, No. 4, New York, 1975, p. 20.

8. Projects Saucer, Sign, Grudge and Blue Book spawned smaller, related projects, whose work was not necessarily shared with the parent project. These included Projects Golden Eagle, Henry, Stork and White Stork.

9. Saunders, Dr David R. and Harkins, R. Roger, *UFOs? Yes!: Where the Condon Committee Went Wrong*, Signet, New York, 1968, p. 105.

10. Letter, 1 December 2005.

11. Personal interview, Raleigh, North Carolina, 23 October 2004.

12. Air Force Regulation No. 200–2, 'Intelligence: Unidentified Flying Objects Reporting (Short Title: UFOB)', Department of the Air Force, Washington, 18 August 1954.

13. Skow, Brian and Endres, Terry, 'The 4602nd Air Intelligence Service Squadron and UFOs', *International UFO Reporter*, Vol. 20, No. 5, Winter 1995, pp. 9–10.

14. Air Force Regulation No. 200–2.

15. Fowler, Raymond E., *UFOs: Interplanetary Visitors*, Exposition Banner, New Jericho, NY 11753, 1974, pp. 288–91.

16. Pratt, Bob, 'Conversations with Major Donald Keyhoe'. www.bobpratt.org/keyhoe.html

17. Ibid.

18. Stringfield, op. cit., pp. 143–4.

19. Pratt, op. cit.

20. Stringfield, Leonard H., *Situation Red, The UFO Siege*, Doubleday, New York, 1977, p. 142.

21. *Chicago Tribune*, 28 August 1953.

22. Gourley, Jay, *The Great Lakes Triangle*, Fawcett, Greenwich, CT, 1977, p. 33.

23. Heath, Gord, 'What Really Happened to Lt. Gene Moncla?' *UFOBC Quarterly*, Vol. 8, No. 1, Winter 2003, pp. 7–14. www.ufobc.ca

24. Ibid.

25. Ibid.

26. Keyhoe, Major Donald E., *The Flying Saucer Conspiracy*, Hutchinson, London, 1957, pp. 11–19.

27. Keyhoe, Major Donald, *Aliens from Space: The Real Story of Unidentified Flying Objects*, Panther, UK, pp. 35–6.

28. Gourley, op. cit., pp. 44–5.

29. Ibid., p. 31.

30. Ibid., pp. 57–8.

31. Keyhoe, *The Flying Saucer Conspiracy*, pp. 48–9.

32. Wilkins, Harold T., *Flying Saucers Uncensored*, Arco, London, 1956, pp. 136–7.

33. Carpenter, Joel, 'The Lockheed UFO Case, 1953', *International UFO Reporter*, Vol. 26, No. 3, Fall 2001, pp. 3–9, 33.

DEPARTMENT OF DEFENSE
OFFICE OF PUBLIC INFORMATION
WASHINGTON 25, D. C.

26 January 1953

Henry Holt & Company
383 Madison Avenue
New York 17, N.Y.

Dear Sirs:

This will acknowledge your letter of recent date regarding
a proposed book on "flying saucers" by Major Donald E. Keyhoe,
U. S. Marine Corps, retired.

We in the Air Force recognize Major Keyhoe as a responsible,
accurate reporter. His long association and cooperation with the
Air Force, in our study of unidentified flying objects, qualifies
him as a leading civilian authority on this investigation.

All the sighting reports and other information he listed have
been cleared and made available to Major Keyhoe from Air Technical
Intelligence records, at his request.

The Air Force, and its investigating agency, "Project Bluebook,"
are aware of Major Keyhoe's conclusion that the "Flying Saucers" are
from another planet. The Air Force has never denied that this
possibility exists. Some of the personnel believe that there may
be some strange natural phenomena completely unknown to us, but that
if the apparently controlled maneuvers reported by many competent
observers are correct, then the only remaining explanation is the
interplanetary answer.

Very Truly Yours

Albert M. Chop
Air Force Press Desk

'We in the Air Force recognize Major Keyhoe as a responsible, accurate reporter
... if the apparently controlled maneuvers reported by many competent observers are
correct, then the only remaining explanation is the interplanetary one.' A letter from a
US Air Force Press Officer replying to an inquiry by Keyhoe's publisher.

(US Department of Defense)

UFO Report
▆▆▆ 53-2

Attachment 10

Brief Sworn Statement

by witness

I, ▆▆▆▆▆▆▆▆▆do solemnly swear that during a special
assignment with the U.S. Air Force on May 21, 1953, I assisted in
the investigation of a crashed unknown object in the vicinity of
Kingman, Arizona.

The object was constructed of an unfamiliar metal which
resembled brushed aluminum. It had impacted 20 inches into the
sand without any sign of structural damage. It was oval and about
30 feet in diameter. An entranceway hatch had been vertically
lowered and opened. It was about 3½ feet high and 1½ feet wide.
I was able to talk briefly with someone on the team who did look
inside only briefly. He saw 2 swivel seats, an oval cabin, and a
lot of instruments and displays.

A tent pitched near the object sheltered the dead remains of
the only occupant of the craft. It was about 4 feet tall, dark
brown complexion and had 2 eyes, 2 nostrils, 2 ears, and a small
round mouth. It was clothed in a silvery metallic suit and wore a
skull cap of the same type of material. It wore no face covering
or helmet.

I certify that the above statement is true by affixing my
signature to this document this day of June 7, 1973.

Signature   : ▆▆▆▆▆▆▆

Date Signed : ___June 7, 1973___

Witnessed by: ▆▆▆▆▆▆▆

Date Signed : ___June 7, 1973___

An affidavit signed by Arthur Stansel, hitherto known as 'Fritz Werner', witnessed by
investigator Raymond E. Fowler, testifying to having assisted in the investigation of a
crashed disc in the vicinity of Kingman, Arizona, in May 1953. On several occasions
Stansel has hinted that he himself, as opposed to 'someone on the team', looked
inside the craft. *(Raymond E. Fowler)*

- 5 -

November 1953 to November 1958

Employer: Wright Air Development Center, Aircraft Laboratory, Wright-Patterson AFB, Ohio

Position: Supervisory Engineer

Duty Summary: As Chief of Alighting Devices for Aircraft Laboratory, had technical cognizance over all research, development, design, and testing of Air Force landing gear, skis, skids, cross-wind gear, and associated controls and instruments. Project conceiver and coordinator for Task Force SLIDE held in the Arctic Ocean, Greenland, and Minnesota. Primary accomplishments were in the area of organizing large task forces of military, civilian, and contractor personnel for projects whose annual costs averaged $700 million.

June 1949 to November 1953

Employer: Air Material Command, Installations Division, Wright-Patterson AFB, Ohio

Position: Mechanical Engineer

Duty Summary: Performed engineering design of Air Force engine test cells. Also performed research and development of techniques for determining blast effects on buildings and structures. Was Project Engineer for Air Force Buildings and Structures portion of Operation Upshot/Knothole held at the Atomic Proving Ground, Nevada.

PUBLICATIONS

"Dynamometer vs Propeller Loading for Engine Testing," AMC, 1953

"Design Aspects of Space Vehicles" (Co-Author), WADC, 1958

"A Digitized Control System for Minuteman Missile," Curtiss-Wright, 1961

"AN/USQ-28 Photo Navigation Viewfinder Simulator," Autometric Corporation, 1962

A page from Arthur Stansel's CV listing his employment details during the relevant period. He has authored other publications in addition to those cited here. In 1973, when he signed the affidavit, he worked as Aerospace Programs Manager with the Raytheon Company (Equipment Division). *(Raymond E. Fowler)*

THE WHITE HOUSE
WASHINGTON

July 13, 1953

MEMORANDUM FOR GENERAL TWINING

The President expects you to attend the Extraordinary
Meeting of the National Security Council in the Broadcast
Room of the White House, Thursday, July 16, at 9:00 A.M.
The program will be explained in detail at the meeting.
It is advisable not to plan any other engagements before
6:00 P.M. on that day.

· Due to the nature of the Meeting, it is necessary to
take special security precautions and to maintain absolute
secrecy regarding participation in, as well as the substance
of, the Meeting. It is requested that you enter the White
House grounds via the Southeast Entrance not later than
8:45 A.M. and descend from your car at the South (Diplomatic)
Entrance of the Mansion. Your car should be discharged and
not wait anywhere in the vicinity of the White House.

The President expects you to lunch with him at the
White House at 12:30 P.M.

In order to avoid communication on this subject, it is
understood that in the absence of contrary word your concur-
rence in the above arrangements is assumed.

ROBERT CUTLER
Special Assistant
to the President

A hitherto Top Secret memorandum from the White House to General Nathan
Twining in July 1953, which probably relates to a meeting of the MJ-12 group.
(*The National Archives, Washington*)

July 14, 1954

~~TOP SECRET RESTRICTED~~
~~SECURITY INFORMATION~~

MEMORANDUM FOR GENERAL TWINING

SUBJECT: NCC/MJ-12 Special Studies Project

    The President has decided that the MJ-12 SSP briefing should take place during the already scheduled White House meeting of July 16, rather than following it as previously intended. More precise arrangements will be explained to you upon arrival. Please alter your plans accordingly.

    Your concurrence in the above change of arrangements is assumed.

ROBERT CUTLER
Special Assistant
to the President

DECLASSIFIED
Authority *ND 85701.3*
By SMITH NARA Date 1/12/87

A memorandum for General Twining relating to a briefing of the MJ-12 group.
(The National Archives, Washington)

*AFR 200-2
1-5

AIR FORCE REGULATION }
NO. 200-2 }

DEPARTMENT OF THE AIR FORCE
WASHINGTON, *12 AUGUST 1954*

INTELLIGENCE

Unidentified Flying Objects Reporting (Short Title: UFOB)

1. Purpose and Scope. This Regulation establishes procedures for reporting information and evidence pertaining to unidentified flying objects and sets forth the responsibility of Air Force activities in this regard. It applies to all Air Force activities.

2. Definitions:

a. *Unidentified Flying Objects (UFOB)*—Relates to any airborne object which by performance, aerodynamic characteristics, or unusual features does not conform to any presently known aircraft or missile type, or which cannot be positively identified as a familiar object.

b. *Familiar Objects*—Include balloons, astronomical bodies, birds, and so forth.

3. Objectives. Air Force interest in unidentified flying objects is twofold: First as a possible threat to the security of the United States and its forces, and secondly, to determine technical aspects involved.

a. *Air Defense.* To date, the flying objects reported have imposed no threat to the security of the United States and its Possessions. However, the possibility that new air vehicles, hostile aircraft or missiles may first be regarded as flying objects by the initial observer is real. This requires that sightings be reported rapidly and as completely as information permits.

b. *Technical.* Analysis thus far has failed to provide a satisfactory explanation for a number of sightings reported. The Air Force will continue to collect and analyze reports until all sightings can be satisfactorily explained, bearing in mind that:

(1) To measure scientific advances, the Air Force must be informed on experimentation and development of new air vehicles.

(2) The possibility exists that an air vehicle of revolutionary configuration may be developed.

(3) The reporting of all pertinent factors will have a direct bearing on the success of the technical analysis.

4. Responsibility:

a. *Reporting.* Commanders of Air Force activities will report all information and evidence that may come to their attention, including that received from adjacent commands of the other services and from civilians.

b. *Investigation.* Air Defense Command will conduct all field investigations within the ZI, to determine the identity of any UFOB.

c. *Analysis.* The Air Technical Intelligence Center (ATIC), Wright-Patterson Air Force Base, Ohio, will analyze and evaluate: All information and evidence reported within the ZI after the Air Defense Command has exhausted all efforts to identify the UFOB; and all information and evidence collected in overseas areas.

d. *Cooperation.* All activities will cooperate with Air Defense Command representatives to insure the economical and prompt success of an investigation, including the furnishing of air and ground transportation, when feasible.

5. Guidance. The thoroughness and quality of a report or investigation into incidents of unidentified flying objects are limited only by the resourcefulness and imagination of the person responsible for preparing the report. Guidance set forth below is based on experience and has been found helpful in evaluating incidents:

a. Theodolite measurements of changes of azimuth and elevation and angular size.

b. Interception, identification, or air search

---

*This Regulation supersedes AFR 200-2, 26 August 1953, including Change 200-2A, 2 November 1953.

The first page from US Air Force Regulation No. 200-2, 12 August 1954.

(The National Archives, Washington)

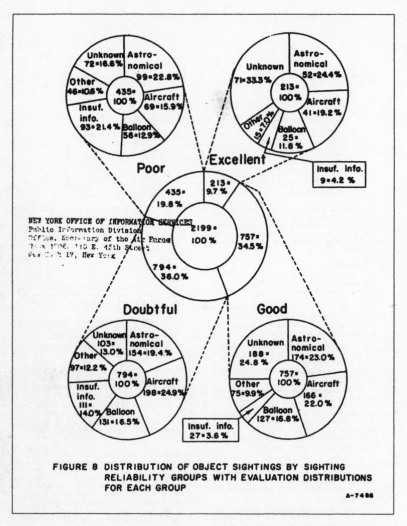

FIGURE 8 DISTRIBUTION OF OBJECT SIGHTINGS BY SIGHTING
RELIABILITY GROUPS WITH EVALUATION DISTRIBUTIONS
FOR EACH GROUP

A-7486

A page from Project Blue Book Special Report No. 14 (5 May 1955). Note that the highest number of 'unknown' sightings are in the categories of 'good' and 'excellent' reliability – at variance with the US Air Force's official position. *(US Air Force)*

14. SPECIAL POWERS

In early 1954 airline pilots in the United States who sighted UFOs became subject to military restrictions contained in a Joint Army-Navy-Air Force Publication (JANAP), promulgated by the Joint Chiefs of Staff, and could find themselves liable to prison terms of up to ten years and/or fines of $10,000 if they discussed their sightings with the media or the public. These restrictions were first imposed during a conference between airline representatives and intelligence officers of the Military Air Transport Service (MATS) in Los Angeles on 17 February 1954.[1] (MATS – now MAC, the Military Airlift Command – is the USAF's major command that relates to and conducts liaison with civilian commercial aviation.)

The subject of JANAP 146 was 'Communication Instructions for Reporting Vital Intelligence Sightings (CIRVIS)'. Unidentified flying objects are listed separately from aircraft and missiles. Citing Espionage Laws, the order states that, 'The unauthorized transmission or revelation of the contents of CIRVIS reports in any manner is prohibited.'[2] Though few civil pilots were adversely affected by this regulation, airline companies.discouraged public disclosure of sightings, sometimes threatening pilots with loss of their jobs.

Alarming aerial encounters, mostly involving military aircraft, continued unabated. L. Fletcher Prouty, a retired US Air Force colonel, is a distinguished author of several authoritative books on intelligence matters. A pilot in the Second World War, he spent his last nine years of service in the Pentagon as the official focal-point officer, first for the Air Force and then for the entire Defense Department, with the CIA (clandestine operations). He was also one of five USAF officers who established the North American Aerospace Defense Command (NORAD). I interviewed him in Washington in 1994.

When commanding an Air Force heavy transport squadron in Tokyo in 1953–54, Prouty received an intriguing message from the Pentagon:

Our crew was covering nearly half the world, every day, back and forth. And one day, I got an official wire from Headquarters, Air Force

– a top-secret wire, for 'my eyes only' – that if ever any of my crewmen saw something that they did not recognize and could not rationalize – in flight – they were to report to me and I was to get sworn statements and to put those statements in an envelope and to ship them to a certain office in the Pentagon ... commanders in relevant positions got the same order, and we got them all over the world.

One day a crew came in, six to seven months later. They'd been on a flight from Hawaii to Tokyo, that in those days took twenty-four hours, landing at Midway Island for fuel. And, as I recall, between Midway and Tokyo they saw something. So the commander came in [and] he had a twelve-man crew and they were all standing behind him. He said: 'We all saw this thing last night, and it persisted; it stayed there, it went with us, it went off.' So immediately I said: 'Stop!' I put them in twelve separate rooms in the barracks. I put a military policeman with each one, I put a recorder with each one, and then put copies of the questions into the rooms, and each one had to answer the questions *after* they had told their own narrative story. So then I wrapped it all up in a bundle and shipped it to Washington – and never heard another word about it.

Colonel Prouty told me that, in addition to the crew, all sixty passengers observed the large unknown object, which flew close beside the C-54 transport for *over an hour* at its altitude of 9,000 feet.[3]

A more frightening top-secret incident involving an Air Force transport flying at night between Hawaii and Japan occurred in 1958. 'Without any warning, there was a blinding flash, like an explosion, near the transport,' reports Major Donald Keyhoe. 'Then the plane's radar picked up a UFO pacing the plane. The captain fired a challenge rocket, and a red flare came in answer, followed by a second, blue-green explosion, then a final red flare.' Keyhoe continues:

No damage was done, and the UFO soon went off the radar, but the alarmed crew stayed on watch the rest of the night. In a verbatim copy of the AF Intelligence debriefing, confidentially given to me by an AF source, the captain said he was convinced they were 'shot at'. The Intelligence debriefing officer, a colonel, added another, more ominous statement: 'The entire crew ... were aware of the incidents in which multi-engined Air Force transports have disappeared while flying between — and—. The crew believed that what happened to them was related to the previous disappearances.' Several AF planes had vanished between Guam and Japan, and the inked-out words evidently were the names of those locations.[4]

Leonard Stringfield learned in 1955 from an Air Force major of another disturbing incident that had occurred sometime within this time frame. 'I can't give you all the details,' began the major, 'but one case scares the hell out of me. And, for God's sake, don't use my name.'

> This case happened in Iceland while I was stationed there with the Air Force. It began when radar picked up two UFOs approaching our base at fast speed. In the area we had a jet fighter on a routine mission, so Operations vectored it in for intercept. We heard the pilot confirm the UFO on radio, then suddenly we lost contact. The next thing we saw was the jet plunge into the water. The waters were shallow and we recovered the jet and the bodies of the two airmen.
>
> We couldn't explain the crash, and there were a number of other things we couldn't explain. Anyway, the case was closed when the adjutant notified the next of kin that the officers were killed while flying on a *routine training mission* . . .[5]

An R7V-1 Super Constellation four-engined military transport with forty-two passengers on board mysteriously vanished en route from its base at Patuxent River Naval Air Station, Maryland, to Lajes in the Azores, on 30 October 1954. In his book *Into the Bermuda Triangle*, Gian J. Quasar, a pilot and leading authority on this subject, reports that messages from the plane were routine up to the point when it passed Bermuda. Nothing further was heard.

An intensive search failed to recover any bodies or even a single item of wreckage. Although there is no evidence to link this disaster with nefarious UFO activity, I am convinced that the disappearance of hundreds of planes and ships in the Bermuda Triangle – like the Great Lakes Triangle and various other locations around the world – is indeed related to such activity. Concluded the Naval Board of Inquiry:

> It is the opinion of the Board that R7V-1 BuNo [Bureau of Aeronautics number] 128441 did meet with a sudden and violent force, that rendered the aircraft no longer airworthy, and was thereby beyond the scope of human endeavour to control. The force that rendered the aircraft uncontrollable is unknown . . .[6]

'TAKE US TO YOUR LEADER'

Why, I am often asked, do aliens not contact our leaders? It would seem that they have.

Rumours persist that on 20 February 1954, President Dwight D. Eisenhower was spirited away during a Palm Springs vacation for a meeting with aliens at the top-secret Edwards (then Muroc) Air Force Base, California. Desmond Leslie, a former RAF pilot and co-author of an early book on the subject, learned from a USAF officer that a disc, estimated to be 100 feet in diameter, had landed on the runway on a certain day. Men returning from leave were suddenly not allowed back on the base. The disc was allegedly housed under guard in Hangar 27, and Eisenhower was taken to see it.[7] Circumstantial evidence suggests that something extraordinary did indeed happen that day.

Gabriel Green, an American researcher, spoke to a military officer who claims to have witnessed the arrival of the craft at Muroc. 'At the time I was engaged in firing practice, under the command of a general,' said the officer. 'We were shooting at a number of targets when suddenly five UFOs came flying overhead. The general ordered all the batteries to fire at the craft. We did so, but our fire had no effect on them. We stopped firing, and then we saw the UFOs land at one of the base's big hangars.' Two other witnesses, Don Johnson and Paul Umbrello, also claim to have witnessed one of the disc-shaped craft near Muroc on the evening of 20 February.[8]

Lord Clancarty, better known as Brinsley Le Poer Trench, the pioneering UFO author, spoke to a USAF test pilot, a retired colonel, who claimed to have been present at Muroc during the Eisenhower visit. 'The pilot says he was one of six people at the meeting,' Lord Clancarty told a reporter. 'Five alien craft landed at the base. Two were cigar-shaped and three were saucer-shaped. The aliens looked human-like, but not exactly,' he said, adding that they had the same proportions as humans and were able to breathe our atmosphere. They did not say where they came from. The aliens spoke English, and supposedly informed the President that they wanted to start an 'educational programme' for the people of Earth in order to make mankind more aware of their presence here.[9]

Unnerved, Eisenhower reportedly indicated to them that he did not think the world was ready, and that such a revelation would create a very difficult situation for everybody. According to the test pilot, the aliens seemed to understand. They indicated that they would continue to make further isolated contacts with humans. A demonstration of their ability to overcome gravity and to make their craft invisible ensued. 'This disturbed the President greatly,' said the pilot, 'because now none of us could see them, although we knew they were there.'[10]

Others present are said to have included Franklin Allen of the Hearst

Newspapers, Cardinal James MacIntyre, bishop and head of the Catholic Church in Los Angeles, and Edwin Nourse of the Brookings Institution (who had been President Truman's financial adviser).[11] The security check before the event is stated to have taken about six hours.[12]

Whatever the truth, Eisenhower, who had been staying with his friend Paul Roy Helms at the Smoke Tree Ranch in Palm Springs, ostensibly for a golfing holiday, 'disappeared' for four hours on 20 February, leading to pandemonium when he failed to turn up for a press conference. The official explanation? Eisenhower had lost a cap on a tooth, necessitating a trip to a local dentist. No evidence for the dental trip (such as White House memos) has ever emerged.[13]

I have learned from a reliable source that sometime after the Eisenhower incident, two scientists were taken by jeep to a meeting with aliens 'somewhere in the desert'. A friend of the source rode 'shotgun' in the jeep, together with his buddy in the military. At the rendezvous point was a landed disc, and the scientists went aboard. Supposedly, a discussion on a 'transfer of technology' ensued for a couple of hours. At the time, the source's friend worked for a small military detachment and held Alpha clearance: he later became a CIA officer.

No additional details are available to me. However, the information tends to corroborate what I have learned from other sources: that since the 1940s communications with an elite group of US military and scientific intelligence personnel have been established, and that there has been a transfer of technology. That an arranged meeting with a president of the United States might subsequently have taken place seems entirely logical to me, given the potentially grave nuclear situation facing Earth.

Another alien encounter in 1954 was reported by Air Marshal Sir Peter Horsley, a former pilot who flew numerous types of aircraft during and following the Second World War (such as the Mosquito, Spitfire, Meteor, Hunter, Lightning and Vulcan). Sir Peter had been Deputy Commander-in-Chief, RAF Strike Command, and spent seven years in the service of HM the Queen and HRH Prince Philip, Duke of Edinburgh, as equerry. It was during this latter period that Sir Peter had an experience that had a profound effect on him – a two-hour meeting with an apparently extraterrestrial human being – as revealed in his autobiography, *Sounds From Another Room*,[14] and published in an extensive account in my *Alien Base*.

Sir Peter shared his interest in the UFO mystery with Air Chief Marshal Sir Arthur Barratt, who introduced him to a British Army friend, a General Martin, who believed that aliens were trying to warn us of the perils of nuclear war. One day in 1954, Martin invited Sir Peter to meet a 'Mrs

Markham' that night at her London flat in Chelsea. Martin did not attend the meeting. There, in a dimly lit room, Sir Peter was introduced to a mysterious 'Mr Janus'.[15]

Without any preliminaries,' writes Sir Peter, 'Mr Janus dived straight into the deep end by asking me to tell him all I knew about flying saucers ... At the end [I] asked Janus what his interest was. He answered me quite simply, "I would like to meet the Duke of Edinburgh."' Somewhat taken aback, Sir Peter replied that this would not be easy. 'I was about to add particularly for security reasons but thought better of it ... here the strangeness of it all started – the man's extraordinary ability to read my thoughts.' Asked why he wanted to meet Prince Philip, Janus replied: '[He] is a man of great vision ... who believes strongly in the proper relationship between man and nature which will prove of great importance in future galactic harmony.'

Janus began by pointing out that man was 'now striving to break his earthly bonds and travel to the Moon and the planets beyond':

Man in his journeys through the universe may find innumerable centres of culture far more ancient than his own ... He will discover a wealth of experiences infinitely more startling and beautiful than can be imagined: an infinite variety of agencies and forces as yet unknown ... even other universes with different space and time formulae ... Man invading space for material gain or personal glorification alone will gain nothing.

'The Earth is going through a Dark Age at the moment,' Janus went on. 'Material possessions count more than a Man's soul.'

Like a child, Man is preoccupied with his technological toys, which he believes will bring him riches and happiness. This shows up in the superficiality of his culture and a careless disregard for nature. In his greedy quest for more complex machines Man is prepared to sacrifice almost anything – his natural environment, animals and even his fellow humans. The dreadful spectre of blowing up his world hardly makes him falter in this headlong rush.

Janus expounded on cosmogony – the origin of life in the universe – referring to the so-called 'big bang' as 'the generally accepted theory' of an expanding universe that 'originated from the giant explosion of a vast area of high-density gas which contained all the elements necessary for life and matter':

If you accept the theory of the expanding universe you accept that it is an ocean of galaxies with solar and planetary systems similar to our own. By the laws of probability there must be millions of planets in the universe supporting life, and within our own galaxy thousands supporting life more advanced than on Earth . . .

Earth is a young planet with its Sun a young mother . . . imagine a galactic solar system somewhere in space with conditions similar to Earth except that its Sun is in the autumn of its life. Provided its inhabitants have survived wars and alien invasion, it is impossible to imagine what super-technology and cultural advancement they have reached . . .

Janus accurately predicted our own technological developments, in that 'perhaps in twenty years' time manned rockets will be commonplace and the Earth will be girdled by satellites of all sorts and sizes', and that there would be 'great strides in the miniaturization of all our present technology, advances in navigational guidance and communication over vast distances'.

Why then were aliens coming here? 'The answer is that this traffic is only a thin trickle in the vast highways of the universe,' explained Janus. 'The Earth after all is a galactic backwater inhabited by only half-civilized men, dangerous even to their neighbours . . .'

Most of these vehicles are robot-controlled space probes monitoring what is going on. Some are manned in order to oversee the whole programme and to ensure the probes do not land or crash by accident. They must also ensure that evidence of their existence is kept away from the vast majority of Earth's population . . . the basic principle of responsible space exploration is that you do not interfere with the natural development and order of life in the universe any more than you should upset or destroy an ant heap or bee-hive . . .

You will have to grow a lot older and learn how to behave on your own planet, if indeed you do not blow yourselves up between times, before you are ready for galactic travel.

'Since time immemorial,' Janus went on, 'there have been tales of vessels coming out of the sky bringing strange visitors. Observers do come among you and make contact on a very selective basis where they judge that such contact could not harm either party.'

These observers have studied Earth for a long time. With advanced medical science they have been fitted with the right sort of internal equipment to allow their bodies to operate normally until they leave.

It is not very difficult to obtain the right sort of clothing and means to move around quite freely ... While you are still far away from travelling in deep space, such contacts will be infrequent and must be conducted in strict secrecy ...

The observers have very highly developed mental powers, including extra-sensory, thought reading, hypnosis and the ability to use different dimensions ... and rely solely on their special powers to look after themselves.

'What was Janus?' Sir Peter asked himself after the meeting. 'Was he part of an elaborate hoax or plot ... an imaginative prophet of the future or what he had insinuated – an observer?'

Sir Peter wrote a verbatim report of the meeting and gave it to Lieutenant-General Sir Frederick 'Boy' Browning, Treasurer to Prince Philip. He never saw General Martin, Mrs Markham or Janus again.[16]

In my first meeting with Sir Peter, I asked him for more details about Mr Janus. 'Somehow, he was difficult to describe,' he began. 'What made it strange is that I have no lasting impression of him: he seemed to fit perfectly in his surroundings. If I have any impression of him, it was his quiet voice which had a rich quality to it. He looked about 45 to 50 years old [and] was dressed in a suit and tie. He was quite normal in every way, except that he seemed to be tuning in to my mind, and gradually took over the conversation ... by the end of the meeting, I was quite disturbed, really.'

'And what of the reaction at Buckingham Palace?' I queried.

'Michael Parker, Prince Philip's private secretary, thought it a joke,' he replied. 'But Prince Philip had an open mind.'[17]

In my second and last meeting with Sir Peter Horsley at his home in 2000, he revealed that, in addition to being disturbed by the realization that Janus was reading his mind, he was even more disturbed by the fact that this extraordinary man 'knew all Britain's top-secret nuclear secrets'.[18]

During a meeting on 7 October 1955 in New York with Mayor Achille Lauro of Naples, General Douglas MacArthur, a famed Army General in the Second World War, made some extraordinary comments regarding the future of warfare on Earth.

'He thinks that another war would be double suicide and that there is enough sense on both sides of the Iron Curtain to avoid it,' said the Mayor. 'He believes that because of the developments of science all the countries on Earth will have to unite to survive and to make a common front against attack by people from other planets.'[19]

What MacArthur could not reveal, of course, was that we were already engaged, if not in a war, then in a conflict.

REFERENCES

1. Fowler, Raymond E., *Casebook of a UFO Investigator*, Prentice-Hall, Englewood Cliffs, New Jersey, 1981, pp. 182–3.
2. JANAP 146(c), Joint Chiefs of Staff, Joint Communications, Electronics Committee, Washington, DC, 10 March 1954.
3. Personal interview, Washington, 16 February 1994.
4. Keyhoe, Major Donald E., *Aliens from Space: The Real Story of Unidentified Flying Objects*, Panther, UK, 1975, p. 193.
5. Stringfield, Leonard H., *Situation Red, The UFO Siege!* Doubleday, New York, 1977, pp. 138–9.
6. Quasar, Gian J., *Into the Bermuda Triangle: Pursuing the Truth Behind the World's Greatest Mystery*, McGraw-Hill, 2004. p. 26.
7. *Valor* magazine, 9 October 1954, and confirmed to the author by Desmond Leslie.
8. Rivas, Juan A. Lorenzo, 'President Eisenhower's "ET" Encounter: What Really happened at Muroc Base?' *Flying Saucer Review*, Vol. 44, No. 3, 1999, pp. 2–5.
9. Picton, John, 'Eisenhower Was Visited by UFO, British Lord Claims', *Toronto Star* (date not available, but the story was confirmed to the author by Lord Clancarty).
10. Rivas, op. cit.
11. Another attendee is reported to have been Commander Charles L. Suggs (US Navy), according to his son, who was interviewed by the researcher William F. Hamilton.
12. Commentary by Gordon Creighton in Rivas, op. cit.
13. Berlitz, Charles and Moore, William, *The Roswell Incident*, Granada, London,1980, pp. 119–28.
14. Horsley, Sir Peter, *Sounds From Another Room: Memories of Planes, Princes and the Paranormal*, Leo Cooper, London, 1997.
15. In Roman mythology, Janus was the 'guardian of gates and doorways and especially of the State in time of war; represented with two faces, one at front and one at back of his head'. (*The Reader's Digest Great Encyclopaedic Dictionary*, The Reader's Digest Association/Oxford University Press, 1964/1962, p. 465.)
16. Horsley, op. cit., pp. 180–96.
17. Personal interview, Hampshire, 21 September 1997.
18. Personal interview, Hampshire, 16 May 2000.
19. 'M'Arthur Greets Mayor of Naples', *New York Times*, 8 October 1955.

THE NEW YORK TIMES, SATURDAY, OCTOBER 8, 1955.

M'ARTHUR GREETS MAYOR OF NAPLES

Lauro Quotes Him as Saying Wars Between Nations Are Now Obsolete

Mayor Achille Lauro of Naples, which was badly damaged in World War II, called on General of the Army Douglas MacArthur yesterday and received the general's cheering opinion that war between countries on this earth was probably obsolete.

However, war between the planets may replace it, in the general's opinion, Mayor Lauro reported afterward.

The Neapolitan Mayor, who is stopping at the Waldorf-Astoria Hotel during his four-day stay in New York, was scheduled to visit General MacArthur, who resides at the hotel, briefly for an exchange of greetings.

"I am delighted that General MacArthur did me the honor of allowing me to remain for forty-five minutes," Signor Lauro said. "I am also delighted that he is pleased with the Neapolitan workers in his factory in my city."

Sperry Rand Corporation, of which General MacArthur is chairman of the board, recently built a plant in Naples employing 600 persons. It is to be expanded to employ 2,000.

Factors for Uniting World

General MacArthur described himself as "a confirmed optimist" regarding the possibility of another world war, Mayor Lauro said.

"He thinks that another war would be double suicide and that there is enough sense on both sides of the Iron Curtain to avoid it," the Mayor went on.

"He believes that because of the developments of science all the countries on earth will have to unite to survive and to make a common front against attack by people from other planets."

The politics of the future will be cosmic, or interplanetary, in General MacArthur's opinion, the Mayor continued. He quoted the military leader as saying that a thousand years from now today's civilization would appear as obsolete as the stone age.

During the visit the two men discussed Dr. Albert Einstein.

"General MacArthur said he admired him as a scientist although not as a politician," Signor Lauro said.

"He quoted Einstein's reply when asked what weapons would be used in a third world war—that he did not know what weapons would be used in a third world war but that a fourth global conflict would be fought with sticks and stones."

Rapprochement With Soviet

Mayor Lauro said General MacArthur was optimistic even about the differences between the Soviet Union and the democracies. He quoted the general as saying:

"The Soviets and the democracies will adopt the best characteristics of each other, and, in the process of many years, there will not be a strict line of demarcation between their ideals; therefore no causes for war between them."

General of the Army Douglas MacArthur's comments, quoted by Mayor Achille Lauro of Naples, that 'because of the developments of science all the countries on Earth will have to unite to survive and to make a common front against attack by people from other planets'. (The *New York Times*, 8 October 1955)
And in a speech in 1962 to the US Military Academy at West Point, MacArthur warned of 'ultimate conflict between a united human race and the sinister forces of some other planetary galaxy'.

15. 'UFO'S — SERIOUS BUSINESS'

At a lecture in 1956 Frank Edwards, a noted newsman and author of two books on UFOs, revealed details of an Air National Guard F-51 crash during a UFO interception – and one that bears uncanny similarities to the Mantell crash of 7 January 1948.

The story begins on 8 January 1956 – almost exactly eight years after the Mantell disaster – when Ground Observer Corps (GOC) personnel at Bedford, Indiana, about 50 miles south of Indianapolis, spotted five flying objects circling around. Shortly before, they had also been seen over Lafayette, Indiana, about 90 miles to the west, then south of Bedford, where they were watched by more than 300 people.

'The objects followed the usual pattern,' said Edwards, 'disk-shaped, about 25 feet in diameter, glowing and changing colour from faint orange to yellow and red. They sent jets from Louisville [Kentucky] up to chase them, but as soon as the jets got within 15 or 20 miles the objects took off, going northward, and left there at high speed and disappeared at great altitude in a matter of seconds.

> Three weeks later, on January 31st, just before I went on the air, I got a call from our Bloomington studio. They said, 'We've got a picture for you of the wreckage of a National Guard plane that crashed down here this afternoon between Bloomington and Bedford. The pilot was killed.' It turned out that the pilot was a fellow who I happened to know, Colonel Lee Merkel, a veteran flyer and a wonderful guy . . . the jets had been up again after unidentified objects south of Bloomington, just as on the 8th, and again the jets lost them. But Col. Merkel, who was in charge of the National Guard base down at Louisville, had taken off in an F-51 Mustang, a propeller-driven job. He had oxygen tanks, and the plane was in excellent condition. He had gone up because he could fly longer than the jets, and the jets were trying to vector him in on the UFOs.
>
> Finally, [Merkel] reported back to the tower at Louisville, by radio, that he could see an object moving along the edge of a cloud some distance ahead and above him, and he took after it. According to the

reports he made to the tower, it was climbing, but he was following it. He gave no description of it, other than to say he could see it glowing and blinking. When he got to about 30,000 feet, he said he thought he was gaining a little on it, and it was then below him. The tower heard no more from him after that.

A few minutes later, his plane exploded at low altitude about 500 feet right above a farmhouse, and the debris scattered all over the fields for a quarter of a mile. It was a terrific blast. I find it hard to believe that the explosion of the plane's gasoline, in those thin aluminium tanks, could possibly have had that much power.

'I'm inclined to think that we have here a repetition of the tragedy of Capt. Thomas Mantell, who was killed at Fort Knox, Kentucky, in January 1948,' declared Edwards. 'I think that after eight years, just a bit north of the original spot, we've had another incident of the same kind. It never made the papers. On November 11, 1954, an unknown object had appeared in the very same area, and Col. Merkel had chased it unsuccessfully. That made front-page headlines in Louisville. But when Merkel died, fourteen months later on a similar mission, not a paper mentioned that he had been chasing something when his plane mysteriously crashed.'[1]

In 1956, the US Navy issued orders to its pilots to engage UFOs in combat if the objects appeared hostile. Operational procedures for a 'UFO scramble', given by a briefing officer to pilots at Los Alamitos Naval Air Station in California, were highly classified, and most officers there refused to discuss the matter.[2]

That military pilots should have been ordered to attack, as opposed to intercept, craft of such obviously superior technology is surprising. By this time, it must have become painfully obvious to military leaders that such a policy was counter-productive, given that many pilots had lost their lives in crashes or disappeared with their planes during confrontations.

A PHOTO-RECONNAISSANCE COUP

One of the most extraordinary aerial encounters took place in late 1956. It was an encounter that yielded a great deal of photographic proof – all of which, of course, remains under wraps to this day.

One morning a giant Convair RB-36H 'Peacemaker' bomber, powered by six piston engines and four outboard-mounted jet engines, took off on a photo-reconnaissance training flight. The plane, of the 718th Squadron, 28th Strategic Reconnaissance Wing, was based at Ellsworth AFB, Rapid

City, South Dakota, and on board were seventeen crew plus a five-man relief crew, commanded by Lieutenant Colonel Lenny Marquis.

According to First Lieutenant (later Lieutenant Colonel) Jimmie Lloyd, serving on this flight as a substitute navigator in the nose, the plane was flying near its top speed of 423 mph in straight and level flight at nearly 40,000 feet, probably near the North Dakota state line, when the incident occurred. At the time, its six remotely controlled gun turrets were in the stowed position. Suddenly the left scanner (observer) in the aft compartment saw a metallic disc fly towards the plane.[3]

'We looked out, and most of the crew did,' said Lloyd, 'and there was this, very obviously, a flying saucer.'

It had a dome on top that was some kind of observation dome that had some portholes around it and it was circular in shape; I would say approximately 100 feet in diameter, and flying just a few hundred yards off our wingtip in formation with us, which it did for quite some period of time – [5 to 8] minutes, I would say. We called a radar site on the ground [and] they did confirm that there was an object flying in formation with us.

We took pictures of it. We had all been issued [with 35mm] Haine cameras and binoculars and a special reporting form in conjunction with Project Blue Book. We had a discrete frequency that we could report these sightings to, and we did.[4]

'The length-to-height ratio of the UFO was about 8:1,' reported Dr Richard Haines and Franklin Carter, 'and a low dome, about one-third the length of the object, was located at the centre of the top surface, which was only slightly curved [and] had three round openings or light sources ... The object seemed to have an almost flat or slightly concave bottom surface. Its vertical sides were populated by many separate round sources of light, each of a different colour [and] the surface of both the main body and raised dome appeared in "light golden" hue.

'After five to eight minutes, the UFO suddenly accelerated horizontally in parallel with the B-36 and then rose at about 30 degrees above the local horizontal without pitching up or down ... All of the peripheral bluish lights became much brighter and definitely greenish as the object accelerated out of sight in several seconds.'[5]

'When we got on the ground,' Lloyd told Franklin Carter, 'we had to turn in all of our logs, equipment, everything, to an intelligence unit called Reci-Tech [Reconnaissance Technology] which was a central processing unit for the whole wing.

'We were debriefed by Intel officers, reminded that we all held top-
secret clearances, and that we couldn't reveal any of this information for a
period of twelve years. Then, several weeks later, we were debriefed again
by some officers from higher headquarters who reminded us also of the
same; and in fact, when I was discharged back in 1960 from the active Air
Force into the active reserves, I was also reminded *again* of the 12-year
period . . .'[6]

It is unfortunate that the precise date of the incident in late 1956 could
not be recalled, though Dr Haines notes that many different UFO sightings
were reported in newspapers in both South and North Dakota in November, including one on the 25th involving an interception from Ellsworth
AFB, confirmed on airborne radar as well as by the 740th Air Control and
Warning Squadron.[7]

AIRCRAFT VANISHES DURING INTERCEPTION

Ellsworth Air Force Base also features in the following case, said to have
occurred in the late spring of 1957, involving an object similar to that
reported by the RB-36 crew. In 1996 Dr Irena Scott, a UFO investigator
who has worked for the Defense Intelligence Agency (DIA), the Battelle
Memorial Institute and the Ohio State University Medical School, received
a letter from Wallace Fowler, Airman Second Class, a former parachute-
rigger based at Ellsworth who witnessed the initial stages of the incident.

Sometime between 18:30 and 19:00 Fowler was sitting on the front
steps of his barracks when an extraordinary object appeared out of nowhere,
directly above him. 'It was saucer-shaped and silver in colour,' reports
Scott. 'On the top side of the saucer was a dome with what appeared to be
portholes, behind which he could see moving shadows. The larger lower
part of the saucer was metallic in appearance, and it was constantly
changing colour. The object, which he estimated to be about the size of a
house, hovered there motionless.'

'I got up and stood there staring at this thing,' Fowler reports. 'I can't
say that I experienced fear because this was such a beautiful sight, and I
was too young to be scared . . . After this stand-off for about two to three
minutes, I remember saying these words [to myself]: "You can come down
here if you want, mother—er. Then it will be me and you". Now strange as
it may sound, or maybe [it was] a coincidence, but this thing took off as if
it was reading my mind. It went straight up at an unbelievable speed.'

'Wallace ran for the hangars and the base control tower,' Scott's report continues. 'As he neared the hangars he saw a number of pilots running toward their planes. Obviously others had seen the object as well. When he entered the hangar he noticed the telephones all seemed to be ringing, and there was a lot of activity as people ran to ready the aircraft for take-off. Wallace went up into the control tower ... telephones were ringing there too, so he was ignored.'

After the planes took off, Fowler listened in as a controller talked to one of the pilots who had been scrambled. 'I heard the pilot say these words: "This thing acts as if it is playing games with us. It sits and waits on us, and when we get close it takes off and leaves us like we are standing still." So [the controller asked them if they could] get close enough to see what it was made of.' The pilot replied that the object was ahead of them and seemed to be waiting again. It appeared to be metallic, he said shortly afterwards. All of a sudden a crash was heard over the intercom. The pilot could no longer be contacted.

Fowler was asked to leave the control tower. 'An officer told everyone before they left not to talk about what they had seen and heard,' says Scott. 'Not much was said regarding the incident, but he does remember one of the pilots saying that an aircraft which had pursued the object had [gone] missing and the wreckage was never found.

'Wallace now has cancer and emphysema. He realizes that his story may still be classified, but he doesn't want to go to his grave with this secret.'

'I can let it all hang out,' said Fowler. 'Can't do me no harm now. My desire is for someone to find out what family lost a loved one in the year 1957 [at] Ellsworth Air Force Base ... It would be interesting to hear what they told the family for the cause of his death.'[8]

LANDINGS OBSERVED BY MILITARY OFFICERS

Shortly before 08:00 on a September morning in 1956, a domed, disc-shaped craft is reported to have landed within the White Sands Proving Ground, 12 miles west of Holloman AFB, Alamogordo, New Mexico, and 50 yards from US Highway 70. Radios and ignition systems of passing cars went dead, as witnesses including two USAF colonels, two sergeants and dozens of base personnel observed the craft before it took off with a 'whirring' sound. Air Force Intelligence officers and CIA experts allegedly arrived at the scene from Washington, DC, and all the base personnel were assembled in a hangar, debriefed and then sworn to secrecy. A cable from the evaluation team to the Pentagon stated that the craft was 'definitely not any type of aircraft under development by the US or any foreign terrestrial power'.[9,10]

In *Beyond Top Secret*, I published a brief account of the landing of a flying disc at the top-secret Edwards AFB in 1957, as related by Gordon Cooper, the late pilot and astronaut, who confirmed the essential details for me. Since then, more details are revealed in Cooper's autobiography, *Leap of Faith*. At the time of the incident, he was assigned to the Fighter Section of the Experimental Flight Test Engineering Division at Edwards as test pilot and manager.

'On May 3, 1957,' Cooper reports, 'I was a captain and had a crew out filming an Askania-camera precision landing system we had installed on the dry lake bed. The Askania automatic system took pictures – one frame per second – as a plane landed to measure its landing characteristics. The two cameramen, James Bittick and Jack Gettys, arrived at Askania number four site a little before 8 a.m., armed with still and motion picture cameras.

> Later that morning they came running in to tell me that a 'strange-looking saucer' had come right over them. 'It didn't make any noise at all, sir,' one of them said . . . They were accustomed to seeing America's top-performance aircraft taking off, screaming low overhead, and landing in front of them on a daily basis. Obviously what they had seen was something quite different, and it had unnerved them both.
>
> They told me they had just about finished their work when the saucer flew over them, hovered above the ground, extended three landing gears; then set down about 50 yards away. They described the saucer as metallic silver in colour and shaped somewhat like an inverted plate . . . After my own UFO experiences in Europe, I was not about to discount any of these stories . . . These two cameramen were trained photographers and had cameras and film with them. I quickly asked the obvious question: 'Did you get any pictures?'
>
> They said they had shot images with 35mm and 4-by-5 still cameras, as well as motion picture film. When they had tried to approach the saucer to get a closer shot, they said it lifted up, retracted its gear, and climbed straight out of sight at a rapid rate of speed – again with no sound. They estimated the craft to be about 30 feet across. It had a silver colour [and] seemed to glow with its own luminosity. I told them to get the film to the lab right away.

Checking the regulations for reporting UFOs, Cooper found a special Pentagon number to call. He gave brief details, first to a captain, then to a colonel, and finally to a general. 'He ordered me to have the film developed right away but "don't run any prints" and to place the negatives in a locked courier pouch to be sent to Washington immediately on the base commanding general's plane.'

> I wasn't about to defy the Pentagon general's order about no prints — a surefire way to end my career or, at the very least, lose my top-secret clearance and my test pilot job. But since nothing was said about not *looking* at the negatives before sending them east, that's what I did when they came back from the lab.
>
> I was amazed at what I saw. The quality was excellent ... The object, shown close up, was a classic saucer, shiny silver and smooth — just as the cameramen had reported. I never saw the motion picture film. Before the day ended, all the negatives and movie film had left on the priority flight for Washington.
>
> Considering what the men had seen, and particularly the photographic evidence they had brought back with them of a UFO touching down on Earth, I expected to get an urgent follow-up call from Washington, or the imminent arrival of high-level investigators. After all, a craft of unknown origin had just overflown and landed at a highly classified military installation. Strangely, there was no word from Washington, and no inquiry was launched. Everything was kept under wraps, as if the incident never happened ...[11]

Reports on the incident did leak out and appeared in several newspapers, though evidently they were based on a watered-down version of events provided by the Air Force source. The *Los Angeles Times*, for example, reported that:

> Camera studies of an unidentified flying object photographed at Edwards Air Force Base last Friday [May 3] are being analyzed by the Air Technical Intelligence Center at Wright-Patterson AFB, Dayton ... Spokesmen at the secret desert test center north of Los Angeles would only say that the object was spotted by two civilian photo theodolite operators. They tracked the object and took pictures ... Films and information were dispatched immediately to the intelligence center.
>
> Unofficial reports said the object appeared round, that it caught the morning sun and that it moved but not at any great speed. There were no estimates as to its size or altitude ...[12]

Apparently, jets at Edwards AFB had been scrambled, but by the time they arrived in the area the disc had gone. Following the incident, possibly the next working day, three officers showed up at the Askania tracking station and interviewed Bittick and Gettys, as well as Frank E. Baker, who supervised the station and also observed the craft. 'The officers were insulting, suggesting that the desert sun does things to one's eyes (despite the fact they had film),' says investigator Michael D. Swords in a review of the case (which, oddly, does not allude to Gordon Cooper's testimony). A few prints from the film are in Project Blue Book files (Case #4715, dated 2 – not 3 – May 1957), but they reveal only fuzzy blobs of light. Years later, Baker said he had seen frames of the film that showed what Bittick and Gettys had described.[13]

It was 06:10, 23 November 1957. First Lieutenant Joseph F. Long, a member of the 97th Fighter Interceptor Squadron,[14] was returning by car to Delaware having completed a USAF Advanced Survival School course at Stead AFB, Nevada. According to the report in USAF Blue Book files, Long's car engine began to stall and finally stopped about 30 miles west of Tonopah. The report continues:

... Source got out of his car to investigate. Outside the car he heard a steady high-pitched whining noise which drew his attention to four disc-shaped objects that were sitting on the ground about 300 to 400 yards to the right of the highway ... He walked for several minutes until he was within approximately 50 feet from the nearest object ... The objects were identical and about 50 feet in diameter [see p. 228].

They were disc-shaped, emitting their own source of light causing them to glow brightly. They were equipped with a transparent dome in the center of the top which was obviously not of the same material as the rest of the craft. The entire body of the objects emitted light. They did not appear to be dark on the underside. They were equipped with three landing gears, each that appeared hemispherical in shape, about two feet in diameter and of some dark material.

The Source estimated the height of the objects from the ground level to the top of the dome to be about 10 to 15 feet. The objects were equipped with a ring around the outside which was darker than the rest of the craft and was apparently rotating. When the Source got to within 50 feet of the nearest object, the hum which had been steady in the air ever since he had first observed the objects, increased in pitch to a degree where it almost hurt his ears, and the objects lifted off the ground.

The protruding gears were retracted almost instantly after takeoff; the objects rose about 50 feet into the air and proceeded slowly (about 10 mph) to the north across the highway, contoured over some small hills about a half mile away and disappeared ... The total time of the sighting lasted about 20 minutes. After the objects disappeared, Source examined place where he had first seen them ... [There were] several very small impressions in the sand where the landing gear had obviously rested. Impressions were very shallow and bowl-shaped, triangular in pattern ...

Source returned to his car and the engine started [and he] proceeded immediately to Indian Springs AFB, Nevada, where he reported the sighting to the base Security Officer.

Dr J. Allen Hynek cites a memo in the Blue Book files which, he explains, 'points up the primary reason why the Air Force put as much effort into investigating this case as it did':

'The damage and embarrassment to the Air Force would be incalculable if this officer allied himself with the host of "flying saucer" writers, experts, and others who provide the Air Force with countless charges and accusations. In this instance, as matters now stand, the Air Force would have no effective rebuttal, or evidence to disprove any unfounded charges.'[15]

On a summer evening in 1958, a mechanic at Holloman AFB observed a disc-shaped craft hovering silently over the tarmac. As the craft retracted its 'ball-like' landing gear (like the four craft seen in Nevada earlier in the year), the witness managed to alert another mechanic in time for them both to see it take off at high speed. The USAF representatives who interrogated the witnesses showed them a large book containing over 300 pages of UFO photographs. On identifying the type of craft they had seen, the mechanics were informed that it had also been seen by control tower personnel. Both witnesses were sworn to secrecy.[16,17]

USAF JETS ATTEMPT TO CAPTURE UFO

'Just before dawn, on September 24, 1959,' reported Major Donald Keyhoe, 'a large flying disc descended near Redmond, Oregon, setting off one of the most desperate pursuits the Air Force ever attempted ...'

At 05:00 an unknown glowing object was sighted near Redmond Airport by police officer Robert Dickerson. When it seemed to drop out of the sky he assumed it was a burning plane about to crash, but it suddenly came to a dead stop at a height of about 200 feet, and then climbed up past the airport and hovered north-east of the field. Dickerson drove straight to the airport and reported the UFO to Flight Specialist Laverne Wertz. Through binoculars, Wertz and other Federal Aviation Agency (FAA) personnel observed the disc and noticed odd, coloured 'tongues of

flame' extending and retracting from the rim. The Military Flight Service at
Hamilton AFB, California, was alerted and at 05:18, six F-102 Delta Dagger
jets were scrambled from their Air National Guard base at Portland Airport.

'As they took off,' said Keyhoe, 'the tower radioed the pilots of a B-47
bomber and an F-89 fighter, on routine flights nearby, and ordered them
to join the F-102s in a secret mission. The purpose: to capture the UFO –
and its crew, if one was aboard. All the pilots were grimly aware of the fatal
chases and narrow escapes in other capture attempts. But they also knew
the mission's tremendous importance . . .

'At Redmond Airport, the FAA observers were still watching the UFO
when they heard the roar of jets.' Keyhoe's report continues:

> As the planes dived toward the spacecraft the tongues of flame
> vanished. Then a fiery exhaust blasted from the bottom of the disc.
> Accelerating at terrific speed, it shot straight upward, almost in the
> jets' path. The nearest pilot banked to avoid a collision. As the UFO
> shot up past him another jet, caught in the churning air from the
> machine's exhaust, almost went out of control. Three other pilots
> pulled out of their dives and climbed after the fleeing disc. But even
> with extra speed from their afterburners they were quickly left behind.
>
> As the UFO disappeared in clouds at 14,000 feet, one AF pilot,
> guided by his gunsight radar, climbed after the unseen craft. His
> approach apparently was registered by the disc, for it instantly changed
> course, tracked by height-finder radar at Klamath Falls [Air National
> Guard base]. Even after the AF pilots gave up the hopeless chase, the
> radar operators were still tracking the UFO in high-speed maneuvers
> between 6,000 and 54,000 feet.

'When the pilots landed,' said Keyhoe, 'they were hurried into an
Intelligence debriefing session. After describing the UFO encounter they
were ordered not to discuss the pursuit, even among themselves.'

Hundreds of Redmond citizens had heard the roaring jets and a few
reported an odd glow in the sky. Fearing exposure of the mission, the
Air Force explained the flight as 'a routine check-up, caused by a false
radar return'. When USAF headquarters learned about the disc's 'exhaust',
it was feared that the UFO might be using nuclear power.[18] Laverne Wertz
was ordered to make a flying check for abnormal radioactivity. 'I was
furnished a plane and pilot,' Wertz told reporter Tim Iahn in 1997. 'As I
recall, there were no abnormal readings. The full report was entered on the
log we used at the Flight Service Station and was forwarded to the FAA.'[19]

Worried about this aspect of the story leaking out, Air Force officials issued another explanation: the Redmond object was 'probably a weather balloon'. However, the story did indeed leak out to the media. Unfortunately for the Air Force, Keyhoe's organization, the National Investigations Committee on Aerial Phenomena (NICAP), managed to obtain certified copies of the FAA logs, which described the UFO, its manoeuvres, the strange tongues of flame, the fiery exhaust and the disc's vertical take-off to elude the interceptors. 'They also included the AF confirmations of radar tracking, scrambling of the Portland jets, and the Klamath Falls report on the UFO's evasive operations after the AF attack had failed,' said Keyhoe. When the Air Force learned of NICAP's damaging acquisition, they tried to discredit the FAA officials, and then announced a new explanation: 'witnesses had been misled by the planet Venus' (!) – which remains the official explanation to this day.

'When the Air Force realized that UFOs were spacecraft, in the early years,' said Keyhoe, 'the Air Defense Command was determined to capture one of these machines. This was confirmed to me in a personal conference with General Sory Smith, Deputy Director of Information, and Major Jeremiah Boggs, an HQ Intelligence officer [who] admitted to me that the AF had put out a special order for its pilots to capture UFOs.'

Keyhoe discussed this revelation with an interceptor pilot he knew, who had been involved in two such chases. 'That's a lot nearer the truth than you might think, even if he did make it sound like a joke,' said the pilot. 'In our squadron at least we were told to ram one and bail out, if we could do it without getting hurt. I don't know anyone that tried it – I certainly didn't. After what happened to Mantell a man would be a fool to try a trick like that.'[20]

Indeed. In addition to being a foolhardy venture, it might seem that the Air Force officials responsible for such hare-brained schemes did not have a need to know that several craft had already been either knocked out of the sky or otherwise acquired. But I think it far more likely that the military simply wanted to get its hands on as many craft (or bits of them) as possible, to further its knowledge of alien technology – evidently at the expense of sacrificing the lives of airmen.

Four nights after the Redmond incident, on 29 September, Major R.O. Braswell, flying an Air Force C-47 transport at 6,500 feet over Texas, reported 'a large red fire' that 'looked like an atomic cloud'. 'It was a massive thing, about five degrees above my plane. The base was at an altitude of 12,000 to 15,000 feet; the top was about 16,000 feet.'

At the same time, a Braniff Airways Lockheed Electra, Flight 542, with twenty-eight passengers and a crew of six, was flying at 15,000 feet over

Buffalo, Texas, when witnesses on the ground saw a sudden fiery glow in the sky followed later by a violent explosion. The airliner completely disintegrated. 'I've investigated lots of crashes, but I've never seen one where the plane was so thoroughly demolished, the wreckage so widely scattered and the people so horribly mangled,' said Braniff's chief of operations, R.V. Carleton. 'And there was nothing among the wreckage which indicated a fire or bomb aboard the plane.'[21]

'UFO'S SERIOUS BUSINESS'

Thus was headed an Operations and Training order issued by the Inspector General of the Air Force to every Air Base Commander in the continental United States on 24 December 1959 (see p. 229). It continues:

> Unidentified Flying Objects – sometimes treated lightly by the press and referred to as 'flying saucers' – must be rapidly and accurately identified as serious USAF business in the ZI [Zone of the Interior]. As AFR 200-2 points out, the Air Force concern with these sightings is threefold: First of all, is the object a threat to the defense of the U.S.? Secondly, does it contribute to technical or scientific knowledge? And then there's the inherent USAF responsibility to explain to the American people through public-information media what is going on in their skies.
>
> The phenomena or actual objects comprising UFO's will tend to increase, with the public more aware of goings on in space but still inclined to some apprehension. Technical and defense considerations will continue to exist in this era . . .

The US Air Force may have an 'inherent responsibility to explain to the American people . . . what is going on in their skies', yet it is manifestly obvious that they were doing nothing of the sort. The public, evidently, did not have a need to know.

REFERENCES

1. 'Frank Edwards: Breakaway UFO Reporter', *UFO Magazine* (US), Vol. 14, No. 10, October 1999, p. 35. (With thanks to Richard Hall and the Donald E. Keyhoe Archives.)

2. *News Tribune*, Fullerton, California, 26 June 1956.

3. Haines, Richard F. and Carter, Franklin, 'A 1956 Military Aircraft-UFO Close Encounter', *International UFO Reporter*, Vol. 2, No. 1, Spring 2000, pp. 22–5.
4. Carter, Franklin, 'UFOs Photographed by Air Force Reconnaissance Mission', *UFOCUS*, The Institute for UFO Research, University of Wyoming, Office of Conferences and Institutes, PO Box 3972, Laramie, WY 82071-3972, Vol. 2, No. 4, Summer 1998, pp. 8, 12.
5. Haines and Carter, op. cit.
6. Carter, op. cit.
7. Hall, Richard H., *The UFO Evidence*, NICAP, Washington, DC, 1964, pp. 22, 29 (cited in Haines and Carter, op. cit.).
8. Scott, Irena, *Ohio UFOs (and many others)*, Vol. I, Greyden Press, Columbus, Ohio, 1997, pp. 92–3.
9. Branch, David and Klinn, Robert E., 'White Sands Sightings Kept Secret', *Santa Ana Register*, California, 15 November 1972, p. C-2, cited in *Beyond Earth: Man's Contact with UFOs*, by Ralph Blum with Judy Blum, Corgi, London, 1974, pp. 102–3.
10. 'Cover Up Exposed', *Santa Ana Register*, 23 November 1972, p. A-11, cited in Blum, op. cit.
11. Cooper, Gordon, with Henderson, Bruce, *Leap of Faith: An Astronaut's Journey into the Unknown*, HarperCollins, New York, 2000, pp. 82–6.
12. 'Cameras Track Flying Object Over Desert', *Los Angeles Times*, 9 May 1957, reproduced in an article by Michael D. Swords, *International UFO Reporter*, Vol. 30, No. 1, October 2005, pp. 10–12.
13. Swords, op. cit.
14. Smith, Willy, *On Pilots and UFOs*, The UNICAT Project, 1997, p. 72.
15. Hynek, op. cit., pp. 182–6, citing Project Blue Book Files, #31.
16. Branch and Klinn, op. cit.
17. 'Cover Up Exposed', *Santa Ana Register*, 23 November 1972.
18. Keyhoe, Major Donald E., *Aliens from Space: The Real Story of Unidentified Flying Objects*, pp. 47–9.
19. Iahn, Tim, 'Redman, WA: From Keyhoe's Files', *UFO Magazine* (US), Vol. 14, No. 2, 1999, p. 35.
20. Keyhoe, op. cit., pp. 49–51.
21. Ibid., pp. 184–5.

AIR FORCE STUDIES PHOTOS

Cameras Track Flying Object Over Desert

Camera studies of an unidentified flying object photographed at Edwards Air Force Base last Friday are being analyzed by the Air Technical Intelligence Center at Wright-Patterson AFB, Dayton, O., The Times learned yesterday.

Spokesmen at the secret desert test center north of Los Angeles would say only that the object was spotted by two civilian photo theodolite operators.

They tracked the object and took pictures with the specialized camera equipment. Films and information were dispatched immediately to the intelligence center.

Unofficial reports said the object appeared round, that it caught the morning sun and that it moved but not at any great speed. There were no estimates as to its size or altitude.

Edwards officers would not hazard a guess as to what the object was, although one said it could have been a weather balloon.

"This desert air does crazy things," he added.

An article in the *Los Angeles Times* (9 May 1957) relating to the flying disc that appeared at Edwards AFB, California, on 3 May. In fact, as confirmed by Gordon Cooper, the disc actually landed at the base and was filmed with still and motion picture cameras by two members of his crew, and the sketch is by one of them.

(Michael D. Swords/International UFO Reporter)

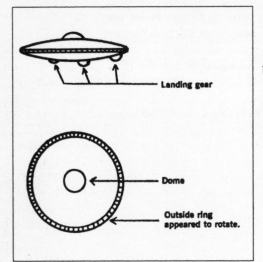

Sketches by Project Blue Book staff based on a report by First Lt. Joseph F. Long of the 97th Fighter Interceptor Squadron, who encountered four landed, disc-shaped craft, 30 miles west of Tonopah, Nevada, on 23 November 1957. Long approached to within 50 feet of the craft. The sighting lasted 20 minutes.

(US Air Force)

OPERATIONS & TRAINING

─── UFO'S SERIOUS BUSINESS ───

Unidentified flying objects - sometimes treated lightly by the press and referred to as "flying saucers" - must be rapidly and accurately identified as serious USAF business in the ZI. As AFR 200-2 points out, the Air Force concern with these sightings is threefold: First of all, is the object a threat to the defense of the U.S.? Secondly, does it contribute to technical or scientific knowledge? And then there's the inherent USAF responsibility to explain to the American people through public-information media what is going on in their skies.

The phenomena or actual objects comprising UFO's will tend to increase, with the public more aware of goings on in space but still inclined to some apprehension. Technical and defense considerations will continue to exist in this era.

Published about three months ago, AFR 200-2 outlines necessary orderly, qualified reporting as well as public-information procedures. This is where the base should stand today, with practices judged at least satisfactory by commander and inspector:

- Responsibility for handling UFO's should rest with either intelligence, operations, the Provost Marshal or the Information Officer - in that order of preference, dictated by limits of the base organization;

- A specific officer should be designated as responsible;

- He should have experience in investigative techniques and also, if possible, scientific or technical background;

- He should have authority to obtain the assistance of specialists on the base;

- He should be equipped with binoculars, camera, Geiger counter, magnifying glass and have a source for containers in which to store samples.

What is required is that every UFO sighting be investigated and reported to the Air Technical Intelligence Center at Wright-Patterson AFB and that explanation to the public be realistic and knowledgeable. Normally that explanation will be made only by the OSAF Information Office. It all adds up to part of the job of being experts in our own domain.

'Unidentified Flying Objects – sometimes treated lightly by the press and referred to as "flying saucers" – must be rapidly and accurately identified as serious USAF business', begins this order, issued by the Inspector General of the Air Force to every Air Base Commander in the continental United States on 24 December 1959. *(US Air Force)*

33.4 HUMAN FEAR AND HOSTILITY

Besides the foregoing reasons, contacting humans is downright dangerous. Think about that for a moment! On the microscopic level our bodies reject and fight (through production antibodies) any alien material; this process helps us fight off disease but it also sometimes results in allergenic reactions to innocuous materials. On the macroscopic (psychological and sociological) level we are antagonistic to beings that are "different". For proof of that, just watch how an odd child is treated by other children, or how a minority group is socially deprived, or how the Arabs feel about the Israelis (Chinese vs Japanese, Turks vs Greeks, etc.) In case you are hesitant to extend that concept to the treatment of aliens let me point out that in very ancient times, possible extraterrestrials may have been treated as Gods but in the last two thousand years, the evidence is that any possible aliens have been ripped apart by mobs, shot and shot at, physically assaulted (in South America there is a well-documented case), and in general treated with fear and aggression. In Ireland about 1,000 A.D., supposed airships were treated as "demon-ships." In Lyons, France, "admitted" space travellers were killed. More recently, on 24 July 1957 Russian anti-aircraft batteries on the Kouril Islands opened fire on UFO's. Although all Soviet anti-aircraft batteries on the islands were in action, no hits were made. The UFO's were luminous and moved very fast. We too have fired on UFO's. About ten o'clock one morning, a radar site near a fighter base

462

picked up a UFO doing 700 mph. The UFO then slowed to 100 mph, and two F-86's were scrambled to intercept. Eventually one F-86 closed on the UFO at about 3,000 feet altitude. The UFO began to accelerate away but the pilot still managed to get to within 500 yards of the target for a short period of time. It was definitely saucer-shaped. As the pilot pushed the F-86 at top speed, the UFO began to pull away. When the range reached 1,000 yards, the pilot armed his guns and fired in an attempt to down the saucer. He failed, and the UFO pulled away rapidly, vanishing in the distance. This same basic situation may have happened on a more personal level.

A page from a chapter on 'Unidentified Flying Objects', which appeared in *Introductory Space Science*, Volume II, a textbook for cadets in use at the US Air Force Academy, Department of Physics, Colorado Springs, from 1968–1970. The chapter, by Major Donald G. Carpenter, contradicts official USAF policy. *(US Air Force)*

16. GLOBAL DEVELOPMENTS

Although UFOs have been reported globally, some countries seem to have attracted more attention than others. One such country is Brazil, and a huge build-up of events was reported there in the mid-1950s.

Chester C. Grusinski, who served on the aircraft carrier USS *Franklin D. Roosevelt* (CVA-42), and whose own experience aboard that carrier appears later in this chapter, reports that on 26 July 1956, two disc-shaped objects were 'suspended in mid-air' over the carrier while it was at anchor in the port of Rio de Janeiro:

> They were over one another [and] had two rows of counter-rotating lights. The upper disk released a fire-ball object that dropped into the top of the lower one. Within seconds they both vanished with tremendous speed. The objects could have been between 75 and 100 feet in [diameter]. And these were seen by Leon Treadwell, Petty Officer Third Class, O.I. [Operations Intelligence] Division. All witnesses involved were told to keep a tight lip on what they saw, and Treadwell had to sign papers that he would tell no-one for 20 years … [On] the 25th or the 27th July 1956, a cigar[like] object was seen and tracked on radar. And the CIC [Combat Information Center] radars said it went off the scope in two sweeps … witnessed by a chief warrant officer, John C. Hau.[1]

At 20:55 on 14 August 1957, a Varig Airlines C-47 cargo plane encountered a luminous object while flying 6,300 feet above the state of Santa Catarina, en route for Rio de Janeiro. Commander Jorgé C. Araujo and his first officer, Edgar O. Soares, reported that suddenly the object was ahead of the plane and then crossed to the right side, following a horizontal trajectory. At this point, the engines began coughing and missing, and the lights in the cabin dimmed and almost went out – it seemed that the whole electrical system of the plane was on the verge of collapse. Everything returned to normal when the object went into a dive and disappeared in cloud. The object, also observed by the radio operator and two stewards, was saucer-shaped with a cupola or dome on top which glowed with an intense green light; the flattened base showed less intense yellowish light.[2]

Another incident occurred on 4 November 1957, involving a Varig C-46 cargo plane flying from Porto Alegre to São Paulo. At 01:40, what looked just like a red light appeared on the port side of the plane. Commander Jean Vincent de Beyssac joked to his co-pilot that at last they were seeing a real flying saucer. Then the object seemed to loom larger. Commander A. Simoes, who interviewed de Beyssac, reports:

> He started to put his plane into a left bank, but just before he pressed his rudder the object jumped a 45-degree arc on the horizon and became larger. De Beyssac started pursuit and was about midway in his left 80-degree turn when the object became even brighter and suddenly he smelled something burning ... all at once his ADF [automatic direction finder], right generator and transmitter 'burned' out. The 'thing' disappeared almost instantly, while the crew looked for fire. De Beyssac turned on his emergency transmitter and reported the incident to Porto Alegre control; then he turned his ship around and headed back to Porto Alegre.

After submitting a written report, de Beyssac went home and got drunk. That same day, Varig issued an order forbidding its pilots to discuss UFO sightings with the media.[3]

A quarter of an hour or so after the C-46 incident, things started hotting up – literally – in Brazil. At 02:00 on 4 November 1957, at the Brazilian Army's Itaipu Fortress at São Vicente, near Santos, two sentries were struck by an unbearable wave of heat emanating from a large disc-shaped object hovering above them while emitting a humming sound. One sentry fainted and the other yelled for help. Inside the garrison, the electrical systems failed completely; even the back-up system would not work. Both soldiers received first- and second-degree burns. The authorities reacted desperately, as Dr Olavo Fontes, one of the world's leading investigators at that time, reports:

> Next day the commander of the fortress issued orders forbidding the whole garrison to say anything about the incident to anyone ... Intelligence officers came and took charge, working frantically to question and silence everyone ... The fortress was placed in a state of martial law, and a top-secret report was sent to QG [headquarters]. Days later, American officers from the US Army Military Mission arrived at the fortress, together with officers from the Brazilian Air Force, to question the sentries and other witnesses involved. Afterwards

a special Air [Force] plane was chartered to bring the two burned sentries to Rio Janeiro [where] they were put in the Army's Central Hospital (HCE), completely isolated from the world behind a tight security curtain.[4]

As Chief of the Brazilian Air Force General Staff information service, Colonel João A. Oliveira had headed Brazil's first official military inquiry into UFOs in the mid-1950s. Later promoted to the rank of Brigadier-General, he was interviewed about the subject by the Brazilian press in February 1958. 'The flying saucer is not a ghost from another dimension or a mysterious dragon,' he declared. 'It is a *fact* confirmed by material evidence. There are thousands of documents, photos, and sighting reports demonstrating its existence . . .'[5]

Dr Fontes was the Brazilian representative of the Aerial Phenomena Research Organization (APRO), a major worldwide UFO organization founded by Coral Lorenzen in 1952. In a long letter to Lorenzen in February 1958, Fontes revealed a great deal of information provided to him unofficially by Brazilian Air Force and Navy intelligence officers anxious to obtain Fontes's collaboration. Relevant to UFO hostility, for example, Fontes learned the following during a meeting with two Navy sources:

. . . We have already lost many planes attempting to shoot down one of them. We have no defence against them. They outperform easily any of our fighters . . . Guided missiles are also useless: they can fly still faster than any of them and can even manoeuvre around them, as if they were toys; or they can interfere with their electronic instruments and make them useless soon after launch; or, if they like, they can explode them before they reach their [target]. They have [caused] the crash of military planes (propeller or jet type) and airliners by stalling their engines through interference with their electric systems (we don't know yet if this is a side effect of their powerful magnetic field, or the result of some kind of weapon – possibly a high-frequency beam of some sort).

They have also a horribly destructive long-range weapon which has been used mercilessly on our jet fighters. In one case, for example, a US Navy interceptor with a crew of two was scrambled to go after a UFO. Their mission was, as usual, to make it land or to shoot it down – if necessary. They used their guns. The answer was immediate and terrifying: instantly all metallic parts of their plane were disintegrated into thousands of fragments, and they found themselves suddenly seated in the air (non-metallic pieces or objects weren't affected): one of them was killed but the other lived to tell the story. We have evidence that this tremendous weapon is an ultra-sonic beam of some sort, which disrupts the molecular cohesion of any metallic structure. They have means to paralyse our radar systems too, to interfere with our radios and television, and to short-circuit our electric power-plants . . .

'There is an exchange of information through intelligence services, and top-secret conferences are held periodically to discuss new developments,' Fontes was told. 'The Brazilian Navy, for example, receives monthly classified reports from the US Navy, and sends back to them any information available . . . Here in Brazil only the persons who work on the problem know the real situation: intelligence officers in the Army, Navy and Air Force; some high-ranking officers in the High Command; the National Security Council and a few scientists whose activities are connected with it; and a few members of certain civilian organizations doing research for military projects.

'All information about the UFO subject from the military is not only classified or reserved for official use: it is top-secret. Civilian authorities and military officers in general are not entitled to know. Even our President is not informed of the whole truth . . .' In this regard, Dr Olavo Fontes was informed by his Brazilian Navy intelligence sources about the state of play at that time:

> Military authorities throughout the world are agreed that the people are not entitled to know anything about the problem. Some military groups believe that such knowledge would be a tremendous shock – enough to paralyze the life in our countries for many years . . . The probability of hostile UFO interference is still estimated as 90 per cent; there is a 10 per cent probability that their hostility is only a consequence of our attacks against their ships: because of this possibility, we are attempting now to make them aware that we would like to make a peaceful contact – so, the orders (now) are to avoid any further attacks against their craft. This policy has been adopted generally, with the exception of some countries which still have fools in their Air Forces who think otherwise.[6]

CLOSE ENCOUNTER ON AIRCRAFT CARRIER

Chester C. Grusinski (mentioned earlier) served on the aircraft carrier USS *Franklin D. Roosevelt* (CVA-42) from 1958 to 1960. The incident he was involved with occurred one night in September 1958, as the ship was sailing in the Caribbean on a 'shake-down' cruise out of the US Navy base at Guantánamo Bay, Cuba. 'We're out at sea, it was dark – eight or nine o'clock', said Grusinski, a nineteen-year-old fireman's apprentice at the time.[7]

> I was down below decks. There was a bunch of men who came running up from the engine room, and a couple of minutes later another bunch came running up and I followed them all the way up to the flight deck. They were watching a small light that was following our ship. Then the light approached our ship. It came in close enough that I could see a row of windows and the figures watching us from inside. The impression I got was that those figures were not human beings.[8]

'I was kind of shocked because I wasn't expecting something like that,' Grusinski told reporter Gerald Scott. 'Then, while we were looking at it, it turned a red-orange colour and took off . . . It could've been a few minutes, or it might've been quite a while – I've got no idea. But I could feel the heat on my face when it came up. It was cigar-shaped. It came up close to the [carrier's] island superstructure. Then it took off and I went down below decks. The next day, I was drinking a lot of water. I felt like I was dehydrated . . . I found out later that we also lost power on the ship the night it happened.' Grusinski estimates that 25 of the 3,000 crewmen witnessed the event.[9]

'The ship's manoeuvres stopped suddenly for some unknown reason during the UFO sighting,' Grusinski told me. 'The next day I got up early to see the ship's plan of the day. There was nothing about the last night's sighting. Years later the Executive Officer (1958–59), who was aboard the ship, said in a letter that he knew nothing of the sighting; and there was nothing in the deck logs.

'Special investigators came aboard to investigate gambling below decks – that was the excuse they used. I found out later they were CIA. And a bunch of men – possibly witnesses – got transferred off the ship.'[10]

Grusinski also found out later that CVA-42 was one of only three aircraft carriers in the Navy's fleet that was equipped to carry nuclear weapons, and 'the first and only carrier at the time allowed to transport the H-Bomb'. He feels this might have been a reason why the USS *Franklin D. Roosevelt* attracted so many UFO sightings.

'Chet' Grusinki's Freedom of Information requests have drawn a blank. 'I got a copy of the ship's deck logs from the years 1958–59; a lot of information was blackened out,' he said. 'When I was looking for information on the 1958 sighting, a commander who was on the *FDR* the same time period that I was told me that I was not supposed to even mention something like this...'[11]

A TRAGIC INTERCEPTION IN JAPAN

Physicist Dr Bruce Maccabee has learned of an incident involving a USAF jet based in Japan in the spring of 1959, related to him by a former lieutenant colonel, a weather officer then stationed at the headquarters of the Fifth Air Force, Yokota Air Base, near Tokyo.

Four F-106 Delta Dart jets stationed in Okinawa and Misawa, Japan, had been instrumented specifically to track and fire on unidentified flying objects. During a visit by the officer to the combat-operations centre at dusk one evening, two F-106s were scrambled to intercept a UFO that had been plotted on radar south of Misawa. Only one jet took off, however, because the other F-106 had developed an instrument malfunction. 'And so the pilot climbed on out and said he was clear on top,' the officer related. 'Because there was a general interest in the command centre in what was happening, they put it on a speaker system. I could hear the down-link from the pilot. The radarscope operators had a tie-in with the Misawa operators on the radars, and they were the only ones who could hear the ground link-up, so I could hear only half the conversation.'

> Basically they were vectoring him in, and he said something like 'I've got it in sight', and he described what appeared to be a circular object that was hovering. It was metallic and had a cockpit on top ... he asked if he should make a firing pass [and] so they called the Pentagon to get authority, and the word came back, yes, make a firing pass ... So the pilot said, 'Will roll in,' and he rolled in and he fired the [missiles] off. Then all of a sudden his voice went into a high falsetto. It was real strange. He blurted out that he had fired, and they had detonated but did not hit it; they detonated just at the edge of it ...
>
> And then he says, 'They've turned on some kind of beam, and they're turning ... They're coming after me.' And then he went into a vertical diving maneuver. And the radar operators started screaming out that it was moving and vectoring towards him, and they started counting out the ranges as it was coming down. The pilot was just breathing heavily and obviously under great stress but controlled, and

he said, 'It's moving closer'. And he just kept describing how it kept gaining on him and this beam was coming towards him. And then the radar operators said, 'Contact'. The two blips matched! And a radar operator said, 'My God, there's no separation ... The thing has stopped. It's just a single blip hovering, but there's nothing else'. [Subsequently the blip also disappeared.]

'For four days after that,' said the officer, 'I gave weather briefings every day for a search up there. They never did find anything...'[12]

BEHIND THE IRON CURTAIN

In the spring of 1959, Soviet PVO (Air Defence) personnel had observed UFOs circling and hovering for more than twenty-four hours above Sverdlovsk, the headquarters of a surface-to-air missile unit. Fighters sent to intercept reported that the UFOs easily outmanoeuvred them, and zigzagged to avoid their cannon fire.[13]

In Czechoslovakia, Commander Duchon and another officer named Bezác, belonging to 'a certain unit' of the Czechoslovak Air Force, were driving towards 'a certain airfield' (location presumably censored by the then Communist government) to supervise some night-flying exercises. It was about 20:00 on 16 November 1959. At a distance of some 10 kilometres from the airfield, their car engine stalled. As Duchon got out to check, a 'light, sapphire-coloured band' could be seen moving at extremely high speed at an altitude of 500 to 800 metres. The coloured band remained behind for a few seconds, apparently in the wake of some unidentified flying object. There was no sound.

The car eventually restarted and the airmen proceeded to the airbase, where they learned that a number of pilots and ground personnel had observed a 'flaming ball' in the sky at 20:05, which flew silently over the base at a terrific speed, described a 90-degree turn, and then came back over the base. The object was tracked on radar at an altitude of 1,000 metres on its return flight over the base; its size was approximately twice that of the largest known bomber. Aircraft held in emergency preparedness at the base received orders to intercept, but for some unaccountable reason they were unable to take off before the object had disappeared from the radarscope and from the view of ground observers.

One minute later the object returned, this time remaining motionless for two minutes over the runway at a height of 100 metres before accelerating at a fantastic speed and disappearing. During this time, observations through binoculars were made by control-tower staff and anti-aircraft gun personnel. All described the object as a disc no less than 150 metres in diameter, with a glowing band around it. 'Unsuccessful attempts were made to contact it by radio in Russian and English and also in the international aviation code,' reported the Czechoslovak journal *Kridla Vlasti* (The Power of Wings). 'The air and soil were immediately tested for radioactivity, but no trace of such was found.'[14]

The latter statement suggests to me that the Czechs – perhaps via the Soviets – were aware of the news item relating to the radioactivity tests following the Redmond, Oregon, incident two months earlier.

According to Alexander Platskin, a former member of 'Institute 22', the Soviet Government's vast, top-secret UFO research programme set up in 1977 (to be discussed later), between the mid-1950s and mid-1960s about 15,000 sightings were reported by pilots, of which most could be explained, he said.[15]

Around the world, the reports continued. Governments, understand-ably anxious to avoid societal disruption, continued officially to dismiss the reality of alien intrusions. Behind the scenes, military and intelligence leaders – knowing more about the situation than their political masters – remained confounded and disturbed.

REFERENCES

1. *Michigan MUFON Newsletter* (date not known).
2. Lorenzen, Coral E., *The Great Flying Saucer Hoax*, William-Frederick, New York, 1962, p. 146–7.
3. Ibid., p. 147–8.
4. Fontes, Dr Olavo T., *The APRO Bulletin*, September 1957, Aerial Phenomena Research Organization, Alamogordo, NM, in Jules Lemaitre, 'A Strange Story from Brazil', *Flying Saucer Review*, Vol. 6, No. 1, January–February 1960, pp. 9–11.
5. *O Globo*, Rio de Janeiro, 28 February 1958.
6. Letter from Olavo Fontes MD to Coral Lorenzen, 27 February 1958.
7. Scott, Gerald, 'Close Encounter: Area Autoworker is "Mr UFO"', *Motor City News*, Detroit, 17 August 1998, p. 1B.
8. *Michigan MUFON Newsletter*.
9. Scott, op. cit.
10. Letters, 26 November 1992 and 27 September 1998.
11. *Michigan MUFON Newsletter*.

12. Maccabee, Bruce, 'Hiding the Hardware', *International UFO Reporter*, Vol. 16, No. 4, September–October 1991, pp. 8–9.
13. 'UFOs over Russia', *Flying Saucers*, No. 47, Palmer Publications, Amherst, Wisconsin, May 1966, pp. 6–10.
14. *Kridla Vlasti*, No. 26, 22 December 1959, translated in *Flying Saucer Review*, Vol. 6, No. 4, July–August 1960, pp. 31–2.
15. *Soviet UFO Secrets Revealed*, a documentary for the History Channel produced by Bill Brummel Productions, Inc.

PART THREE

1960—2006

17. BLACKOUT

In the early 1960s two former CIA officials – both on the board of Major Donald Keyhoe's National Investigations Committee on Aerial Phenomena (NICAP) – wrote strong supportive statements for UFO reality, contradicting the official position of the US Government. Colonel Joseph J. Bryan III, founder and first chief of the CIA's Psychological Warfare Staff, outlined his evaluation of the problem in an open letter to Keyhoe, which was sent to Congress:

> I am aware that hundreds of military and airline pilots, airport personnel, astronomers, missile trackers and other competent observers have reported sightings of Unidentified Flying Objects . . . It is my opinion that: The UFOs [are] devices under intelligent control. Their speeds, maneuvers and other technical evidence prove them superior to any aircraft or space devices now produced on Earth. These UFOs are interplanetary devices systematically observing the Earth, either manned or under remote control, or both.
>
> Information on UFOs, including sightings reports, has been and is still being officially withheld. This policy is dangerous, especially since mistaken identification of UFOs as a secret Russian attack might accidentally set off war . . .[1]

'It is time for the truth to be brought out in open Congressional hearings,' declared Vice Admiral Roscoe Hillenkoetter, former Director of the CIA, in a letter to Keyhoe dated 22 August 1960, also sent to Congress. 'Behind the scenes, high-ranking Air Force officers are soberly concerned about the UFOs. But through official secrecy and ridicule, many citizens are led to believe the unknown flying objects are nonsense.' He also charged that 'to hide the facts, the Air Force has silenced its personnel' through issuance of a regulation (see p. 260). 'I urge immediate Congressional action to reduce the dangers from secrecy about Unidentified Flying Objects,' he continued. 'Two dangers are steadily increasing: 1. The risk of accidental war from mistaking UFO formations for a surprise Soviet attack. 2. The danger that the Soviet Government may, in a critical moment, *falsely* claim the UFOs as secret Russian weapons against which our defences are helpless.'[2] (See p. 261.)

USAF PILOTS' SIGHTINGS REVEALED

Pilots generally are reluctant to go public with their encounters, even if no longer duty-bound by their security oaths. There are exceptions, as we have seen earlier, and in 1999, details emerged of an experience that occurred in late 1959 or early 1960, when General Curtis LeMay, then Vice-Chief of Air Staff, conducted an exercise to test his bombers' capability to penetrate United States air defences. An F-89J Scorpion jet instructor pilot (name on file with the Mutual UFO Network) and his radar observer, First Lieutenant Joe Meyer, had successfully 'intercepted' a B-47 and were descending to land at James Connally AFB, Waco, Texas, when they encountered an unknown target.

'The night was crystal clear with visibility unlimited [and] I arrived just north and west of Waco at 22,000 feet,' said the pilot. 'I noticed a light way out to my right, and level with us, over Waco. I pointed this out to Joe [and] continued my turn while watching the pinpoint of light. It didn't move as I swung into it. I added power, levelled off, and put the object on my jet's nose. At 12 miles, Joe told me he had picked up the object [and] in a moment he had a lock-on, and my pilot's [radar]scope lit up to show a collision course to fly for firing our 2.75-inch rockets.' The report continues:

> Although unarmed, the attack radar presented information as if we were armed. Joe gave me course and overtake information and, as we approached, I could see that the object had four extremely bright blue-white round dots of light on the side that I could observe. I checked my true airspeed [TAS] against the overtake ring on my scope, as by now we were down to 10 seconds to fire.
>
> Our overtake and my true airspeed were identical, meaning that the object was standing still. I was reading 275 TAS. I tried to measure the width of the object against my wingspan and came up with something around 25–30 feet. Joe and I estimated the height at 8–9 feet. By now we were down to five seconds to fire and on a collision course with the object. I wondered what the hell I was going to do.
>
> We concluded it was a UFO. I remember that the technique of ramming, which was taught as a last resort, came into my mind. Instantly, the dot on my scope flew up and I heard the radar antenna

hit the stops . . . I looked up to see the object climbing straight up at an incredible speed. Within a few seconds we were directly under where the object had been, and Joe and I looked straight up into its belly, which was round and, again, a brilliant blue-white . . . When I flew directly below the spot where the object had been, I anticipated hitting the 'wash' [but] to our surprise there was none.

As we watched, the vehicle rapidly became smaller and smaller until it was like a star in the sky, then it went out of sight. Joe and I estimated that we lost sight of it in excess of 90,000 feet. We were extremely shaken up by the event and swore each other to secrecy, as we knew if we mentioned what had just happened we would be branded as nuts . . . and probably grounded.[3]

In the summer of 1961, Captain Robert Filler and his wingman, Lieutenant Phil Lee, based with the 82nd Fighter Interceptor Squadron at Travis Air Force Base, California, were scrambled in their F-102 Delta Dagger jets to intercept a target. The case is published here for the first time.

'The planes that we had on alert were all peaked up: all the radar was 20 miles and the weapons systems worked at 20 miles,' Filler told me. 'When they gave us the altitude, I thought, well, that's fairly high for anything we've ever run an intercept on – I'm going to guess around 50,000 feet. The people that were controlling us on the ground said that we were getting close to 20 miles out. On most of the missions I rarely get a contact at 20 miles – the radars aren't peaked up all the time. Our approximate position was north of Travis, up in the mountain area close to the Sacramento Valley.'

I got a contact at 20 miles and got a lock-on – that means the weapons system is locked on to the target, and you get a speed indication of the target. Speed indication was zero – it was stationary. At five miles, roughly, I have this 'steering dot' – which tells you where to fly your airplane to the target – and it takes off and goes to the top of the scope, which means it's going up into a higher altitude. We get to see nothing, except that both of us had it on radar.

I start timing it. And the timing, as the steering dot is going to the top, where it breaks lock and loses contact, is constantly the same. And that is, 20 miles in two seconds, which comes out as almost 36,000 mph!

So after we landed, I picked up the phone and called the radar control room, 'What was *that*?' 'We don't know,' they said. 'It came in from outer space. We saw it come in, we saw it stop, and we watched it stationary for 30 minutes. Then we made the decision to scramble the two fighters at Travis to go in and identify it.' We asked our squadron commander if we ought to make a written report, and he said no. We heard nothing from division, nothing from the people who made the decision to scramble us in the first place.

So later I said to my wingman that maybe it's a good idea that we just don't talk about this, because at the time I thought we'd run into something that Air Defense Command knew nothing about, that was American – something top secret.[4]

ELECTRICAL INTERFERENCE

A few months later, in the summer of 1961, new surface-to-air missiles were being set up near Rybinsk, 150 kilometres from Moscow, as part of the Moscow air-defence network. According to science reporter Alberto Fenoglio, a huge disc-shaped object appeared at an estimated altitude of 20,000 metres, surrounded by a number of smaller objects. 'A nervous missile battery commander panicked and gave – unauthorized – the order to fire a salvo at the giant disc,' Fenoglio reported.

> The missiles were fired. All exploded when at an estimated distance of some two kilometres from the target, creating a fantastic spectacle in the sky. A second salvo followed, with the same result. The third salvo was never fired, for at this point the smaller 'saucers' went into action and stalled the electrical apparatus of the whole missile base. When the smaller discoidal UFOs had withdrawn and joined the larger craft, the electrical apparatus was again found to be in working order.[5]

Massive power failures have long been associated with UFO activity. On 18 April 1962, Stead AFB, Nevada, admitted that a huge object of unknown identity had landed near an electric power station in Eureka, Nevada, knocking out the power station for more than an hour. This news was withheld until service was restored, after the mysterious object took off. Nellis AFB, Nevada, admitted that the object had been tracked on radar from as far east as Oneida, New York, and that it had been chased by armed interceptor jets from the Phoenix Air Defense Command. Reportedly it 'exploded' with terrific force after it took off, lighting up the streets of Reno. The object was seen as far west as California, and then disappeared from radar.[6]

SIGHTINGS BY X-15 ROCKET PILOTS

During a lecture at the Second National Conference on the Peaceful Uses of Space Research in Seattle on 11 May 1962, NASA pilot Joseph A. Walker said that it was one of his appointed tasks to detect unidentified flying objects during his flights in the rocket-powered X-15 aircraft. He referred to UFOs he had filmed during his record-breaking 50-mile-high flight a few weeks previously.[7] Leonard Stringfield was given further details by a NASA test engineer who had worked on the X-15 programme at Edwards Air Force Base, California.

On 30 April 1962, two disc-shaped objects overtook Walker's X-15 as it was climbing at 3,400 mph at an altitude of about 200,000 feet. 'Two UFOs just passed overhead,' Walker reported, according to the engineer, who was in the Flight Research Center (FRC) control room at the time. No other details were supplied by the pilot. The aft fuselage cameras on the X-15 caught the UFOs on film, which was later seen by the engineer during the post-flight debriefing. The film clearly showed two white or silver disc-shaped aircraft flying in tight formation, rapidly overtaking the X-15 from behind and passing overhead, possibly 100–200 feet above the plane.[8]

At the Seattle conference, Walker revealed that it was the second occasion on which he had filmed UFOs in flight. 'I don't feel like speculating about them,' he said. 'All I know is what appeared on the film . . .'[9]

On 17 July 1962, Major Robert White piloted an X-15 to its maximum altitude of 314,000 feet when, according to Stringfield's source, White reported to NASA FRC Control that 'several' UFOs were flying in formation with him. Twenty other control-room personnel overheard the communication.[10] 'There *are* things out there. There absolutely is! [sic],' *Time* magazine quotes Major White as having reported excitedly over his radio.[11]

ALIEN CONTACTS REPORTED BY USAF PERSONNEL

Forty-five-year-old Sidney Padrick, a TV and radio technician and private pilot, served in the US Air Force during the Second World War and later with the Air Force Reserve. At 02:00 on 30 January 1965 he encountered a craft of unknown origin near his home at Manresa Beach, near Watsonville, 75 miles south of San Francisco. The craft, about 75 feet in diameter and 30 feet high, had come to rest just above the ground. Padrick panicked and began to run, and then a voice came from the craft: 'Do not be frightened, we are not hostile.' Padrick continued to run. The voice repeated the phrase, and then added: 'We mean you no harm,' and invited him to come on board. As he approached cautiously, a door opened and he went inside, finding himself in a small compartment. Another door slid open and he entered, to be met by a man.

'He was no different from me in basic appearance, had clean-cut features, and wore a type of flying suit that covered the body fully,' said Padrick. On board were seven other men, similar in appearance, and one woman, described as extremely pretty. They were all about 5 feet 8 inches to 5 feet 9 inches tall.

By our own standards I would say they all looked between 20 and 25 years old; very young, pert, energetic and intelligent looking. Their features were similar to ours. There was only one feature I noticed that would differ from us greatly, and that was that their faces came to a point, much more than ours. They had sharp chins and noses. Their skin was somewhat of an 'Armenian' colour. Their eyes were all very dark ... there was nothing unusual about them – their brightness, depth or luminescence.

All the men appeared to have very short auburn hair, but it looked as though it had never been cut – it looked like a natural growth. The lady had long hair and it was pushed down inside her clothing ... Their fingers were a little longer than mine [and] the fingernails looked as if someone had just given them a manicure.

All of them were wearing two-piece suits – slip-on type – light bluish-white in colour [and] no buttons or zippers that I could see. The bottom section actually included the shoes – it looked like boots which continued on up to the waistline, without any break around the ankles ... There was a large band in the middle, and large cuffs, and a very large collar that came down with a 'V' neck. The collar had a very pretty design on it ... and the neck piece – right around the neck – had a braid of some kind on it ... They had soles and heels [because] I could hear them walking on the rubbery-like floor.

The first man encountered by Padrick acted as spokesman, explaining that he was the only one on board who spoke English.

He had no accent whatsoever. It was just as plain and just as perfectly-spoken English as anyone had ever spoken on this Earth ... Every question I asked him, he would pause for about 25 or 30 seconds before he would answer, regardless of how minor it was. Perhaps he was getting instructions mentally . . . I think if the crew communicated with each other, it was through mental telepathy, because I could see nothing that would indicate communication otherwise.

Each of the occupied rooms had instrument panels on the walls, with crew members concentrating on the instruments. 'They merely glanced around at me when I entered their room, then turned back to their work,' said Padrick.

Some rooms had four or five instruments, others 15 or 20, but they were of a similar type in each room. They were nothing like ours. I didn't get close to any of the walls that had the movable instruments on them, because when I started to advance in the first room he held out his hand for me not to advance . . . I saw markings on some of the instruments; something like a tape moving along, with little tiny dots and dashes on it . . . They [also] had meters, but I could not see dials on them. He said they lit up only when in use.

Padrick was shown an oblong lens, which he took to be part of a viewing system, with a magnified three-dimensional effect. On it he saw an object which he was told was a 'navigation craft'. It looked like a 'blimp'. 'The object was in sunlight, so it had to be pretty far out – I imagine 1,000 miles out, or better . . . he told me that the power source [of the smaller craft] was transferred to them from the other craft, and that it did all the navigation and manipulation through space. He told me they don't measure time and distance as we know it but rather in terms of light. When I asked him how fast they travelled through space, he answered that their speed was limited only by the speed at which they could transfer their energy source.'

After a while Padrick was informed that they had travelled some distance and were now parked in a deserted area, which on subsequent investigation turned out to be near Leggett, California, 175 miles north-west of Watsonville.

After we had landed on the hillside, he told me to step out so that I could come back to the place later – to know this was real and not dreamed. I stepped out alone and walked around the outside of the ship.

I felt the hull. It seemed very hard but not metallic: I never felt anything like it before. The closest thing to it on this Earth I ever felt would be a windshield – Plexiglas . . . I was outside for not more

than three minutes. I got down and looked at the legs it was on and I
tried to find markings on it: I didn't find a mark anyplace.

Padrick asked where the craft and its people came from, and received
a somewhat cryptic reply. 'He told me they were from a planet in back
of a planet which we observe – but we do not observe them. He did not
say we couldn't observe them – he merely said that we didn't observe them
. . . I think their planet is in our solar system.'

The spaceman described his Utopian society to Padrick: 'As you know
it, we have no sickness, we have no crimes, we have no police force. We
have no schools – our young are taught at an early age to do a job, which
they do very well. Because of our long life expectancy we have a very strict
birth control. We have no money. We live as one.'

As to the purpose of the visit, Padrick was told, 'Observation only.'

'I don't think it meant for them to observe us, I think it was for me to
observe them [because] he didn't ask me one thing about myself, and this
leads me to believe that they know about us already . . . He did say they
would come for further observations [and] I think they are observing
people, mostly.'

Padrick was taken to a 'consultation room', in which, for the first time
in his life, he 'felt the presence of the Supreme Being'. 'It's obvious that
they are on a very high scientific level,' he reported, 'but their relation with
the Supreme Being means a lot more to them than their technical and
scientific ability and knowledge. I would say that their religion and their
science are all in one.'

Padrick was taken back to where he had been picked up two hours
earlier. He stepped out of the craft and walked home.

Sid Padrick reported his experience to the Air Force, and was grilled
for three hours by a team headed by Major Damon B. Reeder from
Hamilton AFB (Headquarters, Western Air Defense Force), near Sacramento. The investigators told Padrick he was 'a lucky man': there had been
two instances where hostility had been involved; one the Mantell case, and
the other an incident when an aircraft completely vanished from a radar
screen (as we have learned, there have been many more such incidents).
Tellingly, however, the Air Force informed Padrick that there was more
than one group of UFOs visiting Earth, and that there were friendly as well
as hostile craft, from more than one source.

There were certain details [the Air Force] asked me not to talk about
publicly, but I think in telling it that everything should be disclosed
. . . They didn't want me to say the space people had no money . . .

They didn't want me to divulge their means of communication, and where they got their power from. Also, the man's name – they told me I should never repeat that because it didn't mean anything. The spaceman had said, 'You may call me Xeno'. He didn't say it *was* his name. [Xeno means 'stranger' or 'foreigner' in Greek.][12,13,14]

The official Air Force report, signed by Major Reeder, Base Operations Officer, Hamilton AFB, and forwarded to the Foreign Technology Division at Wright-Patterson AFB, includes further details of Padrick's conversation with Xeno, from which I cite the following:

(1) Q. How did you evade our radar? A. The hull of our spacecraft absorbs energy and will not allow a reflection or harmful penetration . . .
(4) Q. Are you human? A. Yes, we are human, but not your type . . .
(13) Q. How did you pick me for this experience? A. We did not pick you. It was your choice. You are the first person ever to come aboard this ship. We have invited many before but they were frightened away.
(14) Q. If I were a scientist could I have learned more? A. No . . .[15]

In 1967, L.D. 'Pat' Cody, Director of Aerospace Education at Hamilton AFB, reported in a letter to Dr James E. McDonald (an atmospheric physicist and leading UFO investigator at the time) that he had become very interested in the case and had asked Major Reeder to brief his staff on it. 'I understood from the Major,' wrote Cody, 'that he had interviewed several local citizens . . . who vouched for the apparent reliability of Mr Padrick. I understood that Sid was, at that time, in his twentieth year as an Air Force Reservist and was a private pilot with a little over 600 hours of flying time . . .'

In his letter to Cody, McDonald had expressed his scepticism about the case, based on its religious connotation. 'I, too, have been quite sceptical of his story because of the "Supreme Deity" bit,' responded Cody. 'However, I may be a trifle too critical of this religious aspect because of interviews with a few others who claimed "contacts" . . . He seemed sincere to Mrs Cody and to me during the interview and both of us agreed he had either been in this craft or had had such a vivid dream that he believed he had.'[16]

Although I never met the reclusive Sid Padrick (I mistakenly referred to him as 'the late' in *Beyond Top Secret*), based on the taped lecture I have listened to on many occasions, I believe the story to be genuine.

In 1965, Benton Air Force Station, Red Rock, Pennsylvania, was part of the Aerospace Defense Command Interior Radar Defense Zone. On 5

March that year, two Air Force radar technicians were repairing the height-
finder radar antenna, located north-east of the 648th Radar Squadron site.
One of the technicians is the brother of former Chief Master Sergeant
Walter, who relates that 'a small saucer-shaped object landed nearby'.

As they approached the saucer, a beam of light came out and struck
both technicians. That was the last they could remember, and they
failed to report to their command post. Air Policemen went to search
for the two technicians, but they could not be found. All their tools
and equipment were located near the antenna they were fixing. The
Pennsylvania State Police were alerted, and a search of the area began.

Sixteen hours later, a state trooper found the two technicians
walking on Route 487 about 10 miles from the site, south of Lopez.
They seemed dazed, and were transported to a hospital in Williamsport
[and] found to be dehydrated and confused. No alcohol or drugs were
found in their system. They were later transferred to an Air Force
hospital at Stewart AFB, New York. Trace amounts of alpha radiation
were found on their clothing and strange marks were discovered on
their necks.

Special Agents from the [Air Force] Office of Special Investigations
interviewed the technicians. They related their story up to the point of
the beam of light. They could not remember anything after that . . .
they both spent two weeks in the hospital and were released back to
their unit. My brother was re-examined at the Air Force Psychiatric
Center, Sheppard AFB, Texas, in 1966 [where] the doctor asked him if
he thought he was abducted by extraterrestrial visitors! . . . He [now]
won't speak about the incident.[17]

JAPAN AND INDONESIA

On the night of 15 February 1965, a group of US Army and Air Force
officers was being flown to Japan in a Flying Tiger Line aircraft chartered
by the Defense Department. About an hour from Tokyo, the plane's radar
detected three huge, fast-moving objects. A reddish glow then appeared in
the sky to the left, and three enormous oval-shaped objects in close
formation now descended towards the plane. As the captain prepared to
turn, the UFOs veered to one side, abruptly reduced speed and levelled out
– still in close formation – at the plane's flight level (altitude).

'The radar showed they were five miles away, but even at that distance
they looked gigantic,' reported Major Keyhoe. 'As the giant ships continued

to pace the airliner the captain sent a crewman back into the cabin. In a few minutes he returned with an Air Force officer. The Flying Tiger captain had hoped that an emergency message might bring jets from Okinawa, in case of trouble. But the AF man, after an amazed inspection of the huge UFOs, warned him not to try it. Even if the jets arrived in time, they probably would be helpless – and they might cause an attack.'

> For several minutes more the giant spaceships kept on pacing the plane, while the strain built up in the cockpit. Then the formation abruptly angled upward. Accelerating to 1,200 knots, the ships disappeared in seconds. When the plane landed, AF Intelligence sent a coded report to the Pentagon. It had a powerful impact. The AF officer who had viewed the ships had estimated their size, using the five-mile distance as the basis. If he were correct the three spacecraft must have been nearly 2,000 feet in length – possibly even more . . .[18]

It was 18 March 1965. At around 19:00, three workers in Fuchu, near Hiroshima, reported sighting a strange object over Yuki Town, 'shaped like a triangle whose top radiated a brilliant light'. At 19:06, Captain Yoshiharu Inaba was flying a TOA Airlines Convair 240 from Osaka to Hiroshima, Japan, at an altitude of some 2,000 metres. Weather conditions were good, with a full moon. Suddenly, a 'mysterious, elliptical, luminous object' appeared, just after the plane passed Himeji. 'The object followed for a while,' said Inaba, 'and then stopped for about three minutes, and then followed along my left wing across the Inland Sea for a distance of about 90 kilometres . . . then disappeared.'

Initially fearing a collision, Inaba made a 60-degree turn to the right. Immediately, the object made an abrupt turn and positioned itself alongside the port wing. Emitting a greenish light, the object affected the automatic direction finder (ADF) as well as the radio. As the co-pilot, Tetsu Majima, tried unsuccessfully to contact the Matsuyama tower to report the incident, he heard frantic calls from the pilot of a Tokyo Airlines Piper Apache, Joji Negishi, who said he was being chased by a mysterious luminous object while flying along the northern part of Matsuyama City.

According to a message relayed from the *New York Times* office in Tokyo to the TOA Airlines office, a group of 'flying saucer experts' from the US Defense Department, the Federal Aviation Administration and the Palomar Observatory (California) was being sent to Japan to interview Inaba and Negishi. 'The American mission is believed to be interested in the case,' it was reported, 'because there have been several mysterious aviation accidents and flying saucers might have been involved.'[19,20,21]

'UFOs sighted in Indonesia are identical with those sighted in other countries,' declared Air Marshal Roesmin Nurjadin, Commander-in-Chief of the Indonesian Air Force (now Indonesian National Defence-Air Force) in 1967. 'Sometimes they pose a problem for our air defence, and once we were obliged to open fire on them.'[22]

The most active periods for UFO reports in Indonesia were 1953–4 and 1964–5, according to Air Commodore J. Salutun, former Member of Parliament and Secretary of the National Aerospace Council of the Republic of Indonesia. Salutun has confirmed the incident referred to by Air Marshal Nurjadin: 'The most spectacular UFO incident in Indonesia occurred when, during the height of President Sukarno's confrontation against Malaysia, UFOs penetrated a well-defended area in Java for two weeks at a stretch, and each time were welcomed with perhaps the heaviest anti-aircraft barrage in history.' He added:

> I am convinced that we must study the UFO problem seriously, for reasons of sociology, technology and security. The study of UFOs may lead to new and revolutionary concepts in propulsion and space technology in general, from which our present state-of-the-art may benefit. The study of UFOs is a necessity for the sake of world security in the event we have to prepare for the worst in the space age, irrespective of whether we become the Columbus or the Indians . . .[23]

A DEMONSTRATION OF POWER

During Congressional hearings on UFOs before the House Committee on Science and Astronautics in July 1968, physicist Dr James E. McDonald felt obliged to report that the vast north-east American power blackout of 9 November 1965 may have been caused by UFO activity. 'There were [UFO] reports all over New England in the midst of that blackout,' he stated. 'It is rather puzzling that the pulse of current that tripped the relay on the Ontario Hydro Commission Plant has never been identified . . . Just how a UFO could trigger such an outage on a large power network is, however, not clear. But this is a disturbing series of coincidences . . .'[24]

Were aliens responsible? Legendary Hollywood actor Stuart Whitman believes so. Alone in his hotel room in New York City during the blackout, he was awoken just before dawn by a whistling sound outside his twelfth-floor window. Two strange objects could be seen. 'One of them was orange and the other was blue,' he explained to reporter Vernon Scott. 'They gave off a strange luminescent light, so I couldn't see if there were portholes or who was in them.

Then I heard them speaking to me as if they were on a loudspeaker. They spoke to me in English. It may not have been audible to anyone else: I was probably tuned into the right wavelength. They said they wanted to talk to me because I appeared to have no malice or hate in my soul. They said they were fearful of Earth because Earthlings were messing around with unknown quantities and might disrupt the balance of the universe or their planet.

They said the blackout was just a little demonstration of their power, and that they could do a lot more with almost no effort. It served as a warning. They said they could stop our whole planet from functioning. They asked me to do what I could to fight malice, prejudice and hate on Earth, and then they took off. I felt elated. I wasn't even shocked. I was standing by the window and awake the entire time. I don't know why they picked me as a contact. But I'll swear off a Bible that I saw them out there and that they talked to me . . .[25]

CRASH-LANDING AT KECKSBURG

A month after the vast north-east American power blackout, one of the best-attested incidents involving the crash-landing of an unknown craft occurred, close to the Pennsylvania village of Kecksburg. Initially reported as a fiery object by numerous witnesses in nearby states and Canada, the craft came down at 16:45 on 9 December 1965. US Army personnel and many state police arrived and cordoned off the area. Just before it crash-landed, the object described a series of controlled manoeuvres. Hundreds drove to the site to see what had happened. Later, personnel from the USAF's 4602nd Air Intelligence Service Squadron arrived. After a search covering a 75-acre area and lasting until 02:00 the following morning, the Air Force announced that nothing had been found, explaining the incident as 'a meteor or meteors'.

Stan Gordon, a UFO researcher who became the leading investigator of the case, interviewed numerous witnesses over a period of decades. One witness told Gordon that the object passed about 200 feet above him, moving about as fast as a light plane. Another witness described the object as an acorn-shaped, brownish object which 'made a hissing sound as it spewed greenish fire from its rear'. Another witness, Bill Bulebush, saw the object hesitate and make a turn before descending in the woods.

Firefighter James Romansky was one of the first to get really close to the object before the authorities arrived. 'He said he saw a bronze-coloured, acorn-shaped object with no windows, doors, or seams, partially buried in a gully,' reports Leslie Kean (pronounced 'Kane'), a respected investigative journalist who has also made a thorough study of the case. 'It was about 10–12 feet tall, large enough for a man to stand up in, and 8–12 feet in diameter. Romansky said he saw strange symbols that looked like Egyptian hieroglyphics on the back, or "bumper area" of the acorn. He stayed on the scene with a group of firemen until ordered to leave by two men in trench coats, followed by the uniformed military.'

Hundreds of people, including the media, witnessed the military and police presence that night, and some witnessed the arrival of a small convoy of trucks entering the ravine where the object had crash-landed. The military threatened civilians with guns if they got too close to the barricade. Later, witnesses observed an object being whisked away at speed on the back of a flat-bed tractor-trailer truck. 'Jerry Betters said he was harshly ordered at gunpoint to leave the area after he and his friends caught a glimpse of an acorn-shaped object [that was] on the back of an Army flatbed truck as it struggled up through a field,' Kean's report continues. The object was not fully covered and Betters was able to see what looked like hieroglyphs on the back of the object, like the markings described by Romansky (see plates).

Another witness who gained access to the site before the authorities arrived was John Murphy, news director for the local radio station WHJB, who is reported to have taken several photographs of the object. Later that evening, a state police officer confirmed to Murphy the presence of a blue object, 'pulsating' and with a light on it, matching descriptions by other witnesses of 'blue lights' in the woods. 'In the weeks that followed,' says Kean, 'Murphy became obsessed with the case and developed a radio documentary [that] included interviews conducted that night. One day, he received an unexpected visit from authorities in plain clothes. [His] tapes were confiscated; no one knows what happened to the photographs.' Some interviewees, too, were apparently visited by the same authorities, and became reluctant to discuss the matter further. A news blackout had been imposed.

'In the 1980s, investigators obtained copies of the Air Force Project Blue Book file on the case,' continues Kean. 'A handwritten memo stated that a "three-man team" was sent out from Oakdale, Pennsylvania, "to investigate and pick up an object that started a fire". The files say that members of the 662nd Radar Squadron searched until 2 a.m. and *found nothing*.'

James Oberg, a noted UFO debunker who works for NASA, originally claimed that the real explanation for the Kecksburg object is that it was part of Cosmos 96, a failed Russian *Venera* (Venus) probe that the US Air Force Space Command reported had re-entered Earth's atmosphere over Canada at 03:18 the same day. However, the timing does not match. In an April 2005 response to a request from Leslie Kean, Nicholas L. Johnson, chief scientist for orbital debris at NASA's Johnson Space Center, informed Towers Productions (then producing a documentary for the History Channel), 'No part of Cosmos 96 could have landed in Pennsylvania in the local afternoon of 9 December 1965.'

Leslie Kean spearheaded a Freedom of Information Act (FOIA) effort that was part of a 'UFO Advocacy Initiative' pioneered by the Sci-Fi Channel, which for a few years supplied unprecedented resources to the investigation of government records on a selected case involving physical evidence. The Kecksburg incident satisfied many criteria to establish it as an ideal case. Geoarcheological and geomorphological evidence showed that damage dating back to 1965 was evident in trees at the site, as revealed in the Sci-Fi Channel's excellent documentary on the Kecksburg case, *The New Roswell: Kecksburg Exposed*, first aired in November 2003. A Washington law firm assisted with FOIA appeals and possible lawsuits, and others, including the public relations firm PodestaMattoon, joined the initiative, now called the Coalition for Freedom of Information (CFi – see www.freedomofinfo.org). In December 2003, a lawsuit was filed against NASA with Leslie Kean as plaintiff since, she says, the Agency had denied having certain records which CFi knew it had in its possession.[26]

Leslie Kean told me that she was particularly interested in NASA's 'Fragology Files' from 1962 to 1967, described as 'reports of space objects' recovery, [and] analysis of fragments to determine national ownership and vehicle origin'. 'Although a notation on one of the records for these files says that the files were at the Federal Records Center in 1994,' she says, 'NASA states that the files have been missing since 1967.'[27] As of this writing, the court is still considering the case.

'The CFi Kecksburg initiative won the support of Washington insider John Podesta, President Clinton's former Chief of Staff,' says Kean. 'Podesta was instrumental in the declassification of 800 million [!] pages of documents during the Clinton administration.'

'This initiative will help keep the pressure on,' declared Podesta at a Sci-Fi Channel press conference at the National Press Club in October 2002. 'I think it's time to open the books on questions that have remained

in the dark, on the question of government investigations of UFOs. It's
time to find out what the truth really is that's out there. We ought to do it
because it's right; we ought to do it because the American people quite
frankly can handle the truth; and we ought to do it because it's the
law . . .'[28, 29]

REFERENCES

1. Edwards, Frank, *Flying Saucers – Here and Now!*, Lyle Stuart, New York, 1967,
   pp. 42–3.
2. Keyhoe, Major Donald E., *Aliens From Space: The Real Story of Unidentified Flying
   Objects*, Panther, St Albans, UK, 1975, pp. 102–3.
3. 'Pilot finally reveals UFO encounter', *MUFON UFO Journal*, No. 375, July 1999,
   p. 17.
4. Telephone interview, 11 August 2003.
5. 'UFOs over Russia', *Flying Saucers*, No. 47, Palmer Publications, Amherst,
   Wisconsin, May 1966, pp. 6–10.
6. Kovalenko, Ann, 'Saucer Said Responsible In Blackout', *Sunday Call-Chronicle*,
   Allentown, Pennsylvania, 19 December 1965, p. B-8. Regarding power blackouts
   in the vicinity of USAF bases, I have been informed via a CIA UFO specialist that
   Glasgow AFB, Montana, eventually had to be closed (in 1968) following many
   instances of power failures, ostensibly 'because UFOs would hover over high-
   tension wires and and cause electrical shutdowns'.
7. *Le Matin*, Paris, 13 May 1962.
8. Stringfield, Leonard, 'Roswell & the X-15: UFO Basics', *MUFON UFO Journal*,
   No. 259, November 1989, pp. 6–7.
9. *Le Matin*, op. cit.
10. Stringfield, op. cit.
11. *Time*, 27 July 1962.
12. Lecture by Sid Padrick, Reno, Nevada, 10 July 1966.
13. *The Little Listening Post*, Washington, DC, Vol. 12, No. 3, 1965.
14. Clark, Jerome, 'Two New Contact Claims', *Flying Saucer Review*, Vol. 11, No. 3,
    1965, pp. 20–2.
15. Report by Major Damon B. Reeder, Base Operations Officer, Headquarters,
    Hamilton AFB and 78th Combat Support Group, CA 94935, 10 February 1965.
16. Letter from L.D. 'Pat' Cody, Director of Aerospace Education, USAF Liaison
    Office, Hamilton AFB, to Dr James E. McDonald, Senior Physicist, The University
    of Arizona, Tucson, 25 August 1967.
17. Filer's Files #36, 9 September 1999. www.nationalufocenter.com

18. Keyhoe, op. cit., pp. 149–50.
19. *Japan Times*, Tokyo, 21 March 1965.
20. *Mainichi Daily News*, Tokyo, 22 March 1965.
21. *Mainichi Daily News*, 23 March 1965.
22. Letter to Yusuke J. Matsumura from Air Marshal Roesmin Nurjadin, Commander-in-Chief, Indonesian Air Force, Djakarta, 5 May 1967.
23. Letter from Air Commodore J. Salutun, published in *UFO News*, Vol. 6, No. 1, 1974, CBA International, Yokohama, Japan.
24. Fuller, John G., *Aliens in the Skies: The Scientific Rebuttal to the Condon Committee Report*, G.P. Putnam's Sons, New York, 1969, p. 87.
25. Scott, Vernon, 'Big Blackout? Blame Spacemen', *Toronto Daily Star*, 24 December 1965.
26. Kean, Leslie, 'Forty Years of Secrecy: NASA, the Military, and the 1965 Kecksburg Crash', *International UFO Reporter*, Vol. 30, No. 1, October 2005, pp. 3–9, 28–31.
27. Various communications, January 2006.
28. Kean, op. cit.
29. Regarding information withheld by NASA, in *Apollo 11: The Untold Story*, first shown on Channel Five in July 2006, astronaut Edwin 'Buzz' Aldrin revealed that Apollo 11 encountered a UFO during its flight to the moon. 'There was something out there that was close enough to be observed, and what could it be?' he began. Mike [Collins] decided he thought he could see it in the telescope [and] when you made it real sharp it was sort of bell-shaped . . .

    'Obviously the three of us were not going to blurt out, "Hey, Houston, we've got something moving alongside of us and we don't know what it is . . . Can you tell us what it is?" We weren't about to do that, because we knew that those transmissions would be heard by all sorts of people and, who knows, somebody would have demanded we turn back because of aliens or whatever the reason is.'

    The event remains unexplained, as confirmed by Dr David Baker, Apollo 11 Senior Scientist.

THE NEW YORK TIMES, SUNDAY, FEBRUARY 28, 1960.

AIR FORCE ORDER ON 'SAUCERS' CITED

Pamphlet by the Inspector General Called Objects a 'Serious Business'

WASHINGTON, Feb. 27 (UPI)—The Air Force has sent its commands a warning to treat sightings of unidentified flying objects as "serious business" directly related to the nation's defense, it was learned today.

An Air Force spokesman confirmed issuance of the directive after portions of it were made public by a private "flying saucer" group.

The new regulations were issued by the Air Force Inspector general Dec. 24.

The regulations, revising similar ones issued in the past, outlined procedures and said that "investigations and analysis of UFO's are directly related to the Air Force's responsibility for the defense of the United States."

Committee Reveals Document

Existence of the document was revealed by the National Investigations Committee on Aerial Phenomena.

The privately financed committee accused the Air Force of deception in publicly describing reports of unidentified flying objects as delusions and hoaxes while sending the private admonition to its commands.

Vice Admiral R. H. Hillenkoetter (Ret.), a committee board member and former director of the Central Intelligence Agency, said in a statement that a copy of the inspector general's warning had been sent to the Senate Science and Astronautics Committee.

"It is time for the truth to be brought out in open Congressional hearings," he said.

The Air Force confirmed that the document had been issued.

A spokesman said it was put out by Maj. Gen. Richard E. O'Keefe, acting inspector general at the time, to call attention to revised Air Force regulations concerning unidentified flying objects.

The statement was included in an "operations and training" pamphlet circulated at intervals to bring commands up to date.

Pentagon aides said the new regulations covering seven printed pages, made no substantive change in policy, but had been rewritten as a matter of course.

The Air Force has investigated 6,312 reports of flying objects since 1947, including 183 in the last six months of 1959. The latest Air Force statement, issued a month ago said "no physical or material evidence, not even a minute fragment of a so-called flying saucer, has ever been found."

Admiral Hillenkoetter said that "behind the scenes, high-ranking Air Force officers are soberly concerned about the UFO's."

"But through official secrecy and ridicule, many citizens are led to believe the unknown flying objects are nonsense," the retired admiral said. He charged that "to hide the facts, the Air Force has silenced its personnel" through the issuance of a regulation.

An article in the *New York Times* (28 February 1960). 'Behind the scenes, high-ranking Air Force officers are soberly concerned about the UFOs,' said former CIA Director Vice Admiral Roscoe H. Hillenkoetter. 'But through official secrecy and ridicule, many citizens are led to believe the unknown flying objects are nonsense.'

CONGRESSIONAL RECORD — APPENDIX *September 2* 1960

NICAP UFO Report

EXTENSION OF REMARKS
OF
HON. LEONARD G. WOLF
OF IOWA
IN THE HOUSE OF REPRESENTATIVES
Wednesday, August 31, 1960

MR. WOLF. Mr. Speaker, under leave to extend my remarks, I include an urgent warning by Vice Adm. R. H. Hillenkoetter, former Director of the Central Intelligence Agency, that certain potential dangers are linked with unidentified flying objects—UFO's. Admiral Hillenkoetter's request that Congress inform the public as to the facts is endorsed by more than 200 pilots, rocket, aviation, and radar experts, astronomers, military veterans, and other technically trained members of the National Investigations Committee on Aerial Phenomena. Among them are Rear Adm. H. B. Knowles; Col. Joseph Bryan III, U.S. Air Force Reserve; Lt. Col. Jas. McAshan, USAFR; Lt. Col. Samuel Freeman, U.S. Army Reserve. Aviation; Mr. J. B. Hartranft, president, Aircraft Owners Pilots Association; Capt. R. B. McLaughlin, Navy missile expert; Mr. Frank Rawlinson, physicist, National Aeronautical and Space Agency; Dr. Leslie Kaeburn, space consultant, University of Southern California; former Air Force Maj. William D. Leet, with three officially reported UFO encounters while an Air Force pilot; Frank Halstead, 25 years as curator, Darling Observatory; Rear Adm. D. S. Fahrney, former chief of the Navy missile program; Col. R. B. Emerson, U.S. Army Reserve, head of Emerson Testing Laboratories; Prof. Charles A. Maney, astrophysicist, Defiance University; Capt. W. B. Nash, Pan American Airways.

The "NICAP Report on Secrecy Dangers," with documented evidence on UFO's, was first submitted confidentially to me, and to several other Members of Congress, including Senator LYNDON JOHNSON. In a reply to NICAP, July 6, 1960, Senator JOHNSON stated that he had ordered the staff of the Senate Preparedness Investigating Subcommittee to keep close watch on UFO developments and to report on any recent significant sightings and the Air Force investigations of such sightings.

Although I have not had time for a detailed study, I believe the conclusions of these experienced NICAP officials should be given careful consideration. Certainly their sober evaluations should be completely disassociated from the obvious frauds and delusions about UFO's which unfortunately have been publicized. The NICAP report is stated to be the result of a 3-year investigation—its conclusions based only on verified visual, radar, and photographic evidence by trained, reputable observers.

On August 20, 1960, NICAP sent me the following statement to be added to the original report:

There is a growing danger that UFO's may may be mistaken for Soviet missiles or jet aircraft, accidentally causing war. Several Air Defense scrambles and alerts already have occurred when defense radarmen mistook UFO formations for possible enemy machines. NICAP agrees with this sober warning by Gen. L. M. Chassin, NATO coordinator of Allied Air Services:

"It is of first importance to confirm these objects * * * the business of governments to take a hand, if only to avoid the danger of global tragedy. If we persist in refusing to recognize the existence of these UFO's, we will end up, one fine day, by mistaking them for the guided missiles of an enemy—and the worst will be upon us."

Today, this danger may surpass the one cited in NICAP's report: That the U.S.S.R. might spread false rumors that the UFO's are secret Red devices which have mapped all the U.S. and allied targets and could be used in surprise-attack weapons. (Some Americans already suspect hidden fear of UFO's as the reason for secrecy.)

We are sure you will agree it is imperative to end the risk of accidental war from defense forces' confusion over UFO's. All defense personnel, not merely top-level groups, should be told that the UFO's are real and should be trained to distinguish them—by their characteristic speeds and maneuvers—from conventional planes and missiles. This is not in effect today.

Second, the American people must be convinced, by documented facts, that the UFO's could not be Soviet machines.

Certainly every Member of Congress will agree that any such danger of accidental war—even if slight—must be averted in every possible way. It is also important to prevent any unfounded fear that the UFO's, are secret enemy devices.

After discussing the subject with colleagues, I am certain that there is real concern by many Members of Congress. Without necessarily accepting all the conclusions of the NICAP Board of Governors and technical advisers, we are convinced that a thorough study of the UFO problem should be made. Pending such action, I believe that publication of the NICAP report will help to reduce the dangers cited by Vice Admiral Hillenkoetter and the other NICAP officials.

For those Members desiring to do so the previously mentioned confidential report can be obtained upon request at the National Investigation Committee on Aerial Phenomena, 1536 Connecticut Avenue NW., Washington, D.C.

The urgent recommendations of the National Investigations Committee on Aerial Phenomena (NICAP) brought to the attention of the US Congress, 31 August 1960.

(United States Congress)

18. A POSITIVE THREAT

On 9 April 1964, the Gemini-Titan I was launched from Complex 19 at the Cape Canaveral US Air Force Missile Test Range in Florida. Clark C. McClelland, a young designer working for the Titan II Launch Operations Team in Hangar 'U', was assigned to work with an engineer called Chuck at the time. 'We had a problem happening with the first stage of the Titan and called it "Pogo",' McClelland reports.

> Several previous test flights were flown and the effect showed up at lift-off. It acted like a Pogo stick (up and down motion) as the vehicle rose into the sky ... Chuck and I were to attach measurements to the booster and determine how or what could be done to stop the Pogo effect. Several modifications had been made and this flight would prove if we were approaching the correction of the difficulty ...
>
> The rocket lifted off and began to return data which indicated that the modifications Chuck and I had designed had reduced the Pogo effect significantly ... As the Gemini capsule entered orbit, the RCA world tracking team began to realize that 'our' capsule was not alone, as viewed through their incoming telemetry, visual theodolite and other high-powered optical data. Our capsule had four 'visitors' ...
>
> NASA, the USAF and Martin-Marietta who built the Titan II were all puzzled ... the intelligent determination was that we had other physical objects there with our Gemini capsule. Total silence filled the launch control area ... 'What about UFOs?' It was as if I had taken the Lord's name in vain. The silence deepened ... Cold stares came at me from the NASA brass and USAF officers. Actually, the only obvious answer was what I had so blatantly stated – they were UFOs!

Several hours after the objects departed their single orbit rendezvous with the Gemini capsule, says McClelland, a shadowy group of personnel arrived on the scene.

> One thing was certain, this group was at the Cape for no other reason than the Gemini/Titan mission and its guests ... They wore no uniforms yet acted as if they were military. They spoke of returning to

Washington, DC ... To make a long story short, NASA, USAF, Pentagon, White House, NSA, etc., all determined that [the event] had to be eventually explained as normal activity [and] the official determination was that the objects were the torn particles or remains of the Titan upper stage that apparently entered orbit with the Gemini capsule. I was at the news conference and I nearly began to laugh. How could a broken stage overtake the capsule and stop slightly ahead of the capsule to accompany it for an entire orbit round the Earth? But I held my laugh to save my job ...[1]

First Lieutenant Robert Jacobs was Officer-in-Charge of Photo-optical Instrumentation in the 1369th Photographic Squadron at Vandenberg AFB, California, in September 1964, when a UFO was responsible for the destruction of an Atlas-F intercontinental ballistic missile (ICBM) during a test firing. The incident was recorded by a 35mm movie camera attached to a high-powered telescope at the tracking site near Anderson Peak, 124 miles from Vandenberg.

Jacobs took the exposed cans of film to the processing laboratory at Vandenberg. A couple of days later he was ordered to report to the office of Major Florenz J. Mansmann, chief science officer of the unit. A projector had been set up and a group of people was present at the meeting as the film rolled. Towards the end, Mansmann ordered Jacobs to watch carefully. 'At that moment the most remarkable vision of my life came on the screen,' reports Jacobs:

Another object flew into the frame from left to right. It approached the warhead package and *manoeuvred around it*. That is, this thing flew a relative polar orbit around our warhead package, which was itself heading toward the South Pacific at some 18,000 mph ... it emitted four distinct, bright flashes of light at approximately the four cardinal compass points of its orbit. These flashes were so intense that each 'strike' caused the [Image Orthicon] tube to 'bloom' or form a halo around the spot ...

The object departed the frame in the same direction from which it had come. The shape of the object was that of a classic 'flying saucer'. In the middle of the top half was a dome [from which] or just beneath it, seemed to issue a beam of light which caused the flashes described. Subsequently the [dummy nuclear] warhead malfunctioned and tumbled out of suborbit hundreds of miles short of its target.

The film was run through several more times. Jacobs was allowed to examine the frames with a magnifying glass, and then ordered to say nothing about the footage, which was turned over to two men in plain clothes from Washington. When the story finally broke years later, Mansmann (later a research consultant at Stanford University) categorically verified Jacobs's account.[2,3]

Sightings of UFOs were commonly reported during ICBM test launches. From 1965 to 1967, for instance, Richard Bowen tracked Minuteman and Titan missile launches at the Kennedy Space Center, Florida, as an assistant superintendent for range operations with Pan American World Airlines. He claims he saw 'bogeys' approaching a Titan the first time he sat in front of a radar screen. 'You'd see these things coming in,' he told reporter Billy Cox, 'pulling 90-degree turns at speeds of [about] 9,000 mph. And I'm going, "Look at this! Look at this!" And the rest of the guys are saying, "Relax, it happens every launch" . . .'[4]

In 1966, UFOs were reported hovering over a number of ICBM sites. The North American Aerospace Defense Command (NORAD – formerly USAF Air Defense Command) is responsible for protecting the North American continent from attack by enemy missiles or aircraft. While the vast majority of the 25,000 observations each day that are recorded by NORAD's Space Detection and Tracking System (Spadats) and the Naval Space Surveillance System turn out to be readily identifiable, a certain percentage are classed as 'uncorrelated observations',[5] of which there have been literally millions since the early 1960s. Assuming that the majority of these, too, can be explained, that still leaves thousands of possibly bonafide UFO reports. Tellingly, a document relating to NORAD's Unknown Track Reporting System (NUTR) states that 7,000 trackings of unknown objects had been recorded since 1971, but nearly all these reports are exempt from disclosure (see p. 275). But quite a number of documents have been released relating to the many intrusions occurring over Strategic Air Command (SAC) bases – including nuclear missile bases – such as the following incidents.

On the nights of 24–25 August 1966, unidentified objects were observed for a total of some *three-and-half hours* above the Minuteman intercontinental ballistic missile (ICBM) silos at Minot AFB, North Dakota. 'The organizations assigned to operate and protect the missile installations at Minot were the 91st Strategic Missile Wing (SMW), the 862nd Combat Support Group (CSG), and the 786th Radar Squadron,' reports Robert L. Salas, co-author of *Faded Giant*, a book detailing numerous such instances, including one at another base the following year. 'The Minot UFOs were witnessed by multiple observers at three widely separated missile sites and were confirmed by radar.'[6]

The following extracts from a six-page USAF report by the Base Director of Operations (p. 276) are revealing:

... Capt Smith (Missile Combat Crew Commander) on duty at Missile Site (MIKE Flight) 60 feet underground indicated that radio transmission was being interrupted by static, this static accompanied by the UFO coming close to the Missile Site. When UFO climbed, static stopped ... At 0512Z, UFO climbed for altitude after hovering for 15 minutes. South Radar base gave altitude as 100,000 feet, NW of Minot ... At this time a strike team reported UFO descending ... The UFO then began to swoop and dive [and] appeared to land 10 to 15 miles South of MIKE 6 ... When the [strike] team was about 10 miles from the landing site, static disrupted radio contact with them ... Another UFO was visually sighted and confirmed by radar ...[7]

On 5 March 1967, NORAD tracked an uncorrelated target descending over the missile site at Minot AFB. Strike teams were notified immediately and they sighted a metallic-appearing, disc-like object with bright flashing lights moving slowly over the site. Three armed trucks chased the intruder until it stopped and hovered at 500 feet. The teams had orders to capture the UFO undamaged if it landed, but it then began circling over a launch-control facility. F-106 Delta Dart interceptors were about to be scrambled when the UFO climbed vertically and disappeared.[8]

In the early hours of 17 March 1967, Robert Salas, on duty as Deputy Missile Combat Crew Commander in the underground Launch Control Facility (LCF) at Malmstrom AFB, Montana, received a call from his non-commissioned officer (NCO) in charge of site security. 'He said that he and other guards had observed some unidentified flying objects in the vicinity [which] had overflown the LCF a few times [though] he could only distinguish them as "lights" at this time,' reports Salas. 'At the time, I believed the first call to be a joke.'

Five or ten minutes later, I received a second call from my security NCO. This time he was much more agitated and distraught. He stated that there was a UFO hovering just outside the front gate! He wanted to know what he should do ... As we were talking, he said he had to go because one of the guards had been injured. I immediately woke my commander ...

Within seconds, our [Minuteman] missiles began shutting down from 'Alert' status to 'No-Go' status. I recall that most, if not all, of our missiles had shut down in rapid succession. Normally, if a missile went off alert status, it was due to a power outage at a particular site

... It was extremely rare for more than one missile to go off-line for any length of time. In this case, none of our missiles came back on-line. The problem was not lack of power; some signal had been sent to the missiles which caused them to go off alert.

After we reported this incident to the command post, I phoned my security guard to determine what had happened topside [i.e., at the surface]. He informed me that the guard who had approached the UFO had been injured – not seriously ... We were relieved by our scheduled replacement crew later that morning. The missiles had still not been brought on-line by on-site maintenance. Once topside, I spoke directly with the security guard about the UFOs. The only additional detail he added, that I recalled, was that the UFO had a red glow and appeared to be saucer-shaped [and] hovering silently.

'When my commander and I returned to the base, we discussed the incident with our squadron commander and an investigator from Air Force Office of Special Investigations (AFOSI). The Colonel was just as shocked about the incident as we were.' Salas later recalled his commander telling him, 'The same thing happened at another flight' (Echo Flight). 'The Echo Missile Combat Crew Commander related that prior to the shutdown of all his missiles he had received more than one report from security patrols and maintenance crews that they had seen UFOs; one was directly above one of the LFs [launch facilities] in Echo Flight.'[9]

Former airman James J. Ortyl was assigned to Malmstrom AFB at the time of the incidents, and confirmed the following to Salas and, on another occasion, to me:

In March 1967, while on day shift duty at LCF 'K', three or four security team members including myself were engaged in a conver-sation at the dispatch office [when] I observed an unidentified flying object pass over the entrance gate and fly in close proximity past the window ... At least two other air policemen acknowledged seeing the same thing. The object appeared red or red-orange in colour and glowed much like a ball of fire ... I could not detect a distinct shape or structure. It seemed to have a round appearance to it ...[10]

Minot Air Force Base, North Dakota, where incidents involving UFOs and intercontinental ballistic missiles occurred as recounted earlier, was again the scene of an extraordinary intrusion by an unknown craft on 24 October 1968. Bradford Runyan Jr was flying in the right seat as an instructor co-pilot of a B-52H bomber, approaching the base, when he was requested to 'check on something in the area' and given a heading to follow. 'When I asked what I was looking for,' wrote Runyon, 'I was told I would know it if I found it.' The report he sent to me continues:

> Minutes later my nav [navigation] team had an object on their radarscopes approaching from the right rear of our plane at such a high rate of speed that they thought a collision was imminent. The object stopped off our right tail momentarily, then moved to the left side of our plane. We lost radio contact with the base, and decided to land the plane. The UFO stayed with us until within 10 miles of the base where it set down on the ground and our UHF radios came back on. We were instructed to go back and overfly the object, which we did, again losing radio contact with the base when we flew over the object.
>
> At a briefing the following day I was told that a 20-ton concrete lid had been removed from a missile silo and both outer and inner alarms had been activated. Our aircraft film showed a radar return about five times as large as a KC-135 tanker and a closure rate of about 3,000 mph. Ground crews saw the object join with us, and recently a retired CIA person sent to investigate the incident told me that Blue Book lied, and that it was a UFO.

Runyon had overflown the object at 2,000 feet. 'Looking down on the object when it was on the ground,' he explained, 'the body was several hundred feet long and glowed dark orange in colour, like molten steel. The crescent moon-shaped part was connected to the body with a space in between. Blue and green lights appeared to be inside the crescent-shaped part as we passed over the object . . .'[11]

INTERNATIONAL COLLABORATION

By 1967, the stockpile of nuclear weapons in the United States alone reached its zenith – 30,893 compared to 6,444 ten years previously.[12] I believe it is no coincidence that 1967 also saw a huge increase in UFO sightings around the globe. And the intrusions at intercontinental ballistic missile sites continued in ensuing years, on one occasion bringing the USA and the USSR to the brink of a nuclear exchange, as we shall learn in a later chapter. Posing as they did an insuperable problem, these intrusions nonetheless led to a positive outcome behind the scenes – an unprecedented degree of collaboration between the superpowers.

On 18 October 1967, the first meeting of the UFO section of the All-

Union Committee on Cosmonautics of the DOSAAF (All-Union Voluntary Society for Co-operation with the Army, Navy and Air Force) took place in Moscow, attended by 400 people. Members included a cosmonaut and many scientists and astronomers, as well as 200 qualified observers stationed throughout the USSR.[13]

On 10 November 1967, two DOSAAF representatives, retired Soviet Air Force Major-General Porfiri Stolyarov, and Dr Felix Zigel of the Moscow Aviation Institute, appeared on Moscow Central Television to announce the formation of the committee, at the conclusion of which Zigel stated: 'Unidentified Flying Objects are a very serious subject which we must study fully. We appeal to all viewers to send us details of any observations of strange flying craft seen over the territories of the Soviet Union. This is a serious challenge to science, and we need the help of all Soviet citizens . . .'[14]

The committee was inundated with letters from the public, including over 200 good reports. Perhaps the authorities had not anticipated such a response. By the end of November 1967, the DOSAAF Central Section of the All-Union Committee of Cosmonautics, chaired by Army General A.L. Getman, adopted and passed a resolution on the dissolution of the UFO Section (none of whose members were either invited to the meeting, or ever informed as to the reason for this decision).[15]

Reactions to the formation of the Stolyarov Committee, and what it implied, were worldwide. Clearly, the USSR's more conservative scientists were thoroughly embarrassed by the whole affair. However, in an article in the *New York Times*, Dr Zigel appealed for international scientific co-operation on the matter. 'Unfortunately, certain scientists, both in the Soviet Union and the United States, deny the very existence of the problem, instead of trying to solve it,' he declared. 'The UFO problem is a challenge to mankind. It is the duty of scientists to take up the challenge . . .'[16]

The British Government, apparently, was among the first to take up the challenge. According to a US Defense Intelligence Agency (DIA) attaché's report, for instance: 'On 12 December 1967, the British Embassy was directed by London [Foreign Office] to further investigate the subject with a view to cooperating with the Soviets in observation teams for UFOs'. The British Scientific Counsellor in Moscow was told, however, that the commission would soon be disbanded.[17]

Zigel was ordered to terminate his research, and forbidden from meeting Western journalists.[18] The Americans, in particular, were keen to talk to him, since a new official UFO project had been established at the University of Colorado, headed by Dr Edward Condon and commissioned by the US Air Force. But no replies were forthcoming. Paradoxically, although forbidden to carry out his 'dissident' research, Zigel (together with another top investigator, Yuri Fomin) was invited to give classified lectures on the subject to government and military officials – including the KGB.

In 1979, Victor Marchetti, former Executive Assistant to the Deputy Director, Central Intelligence Agency, wrote that:

> If it were concluded that UFOs were not of terrestrial origin but, rather, vehicles from outer space, the CIA and US Government, aware that the phenomenon was of a worldwide nature, would seek co-operation in the investigation from the Earth's other technically advanced nations, such as the United Kingdom, France, Germany, and even the USSR. The CIA would function as the US Government's agent, just as the KGB would be the USSR's, MI6 would be the UK's, and so on. These agencies ... are quite accustomed to co-operating with each other on matters of mutual interest.[19]

Dorothy Kilgallen, the noted American journalist cited earlier, learned from her British military sources in 1954 that: 'Flying saucers are regarded as of such vital importance that they will be the subject of a special hush-hush meeting of the world military heads next summer.'[20]

By 1955, the Soviet Ministry of Defence had created the UFO Research Committee, which classified UFO reports at a top-secret level. According to Yuri Stroganov, heads of the intelligence services of the USSR, Great Britain, United States and France held secret meetings in Geneva throughout 1956. There they reached an agreement regarding a policy of secrecy on 'the UFO problem', reportedly including: the pressurizing of witnesses (including death threats) to refrain from talking about their experiences; fabrication of false 'explanations' for sightings; the creation of a mechanism to ignore or play down the subject, involving the complicity of the military and scientific community as well as the media; and the infiltration of UFO research groups.[21]

In 1965, writer George Langelaan, a former officer of the French secret service (known at that time as the SDECE – Service de Documentation Extérieure et de Contre-Espionnage) revealed to a French journalist that the Russian and American secret services had collaborated on the problem, and had concluded: 'The flying saucers exist, their source is extraterrestrial, and the future – relatively quite soon – should permit confirmation of this statement.'[22]

No such confirmation was forthcoming for many years. President Mikhail Gorbachev has confirmed, for instance, that at the Geneva Summit in 1985 with President Ronald Reagan, the subject of collaboration was discussed. 'The US President said that, if the Earth faced an invasion by extraterrestrials,' Gorbachev remarked in 1987, 'the United States and the Soviet Union would join forces to repel such an invasion. I shall not dispute the hypothesis, though I think it's early yet to worry about such an intrusion . . .'[23]

REFERENCES

1. McClelland, Clark C., 'Four Guests with Gemini'. www.stargate-chronicles.com
2. Jacobs, Bob, PhD, 'Deliberate Deception: The Big Sur UFO Filming', *MUFON UFO Journal*, No. 249, January 1989, pp. 3–8.
3. Crain, T. Scott Jr, 'UFO Intercepts Rocket', *MUFON UFO Journal*, No. 225, January 1987, pp. 5–6.
4. Cox, Billy, 'Locals tell tales of UFO sightings', *Florida Today*, Melbourne, Florida, 6 July 1997.
5. Fawcett, Lawrence, and Greenwood, Barry, *Clear Intent: The Government Coverup of the UFO Experience*, Prentice-Hall, Englewood Cliffs, New Jersey, 1984, pp. 9–11.
6. Salas, Robert and Klotz, James, *Faded Giant: The 1967 Missile/UFO Incidents* (revised edition), privately published by the authors, 2004, pp. 5–6. Available from Jim Klotz, PO Box 832, Mercer Island, WA 98040. mail@cufon.org
7. Report from Headquarters 862nd Combat Support Group (SAC), Minot AFB, North Dakota 58701, 30 August 1966 (reproduced in *Faded Giant*).
8. Fowler, Raymond E., *Casebook of a UFO Investigator*, Prentice-Hall, Englewood Cliffs, NJ, 1981, p. 187.
9. Salas, Robert L., 'Minuteman Missiles Shutdown', *MUFON UFO Journal*, No. 345, January 1997, pp. 15–17. See also *Faded Giant*.
10. Salas and Klotz, op. cit., pp. 31–2.
11. Report received from Bradford Runyan Jr, dated 11 February 2000, amended in 2005.
12. Light, Michael, *100 Suns: 1945–1962*, Jonathan Cape, London, 2003. Hobana, Ion, and Weverbergh, Julien, *UFOs from Behind the Iron Curtain*, Souvenir, London, 1974, p. 25.
13. Creighton, Gordon, *Flying Saucer Review*, Vol. 13, No. 6, 1967, p. 2.
14. Ibid. Hobana and Weverbergh report that Stolyarov, not Zigel, made the concluding statement.
15. Brill, Joe, 'UFOs Behind the Iron Curtain', *Skylook*, No. 86, Mutual UFO Network, January 1975.

16. *New York Times*, 10 December 1967.
17. Defense Intelligence Agency report, 19 January 1968.
18. Creighton, op. cit., p. 10.
19. Marchetti, Victor, 'How the CIA Views the UFO Phenomenon', *Second Look*, Washington, DC, Vol. 1, No. 7, May 1979, pp. 2–5.
20. *Los Angeles Examiner*, 23 May 1955.
21. Stonehill, Paul, *The Soviet UFO Files*, Bramley Books, Quadrillion Publishing Ltd, Godalming, Surrey, GU7 1XW, UK, 1998, p. 41.
22. *Sud-Ouest*, Bordeaux, 17 February 1965.
23. Speech at the Grand Kremlin Palace, Moscow, 17 February 1987, cited in *Soviet Life*, May 1987, p. 7A.

NASA
National Aeronautics and
Space Administration

INFORMATION SHEET

Number 78-1

Prepared by:

LFF-3/Public Services Branch
Office of External Relations
NASA Headquarters
Washington, DC 20546

UNIDENTIFIED FLYING OBJECTS

The information contained here has been compiled to respond to queries on Unidentified Flying Objects directed to the White House as well as NASA.

NASA is the focal point for answering public inquiries to the White House relating to UFOs. NASA is not engaged in a research program involving these phenomena, nor is any other government agency.

Reports of unidentified objects entering United States air space are of interest to the military as a regular part of defense surveillance. Beyond that, the U.S. Air Force no longer investigates reports of UFO sightings.

February 1, 1978

A NASA information sheet perpetuating the myth that no government agency is engaged in UFO research. NASA itself has always been involved in UFO investigations: in June 1967, for instance, Kurt Debus, Director of the John F. Kennedy Space Center (KSC), issued management instructions mostly related to the processing of UFO reports (see following page). *(NASA)*

KMI 8610. 4
June 28, 1967

(4)   Refer all inquiries from news media to the Public
      Information Branch.

(5)   Consult with the Senior Scientist, KSC, on all
      sightings reported.

(6)   Call in unidentified flying object reports to the Patrick
      Air Force Base Command Post, telephone 494-7001.

d.   All written communications received from persons or activities
     reporting a sighting will be immediately transmitted to the
     Senior Scientist, KSC.

RESPONSIBILITIES

a.   Test Support Management Office will be responsible for:

(1)   Developing and maintaining a capability for receiving,
      screening, and processing reports of sightings, as
      defined in paragraph 4, on a 24-hour-day, 7-day-week
      basis.

(2)   Ensuring close liaison with the Senior Scientist, KSC,
      and the Public Affairs Office on matters pertaining to this
      Instruction.

(3)   Coordinating with the Senior Scientist, KSC, as soon as
      possible after a reported sighting to determine the action
      to be taken.

b.   The KSC Scheduling Branch, Test Support Management Office,
     will be responsible for maintaining a 24-hour-day, 7-day-week
     capability for receiving, screening, and processing reports
     of sightings, in accordance with paragraph 5c.

c.   The Senior Scientist, KSC, will be responsible for:

(1)   The overall monitoring of the space vehicle fragment
      sighting program at KSC.

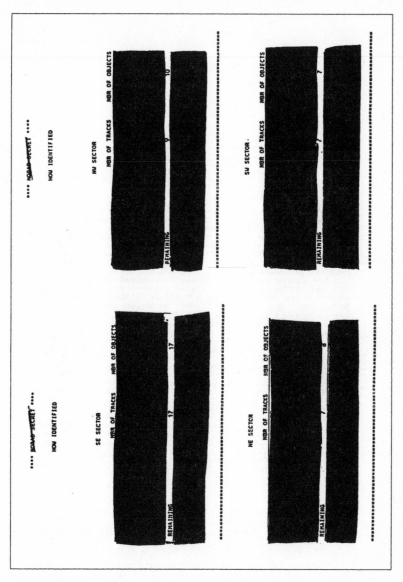

Censored details from the records of North American Aerospace Defense Command's Unknown Track Reporting System, classified NORAD SECRET. 7,000 unknown objects were tracked from 1971–1990, for example, but details remain secret in most cases. *(NORAD/Citizens Against UFO Secrecy)*

a. Ceiling: 1 - Ø to Clr.

b. Visibility: 15+.

c. Amount of cloud cover: 1/10 to 0.

d. None. | d. Thunderstorms in area? |

e. Vertical temperature gradient: See par g(2).

h. None. | h. Other unusual activity or conditions? |
            | i. Interception/identification measures? |

i. One (1) F-106, assigned 5th Fighter Interceptor Squadron (ADC)
one (1) KC-135, assigned 450th Bomb Wing (906AREFS) Minot AFB, NDak.

j. One (1) KC-135 in area. | j. Air traffic in area? |

k. SHAW, CHESTER A.; JR., Major, USAF, Base Director of Operations.
Comments: Capt Smith (Missile Combat Crew Commander) on duty at Missile
Site (MIKE Flt) sixty (60) feet underground indicated that radio transmission was being interrupted by static, this static was accompanied by
the UFO coming close to the Missile Site (MIKE Flt). When UFO climbed,
static stopped. The UFO appeared to be S.E. of MIKE 6, range undetermined.
At 0512Z, UFO climbed for altitude after hovering for 15 minutes. South
Radar base gave altitude as 100,000 feet, N.W. of Minot AFB, NDak. At
this time a strike team reported UFO descending, checked with Radar Site.
they also verified this. The UFO then began to swoop and dive. It then
appeared to land 10 to 15 miles South of MIKE 6. "MIKE 6" Missile Site
Control sent a strike team to check. When the team was about 10 miles
from the landing sight, static disrupted radio contact with them. Five
(5) to eight (8) minutes later, the glow diminished and the UFO took off.
Another UFO was visually sighted and confirmed by radar. The one that
was first sighted passed beneath the second. Radar also confirmed this.
The first, made for altitude toward the North and the second seemed to
disappear with the glow of red. A3C SEDOVIC at the South Radar base
confirmed this also. At 0619Z, two and one half (2½) hours after first
sighting, an F-106 interceptor was sent up. No contact or sighting was
established. The Control Tower asked the Aircraft Commander of a KC-135
which was flying in the local area to check the area. He reported nothing.
The Radar Site picked up an echo on radar which on checking was the KC-135.
No other sightings. At 0645Z discontinued search for UFO.

l. None.

| k. Position, title & comments of preparing officer |

CHESTER A. SHAW, Jr., Major, USAF
Base Director of Operations

3

Part of a US Air Force report by Major Chester A. Shaw regarding intrusions
by UFOs at Minot AFB, North Dakota, in August 1966.
(From *Faded Giant* by Robert Salas and James Klotz)

KP3u5

PTT ZYUW RUWMADA6076 3030429-ZZZZ--RUEDFIF.

ZNY ZZZZE

P 230042Z OCT 6b

FM 662 CMBT SPT GP MINOT AFB NDAK

TO RUWMFVA/ADC ENT AFB COLO

RUWTEMB/WIADIV MALSTROM AFB MONT

RUEDFIF/FTD WPAFB

RUEFHQA/CSAF

BT

UNCLAS E F T O BO.SEC I OF II.

FOR TDPT (UFO). FOR AFRDC. FOR SAF-OI. SUBJ: UFO REPORT.

A. DESCRIPTION OF THE OBJECTS. (1) SHAPE WAS DESCRIBED BY

VISUAL SIGHTING AS "JUST ABOUT ROUND, A LITTLE OBLONG IF ANYTHING".

THE SHAPE OF AN AIRBORNE B-52 RADAR SCOPE WAS VERY SHARP AND

IRREGULAR AND AT TIMES RECTANGULAR. (2) VISUAL SIGHTING

COMPARED OBJECT SIZE TO BE EQUAL TO THE SUN, VERY LARGE, TOO BIG

FOR AN AIRCRAFT. RADAR SIGHTING DESCRIBES THE SIZE ON THE SCOPE

TO BE LARGER THAN THAT OF A KC-135 DURING AERIAL REFUELING.

(3) COLOR WAS A VERY BRIGHT RED ORANGE MOST OF THE TIME. (4)

THE INITIAL SIGHTING WAS ONE OBJECT. THE ONE OBJECT WAS JOINED BY

ONE OTHER LIKE OBJECT FOR A SHORT TIME. THE AIRBORNE RADAR

The first page of a report by Project Blue Book on the sighting of UFOs at Minot AFB, North Dakota, in May 1968. One object approached an incoming B-52H Stratofortress bomber at high speed and then landed at the base, causing communications failure when the bomber flew over it. The object was described by the co-pilot as 'several hundred feet long'. *(The National Archives, Washington, via Tom Tulien)*

19. ENCOUNTERS AT SEA

While numerous reports of sightings by air force personnel around the world have been released officially, the same cannot be said of naval reports. This has led to a false assumption that very few such incidents have occurred.

On the evening of 30 July 1967, the Argentine steamer *Naviero* was some 120 miles from the Brazilian coast, opposite Cape Santa Marte Grande in the state of Santa Catarina, when Captain Julián Lucas Ardanza was alerted by his crew to the presence of a mysterious submarine. Arriving on deck, Ardanza could see a shining object in the sea. Cigar-shaped, with an estimated length of over 100 feet, it emitted a powerful blue and white glow. No noise could be heard, no wake could be seen in the water, and there was no sign of a periscope, railing, conning tower or any other superstructure, such as would be expected of a conventional submarine. It paced the ship for fifteen minutes before suddenly diving, passing right underneath the *Naviero* and vanishing in the depths, glowing brightly as it went.

In subsequent interviews with the Argentine press, Chief Officer Carlos Lasca described the object as 'a submergible UFO with its own illumination', and the Argentine maritime authorities officially classed it as an 'Unidentified Submarine Object'.[1]

At 19:51 on the evening of 4 October 1967, on the outskirts of Royal Canadian Naval Air Station Shearwater, two men reported strange lights in the sky. At 21:00 on the ship MV *Nickerson*, 32 nautical miles south of Sambro, Nova Scotia, four objects about 16 miles to the north-east were seen on the radarscope and visually, as four brilliant red lights which appeared to be on or just above the water. Don Ledger, a private pilot and co-author of *Dark Object*, a book detailing these and the more significant events which followed, reports that the red lights appeared to be 'spaced out in a box formation, about six miles on a side ... Occasionally one of the lights would flare up to such an intensity that it would leave an after-image ...' Eventually one of the red lights climbed and passed directly over the ship.

At around 23:20, something plummeted into Shag Harbour, a village on the south-eastern coast of Nova Scotia. Witnesses reported to the Royal Canadian Mounted Police (RCMP) that they thought an aircraft had crashed. Laurie Wickens and four friends were driving in the area when they spotted a large object with four sequential flashing amber-coloured lights above and in front of their car. It looked as though the object was coming down into the harbour.

On reaching the harbour, Wickens and his friends jumped out of their car and ran to the water's edge, where a 'dark object' could be seen floating or hovering just above the water. 'The flashing lights had extinguished, to be replaced with one pale, constant yellow light that seemed to be on top of the object, located about 800–900 feet from their position and drifting with the ebb tide,' reports Ledger.

Wickens contacted the RCMP detachment in Barrington Passage and informed them that a big plane or small airliner had crashed into the Sound, a body of water adjacent to Shag Harbour. Shortly after Wickens reported the incident, others, including Mounties, also reported having seen a strange craft. They soon joined Wickens's group and others on the beach and watched the strange craft, estimated to be about 60 feet across, as it drifted out to sea and appeared to submerge. The UFO had now become a USO.

One of the boats sent out to investigate encountered thick, glittering yellow bubbly foam near the location of the impact, stretching down the Sound for half a mile. A smell of sulphur pervaded the area. When touched, the foam left an oily residue on the skin. Later on, a Coastguard cutter also joined the search. Nothing more was found. The Royal Canadian Air Force's (RCAF) Air Desk in Ottawa classed the 'dark object' as a UFO report,[2] as did the Rescue Co-ordination Centre in Halifax, having eliminated the possibility of a crashed plane.

On 6 October, four divers from the Royal Canadian Navy's Fleet Diving Unit arrived and began to search the seabed. A number of fishermen reported that the divers brought up some material, and it was rumoured that this material was shipped to the Naval Armament Depot. 'As puzzled as the Royal Canadian Navy and Air Force were, they apparently were not curious enough to seek solutions to an obviously solid UFO sighting,' says Ledger, '[and] the Shag Harbour incident, like the Dark Object itself, had sunk into oblivion.'

Twenty-five years later, Chris Styles, one of the eyewitnesses to the Shag Harbour incident and co-author of Dark Object, began to investigate the case in depth, following some advice from researcher Stanton Friedman, who lived in New Brunswick. Styles and a friend set about trawling through archives, including microfilm, and struck paydirt when they discovered a priority message to Canadian Forces Headquarters from the Rescue Co-ordination Centre in Halifax, advising that a UFO had impacted the waters of Shag Harbour. Other official documents surfaced, leaving no doubt that officialdom was dealing with a genuine UFO.

The most interesting information to emerge concerned events following the disappearance out to sea of the 'dark object'. 'Harry', one of the divers involved, disclosed that another search had been initiated in the waters off Shelburne Harbour, some 30 miles to the north-east. Sonar and other soundings had pinpointed the object's position, 300 yards from shore. 'We knew there was something down there, and we knew it wasn't anything from here,' he said, 'but I'm not going to say anything else.'

A 'knowledgeable' RCAF source disclosed that NORAD's then alternate operations centre at North Bay, Ontario, had scrambled fighters to intercept what was originally thought to be an incoming intercontinental missile. 'He was advised that the object was travelling at 7,500 miles per hour, which is about Mach 10,' explains Ledger. 'In 1967 we had no aircraft that could move that fast, and we still don't today. Suddenly it stopped and hovered for some moments, then continued on its course at 4,400 miles per hour before slowing to a moderate speed and impacting into Shag Harbour.'

According to Colonel Calvin Rushton, former base commander at Canadian Forces Station Barrington, the object had entered Earth's atmosphere over Siberia. After submerging in the Sound at Shag Harbour, it proceeded out to sea, where it was detected by hydrophones at the top-secret Canadian Forces Station Shelburne, then one of over sixty worldwide submarine detection bases (using the Sonar Surveillance System). Having rounded Cape Sable Island it then headed north-east up the coast and came to rest a few miles off Shelburne, above the magnetic anomaly detection (MAD) grid feed. (These mostly airborne detectors register the magnetic anomaly created by the movement of a submarine's mainly ferrous hull as it passes through the 'lines of force' of Earth's natural magnetic field.)

A flotilla of six or seven Canadian and American ships, including a barge, were tasked to the site and anchored above the object – and *another* that had joined it – for seven days off Government Point. Divers photo-graphed both objects, and hydrophones and other sensors were lowered to study them. During this period, Canadian armed forces soldiers blocked access to both the Shelburne base and Government Point. While some of the ships were diverted to chase a possible Soviet submarine, one and possibly both objects headed south, still submerged, and then became airborne and headed out over the Gulf of Maine.

Information suggests that some material evidence may have been recovered and taken away by barge. In any event, further searches of the seabed organized by the authors and the *Sightings* television production team, who made a documentary on the case in 1995, yielded no supportive material evidence. The case per se, however, remains one of the most compelling on record.[3]

The following crucially significant case has received little coverage, apart from publication in a specialist UFO journal many years ago (a fate that has befallen many of the first-rate cases cited in this book). I am glad to introduce it here, thanks to the veteran Australian researcher Bill Chalker, who has also provided me with additional details.

Not long after midnight on or around 23 October 1969, *Aguila*, a barque-type transport ship of the Chilean Navy, at sea 350 miles off Valparaiso, was heading generally north-east at a speed of 20 knots, when the Combat Information Centre in the ship reported a long-range, airborne contact by radar. A minute later, at 00:44, the contact had reduced the distance to 400 nautical miles; at 00:45, to 150 miles, closing from 332 degrees true. Whatever the type of target, it was then closing at an incredible 213 miles per minute – or 12,780 mph (statute).

At 00:47, at a distance of 12 miles, the single contact appeared on the radarscope as six separate targets. When visual contact was made with the targets, the ship's commander was summoned to the bridge. According to the witness, Lius, one massive object, accompanied by five smaller objects, approached the ship. The large object was rectangular, with 'semicircles' in the side, as if scooped out. It was bathed in brilliant light. 'The thing must have been metallic,' Lius told Chalker. 'It was bigger than the frigate, which was [113] metres long.' The five smaller objects were bluish in colour and egg-shaped, no more than 8 feet in diameter and 5 to 6 feet in depth.[4]

When the objects had closed to a distance of approximately 2,000 yards, three of the smaller objects went portside of the main object and two went to starboard. At times, these smaller objects appeared to be flying in 'elliptical circles, backwards and forwards between the big one and our vessel', said Lius. 'The main thing did not change direction – if it had been in the sea, there would have been a collision.'

When the large object was at a distance of 300 yards, a humming sound could be heard. At this point, the frigate's power cut out for a short while, as the huge object passed overhead. 'What the hell was that?' asked the commander, as he came to the bridge. 'You could see the whole thing, the light was so strong,' said the witness. 'You could see the water, the funnel-head, the head of the ship, the towers, everything. Everybody on the bridge was sort of listening to the noise. I don't know [exactly] how long this thing took to go across.'

The light underneath the main, rectangular object was predominantly red, and 'beetroot (crimson) red lights' seemed to be moving back and forth inside it. A 'half-circle crescent' or scoop-shape could be seen underneath, as well as what looked like 'corn-cobs' on the side. Green or turquoise lights along the side seemed to be pulsating. After the object had passed over the ship and was at a distance of about 200 yards, power on the ship returned to normal. The smaller objects, which never came closer than 500 to 1,000 yards, went around the ship and joined up with the larger one. Finally, at a distance of about 2 miles, the large object simply vanished. The only residue, interestingly, was what appeared to be small, floating pieces of metallic paper.

According to Lius, all on board were ordered by the commander not to comment on what they had seen. Several entries had been made in the ship's log by the officer of the deck regarding the incident, but when this officer awoke after retiring from his shift, he found only normal entries in what appeared to be his own handwriting. There was no mention of the incident. Due to an accident to the left-handed officer's hand, he was obliged to use his right hand for writing. He had to use considerable pressure, so that an imprint was always left on the page underneath. No such impressions appeared in the log.

The frigate eventually arrived at the port of Valparaiso. After breakfast the men on duty during the incident were asked to report to the ship's commander, who said that some people would interview them. The visitors, two Chilean Navy officers and four Spanish-speaking Americans in civilian clothes – the latter from the US Naval Attaché's office – questioned the witnesses in separate rooms in an ordnance store at the port. 'Explain what happened last night,' they ordered Chalker's witness. He related the incident.

'No, you didn't see that!' came the response.

'That's what we saw,' protested the witness.

'No, you didn't see it. Go walk around here, smoke if you like, but remember, you didn't see anything. You know nothing.'

'Are we under arrest or what?' the witness asked one of the Chilean Navy men, a tactical commander.

'No, you are not.'

'Then why are we here, then?'

'You are under orders. These people just want to talk to you, to put you on the right track.'

The witnesses were not asked by the questioners to relate the story in detail: it was evident from their questions that they were aware of what had happened. 'They also had a radar-plot blueprint,' the witness claimed.

'According to my informant,' said Chalker, 'the group were not talking to him to find out what had happened, but rather they were telling him it never happened, to forget about it. This went on for two days. Every two hours, the guy would come up [and say],"What do you think now?" He was more than "cranky" with this bloke. "We couldn't come out [and] we had arguments," he said. "They didn't have the right to do what they were doing." ' The witness was threatened as well, reports Chalker:

> My informant told them he would complain when he got out. He was told that if he did that, it would be the end of him. He never saw the other witnesses at all during the two days. He was not allowed to sleep until he signed a document they put in front of him. After he signed it, he was taken by jeep to another location. One week later he was transferred unexpectedly from frigate duty. He never saw the others again.

'The witness was very convincing in his re-telling,' concluded Bill Chalker. 'He seemed not to be telling a story, rather, he was passionately relating something that had happened to him.'[5] Understandably, Chalker still refuses to disclose the surname of his informant. 'He has served his term of service, but fears that if it got out that he was responsible for leaking details of the incident, enforced military service could be used as a form of censure.'[6]

A USO IN VIETNAM

While serving on the US Navy destroyer USS *Leary* (DD-879) during its 1969 Western Pacific (WESTPAC) Cruise in the Vietnam War, Ensign Will Miller, US Naval Reserve (now retired at the rank of commander) and some crew members had a night-time encounter with an unidentified submergible object (USO). 'At the time of the incident, we were positioning ourselves in the Gulf of Tonkin for a shore bombardment mission,' Miller recounted when I met him in 2005.

We were a gunfire-support ship, and because we were approaching fishing grounds offshore, we had to be on the alert for wooden Vietnamese fishing craft. These boats had lights on their bows with which to attract their catch in the dark, and trailed fishing nets behind them. It was a hazy night, so I told the Port lookout to let me know when he saw the fishermen's bow light change from just a diffused glow in the distance to a brighter glow with an intense center light. We would then turn the ship to avoid the vessel. 'I see the glow,' the lookout reported, and I took a bearing to the light.

However, the light suddenly moved from above the water to *below* it, and moved rapidly toward our destroyer at 45 degrees to the bow, passing directly beneath the ship. We ran to the starboard side to see if the object had emerged, but there was nothing. Nothing was seen on our sonar, our surface radar, our ECM [electronic countermeasure] system. Whatever the object was, it wasn't a submarine. We decided against waking the Captain, but I directed that a Deck Log entry be made of the event, since we were required, like all naval vessels, to report any unusual observations such as this.

All the ships' original logs were always re-transcribed for official submission. Years later, I reviewed USS *Leary*'s logs at the Naval Historical Center for the period of the incident, but there was absolutely no record of the event in the official log book.[7]

Many UFO events were reported during the Vietnam War. General George S. Brown, former US Air Force Chief of Staff, for example, confirmed that in the early summer of 1968 and in 1969 what were initially thought to be enemy helicopters were fired on by elements of the Army, but that 'there was no enemy at all involved'. (See p. 294.)

GIANT UFO DISRUPTS OPERATIONS ON US AIRCRAFT CARRIER

James M. Kopf (YN3) served as a communications specialist – with Top Secret Crypto clearance – on the aircraft carrier USS *John F. Kennedy* (CVA-67, now CV-67) of the US Sixth Fleet. One evening in June/July 1971, the carrier was approaching the completion of an Operational Readiness Exercise (ORE) in the Caribbean when an incident occurred following an eighteen-hour period simulating General Quarters ('battle stations').

'I was in the Communications Center, and we had several different areas there in main communications,' Kopf explained to me during our meeting in 2005.

We had ship-to-ship teletype circuits, ship-to-shore teletype circuits, and what they called the Fleet Broadcasts, and these consisted of four primary channels and four alternate channels – eight teletypes altogether. There were two rows; the primaries were the top row, the alternates the bottom row. My job at the time was to monitor the messages as they came in. We had a big 'guard list' hanging up on the walls, and any messages which weren't on that guard list I simply removed and filed on a clipboard, in chronological order.

These messages were susceptible to 'garble', and when this happened I would immediately call the next room – Facilities Control – and they would fine-tune the receivers and then check the equipment to try and keep the garble from coming through. If one started acting up, normally the second one was good because they use different frequencies and could be fixed by patching the two frequencies up. But this particular evening, at around 20:30, they all started playing up – they were all typing garbage. I called Facilities Control and said that all my fleet broadcasts were out. And the response was that *all* communications were out! You could hear people yelling at each other.

I don't know how many minutes went by, but we had a pneumatic tube which went up to the signal bridge, which is located on top of the 'island' – the Navigational Bridge. And over this intercom we heard someone (a boatswain's mate) on the bridge say, 'It's God – it's the end of the world!' There were five of us sailors in the communications centre, and we kind of looked at each other. Then a more rational voice (from a signalman) got on the intercom: 'Man, there's something hovering over the ship!' So, a guy named Dennis Jordan looked at me and said, 'Let's go up!'

The communications centre is amidships, under the flight deck. We went through Facilities Control and down a passageway that leads to the catwalk on the edge of the flight deck, on the port side of the ship. And we looked toward the 'island', and up in the sky there's this huge, glowing sphere, at an elevation of between 60 and 70 degrees. This thing was kind of an orangeish colour – it pulsated, slowly, between an orange and a lighter yellow. There was no sound. It must have been pretty big – you couldn't tell just how big because there was no point of reference, but anyway, it seemed huge. Dennis and I only got to see it for less than a minute at most, because then General Quarters sounded and we had to get back to our battle station.

I don't remember exactly how long it was, but shortly the messages started to return to normal. We remained in General Quarters for

about two hours, and then returned to normal Standing Orders. I
didn't get to bed before 04:00 – we were all talking about it. A friend
who worked on the radar console in the Combat Information Center
(CIC) told me that all the radarscopes were glowing, and then cut out
altogether. The signalman who first alerted us to the object hovering
above the ship told me that someone had to be taken to the sick bay
and sedated: I assumed that was the boatswain's mate who yelled
about God and the end of the world.

I also learned from a guy on the bridge that, during the approximately 20 minutes the object hovered over the ship, none of the
compasses was working properly, and that most electrical components
and systems stopped functioning. The two F-4 Phantom jets on Ready
Combat Air Patrol (CAP) – always in a state of high readiness – would
not start.

There were 5,000 men aboard the carrier, but I don't think there
were more than eighteen men who saw this thing, the reason being
that everyone was so exhausted from the flight operations involved in
the Exercise, and they were either trying to get something to eat or to
sleep. And I learned that the Commanding Officer, Captain Ferdinand
B. Koch, was freaked out: he felt so helpless because the air defenses
didn't work. I believe that photos were taken of the object by officers
from IOIC – Integrated Operations Intelligence Communications. I
also heard that three or four plain-clothed men came aboard the ship,
and interviewed those personnel who had seen the object. Dennis and
I were not interviewed, maybe because so few people knew that we
had seen it.

I think it was two days later that the Commanding Officers and
Executive Officers came on our closed-circuit television to say how
well, overall, we had done in the ORE, and to announce a 30-day
stand-down to allow the crew to go on leave when we arrived in
Norfolk, Virginia. At the end of their briefing, Captain Koch looked at
the camera and said: 'I would like to remind the crew that certain
events that take place aboard a Naval Combatant Ship are considered
classified, and they will not be discussed with anyone without a need
to know.' And that's all he said.

Years later I had an e-mail from a crew member of DP (data
processor) rank who was in charge of certain computers on the ship.
He said he had been awakened and told that the computers were
down, so he went to the computer room to try and get them restarted.
He was told that a UFO had been responsible, which he thought was
a joke – until he read on-line about my experience.

I still don't know what it was we saw. Because it was almost above us, I have wondered if it might have been saucer-shaped, but appearing like a sphere. It looked like something physical . . .[8]

I have discussed the USS *John F. Kennedy* incident, and others involving UFO events reported from aircraft carriers, with Rear Admiral Joseph J. Barth Jr, Commanding Officer of the USS *Forrestal* aircraft carrier (CV-59) from 1975 to 1977. He questions several aspects of the *Kennedy* report. 'As for the glowing sphere hovering over the ship, and the failure of radar and navigational systems,' he told me, for example, 'this is a happening which most certainly would have been reported with some urgency. The report system used by the Navy at that time, and probably still used, is called the OPREP or Operational Reporting System. These reports were numbered One through Four. My guess is that this incident would have generated an OPREP 3. These reports should be available by now. The Ship's Log books are kept in Navy Archives and are normally unclassified.'[9]

I put this to Jim Kopf, who during his tour of duty on the *Kennedy* spent a year and a half in the navigation department, and wrote reports in one of the ship's two logs. 'RADM Barth is correct that a report of the incident would have been sent to an appropriate authority. [However], if there really is a government cover-up on UFO activities, that report will never be seen.'[10] Indeed, this is standard practice.

In a letter to former US Navy submarine officer President Jimmy Carter (who sighted a UFO in 1969), a then serving Navy Cryptologic Officer wrote as follows:

For eight active years, plus six years of enthusiastic interest, I have followed the UFO phenomenon as close as my duties have allowed . . . I have heard of sightings which were experienced aboard Navy ships, on board Naval Stations, and by Navy personnel on their off-duty time. I have heard of cases where Air Force officers would speak quite freely of UFOs over cocktails, but would at the same time state that to mention such officially would probably jeopardize or end their career . . .

I believe that our Government not only needs to make any and all UFO data available, but, further, that official statements should be brought forward declassifying all data [and] that anyone having such information be invited to bring it forward, and should doubt exist as to the information's possible National Security impact, that they forward that information through their respective intelligence service, who would sanitize it for release to interested investigative bodies.

Such an official attitude would prevent ships' OOD's [Officers of the Day] from saying, 'Let's not enter this mess in the deck log' . . . Specifically, there are classified instructions within the Department of Defense and other Departments which require holding back such information which might be found in US Navy ships' deck logs, CIC logs, and/or other records of all classifications.[11]

THE DISAPPEARANCE OF *STING 27*

Bermuda Triangle specialist Gian J. Quasar reports the mysterious disappearance of a Phantom II jet, *Sting 27*, during a short routine flight out of Homestead Air Force Base, south of Miami, Florida, on 10 September 1971. The plane took off at 08:05, and its last radar return was noted at 08:22, 82 miles to the south-east. The jet was in a turn after having come out of Mach 1 speed, explains Quasar. 'At this time "Blissful Control" noticed *Sting 27*'s SIF (Selective Identification Feature) get weaker. "*Sting 27*, your SIF feature is fading. We're having trouble identifying you. Is that you at the boundary of Alpha six?" Lieutenant Norm Northrup, in training under Captain John Romero in the back seat, responded, "Roger, I am in a port turn at this time." Radar confirmed Northrup's message. *Sting 27* turned left to a northerly heading, then right again. "During the right turn, radar contact was lost at 8:22 A.M." states the report.'

No trace of *Sting 27* was ever found, despite searches in the area both by other Phantoms (*Sting 29* and *Sting 30*) and the Coast Guard cutter *Steadfast*. Quasar notes that the official accident report had been considerably censored. 'Even the standard summary sheet,' he writes, 'has been subjected to a skilled razor. This extends even to the answer box for the question "What type of accident?" Usually the answer is "missing/unknown" and does not require editing.' The report implies that some type of collision or impact in mid-air occurred. Tellingly, an 'object' was reported by the other two Phantoms when they were vectored to *Sting 27*'s last radar spot. Quasar continues:

According to the report, only minutes after *Sting 27* vanished, *Sting 29* dropped down to 1,500 feet to get a closer look at an 'area of disturbance' in the ocean and then described it – in the words of the report – as 'an area of water discoloration, oblong in shape, approximately 100 by 200 feet, with its axis running north/south; its southern tip appeared to be below the surface and the northern end appeared to be above'. The report does not offer it as a 'UFO' or its submarine equivalent 'USO', for a gap takes the place of any Air Force opinion or clarification – the explanatory paragraph is neatly hacked out . . .

No trace of discoloration was found by the Coast Guard cutter when it arrived in the area shortly afterwards, and sonar did not reveal any trace of *Sting 27* on the ocean-bed area.[12]

AN INTERNATIONAL INCIDENT

An incident when an unknown craft appeared during a NATO naval exercise off the coast of Russia was revealed by a crew member on board one of three Royal Canadian Navy destroyers at the scene. The incident occurred on a clear September day in 1974, as thirty ships of Allied nations were winding up more than three weeks of manoeuvres off the port of Murmansk. Suddenly, all attention was centred on an elongated aerial object that appeared low over the water on the fringe of the area.

The Canadian crew member, who was about one mile away, described the object as silvery in colour, approximately the size of a DC-8 airliner (length 150 feet, wingspan 142 feet) and with a dome on top. It swayed from side to side as it hovered. While hundreds of crewmen watched and radar sets registered a solid blip from the intruder, aircraft aboard the carrier USS *John F. Kennedy*, flagship of the exercise, were ordered to intercept. As twenty or more jets roared into action, the UFO ascended until it disappeared. The aircraft were then called back. An order went out that those present were not to report what they had seen.

The Canadian crewman added an amusing detail. For three weeks, the NATO manoeuvres had been tracked by two Russian destroyers which had left shortly before the sighting, obviously realizing that the exercise was about to end. However, when the unknown craft appeared, the Russians returned and sent two jets to join the US Navy pack in pursuit of the intruder! 'It was striking evidence,' added the witness, 'that the UFO mystery overrides all national barriers.'[13]

The superpowers were to become increasingly united in a growing concern about the alien intruders.

SOUTH-WEST OF BERMUDA

On 23 April 1976, a certain US Navy destroyer was steaming about 700 miles out in the Atlantic just south-west of Bermuda, bound for Boston. At

02:40, First Lieutenant Hedison (pseudonym), on communications duty, was alerted by the officer of the deck to an unidentified green light low in the sky at 'zero-zero-zero' – dead ahead – through light fog, at an estimated distance of 3 miles. Hedison checked with the ship's Combat Information Center, but nothing had been detected ahead.

Stepping on to the wing of the bridge, Hedison and the bridge lookouts observed the green light drop to within 30 or 40 feet of the ocean surface and appear to head towards them on a collision course. Still nothing had been detected by radar or sonar. Hedison ordered a 90-degree turn to starboard. 'As the ship heeled around,' reported investigator Donald R. Todd, 'the light, now closer and more prominent through the fog, became a solid green glow of considerable size – and had made a similar 90-degree turn to port – and was now pacing the destroyer.'

> Hedison ordered another 90-degree turn to starboard, putting the destroyer now on a reverse course, away from Boston. The UFO likewise turned to starboard, came in closer to within about 50 or 60 feet, and continued to pace the ship. Suddenly the destroyer emerged from the fog, and the radar shack erupted with excitement. A sudden large blip appeared on the scope, and now half of the ship's complement had been awakened and was on the decks, watching.

As Hedison ordered the helmsman to bring the destroyer back to its original heading of 292 degrees, the UFO immediately followed around in a wide, 180-degree arc, and took up position some distance off the destroyer's port beam. At this point, the captain came on the bridge.

> Simultaneously with the Captain's arrival, the UFO rose towards their bows as if going up an inclined plane, and leisurely circled the ship twice. Then once again off the port beam, it descended at moderate speed, heightened its green brilliance, then, tilted at an angle, it entered the water with its leading edge. During the encirclement of the destroyer, the Captain, Lieutenant Hedison, and some of the crew had been observing the UFO-USO with binoculars. Once the object entered the water, it seemed to sink at a gradual angle until only a dim green glow could be distinguished beneath the water.

All personnel on the bridge and deck were advised by the captain to forget the incident, a warning later repeated twice via the general announcing system. According to Hedison, the destroyer's captain made an entry in the ship's log to the effect that his ship had manoeuvred so as to avoid collision in fog with another, unidentified ship, which 'appeared to be a Russian trawler'.[14]

SOVIET NAVAL INTELLIGENCE

In 1977 Dr Vladimir Azhazha, then a Soviet Navy submarine officer specializing in hydroacoustics, was asked by Vice-Admiral Y.V. Ivanov, head of Naval Intelligence, to carry out research into 'hydrospheric aspects of the UFO issue'. One case Azhazha investigated took place on 7 October 1977, when the *Volga*, a 'floating base' ship for submarine maintenance, encountered UFOs 200 miles from the Kola Peninsula in the Barents Sea. 'There were nine in all,' he reported, 'and for eighteen minutes while they were flying around the *Volga*, all radio communications were blacked out.'[15]

Azhazha confirmed that, like other Navy reports on UFO/USO incidents which he studied for ten years, the above report was classified top secret. 'There were too many incidents which could not be denied,' he told Jacques Vallée and Martine Castello in 1990.

> It all began when we tried to understand the nature of certain underwater objects that followed our submarines. At times they even anticipated our maneuvers! Initially, we thought they were American devices. One day such an object came to the surface in a rather spectacular fashion. One of our ice-breakers was working its way in the Arctic Ocean when a brilliant spherical craft suddenly broke out of the ice and flew up vertically, showering the vessel with fragments of ice. All the sailors on deck and the officers on the bridge saw it. And it was hard to deny the hole in the ice![16]

*

In an interview on UC-13 TV in 2002, Admiral Jorge Martinez Bush, former Commander-in-Chief of the Chilean Navy, confirmed that 'UFOs are real'. He cited two observations of UFOs he made during his career, including one when he had been in command of the destroyer *Lord Cochrane* in May 1970. Regarding USOs, he declared: 'There have been submarine contacts impossible to identify, with the characteristics of a submarine – metallic sound and rapid displacement. There are inexplicable things that require a more profound study . . .'[17]

REFERENCES

1. Galíndez, Oscar A., 'Crew of Argentine Ship See *Submarine* UFO', *Flying Saucer Review*, Vol. 14, No. 2, March–April 1968, p. 22.

2. Ledger, Don, 'UFO Crash at Shag Harbour', *International UFO Reporter*, Vol. 22, No. 4, Winter 1997–98, pp. 8–9, 20.

3. Ledger, Don and Styles, Chris, *Dark Object: The World's Only Government-documented UFO Crash*, ed. Whitley Strieber, Dell, New York, 2001.

4. Chalker, Bill, 'EM UFO Incident off Chile in 1969', *The APRO Bulletin*, Vol. 33, No. 3, 1986, pp. 7–8, first published in *International UFO Reporter*, September/October 1985, pp. 4–6.

5. Chalker, *The APRO Bulletin*, Vol. 33, No. 5, 1986, pp. 5–6, also in *International UFO Reporter*, ibid.

6. Chalker, *The APRO Bulletin*, Vol. 33, No. 3, p. 8, also in *International UFO Reporter*, ibid.

7. Personal interview, Tampa, Florida, 12 April 2005.

8. Personal interview, Mount Airy, Maryland, 25 September 2005.

9. Letter, 1 June 2005.

10. Email, 21 July 2005.

11. Bryant, Larry W., *UFO Politics at the White House: Citizens Rally Round Jimmy Carter's Promise*, The Invisible College Press LLC, PO Box 209, Woodbridge, VA 22194-0209, 2001, pp. 44–7. http://www.invispress.com

12. Quasar, Gian J., *Into the Bermuda Triangle: Pursuing the Truth Behind the World's Greatest Mystery*, McGraw-Hill, 2004, pp. 35–6.

13. 'UFO Watches NATO Fleet', *Canadian UFO Report*, Vol. 4, No. 4, Summer 1977.

14. Todd, Donald R., 'Ship's Crew Sees UFO', *The APRO Bulletin*, Vol. 26, No. 11, May 1978, pp. 1–2.

15. Interview with Lawrence Moore and Livia Russell, Moscow, March 1994.

16. Vallée, Jacques, with Castello, Martine, *UFO Chronicles of the Soviet Union: A Cosmic Samizdat*, Ballantine, New York, 1992, pp. 27–8.

17. Huneeus, J. Antonio, 'USOs in Chile and Peru', *Fate*, Vol. 56, No. 1, January 2003, pp. 6–7.

EXCERPTS: PRESS REMARKS CONCERNING UFOs

BY GENERAL GEORGE S. BROWN,

CHIEF OF STAFF, USAF

October 16, 1973

Q. General, one more question. What is the Air Force's position
on the UFO business?

I don't know whether this story has ever been told or not. They
weren't called UFOs. They were called enemy helicopters. And
they were only seen at night and they were only seen in certain
places. They were seen up around the DMZ in the early summer of
'68. And this resulted in quite a little battle. And in the course
of this an Australian destroyer took a hit and we never found any
enemy, we only found ourselves when this had all been sorted out.
And this caused some shooting there and there was no enemy at all
involved but we always reacted. Always after dark. The same thing
happened up at Pleiku at the Highlands in '69. And we found there
that they had moved the radar in and the Army started to work and
we finally got that radar out of there and then they quit worrying
about their problem.

General George S. Brown, Chief of Staff, US Air Force, admits that UFOs were
observed during the Vietnam War. *(The National Archives, Washington)*

20. A GLOBAL PHENOMENON

Since UFO sightings began to proliferate in the Second World War, for decades practically no information was available from the country with the largest population in the world – the People's Republic of China. But in the late 1970s articles started appearing in newspapers and magazines describing sightings going back to the war. It is important to note that the majority of Chinese, living as they did at that time in an isolated society, were unlikely to have been influenced by Western reports about such things, thus making their testimony more compelling.

In 1980 what became the China UFO Research Organization (CURO) was founded, with branches in Beijing, Shanghai and in many provinces. As mentioned in the introduction, CURO is affiliated to the China Association for Science and Technology, and by 1992 had 3,600 full members as well as 40,000 research associates. Even allowing proportionately for its huge population, no other country in the world has matched China in this respect. Moreover, these figures do not take into account the number of Chinese Secret Service personnel engaged in monitoring the phenomenon worldwide. Most of China's UFO researchers are scientists and engineers, and many UFO groups require both a college degree and published research for membership.

In January 1964 many citizens in Shanghai observed a huge cigar-shaped aerial object flying slowly towards the south-west. MiG jet fighters of the People's Liberation Army Air Force were scrambled in pursuit, but failed to force the UFO down. The object was officially explained as an 'American missile'.[1] In early 1968, four artillerymen of the Navy garrison at Luda, in China's northern province of Liaoning, observed a luminous gold, oval-shaped object flying at a low altitude, leaving a thin trail. As it began to climb steeply before disappearing, all communications and radar systems failed, almost causing an accident in the fleet. The naval patrol went on alert, and the fleet commander ordered his men to prepare for combat. Half an hour later communications and radar returned to normal. A two-man coastguard patrol reportedly saw the UFO land on the south coast and fired at it with automatic rifles and machine guns, but soldiers sent to investigate found no trace of the object.[2]

In mid-April 1968, at a construction site in the north Gobi Desert, a battalion of soldiers witnessed the landing of a luminous red-orange disc with a diameter of about 10 feet. A team of motorcycle troops was dispatched from the regiment's headquarters to approach the object, at which point it took off vertically and disappeared. Most witnesses dismissed the object as some kind of Soviet reconnaissance device, since the northern frontier with the USSR passed through the region.[3]

ALGERIA

In 2000, together with my principal associate, the late Graham Sheppard, a retired British Airways captain (who had had two radar/visual-confirmed sightings of UFOs while flying in 1967),[4] I interviewed several important new witnesses in Paris, including Jean-Pierre Morin, a former deputy manager of security for the Centre National d'Etudes Spatiales (CNES, France's equivalent of NASA).

Hammaguir, a military base on a high plateau to the south of Colomb-Béchar in Algeria's Sahara Desert, was used as a French missile testing and development site from the mid-1950s until France was required to evacuate the base in 1967, following Algerian independence. One night in January that year, Morin was with a group of six people, three of them well-known astrophysicists, preparing a rocket for launch the following morning.

'I was driving three members of the team to the launch tower in a Citröen 2CV,' Morin told us. 'When we arrived at a row of buildings, the man next to me pointed out a light in the sky, which at first we took to be a plane. But all the lights of the airfield were out. The light started to come right towards us, though not very rapidly. And then something happened to my engine – it started running "rough", and stopped by itself. Immediately we got out of the car.'

> There was no Moon that night, only millions of stars clearly visible in the desert air. We watched as the light slowly came closer, without making any sound. We got the impression of a very heavy, a very stable object. It seemed to come to within about 500 metres from us, and remained stationary at an elevation of 45 degrees. To me, it was a black object, by contrast with the stars, and it had a cylindrical shape, along the length of which I saw 'flames' of different colours – it was probably the air that was ionized.

We were completely stunned. It seemed to us that it was a very large object, 300 to 400 metres [984 to 1,312 feet] in length. And then I remember a 'tinkling' sound in my ears, like I get when I dive 10 to 12 metres in the sea. I don't know if it was because we were paralysed, but we couldn't communicate. We tried to understand why this object was so silent. Its speed was very slow. What we saw was incredible. After this, it moved on at the same speed, very low.

Then the car with the astrophysicists arrived: they had seen us standing in the road and thought we'd broken down. Astonished, they watched the object with us for about 20 or 30 minutes, as it continued on the same trajectory. Then it angled upwards, heading in the direction of the Orion constellation, and vanished.

Morin's sketch of the object shows a perfect cylinder with sharp ends, the ratio of the measurements approximately 10:1. Thus, assuming a length of 1,000 feet, it would have been 100 feet in diameter.

'I was a young engineer at the time,' Morin explained to us, 'and not all that experienced in the space business. But now, looking back after forty years in the business, I'm certain that that craft was of a technology which we certainly haven't reached today . . .'[5]

MADAGASCAR

During a daylight reconnaissance exercise in May 1967, a detachment of officers serving with the French Foreign Legion in Madagascar observed the landing – in 'falling leaf' motion – of an unknown flying machine. It shone very brightly and was surrounded by 'an intense, dazzling glow' that dissipated when it touched down, on tripod legs. Seven to eight metres in height, the egg-shaped craft had no visible markings, apart from several openings on the base, from which 'flames' emitted. Just as described by the French witnesses to the Algerian event in January that year, the 'flames' were described as 'not normal flames [and] must surely have been something else'.

'There were twenty-three of us Legionnaires, with one officer and four non-commissioned officers,' reported a witness. 'And we were all paralysed. All of us saw the machine land and take off again, *but none of us perceived the lapse of time* . . . when the machine had departed, we all recovered the use of our limbs . . . But when we checked up on the time, it was now 15:15. Two and three-quarter hours had passed without our perceiving it.

'Headquarters ordered us not to approach the landing site, and not to discuss the matter among ourselves. Some specialists arrived from Paris to interrogate us. We were made to swear on oath that we would keep it secret. We were visited by the doctors, and we were made to undergo tests. For two days after the event we all had violent headaches, with a buzzing in the ears and a powerful beating in the area of the temples. We were not told the results of the tests . . .'[6]

CUBA

Shortly after midnight on 14 June 1968, several bursts of machine-gun fire were heard coming from a location in the vicinity of Cabañas, where Cuban soldier Isidro Puentes Ventura was on guard duty. At dawn, Puentes was found unconscious by an Army patrol. He was taken to a hospital in Pinar del Río, where he remained in shock for six days, unable to speak. He was then taken to the Naval hospital in Havana, where he was diagnosed to be suffering from emotional trauma. He remained in shock for a second week.

At the site where Puentes had been posted, Cuban and Soviet intelligence specialists found forty-eight spent cartridges and fourteen bullets apparently flattened by impact with something solid, as well as equally spaced indentations on the ground indicating that a heavy device had landed. Tests revealed that the soil had been exposed to a high temperature. On recovering, Puentes explained that he had come to within 50 metres of a brilliant round object on the ground, with a dome and several 'antennas' on top. Convinced that the device was American, he fired about forty rounds at it. The craft turned orange and emitted a strong whistling sound – Puentes' last recollection before losing consciousness. Soviet intelligence specialists subjected Puentes to a fifty-hour interrogation, after which he was put through fifteen hypnosis sessions. No contradictions were found in his story.[7]

SAUDI ARABIA

On an undisclosed date around 1970, the crew of a US Air Force C-5A Galaxy transport, flying at 500 mph at 37,000 feet, encountered an unknown craft over Maula Idris, Saudi Arabia. Nicholas Crossland recounted for me the testimony of a friend of his, an RAF officer on detachment (name on file) who was flying the plane. The object was described by the pilot as 'semi-spherical, like two saucers joined together, surrounded by the colours red, green, and yellow', and it was estimated to be at about 75,000 feet altitude. At the debriefing, USAF personnel were particularly interested in the colours displayed by the object.[8]

TURKEY

During my participation in an international UFO congress in Istanbul in December 2001, organized by the Sirius UFO Space Sciences Research Centre, I spoke to two retired Turkish Air Force fighter pilots who had encountered UFOs. One was Süleyman Tekyildirim, who told me and Graham Sheppard, also participating in the conference, that on 17 June 1969 his base was alerted to the presence of an unidentified flying object. He was ordered to intercept it in a US-built F-5A Freedom Fighter.

'It was grey, and like an upside-down light bulb,' he told us. 'I flew above it and reported that it was probably a meteorological balloon. As I continued describing it, it moved to my left and moved off at a fantastic speed. Obviously it wasn't a balloon! I did everything I could to try and catch it, but just couldn't keep up. I suggested to the base that F-104 Starfighters would stand a better chance. I also proposed firing at the object – but they forbade that. Eventually it disappeared.'[9]

The other pilot we spoke to was Sefik Ayanoğlu, who said in a newspaper interview that only 25 per cent of Turkish pilots dare to speak publicly about their encounters, but that all UFO reports are collected and studied at Eskisehir Control Centre.[10]

Between 24 and 27 October 1969, sightings of a UFO over Turkey's capital, Ankara, excited much interest. The Turkish Air Force was inundated with reports, and jet fighters were scrambled from Murtad Air Base. The jets closed to within 12,000 metres, but the UFO always maintained a distance by climbing higher. The game of cat and mouse continued over several days. Eventually the base commander himself, Ercüment Gökaydin, flew with the interceptors. 'Our planes reached a height of 35,000 feet,' he wrote in his report, 'but the object was at a height of at least 50,000 feet. It was oval in shape, and a silvery colour. There was no other countries' traffic in the area at the time, or prototypes under test.'

The jets took gun-camera film, which has not been released. One pilot who managed to get closer said the object had three round windows like portholes.[11]

THAILAND

In 1974 a revealing letter was published in the British *Flying Saucer Review* from Sergeant Terry W. Colvin, an officer stationed with a Royal Thai Air Force unit on the Laos border. Colvin had included a report of the sighting of an unknown, structured craft seen in a suburb of Bangkok in the late summer of that year, which he translated in the letter. He continued:

> I am unable to gather more details as I am currently assigned to an isolated signal relay site in N.E. Thailand near the *amphur* (district) town of Mukdahan. But I have hearsay accounts from US Air Force personnel that several of the F-111s lost during combat in S.E. Asia disappeared just as inexplicably as the two which disappeared in the state of Nevada, USA, in 1972.
>
> Also, an F-4 Phantom jet fighter-bomber vanished from radar screens simultaneously, as visual contact was lost by the wingman. No debris was recovered, and enemy fire was not suspected as the incident occurred over Thailand, just a few miles from Ubon Royal Thai Air Force Base.[12]

KOREA

At 10:00 one morning in the autumn of 1974, radar at an Air Defence Artillery site at Binn, South Korea, picked up a fast-moving target. At 700 yards, visual contact was made with a massive, oval-shaped, glowing metallic craft, estimated to be 300 feet in diameter and 30 feet in depth, with red and green pulsating lights moving anti-clockwise around the rim. Suddenly the huge craft came to a halt, at less than 700 yards range, its lights blinking rapidly.

'The Captain of D Battery gave orders to fire the first Hawk missile,' reports Leonard Stringfield. 'Ignited, it started off the pad. In clear view of the men waiting anxiously from a remote-control zone, the missile, according to my informant at the scene, "never made it". It was hit by a beam of intense white light and destroyed. So was the launcher. Both were melted down "like lead toys". In a matter of minutes, the unidentified craft, making a noise like a swarm of bees, departed from Binn at extraordinary speed, and disappeared from the radarscope.

'My informant relates that the captain of D Battery was dumb-founded,' Stringfield continues. 'In everyone's view was a melted mass representing millions of dollars of highly sophisticated equipment. Fortunately, because of the missile base's remote-control mechanism, there were no casualties. The next day, all members of the battalion on duty were summoned to a secret meeting and told by the commanding officer that the disaster was *absolutely hush-hush*. But, regardless of UFO secrecy, the men on the base never felt secure again . . .'[13]

MEXICO

On 3 May 1975, a young Mexican pilot, Carlos Antonio de los Santos Montiel, was harassed by three 10-to-12-foot discs while flying a Piper PA-24 Comanche (XB-XAU). Two of the discs positioned themselves at each wingtip while the third went underneath and bumped the plane, causing damage. The controls were temporarily frozen and the pilot was unable to lower the landing gear. He declared a Mayday. Eventually the discs left, and he was able to fix the landing gear after adjustments to the control lever with a screwdriver. He made a successful emergency landing at Mexico City International Airport.[14]

GERMANY

At about 17:00 on 13 August 1976, D.W., a thirty-three-year-old private pilot, was flying a Piper Arrow PA-28 (R-200) on a heading between Diepholz and Petershagen, Germany, when he noticed a strange light approaching at his 9 o'clock position. 'Initially the UFO seemed to be a great distance away,' reports investigator Dr Richard F. Haines, 'but over a 3–5 minute period, it came closer and closer, taking a fixed position off his left wing for several more minutes at an unknown but apparently near distance.' The very bright object appeared to be oval-shaped, with a yellowish centre and flame-orange boundary.

Suddenly the Piper went into two rapid 360-degree clockwise rolls, from which the pilot recovered manually, losing 500 feet altitude. The magnetic compass was spinning in a clockwise direction so fast that he couldn't read the numbers. The UFO remained alongside. D.W. reported the event to Hannover Airport. A controller confirmed that they were tracking both his plane and another nearby object, and that aircraft would be sent to investigate.

Four minutes later, two US Air Force F-4 Phantom jets flew by, one on either side of the Piper, at an estimated 400–500 mph. Just as the jets arrived, the UFO accelerated forward, and then upward at about a 30-degree angle, and turned right, passing in front of the Piper. It quickly outdistanced the pursuing Phantoms, and was out of sight in seconds.

D.W. was directed to land at Hannover, some 45 miles east-south-east of his position, and ordered to taxi to a special area. Within minutes, a military van without licence plates pulled up to his plane, and five men in suits got out. They would not identify who they worked for. The pilot was taken to an underground room at the airport where a man sat behind a desk. Two of the original men left the room. The others began asking D.W. detailed questions in German about the sighting: he had the impression that one of the men was American.

The questioning went on for about three hours. At one point D.W. was politely asked to read and sign a form printed in German. It stated that he agreed never to disclose the details of his UFO sighting. He declined to sign the form, despite the fact that it was firmly suggested that his licence might be suspended. After this, he was released. 'As would be expected under the circumstances, he was emotionally upset by these events,'[15] writes Dr Haines, a former NASA-contracted research scientist, who is currently scientific director of the National Aviation Reporting Center on Anomalous Phenomena (NARCAP).[16]

IRAN

In two previous books I described in detail the sensational case of the interception of a UFO by F-4 Phantom jets of the Imperial Iranian Air Force over Tehran in the small hours of 19 September 1976. The essential details are contained in a previously secret US Air Force Security Service article (reproduced on pp. 315–17), which references the communications and instrumentation failures experienced by the crew of the first jet, which was forced to return to base. Another F-4 was ordered to intercept. At one point, a second UFO detached from the main one and headed straight for the jet. The pilots attempted to fire a guided missile at it, but a sudden loss of power in the weapons control system prevented them from doing so. Communications were simultaneously lost.

Important additional information not included in that article appeared in a 1994 *Sightings* television documentary, which featured interviews with some of the military personnel involved. It was revealed, for example, that following the abortive attempt by the crew of the second F-4 (commanded by Iran's then 'top-gun' pilot, Major Hussan Jafori) to fire an AIM-9 Sidewinder guided missile at the second object, they feared for their lives and tried to eject from the plane, but the eject circuit malfunctioned. As the F-4 approached for landing at Mehrabad Air Force Base, the larger UFO followed it and then described a low-altitude fly-by over the runway, causing an electrical power failure for several seconds. Twenty-five minutes after the UFO disappeared, it was observed by the pilot of an Egyptian Air Force jet over the Mediterranean Sea, and then later by the crew and passengers of KLM Flight 241 in the Lisbon area. Furthermore, Ron Regehr, an analyst with the US Defense Support Program (DSP) satellite system, revealed that a DSP (nuclear-event monitoring) satellite picked up signals from an 'unidentifiable technology' over Iran on the night in question.

Finally, General Mahmoud Sabahat, former Vice-Commander of the 2nd Tactical Fighter Base, disclosed in the documentary that on the day after the incident he attended a top-secret meeting between the head of the Iranian Air Force and Major General Richard Secord, chief of the US Air Force section in Iran, and other personnel. 'When they heard our report and the report of the pilots,' said Hossein Pirouzi, air-traffic supervisor at Mehrabad, 'they concluded that no country is able to have such a technology, and all of them believed it [must] be [an] object from outer space.'[17]

INDIA

In India, as in China, sightings of UFOs were seldom reported for many years: when I was there in 1964, I learned that it was a 'taboo' subject. But in the 1970s a spate of sightings led to a resurgence of public interest, according to Robert F. Dorr, a retired senior diplomat and leading aviation author. Here follows a brief summary of three events he investigated:

— 11 July 1976 – Two Indian Air Force MiG-21 jets were scrambled near the Pakistani border to intercept what was initially thought to be a Pakistani jet, but the object was doing 2,600 mph, and the two pilots reported an amber, saucer-shaped craft which pulled away before they could catch up with it.
— 11 January 1977 – Near Varanasi (Benares), a UFO 'flap' lasting 45 minutes was observed by thousands. The crew of an Indian Air Force jet transport, 42 miles to the west of the city, encountered three luminescent disc-shaped objects which 'flew past, circled once as if inspecting my airplane, then continued eastward toward Varanasi', the pilot stated.

— 16 July 1977 – As an Air India Boeing 747 (Flight 9) made its final
approach to Calcutta's Dum Dum airport at 23:15, air traffic controllers
noticed a second flying object, closing on the 747. No other aircraft had
been given clearance for an approach. Witnesses on the ground reported a
saucer-shaped object, about the same size as a 747, rushing toward the
airliner. Suddenly, the UFO, dangerously close, was visible to most
passengers, and to the crew. It departed two miles from touch-down.
To Captain Dhingra, the object was a 'strange-looking apparition . . . but
a thing of real substance'.[18]

FRANCE

France's Deterrent Force, known officially as 'la Force de Frappe', included
the Dassault Mirage IVA supersonic bomber, which was capable of carrying
a 60-kiloton nuclear weapon. On 7 March 1977, during a training exercise
for night-time bombing, a Mirage IVA based with the 4th Wing at the
French Air Force (l'Armée de l'Air) base at Luxeuil, encountered unknown
traffic. At 20:34, Colonel René Giraud and his navigator, Capitaine Jean-
Paul Abraham, flying over Chaumont at 30,000 feet, en route to Bordeaux,
were surprised by the sudden presence of a bright light.

'I thought it was the landing light of a Mirage III interceptor jet,'
Giraud told me, when I met him at the Dassault chalet at the Paris Air
Show in 2003. 'But we had not been warned about any other traffic. The
light continued to approach. I contacted the control center at Contrexéville,
but they said that nothing showed up on their radar. "What are you doing?
Are you sleeping?" they said. "Check your oxygen!"

'The light was at our 3 o'clock position. We were flying at about Mach
0.95. I made a hard right-hand turn – but the light always stayed inside the
turn. It was about 1,500 metres away, making a faster speed than our plane.
I turned on a reciprocal, and the light shot off at incredible speed. After
about ten seconds, I said to my navigator, "Look out! It's coming back!"
What struck me particularly, when I said this, was a strong feeling that we
were being observed. It was the first time in my life I had experienced
something like that. But there was no feeling of fear.

'We had the feeling that there was a heavy mass behind the light –
something at least as big as a Boeing 747. I made another hard right-hand
turn, almost to the 6 o'clock position, then a reversal. Again, the light shot
off at tremendous speed – I think at least 6,000 to 7,000 km/h – which is
not possible for a plane. And there was no supersonic bang and no shock-

wave. Neither did we experience any effects on the radio or instruments during the encounter.

'When we landed, we didn't say anything for a week. But the radar staff was intrigued – and they wanted explanations, since they had been following our aircraft's manoeuvres! As a Mirage IV pilot, I wasn't permitted to have a "dog-fight" with another plane – even though we weren't carrying a nuclear weapon at the time.

'I couldn't sleep for a week, because I was so emotionally upset. I was very anxious: had there been another such occasion, I would have resigned from the Air Force. Whatever it was, it wasn't an earthly thing. I believe that their space–time is different from ours, so I don't expect to understand everything. From my point of view, its intention was curiosity. They don't want to harm us. If they're coming from another solar system, I think they're of goodwill . . .'[19]

BAY OF BISCAY

In January 2005, the British Ministry of Defence (MoD) released numerous hitherto classified files on UFOs, anticipating a large volume of requests under provisions of the new Freedom of Information laws, enacted that year. Among them was a case involving a Vulcan B.2 bomber. Originally part of the RAF high-altitude nuclear deterrent force, the Vulcan was later used at low altitude in tactical nuclear/conventional roles.

Before the encounter, at 22:20 on 21 May 1977, three airmen stationed at RAF Waddington, Lincolnshire – where a Vulcan squadron was based – observed a triangular-shaped light moving erratically in the sky. Within minutes the light was tracked as an 'unidentified contact', moving in a zigzag manner, at RAF Patrington, some 50 miles north-east of Waddington. The unknown radar contact registered for four minutes on the radarscopes when suddenly the screens were 'partially obliterated by high-powered interference', which returned to normal once the target had disappeared.[20]

Five days later, on 26 May 1977, at 01:15 local time over the Bay of Biscay, the crew of a Vulcan (XL321), based at RAF Scampton in Lincolnshire, flying at 43,000 feet at a speed of Mach 0.86, observed bright lights approaching their track from the west. As in the Mirage IV case, all five crewmen of the Vulcan (piloted by Flight Lieutenant David Edwards) initially thought the lights were 'similar to aircraft landing lights', though they are described in this case as 'with long pencil beam ahead of lights'.

Extracts (verbatim) from the official signal, sent from RAF Scampton to the MoD, follow:

... HEADLIGHT EFFECT THEN DISAPPEARED AS IF THEY HAD BEEN
TURNED OFF OR RETRACTED OR OBJECT TURNED ONTO
RECIPROCAL TRACK. HOWEVER LARGE ORANGE GLOW REMAINED IN
SKY. GLOW WAS LARGE BUT CREW UNABLE TO ESTIMATE SIZE.
GLOW ALSO HAD BRIGHT GREEN FLUORESCENT SPOT IN BOTTOM
RIGHT HAND CORNER. CAPT AND CO-PLT THEN OBSERVED OBJECT
LEAVING FROM MIDDLE OF THE GLOW ON WESTERLY TRACK AND
CLIMBING AT VERY HIGH SPEED AT ANGLE OF 45 DEGREES. OBJECT
LEFT VERY THIN TRAIL SIMILAR TO CONTRAIL ...

NAV RADAR ... OBSERVED INTERFERENCE ON H2S RADAR
SCREEN FROM SAME DIRECTION AND TOOK R88 CAMERA FILM ...
DISTANCE ESTIMATED 40NM BUT DIFFICULT TO QUANTIFY DUE
LACK OF COMPARISON AND GLOW EFFECT ... GLOW REMAINED
STATIC AND VISIBLE FOR SEVERAL MINUTES. RADAR
INTERFERENCE SIMILAR TO NARROW SPOKE AND IN VARIOUS
OTHER JAMMING LIKE FORMS CONTINUED FROM APPARENT
POSITION OF AFTER GLOW FOR 45 MINUTES AFTER VULCAN HAD
TURNED AWAY ...

RADAR PHOTOGRAPHY SHOWS MINOR ELECTRONIC
INTERFERENCE FROM GENERAL DIRECTION OF SIGHTING ... BOTH
SHOTS OF SUBJECT RESPONSE SHOW ELONGATED SHADOW OF NO
SHOW AREA DOWN RANGE THUS INDICATING LARGE SIZE. NOTE
THAT NAV RADAR CLAIMS THAT OPERATION OF TILT CONROL
DOWNWARDS CAUSED THESE RESPONSES TO DISAPPEAR THUS
INDICATING A LARGE OBJECT ABOVE SURFACE AGAIN POSSIBLY AT
SIMILAR HEIGHT ...

A handwritten note on the first page of the signal reveals that the MoD's Civil Service central UFO desk – then known as S4f (Air) – would not be privy to the results of inquiries by a branch of the Defence Intelligence Staff and RAF Ground Environment (Radar) Operations. It reads: 'Spoke to Mr Thompson DI55b and to Sqn Ldr Nicholas – Ops(GE)2(RAF) – and asked them to look out for this signal particularly. I asked them to forward the report to anyone else who should have it if they thought it to be necessary. S4f(Air) will not know the outcome of their enquiries.'[21]

Moreover, the minutes of a meeting between staff of S4f (Air) and DI55 held at Whitehall in May the previous year (1976) state that, 'since investigations into the defence implications of alleged UFO sightings might involve highly classified material it was agreed that S4f(Air) has no "need to know" about enquiries made by any specialist branch ... It followed that detailed reports on such investigations could not be included in the files which would ultimately be disclosed when UFO reports were opened to the public.'[22]

Was S4f (Air) 'out of the loop'? No, says Nick Pope, who headed the MoD's UFO research effort from 1991 to 1994. 'Had the civil servants really been out of the loop,' he told me, 'they would not have received the signals at all – let alone been designated as the lead division. The comments reflect the fact that Defence Intelligence Staff methods and sources were not shared.'[23]

PORTUGAL

On 17 June 1977, José Francisco Rodriguez, a young pilot based with the 31st Squadron of the Portuguese Air Force (Força Aérea Portuguesa) at Tancos, was flying over the Castelo de Bode dam in a Dornier 27 light aircraft in poor weather, when suddenly an unknown, dark object emerged from the clouds slightly to his right. He banked to the left and radioed to ask if there was any traffic in the area. A reply came back in the negative.

Suddenly the object appeared at the pilot's 11 o'clock position 'no more than six metres away'. It was about 13 to 15 metres in diameter, with a lower section on which could be seen four or five 'panels'. The Dornier's electric directional gyroscope rotated wildly, and then the plane began to vibrate violently and went into an uncontrolled dive. Rodriguez struggled to regain control by pushing the control column forward. Airspeed increased to 140 knots, and then to 180 knots, as the ground loomed nearer. Control was regained when almost 'touching the tree tops', and the plane was landed safely. Such was Rodriguez's state of shock that he had difficulty speaking.[24]

No explanation for the incident was forthcoming, though I did receive an official report that includes this and some other incidents from the Portuguese Embassy in London.

SOUTH AFRICA

Back in 1955, the Air Chief of Staff, South African Air Force (SAAF), admitted that the Department of Defence classified official information on the UFO subject as 'Top Secret – Not to be Divulged'. In 1981, during a visit to Cape Town, I learned from a defence source about a tragic case which involved the disappearance of two SAAF pilots and their aircraft. The incident occurred on the day after the Portuguese Air Force Dornier pilot was harassed.

On 18 June 1977, the two pilots, both with fifteen years and 7,000 hours of flying experience, disappeared over the South Atlantic Ocean 40 miles north-west of Lüderitz Bay (Namibia), together with their Mirage F1-CZ jets. The last radio contact was at 10:48. At about 11:15 the planes simply vanished from the radar screens. It was evident that the pilots were frantically trying to communicate with base: the radio call button was being pressed but no transmission could be heard.

A simple accident – perhaps a collision? Both planes were equipped with standard life-saving gear. A Navy ship was in the area within an hour, and a helicopter within two hours. Weather conditions were good; 3/8ths altocumulus at 25,000 feet and high cirrus at 45–50,000 feet – the altitude at which the Mirages were flying. No trace was ever found of either the pilots or the aircraft.[25]

CHILE

In an interview in 2002, retired General Hernán Gabrielli Rojas described his encounter with a UFO during a training flight over the deserts of northern Chile in 1978 (date not given). He was flying one of a pair of F-5F Tiger II jets of the Fuerza Aérea de Chile (FACh). Not far from Antofagasta, the jets' radar alerted the pilots to the presence of an enormous intruder.

'It was noon, and I was flying with Captain Danilo Catalán – we were both flight instructors,' Gabrielli told journalist Cristián Riffo. 'Accompanying us were avionics technician Fernando Gómez and another trainee. The F-5 is radar-equipped, and a line appeared from side to side; in other words, a trace throughout the bottom side of the screen. A trace for a surface ship, a cruiser, is approximately one centimetre long, but this line went from one side of the screen to the other. I assumed the radarscope had failed, and said as much to Catalán, but his radar also failed. I then advised the ground radar at Antofagasta – and they also picked up the line.

'We were occupied with these details when we looked towards the east – we were flying from north to south in the vicinity of Mejillones – and saw a deformed cigar-shaped object, like a plantain banana. It was swathed in smoke.' The general estimated the size of the object as being comparable to that of a dozen aircraft carriers.

Captain Edward J. Ruppelt, the intelligence officer who was the first head of the US Air Force's Project Blue Book.

Major Donald E. Keyhoe, former US Marine Corps pilot and first exposer of the UFO cover-up. *(Fortean Picture Library)*

Leroy Gordon Cooper, the pilot, pioneer astronaut and UFO researcher, to whom this book is dedicated. While stationed in Germany in 1951, Cooper was scrambled on several occasions to intercept flying discs. *(Flight Data Center)*

The Weather

The Washington Post FINAL

Seventy-fifth Year in the Nation's Capital

NO.   27,801   Phone NA. 6700   MONDAY, JULY 29, 1952   WTOP AM -1500; FM (98.3) TV (CH. 9)   FIVE CENTS

'Saucer' Outran Jet, Pilot Reveals

Above. The *Washington Post* lead story for 29 July 1952. *Right.* Pilots and radar navigators outside their F-94B Starfire interceptors at Newcastle AFB, Delaware, at the time of the UFO air alerts above Washington, DC, July 1952. *(UPI Newspictures)*

An F9F Panther jet of the type flown by Marine 1st Lieutenant Eddy P. Balocco when he was scrambled to intercept a UFO in February 1953 near Edenton, North Carolina. *(US Navy via Philip Jarrett)*

Two F-102 Delta Dagger jets, like those scrambled to intercept a stationary object in the sky over California in 1961. The crew calculated its sudden departure at nearly 36,000 mph. *(US Air Force via Robert F. Dorr)*

In June 1953, a Lockheed F-94C Starfire like this one was scrambled to intercept an unknown target at Otis AFB, Massachusetts. Shortly after take-off the power failed. The pilot ejected safely, without the radar operator, who, along with the aircraft, was never found. *(The National Archives, Washington, DC)*

The mighty Convair B-36 Peacemaker, capable of carrying nuclear weapons, had several encounters with UFOs. One such was in late 1956 over the North/South Dakota border, when all seventeen crew members plus a five-man relief crew saw a 100ft craft with a dome and what appeared to be portholes or lights. *(Don Bishop)*

A radarscope photograph of UFOs off Bermuda, taken from a US Air Force plane on 3 July 1954. *(The National Archives, Washington, DC)*

This UFO was photographed in 1963 by the co-pilot of an AVENSA Airlines DC-4 between Barcelona and Maiquetia in Venezuela. A propeller spinner can be seen in the right foreground, and a highway divides the trees. Fernando de Calvet, a professional topographer and geometrician, demonstrated mathematically that all of the objects in the photograph bear exact relation with each other. *(Aerial Phenomena Research Organisation)*

President John F. Kennedy was allegedly taken on this Air Force One (Boeing VC-137C) to view deceased alien bodies at a US Air Force base in Florida. *(US Air Force)*

An Atlas-F intercontinental ballistic missile. In September 1964, an Atlas with a dummy nuclear warhead, test-fired from Vandenberg AFB, California, was approached by a classic disc-shaped craft which fired flashes of light at it. The warhead malfunctioned and tumbled out of sub-orbit. The event – confirmed by several military personnel – was recorded on 35mm movie film through a high-powered telescope. *(US Air Force)*

A frame from the 8mm colour movie film taken by George Adamski in the presence of Madeleine Rodeffer and other witnesses at Silver Spring, Maryland (near Washington, DC) in February 1965. During a meeting with the author at the Pentagon in May 1998, the Director of the Defense Airborne Reconnaissance Office stated his opinion that this and other frames from the film seemed genuine. *(Madeleine Rodeffer)*

Sketch of the object which crash-landed near the village of Kecksburg, Pennsylvania, in December 1965. *(C. M. Hanna)*

Left. The USS *John F. Kennedy* (CV-67). In June/July 1971 a massive, glowing, spherical UFO appeared over the carrier, disrupting communications and electrical systems. *(US Navy)*
Right. James M. Kopf, one of the witnesses, a communications specialist holding Top Secret Crypto clearance at the time.

The USS *Leary* DD-879, which had an encounter with an unidentified submarine object during the Vietnam War. *(US Navy)*

The Dassault Mirage IVA, France's supersonic bomber capable of carrying a 60-kiloton nuclear weapon. In March 1977, Colonel René Giraud and his navigator encountered a huge UFO, 'at least as big as a Boeing 747', while flying a Mirage IVA over Chaumont. *(Via Philip Jarrett)*

The British Vulcan bomber, designed to carry nuclear weapons. In May 1977, the crew of this Vulcan reported a UFO over the Bay of Biscay. The aircraft – Vulcan B.2 Blue Steel XL321 of 617 Squadron – is shown here at RAF Finningley in 1969. *(Steve Williams)*

Right. A photograph taken in September 1985 of the object which had nearly collided head-on with a Cessna 337 Super Skymaster over the Mojave Desert. *(David J. Hastings)*

Yuri Andropov, former Soviet president and head of the KGB. In 1977/78 he instigated a top-secret ten-year UFO research programme involving four million military officers. *(US Information Service)*

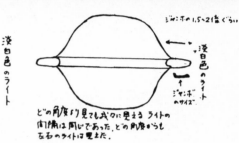

A Japan Airlines Boeing 747-400 cargo jet, and a drawing of the object seen from one of these aircraft over Alaska in November 1986, sketched by Captain Kenju Terauchi. The jumbo jet, shown on the right, was dwarfed by the craft. *(Japan Airlines / Kenju Terauchi)*

淡白色のライト

ジャンボの1.5～2½ぐらい

淡白色のライト

ジャンボのサイズ

どの角度より見ても式々に見えるライトの
間隔は同じであった、どの角度からも
左右のライトは見えた.

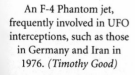

In July 1976, two Indian Air Force MiG-21s, such as the one shown here, witnessed a disc-shaped object on the Pakistan border, which flew away at an estimated 2,600 mph when approached. *(Indian Air Force)*

An F-4 Phantom jet, frequently involved in UFO interceptions, such as those in Germany and Iran in 1976. *(Timothy Good)*

A Chinese Shenyang JJ-6, like the one scrambled to intercept a UFO near Changzhou City in October 1998. The UFO repeatedly played 'cat and mouse' with the jet. Permission to fire at the object was denied. *(Chinese Air Force)*

On 4 January 2004, this Boeing 737–448 of Aer Lingus was allegedly harrassed by a triangular-shaped craft prior to landing at Dublin Airport. The airliner experienced a power drain, there was a great deal of turbulence, the outside air temperature rose to 164° Centigrade and the plane suffered damage to the wings and air brakes. *(Andrzej Krzewski)*

John Podesta, formerly President Clinton's Chief of Staff. 'It's time to open the books . . . on the question of government investigations of UFO's,' he said in 2002. 'We ought to do it because the American people, quite frankly, can handle the truth; and we ought to do it because it's the law.' *(Leslie Kean)*

'UFOs are as real as the airplanes that fly over your head,' said retired Canadian Minister of Defence Paul Hellyer (*right*) in 2005. 'The secrecy involved in all matters pertaining to the Roswell incident was unparalleled . . . so the vast majority of US officials [and] politicians . . . were never in the loop.' *(Ethan Eisenberg)*

It was large, and must have been some 15 to 20 miles away. It moved in the same direction as us. We were heading back from Attack One, which is a combat tactic involving gun cameras – no cannon, missiles, or anything else, so as you can imagine, we were considerably alarmed. We could see a huge thing surrounded in smoke, and from which vapour issued. All of this must have lasted some five minutes. We approached the UFO but it was motionless. It neither approached nor retreated – it merely moved parallel to us. It was quite impressive, and something could be seen concealed behind the smoke.

Although the F-5Fs were equipped with cameras, General Gabrielli did not say if any footage had been obtained. 'The object then disappeared towards Easter Island at an impressive rate of speed,' he recalled. 'The sky cleared, and the lines on the radar vanished. However, there definitely was a physical flying object there.'

In February 2001, a newswire from Agence France Presse reported that the FACh had turned over classified information regarding UFO sightings in Chile – including the Chilean Antarctic – to the US Defense Intelligence Agency.[26]

CHINA

On the evening of 23 October 1978, hundreds of Chinese Air Force pilots and other officers at Lintiao Air Base in Gansu province were watching the beginning of an open-air film, which had started at 20:00, when there was a flurry of disturbance in the audience. 'Several minutes after the show had begun,' reported pilot Zhou Quintong, 'I saw a huge object flying from east to west which flew over our heads.

'It was an immense, oblong object but was not clearly visible. It had two large lamps, like searchlights, in front, shooting out white light forward, and a luminous trail issued from the rear ... The speed was not very great, and it flew in a straight line. It was of a huge size, occupying about 20 to 35 degrees of arc, not very high above the ground and was in sight for two or three minutes.'[27]

Chinese researchers speculated that there could be a connection with the disappearance of the young Australian pilot Frederick Valentich, who two days earlier had vanished with his Cessna 182 (VH-DSJ) shortly after reporting being harassed by a large metallic object over the notorious Bass Strait, en route from Melbourne to Tasmania. According to the transcript of the transmissions between Valentich and Melbourne Flight Service Unit, the pilot's last words were: '. . . ah Melbourne that strange aircraft is hovering on top of me again – it is hovering and it's not an aircraft.'[28] (See p. 318.)

KOREA

It was about 09:00 on a day in March 1979. Two F-4D Phantom jets of the Republic of Korea Air Force (RoKAF) were returning from the annual South Korea/US military exercise, Team Spirit, to Taeku Air Force Base. Lieutenant Colonel Seungbae Lee was piloting one plane and Colonel Byungsun Lim the other, at an altitude of 15,000 feet. On reaching Palkong Mountain, a star-like, apparently stationary object appeared in the distance, which grew in size as the jets approached. It did not register on radar, so the pilots radioed the base – they too were unable to see it on radar. As the pilots approached to within 15 miles of the object, it shot away to the east, and then hovered again.

'The pilots had a close view of the UFO, from about 1,000 feet away,' Sunglyul Maeng, one of Korea's leading UFO researchers, informed me. 'It was radiating bright golden light, like a blast furnace, from the top to the bottom of its disc-shaped body. From its rim, red and blue lights sparkled. It was as big as a jumbo jet. After the F-4s had circled twice above the UFO, it shot away in the direction of the eastern Korean peninsula.'[29]

Maeng gave me this report in 1996, when he was studying engineering at the University of Cambridge. Like other cases from Korea he presented me with, the report was new to me, and as far as I am aware it is published here for the first time outside Korea.

SPAIN

On 11 November 1979, a near miss with an unknown craft, 'approximately the size of a jumbo jet' – as in the Korean case – over Ibiza, Spain, was reported by the crew of a Spanish Air Transport (TAE) Super-Caravelle. Within minutes, a Spanish Air Force (Ejército del Aire) Mirage F1-CE jet from Los Llanos Air Force Base (Albacete) was scrambled to intercept unknown targets in the vicinity of Valencia. It was now 02:20 on 12 November.

Captain-Pilot Fernando Cámara was ordered to identify the lights and prepare his weaponry, but he was unable to locate any targets, and none showed on his radar. However, as the Mirage passed over Valencia at 7,500 metres, a powerful noise of unknown origin, 'like a siren', broke in on all the radio channels. Cámara then caught sight of a strange light, and set off in pursuit. The light would not let him get near it, and still nothing showed on his radar. This happened several times. On the second attempt, the light suddenly accelerated to the same speed as the Mirage (1,110 km/h), maintaining a constant distance from the jet. Cámara attempted to film the object, but his on-board camera jammed. Other instruments seemed to be affected too.

Pegaso Operations Centre ordered Cámara to head for Sagunto (Valencia), where another light appeared. The game of 'cat and mouse' ensued twice more. Finally, running low on fuel, the Mirage returned to base, the object continuing to track the plane and jamming its electronic equipment.[30]

At 17:20 on 17 November, Pegaso Operations Centre detected an unknown track some 40 kilometres south of Morril (Granada), and a Mirage F1 took off from Los Llanos AFB. By the time the jet arrived in the vicinity, the object had disappeared from radar. At 18:16 the pilot was heading back to base when he saw three powerful red-yellow lights in the shape of a triangle about 19 kilometres away. They did not register on radar. In spite of chasing the lights at 1,160 km/h, the Mirage could not close the gap. During his descent into Los Llanos, some childish, laughing voices broke in on the UHF-11 channel that linked the pilot to the Pegaso Operations Centre. 'Hello, how are you? Hello, hello,' they said in Spanish. The interference lasted for thirty seconds, but was not heard at the Centre.[31]

PERU

Two sightings by Peruvian Air Force – Fuerza Aérea Peruana (FAP) – personnel in May 1980, including the interception and attempted destruction of a UFO, are cited in a US Defense Intelligence Agency (DIA) document (p. 320). The source of the information was a Peruvian Air Force (FAP) officer. Extracts follow:

> ... Unidentified flying object in the vicinity of Mariano Melgar Air Base, La Joya (Peru 16805S, 0715306W) ... vehicle was spotted on two different occasions. The first was during the morning hours of 9 May 80, and the second during the early evening hours of 10 May 80 ...

On 9 May, while a group of FAP officers were [flying] in formation at Mariano Melgar, they spotted a UFO that was round in shape, hovering near the airfield. The air commander scrambled a [Sukhoi] Su-22 aircraft to intercept. The pilot, according to a third party, intercepted the vehicle and fired upon it at very close range without any apparent damage. The pilot tried to make a second pass on the vehicle, but the UFO out-ran the aircraft.[32]

PUERTO RICO

Puerto Rico lies within an apex of the legendary Bermuda Triangle, where many mysterious events have occurred, such as those described earlier. On 28 June 1980, two young civilian pilots, José L. Maldonado Torres and José A. Pagán Santos, flying at 1,500 feet in an Ercoupe 415-D (N3808H) on the return leg to San Juan from Santo Domingo in the Dominican Republic, disappeared shortly after transmitting a Mayday distress call. Here follow salient extracts from the transcript contained in the US National Transportation Safety Board (NTSB) accident report (see p. 320):

'Mayday Mayday . . . We are lost . . . we found, ah, a weird object in our course that made us change course about three different times. We got it right now in front of us at one o'clock . . . Right now we supposed to be at about 35 miles from the coast of Puerto Rico . . . We are right again in the same stuff sir . . .'

And that final sentence was the last response heard. An air-sea rescue search failed to locate any wreckage or bodies. Concluded the NTSB: 'The aircraft is presumed ditched at sea and both occupants deceased . . .'[33]

TURKEY

On 14 January 1983 a very bright object appeared in the sky above Adana, southern Turkey, at 19:53, and many people stopped their cars to observe it. Soon the UFO was joined by two US Air Force jets from the NATO base at Incirlik. One of the jets flew in tight circles around the UFO, which dwarfed the fighter in comparison and was described as disc-shaped with a dome underneath. The object accelerated and then disappeared over the Mediterranean Sea, with the jets in pursuit. Witnesses claim that only one jet returned to base. Investigator Eric Saunders learned that: 'Turkish forces were involved in a search-and-rescue mission over the Mediterranean on that date, at the request of the USAF.' Although officials admitted to locals that a plane had been lost, they refused to discuss the circumstances.[34]

And no wonder. Such incidents lie at the core of official secrecy on the subject. How on Earth could our military leaders possibly acknowledge that an ongoing conflict existed with certain implacable alien species, particularly since we lacked effective countermeasures?

REFERENCES

1. Stevens, Wendelle C. and Dong, Paul, *UFOs over Modern China*, UFO Photo Archives, PO Box 17206, Tucson, AZ 85710, 1983, p. 45. See also the chapter on Chinese reports in *Above Top Secret* and *Beyond Top Secret*.
2. Ibid., pp. 48–9.
3. Ibid., pp. 49–50.
4. See *Beyond Top Secret* and *Unearthly Disclosure*.
5. Personal interview, Paris, 12 December 2000.
6. Julien, H., 'A 1967 Landing in Madagascar', *Flying Saucer Review*, Vol. 23, No. 1, January–February 1977, pp. 29–30. A detailed account of this event appears in *Alien Base* by Timothy Good.
7. Vallée, Jacques, with Costello, Martine, *UFO Chronicles of the Soviet Union: A Cosmic Samizdat*, Ballantine Books, New York, 1992, pp. 82–5.
8. Letters, 5/15 December 1995.
9. Personal interview, Istanbul, 15 December 2001.
10. *Posta*, Istanbul, 17 December 2001. Translated by Esen Şekerkarar.
11. Saunders, Eric, *UFO Cases from Turkey*. (Privately published.)
12. Letter from Sergeant Terry W. Colvin, Ubon Royal Thai Air Force Base, Thailand, *Flying Saucer Review Case Histories*, Supplement No. 18, February 1974, p. 17. Published by FSR Publications Ltd, PO Box 585, Rickmansworth, WD3 1YJ, UK. www.fsr.org.uk
13. Stringfield, Leonard H., *Situation Red, The UFO Siege!*, Doubleday, New York, 1977, pp. 135–6.
14. Good, Timothy, *Alien Base: Earth's Encounters with Extraterrestrials*, Century, London, 1998; Avon Books, New York, 1999.
15. Haines, Richard F., 'An Aircraft/UFO Encounter over Germany in 1976', *International UFO Reporter*, Vol. 24, No. 4, Winter 1999, pp. 3–6.
16. National Aviation Reporting Center on Anomalous Phenomena, PO Box 1535, Vallejo, CA 94590. www.narcap.org
17. *Sightings*, Paramount Pictures, 5555 Melrose Avenue, Mae West 146, Hollywood, CA 90038-3197.

18. Drucker, Ronald, (Robert F. Dorr) 'UFO Crisis in India', *UFO Report*, Vol. 6, No. 4, October 1978, pp. 25–7, 45, 65–8.

19. Personal interview, Paris Air Show, Le Bourget, 19 June 2003.

20. The National Archives, DEFE 71/34.

21. The National Archives, DEFE 71/35.

22. The National Archives, DEFE 24/977–979.

23. Note, 18 January 2006.

24. Smith, Dr Willy, 'Unknown Intruder over Portugal', *International UFO Reporter*, Vol. 10, No. 6, November–December 1985, pp. 6–8.

25. Good, Timothy, *Beyond Top Secret: The Worldwide UFO Security Threat*, Sidgwick & Jackson, London, 1996, pp. 276–7.

26. Corrales, Scott, 'Military Implications of UFOs in Latin America and Spain', *Inexplicata*, The Journal of Hispanic Ufology, Issue #12, Winter 2003.

27. Stevens and Dong, op. cit., pp. 119–20.

28. Haines, Richard F., *Melbourne Episode: Case Study of a Missing Pilot*, LDA Press, Los Altos, California, 1987. See also *Above Top Secret* and *Beyond Top Secret*.

29. Letter, 4 June 1996.

30. Crivillén, J. Plana, 'Encounters in Spanish Air-Space between Aircraft and UFOs', *Flying Saucer Review*, Vol. 34, No. 1, 1989, p. 22.

31. Ballester Olmos, Vicente-Juan, 'UFO Declassification in Spain – Military UFO Files Available to the Public: A Balance'; a paper presented at the Eighth BUFORA International UFO Congress, Sheffield Hallam University, 19–20 August 1995.

32. Department of Defense Intelligence Information Report No. 6-876-0146-80, received by the Joint Chiefs of Staff Message Center, 3 June 1980.

33. National Transportation Safety Board Accident File No. MIA-80-D-A079. See also Good, Timothy, *Unearthly Disclosure: Conflicting Interests in the Control of Extraterrestrial Intelligence*, Century, London, 2000, pp. 34–9.

34. Saunders, op. cit.

SECRET

NOW YOU SEE IT, NOW YOU DON'T! (U)

Captain Henry S. Shields, HQ USAFE/INOMP

(S) Sometime in his career, each pilot can expect to encounter strange, unusual happenings which will never be adequately or entirely explained by logic or subsequent investigation. The following article recounts just such an episode as reported by two F-4 Phantom crews of the Imperial Iranian Air Force during late 1976. No additional information or explanation of the strange events has been forthcoming; the story will be filed away and probably forgotten, but it makes interesting and possibly disturbing, reading.

* * * * *

(S) Until 0030 on a clear autumn morning, it had been an entirely routine night watch for the Imperial Iranian Air Force's command post in the Tehran area. In quick succession, four calls arrived from one of the city's suburbs reporting a series of strange airborne objects. These Unidentified Flying Objects (UFOs) were described as 'bird-like', or as brightly-lit helicopters (although none were airborne at the time). Unable to convince the callers that they were only seeing stars, a senior officer went outside to see for himself. Observing an object to the north like a star, only larger and brighter, he immediately scrambled an IIAF F-4 to investigate.

(S) Approaching the city, the F-4 pilot reported that the brilliant object was easily visible 70 miles away. When approximately 25 NM distant, the interceptor lost all instrumentation and UHF/Intercom communications. Upon breaking off the intercept and turning towards his home base, all systems returned to normal, as if the strange object no longer regarded the aircraft as a threat.

SECRET

An article from the US Air Force Security Service *MIJI Quarterly* (MQ 3-78) about the UFOs encountered over the Tehran area by F-4 Phantom pilots of the Imperial Iranian Air Force on 19 September 1976. (*Air Force Electronic Warfare Center via William L. Moore Publications & Research*)

SECRET

(S) A second F-4 was scrambled ten minutes after the first.
The backseater reported radar-lock on the UFO at 27 NM/12 o'clock
high position, and a rate of closure of 150 knots. Upon reaching the
25 NM point, the object began rapidly moving away to maintain a
constant separation distance while still visible on the radar scope.
While the size of the radar return was comparable to that of a KC-
135, its intense brilliance made estimation of actual size impossible.
Visually, it resembled flashing strobe lights arranged in a rectangular pattern and alternating blue, green, red, and orange. Their
sequence was so fast that all colors could be seen at once.

(S) As the F-4 continued pursuit south of Tehran, a second
brightly-lit object (about one-half to one-third the size of the moon)
detached from the original UFO and headed straight for the F-4 at a
high rate of speed. The pilot attempted to fire an AIM-9 missile at
the new object but was prevented by a sudden power loss in his
weapons control panel. UHF and internal communications were
simultaneously lost. The pilot promptly initiated a turn and negative-
G dive to escape, but the object fell in behind the F-4 at 3-4 NM
distance. Continuing the turn, the pilot observed the second object
turn inside of him and then away, subsequently returning to the primary UFO for a perfect rendezvous.

(S) The two UFOs had hardly rejoined when a second object
detached and headed straight down toward the ground at high speed.
Having regained weapons and communications systems, the aircrew
watched the third object, anticipating a large explosion when it struck
the ground. However, it landed gently and cast a bright light over a
two-three kilometer area. The pilot flew as low over the area as
possible, fixing the object's exact location.

(S) Upon return to home base, both crewmen had difficulty in

SECRET

SECRET

adjusting their night vision devices for landing. The landing was further complicated by excessive interference on UHF and a further complete loss of all communications when passing through a 150 degree magnetic bearing from the home base. The inertial navigation system simultaneously fluctuated from 30 to 50 degrees. A civil airliner approaching the area also experienced a similar communications failure, but reported no unusual sightings.

(S) While on a long final approach, the F-4 crew noted a further UFO. This was described as a cylinder-shaped object (about the size of a T-33 trainer) with bright steady lights on each end and a flasher in the middle. It quickly approached and passed directly over the F-4. In answer to the pilot's query, the control tower reported no other air traffic in the area, although they subsequently obtained a visual sighting of the object when specifically directed where to look.

(S) The following day, the F-4 crew was flown by helicopter to the location where they believed the object had landed. This turned out to be a dry lake bed, but nothing unusual was noticed. As the helicopter circled off to the west, however, a very noticeable beeper signal was received, and eventually traced to a nearby house. They immediately landed and asked the inhabitants if anything strange or unusual had occurred the previous night. Yes, they replied, there had been loud noises and a very bright light, like lightning. The helicopter returned to base and arrangements were made to conduct various tests, such as radiation checks, in the vicinity of the house. Unfortunately, the results of such tests have not been reported. (XSO3 2)

SECRET

TIME	FROM	TO	TEXT
:08	FS	DSJ	DELTA SIERRA JULIET CONFIRM THE ER AIRCRAFT JUST VANISHED
:14	DSJ	FS	SAY AGAIN
:17	FS	DSJ	DELTA SIERRA JULIET IS THE AIRCRAFT STILL WITH YOU
:23	DSJ	FS	DELTA SIERRA JULIET (ITS AH NOR) // open microphone 2 seconds // (NOW) APPROACHING FROM THE SOUTHWEST
:37	FS	DSJ	DELTA SIERRA JULIET
:52	DSJ	FS	DELTA SIERRA JULIET THE ENGINE IS IS ROUGH IDLING IVE GOT IT SET AT TWENTY THREE TWENTY FOUR AND THE THING IS (COUGHING)
0912:04	FS	DSJ	DELTA SIERRA JULIET ROGER WHAT ARE YOUR INTENTIONS
:09	DSJ	FS	MY INTENTIONS ARE AH TO GO TO KING ISLAND AH MELBOURNE THAT STRANGE AIRCRAFT IS HOVERING ON TOP OF ME AGAIN // two second open microphone // IT IS HOVERING AND ITS NOT AN AIRCRAFT
:22	FS	DSJ	DELTA SIERRA JULIET
:28	DSJ	FS	DELTA SIERRA JULIET MELBOURNE // 17 seconds open microphone //
:49	FS	DSJ	DELTA SIERRA JULIET MELBOURNE

The last page of the official transcript of communications between the 20-year-old Australian pilot, Frederick Valentich, flying a Cessna 182L (VH-DSJ) over the Bass Strait, and Melbourne Flight Service Unit (FS), prior to his disappearance on 21 October 1978. *(Australian Department of Transport)*

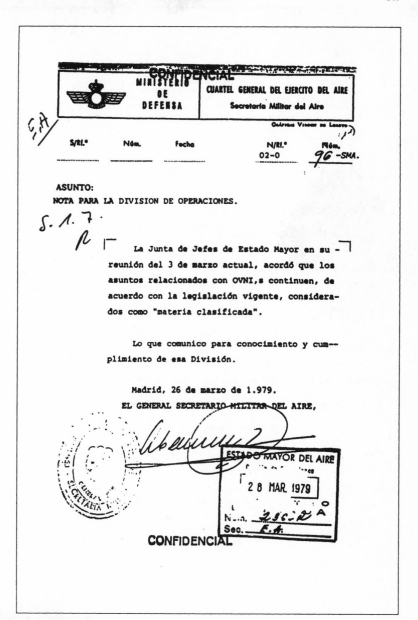

CONFIDENCIAL

| MINISTERIO DE DEFENSA | CUARTEL GENERAL DEL EJERCITO DEL AIRE |
| | Secretaría Militar del Aire |

| S/Rf.° | Núm. | Fecha | N/Rf.° | Núm. |
| | | | 02-0 | 96 -SMA. |

ASUNTO:
NOTA PARA LA DIVISION DE OPERACIONES.

       La Junta de Jefes de Estado Mayor en su reunión del 3 de marzo actual, acordó que los asuntos relacionados con OVNI,s continuen, de acuerdo con la legislación vigente, considerados como "materia clasificada".

       Lo que comunico para conocimiento y cumplimiento de esa División.

       Madrid, 26 de marzo de 1.979.
       EL GENERAL SECRETARIO MILITAR DEL AIRE,

ESTADO MAYOR DEL AIRE
2 8 MAR. 1979
N...
Sec.

CONFIDENCIAL

The UFO subject confirmed by the Spanish Joint Chiefs of Staff in 1979 as a 'classified matter'. *(Ministerio de Defensa/Vicente-Juan Ballester Olmos)*

```
                        DEPARTMENT OF DEFENSE
                             JOINT CHIEFS OF STAFF
                              MESSAGE CENTER

PAGE  ?                                                        18134
8A.        DETAILS: SOURCE TOLD RO ABOUT THE SPOTTING OF AN
UNIDENTIFIED FLYING OBJECT IN THE VICINITY OF MARIANO MELGAR AIR
BASE, LA JOYA, PERU (1680S9, 0715396W). SOURCE STATED THAT THE
VEHICLE WAS SPOTTED ON TWO DIFFERENT OCCASIONS. THE FIRST WAS
DURING THE MORNING HOURS OF 9 MAY 80, AND THE SECOND DURING
THE EARLY EVENING HOURS OF 10 MAY 80.
           SOURCE STATED THAT ON 9 MAY, WHILE A GROUP OF FAP
OFFICERS WERE IN FORMATION AT MARIANO MALGAR, THEY SPOTTED A
UFO THAT WAS ROUND IN SHAPE, HOVERING NEAR THE AIRFIELD. THE
AIR COMMANDER SCRAMBLED AN SU-22 AIRCRAFT TO MAKE AN
INTERCEPT. THE PILOT, ACCORDING TO A THIRD PARTY, INTERCEPTED
THE VEHICLE AND FIRED UPON IT AT VERY CLOSE RANGE WITHOUT
CAUSING ANY APPARENT DAMAGE. THE PILOT TRIED TO MAKE A
SECOND PASS ON THE VEHICLE, BUT THE UFO OUT-RAN THE SU-22.
           THE SECOND SIGHTING WAS DURING HOURS OF DARKNESS.
THE VEHICLE WAS LIGHTED. AGAIN AN SU-22 WAS SCRAMBLED, BUT THE
VEHICLE OUT-RAN THE AIRCRAFT.
8B.        ORIG CMTS: RO HAS HEARD DISCUSSION ABOUT THE
SIGHTING FROM OTHER SOURCES. APPARENTLY SOME VEHICLE WAS
SPOTTED, BUT ITS ORIGIN REMAINS UNKNOWN.
```

A US Defense Intelligence Agency (DIA) report on interceptions of a UFO by Sukhoi Su-22 jets of the Peruvian Air Force in May 1980. *(Defense Intelligence Agency)*

An excerpt from the National Transportation Safety Board Accident File on the disappearance of two pilots, José L. Maldonado Torres and José A. Pagán Santos, together with their Ercoupe 415-D (N3808H), as they were returning to Puerto Rico after a flight from Santo Domingo in the Dominican Republic, on 28 June 1980. The pilots' communications with San Juan International Airport were relayed via Iberia Airlines flight 976. *(National Transportation Safety Board, Washington)*

```
0003:25 GMT    N3808H    Mayday Mayday we are lost we found a strange
                         object in our course

0003:35 GMT    IB976     Station calling Mayday Mayday Iberia nine seven
                         six Iberia nine seven six  go ahead

0003:45 GMT    N3808H    Ah  we are going from Santo Domingo to ah San Juan
                         International but we found (Ah a weird object in
                         our course that made us change course about three
                         different times  we got it right now in front of us
                         at one o'clock our heading is) zero seven zero
                         degrees... our altitude one thousand six hundred
                         at zero seven degrees... our VORs got lost off
                         frequency.

0004:15 GMT    IB976     Station calling one two one five Mayday Mayday
                         Iberia nine seven six go ahead

0004:20 GMT    N3808H    Mayday Mayday this is Air-Coupe three eight zero
                         eight Hotel in flight from Santo Domingo to
                         San Juan Puerto Rico. we have a very weird ah object
                         in front of us that make us lose course... our
                         present heading is one thirty degrees at one
                         thousand five hundred feet sir
```

21. INTRUSIONS AT USAF BASES

On the night of 6 November 1973, at 21:45, a US Air Force security policeman at Kirtland Air Force Base East (formerly Sandia Base), New Mexico, sighted a large glowing object hovering over the nuclear-weapons inspection facility in the Manzano Laboratory area (Sandia National Laboratories). Thus began an astonishing series of incidents from the 1973–4 period which are known to relatively few students of the subject, let alone the general public.

'The object was described as oblate spherical in shape, 150 feet in diameter, golden in colour, and absolutely silent,' reported R.C. Hecker, an investigator for the Aerial Phenomena Research Organization.

> The object was hovering approximately 100 feet over Plant No. 3. The nine other air policemen on duty in that area were alerted to the presence of the intruder. While the other air policemen moved into positions affording views of the object, a call was put through to Kirtland East for assistance. According to my informant (one of the air policemen who saw the UFO), four interceptors (F-101 Voodoos) of the 150th Fighter Group, New Mexico Air National Guard, were scrambled to intercept the object. As the interceptors grouped in the skies over Kirtland AFB West, the object began moving in an easterly direction and passed out of sight over the Manzano Mountains at treetop level (below the radar horizon). By the time the jets had arrived on the scene, the object had vanished.

'I interviewed one of the air policemen who observed the object,' Hecker's report continues. 'He received word of the object's location when the alarm was sounded over his transceiver . . . he said that military officials were upset by the incident. He requested that I not identify the source of my information, due to immediate censoring of the report [and] that officially the sighting had not occurred: there were no references to it in intelligence briefs (which he had access to) in succeeding days.'[1]

At 16:30 on 15 April 1974, a couple observed an object 50–75 feet in diameter at an altitude of about 2,000 feet. 'The object displayed a distinct whirling motion, as it rotated about its central axis,' reported Hecker. 'There was no sound, nor was there any visible means of propulsion ... Immediately south of the witnesses' home is the Manzano Laboratory high-security area [which] is restricted to all private and commercial aircraft below 3,000 feet.'

A month later, a disc is said to have crash-landed on the east side of the Manzano Mountains, less than 30 miles south-west of Albuquerque. Hecker reports:

> At 22:10 hours, May 17, 1974, electronic scanning instruments at the Manzano Laboratory section of Kirtland AFB East registered a tremendous burst of energy in the 250 to 275 megahertz range. The energy was so intense it threw all of their instruments completely off-scale. The burst of energy was first noted in the Earth's upper atmosphere. Before the energy died out, a trajectory was plotted. A recovery team was immediately dispatched to the designated impact area. An area southwest of the small mountain community of Chilili, New Mexico, was cordoned off. A few hours later what was described as a metallic, circular object approximately 60 feet in diameter (before being dismantled for handling) was quietly moved into a hangar at Kirtland AFB.

'I talked with the man who was monitoring the electronic scanning equipment at Manzano [Base] when the initial burst of energy was registered,' continued Hecker. 'This individual has given me leads to sightings in the past which have always proven valid ... After being told of this incident, I was stopped by a man who identified himself as a Kirtland AFB officer. He ordered me to forget everything I had been told about this incident.'[2]

In August–September 1980 a number of instances occurred involving high-frequency jamming of radar and other equipment, as well as several landings of unknown objects in Coyote Canyon, part of a large restricted test range used by the Air Force Weapons Laboratory, Sandia National Laboratories, Defense Nuclear Agency and the Department of Energy (see p. 329). During my research trip to the area in July 1989, Major Ernest E. Edwards, who had been in charge of security at the Manzano Nuclear Weapons Storage Facility at the time, confirmed the contents of these reports, and pointed out to me in person where they had taken place.

As mentioned earlier, I have learned via a credible high-ranking source – now corroborated by another source – that an alien facility was sited in the vicinity of the nuclear-weapons storage area in the Manzano Mountains.

The preponderance of evidence, from the intrusions in 1949 to the cases cited in this chapter, certainly supports that probability.

ALIEN ABDUCTION

Intrusions at US Air Force bases and sensitive nuclear facilities in New Mexico reached a new high in August 1975, when a US Air Force flight mechanic based at Holloman AFB, Alamogordo, claimed to have been abducted by aliens.

On 13 August, after finishing work at 23:30 the previous night, Sergeant Charles L. Moody decided to stay up late to watch a meteor shower (the 'Perseids'), and drove to a location a short distance from his home to do so. After observing a number of bright meteors, something totally unusual appeared.

'At approximately 01:20 hours I observed a dull metallic object that seemed to just drop out of the sky and start to hover with a wobbling motion, approximately 100 feet in front of me,' reported Moody. 'The object was moving slowly toward my car ... I tried to start my car but it was like there was no battery at all.'

At this time the object stopped dead still as if to just hang there in the air. [It] was about 50 feet across and approximately 18 to 20 feet thick at the center, maybe more. At this time I heard a high-pitched sound, something like a dental drill might make at high speed, and just to the right of the center of the object I saw what seemed to be an oblong-shaped window [with] the shadows of what looked to be [two or three] human forms.

At this time the high-pitched sound stopped, and a feeling of numbness came over my body. The fear that I had before left me, and I felt a very peaceful calmness. [Then] the object lifted very fast. It made no sound ... After the object left, my car started perfectly. As I drove off I looked at my watch, and it was now 02:45 hours. It seemed to me that the sighting only lasted one or maybe two minutes. That makes one hour and 25 minutes that I cannot account for ...[3]

Following this incident, Moody broke out in a heat rash on his lower body and suffered pain in his lower back. In early September 1975, two researchers from the Aerial Phenomena Research Organization, Jim Lorenzen and Wendelle C. Stevens (a former USAF test pilot), met Moody and his wife Karon at Alamogordo, and formed a favourable impression. Moody had been anxious that his story should not come to the attention of the Air Force, though he did talk to a friend, Dr Abraham Goldman, a former USAF flight surgeon, who gave him what transpired to be helpful advice regarding the recovery of at least some of his 'missing' memory. In late September, Moody was ordered to be transferred overseas – a move predicted by Lorenzen, whose military background and previous employment at Holloman made him familiar with such security measures.

Before departing a month later, Moody wrote a long letter to Lorenzen, describing what he now recalled of the experience. Selected extracts follow:

... The beings were about five feet tall and very much like us, except their heads were larger and [they had] no hair; ears very small, eyes a little larger than ours, nose small, and the mouth had very thin lips. I would say their weight was maybe between 110–130 pounds. There was speech but their lips did not move. Their type of clothing was skin-tight [without] zippers or buttons [and] black, except for one of them that had on a silver-white looking suit.

There were no names said, but they knew who I was and called me by my proper name – Charles, and did not use my nickname, Chuck. It was like they could read my mind ... I was taken to a room and the elder or leader touched my back and legs with a rod-looking device ... he said there had been a scuffle when they first made contact with me, and he only wanted to correct any misplacement that might have happened ... The inside of the craft was as clean as an operating room [and] the lighting was indirect.

I was thinking to myself, 'If only I could see the drive unit of the craft, how wonderful that would be'. The elder or leader put his hand on my shoulder and said to follow him. We went to a small room that had no fixtures and was dimly lit ... The floor seemed to give way like an elevator. I guess we went down about six feet and what I saw then was a room about 25 feet across, and in the center was what looked like a huge carbon rod going through the roof of the room; around the rod were three what looked like holes covered with glass. Inside the glass-covered holes or balls were what looked like large crystals with two rods, one on each side of the crystal. One rod came to a ball-like top, the other one came to a 'T' type top. I was told that this was the drive unit, and that I could understand it if I tried. There were no wires or cables ...

I was then taken back up through the same way we came down. The leader then told me that this was not their main craft, but only used for observing, and that their main craft was about 400 of our miles above the Earth. And the drive unit on it was different ... I asked if I could go to the main craft, and I was told no, that their time was short, but they could find me any time they desired and that in a short time they would see me again ... And then he told me to be sure and see a doctor soon. And I did ...

'It's not just one advanced race that is studying this planet Earth, but a group of them,' Moody declared. 'They also fear for their own lives, and will protect themselves at all costs. Their intent is a peaceful one, and if the leaders of this world will only heed their warnings we will find ourselves a lot better off than before, and at this time it's not up to us to accept them, but for them to accept us!'"[4]

I do not know what became of Charles Moody, following his transfer abroad (to a US Air Force base in Spain). However, I do know that a psychological stress evaluation (PSE) of him by Charles McQuiston (co-inventor of the PSE) indicated that he was telling the truth. Moreover, Moody held a high-security clearance at Holloman AFB and was involved in the Air Force's Human Reliability Program, where he had been screened by a psychiatrist and declared free of emotional disorders.

LOW-LEVEL INTRUSIONS OVER ICBM BASES

In October and November 1975, a spate of low-level UFO intrusions over Strategic Air Command intercontinental ballistic missile bases in Maine, Michigan, Montana and North Dakota caused widespread official concern, particularly since some of the unknown objects exhibited what is called a 'clear intent' over the nuclear-missile sites. I cite from two official documents:

• *Alert Center Branch, US Air Force Aerospace Intelligence Division, 31 October 1975*
Contacted CIA OPS center and informed them of U/I flight activity over two SAC bases near Canadian border. CIA ... requested they be informed of any follow up activity.

• *Commander-in-Charge, North American Aerospace Defense Command*
This morning, 11 Nov 75, CFS Falconbridge reported search and height radar paints on an object up to 30 nautical miles south of the site ranging in altitude from 25,000 ft to 75,000 ft ... With binoculars the object appeared as a 100 ft diameter sphere ... I have also expressed my concern to [Secretary of the Air Force Office of Information] that

we come up soonest with a proposed answer to queries from the press
to prevent over reaction by the public to reports in the media that may
be blown out of proportion.

PILOTS HARASSED

In 1975, Major Donald Keyhoe disclosed details relating to a case that he
had learned about from his Air Force sources. 'This is a powerful case,
similar to the Kinross case,' said Keyhoe, 'but the location is secret. I can't
even tell you on which coast it happened, or when it happened. But it was
over two years ago.' Leonard Stringfield reports:

'This incident begins with radar picking up a blip that appeared on the
scope as the UFO circled over the airbase. Three jets were scrambled. As
the jets climbed skyward, the UFO continued its circling maneuver; then it
leveled off, heading toward them. Trying to avoid collision, the jets spread
out. Then the UFO accelerated to a higher [altitude], leaving the interceptors under it. Suddenly and inexplicably, the jets vanished from the scope.

Said Keyhoe, 'It was as though the UFO had swallowed up the jets.
Then the UFO made a turn and streaked off the scope. The radar had over
a 200-mile range, but there was no trace of the three jets or the UFO. The
Air Force made the usual extensive search for the missing jets. Nothing!'[5]

In conversation with reporter Bob Pratt in 1978, Keyhoe confirmed the
reliability of his Air Force sources for the story. The three missing planes
were F-102 Delta Dagger jets from a certain Air Force base in Florida.[6]

A shocking case occurred on 6 May 1976 over the restricted military
air corridor north of Cincinnati and east of Wright-Patterson Air Force
Base, Dayton, Ohio, when a pilot was testing a highly sophisticated new
instrument in his plane (type not revealed). According to information
provided to Leonard Stringfield via an engineer who was present at the
debriefing, the incident happened in clear weather during daylight hours.

'Somewhere east of Wright-Patterson AFB,' reported Stringfield, 'the
pilot, making his routine test run, suddenly caught sight of three unidentified silverish objects, flying in formation at an unknown distance ahead.
They were closing in fast toward his aircraft.'

The UFOs, described as huge silver discs with portholes that had a
mirrored effect, suddenly moved in menacingly close. The pilot, fearing
a collision, tried to evade the objects by descending to 1,000 feet . . .
But the three UFOs hung tenaciously close – one on each wing tip, the
other above the fuselage.

The stunned pilot tried evasive action: levelled off and then shot up in a vertical climb to 3,000 feet. But the UFOs stuck to his aircraft and continued their harassment for more than an hour. During this frantic period, all the instruments on the pilot's control panel went 'haywire', and he admitted later that he lost all sense of time.

'According to the engineer,' continued Stringfield, 'the pilot, during debriefing, said he was terrified by the action and confessed that he broke down and cried. The UFOs were confirmed by base radar, probably by a portable unit of the Air Systems Division.'[7]

This incident bears a remarkable resemblance to the one reported by the Mexican pilot Carlos de los Santos Montiel three days earlier, described in the previous chapter.

MAJOR USAF EUROPE EVENTS

No UFO case in the UK has attracted more publicity than the extraordinary events occurring over several nights in Rendlesham Forest, just outside the twin US Air Forces Europe NATO bases at Bentwaters and Woodbridge, Suffolk, in late December 1980. As in the case of the Roswell incident, several documentaries and books have been devoted to the case. The memorandum summarizing these events, sent to the Ministry of Defence (MoD) by Lieutenant Colonel Charles I. Halt, Deputy Base Commander, who also witnessed several of the incidents, is reproduced on page 330. I interviewed Colonel Halt on one occasion and met him on another. At the latter occasion, Nick Pope, who headed the MoD's UFO research effort from 1991 to 1994 and had conducted extensive official investigations into the incident, was present. Halt told us both emphatically that certain US authorities had covered up their investigations.

At one stage witnesses reported that the UFOs beamed lights down on to the hardened bunkers containing nuclear weapons (more of which were then stored at Bentwaters than anywhere else in Europe). Halt and his investigators tape-recorded their communications describing some of these dramatic events. It should be noted that a very similar craft was seen for well over an hour by numerous witnesses (some using binoculars) over south-east London and north-west Kent on 15 December 1980, as it hovered for long periods, occasionally split into five separate elements and then regrouped into a single element. All this took place in a cloudless sky. I myself saw the object for a brief period. Frustratingly, I had neither binoculars nor a camera with me and, as luck would have it, by the time I had dashed home only minutes later and was about to photograph and film it with zoom lenses, it had vanished.[8] They must have known I was coming!

Readers seeking further information are encouraged to read two definitive books on the case: *You Can't Tell the People* by Georgina Bruni,[9] and the updated edition of *Left at East Gate* by Larry Warren and Peter Robbins.[10] Bruni's title was inspired by a brief conversation with former Prime Minister Margaret Thatcher in May 1997, during which Bruni brought up the Rendlesham Forest incident.

'UFOs?' retorted Lady Thatcher. 'You must get your facts right – and you can't tell the people!'

REFERENCES

1. Hecker, R. C., 'New Mexico Reports', *The APRO Bulletin*, Vol. 23, No. 2, November 1973, p. 5.

2. Ibid., p. 6.

3. Lorenzen, L.J., 'The Moody Case', *The APRO Bulletin*, Vol. 24, No. 12, June 1976, p. 6.

4. *The APRO Bulletin*, Vol. 25, No. 1, July 1976, pp. 2, 5–6.

5. Stringfield, Leonard H., *Situation Red, The UFO Siege!*, Doubleday, New York, 1977, pp. 143–4.

6. http://www.bobpratt.org/keyhoe.html

7. Stringfield, op. cit., pp. 145–6.

8. *Above Top Secret* and *Beyond Top Secret*.

9. Bruni, Georgina, *You Can't Tell the People: The Cover-up of Britain's Roswell*, Sidgwick & Jackson, London, 2000.

10. Warren, Larry, and Robbins, Peter, *Left at East Gate: A First-Hand Account of the Rendlesham Forest UFO Incident, Its Cover-up, and Investigation*, Cosimo-on-Demand, New York, 2005.

COMPLAINT FORM	Hq 1 V 0 S		

I   ADMINISTRATIVE DATA

TITLE	DATE	TIME
KIRTLAND AFB, NM, 8 Aug - 3 Sep 80, Alleged Sigthings of Unidentified Aerial Lights in Restricted Test Range.	2 - 9 Sept 80	1200

PLACE
AFOSI Det 1700, Kirtland AFB, NM

HOW RECEIVED

X	IN PERSON		TELEPHONICALLY		IN WRITING

SOURCE AND EVALUATION
MAJOR ERNEST E. EDWARDS

RESIDENCE OR BUSINESS ADDRESS
Commander, 1608 SPS, Manzano
Kirtland AFB, NM

PHONE
4-7516

CR __44__ APPLIES

II   SUMMARY OF INFORMATION

REMARKS

1. On 2 Sept 80, SOURCE related on 8 Aug 80, three Security Policemen assigned to 1608 SPS, KAFB, NM, on duty inside the Manzano Weapons Storage Area sighted an unidentified light in the air that traveled from North to South over the Coyote Canyon area of the Department of Defense Restricted Test Range on KAFB, NM. The Security Policemen identified as: SSGT STEPHEN FERENZ, Area Supervisor, AIC MARTIN W. RIST and AMN ANTHONY D. FRAZIER, were later interviewed separately by SOURCE and all three related the same statement; At approximately 2350hrs., while on duty in Charlie Sector, East Side of Manzano, the three observed a very bright light in the sky approximately 3 miles North-North East of their position. The light traveled with great speed and stopped suddenly in the sky over Coyote Canyon. The three first thought the object was a helicopter, however, after observing the strange aerial maneuvers (stop and go), they felt a helicopter couldn't have performed such skills. The light landed in the Coyote Canyon area. Sometime later, three witnessed the light take off and leave proceeding straight up at a high speed and disappear.

2. Central Security Control (CSC) inside Manzano, contacted Sandia Security, who conducts frequent building checks on two alarmed structures in the area. They advised that a patrol was already in the area and would investigate.

3. On 11 Aug 80, RUSS CURTIS, Sandia Security, advised that on 9 Aug 80, a Sandia Security Guard, (who wishes his name not be divulged for fear of harassment), related the following: At approximately 0020hrs., he was driving East on the Coyote Canyon access road on a routine building check of an alarmed structure. As he approached the structure he observed a bright light near the ground behind the structure. He also observed an object he first thought was a helicopter. But after driving closer, he observed a round disk shaped object. He attempted to radio for a back up patrol but his radio would not work. As he approached the object on foot armed with a shotgun, the object took off in a vertical direction at a high rate of speed. The guard was a former helicopter mechanic in the U.S. Army and stated the object he observed was not a helicopter.

4. SOURCE advised on 22 Aug 80, three other security policemen observed the same

DATE FORWARDED HQ AFOSI	1 V O S	10 Aug 80	AFOSI FORM 58 ATTACHED ☐ YES ☐ NO

DATE	TYPED OR PRINTED NAME OF SPECIAL AGENT	SIGNATURE
8 Sept 80	RICHARD C. DOTY, SA	Richard C. Doty

DISTRICT FILE NO
80 17 8 9 3 - c / 27

DCII RESULTS
NEGATIVE ☑   POSITIVE (See Attached)

AFOSI FORM 1   PREVIOUS EDITION WILL BE USED

Part of an Air Force Office of Special Investigations (AFOSI) complaint form relating to UFO intrusions at the Manzano nuclear weapons storage area in August–September 1980. *(The National Archives, Washington)*

DEPARTMENT OF THE AIR FORCE
HEADQUARTERS 81ST COMBAT SUPPORT GROUP (USAFE)
APO NEW YORK 09755

REPLY TO
ATTN OF: CD   13 Jan 81

SUBJECT: Unexplained Lights

TO: RAF/CC

1. Early in the morning of 27 Dec 80 (approximately 0300L), two USAF
security police patrolmen saw unusual lights outside the back gate at
RAF Woodbridge. Thinking an aircraft might have crashed or been forced
down, they called for permission to go outside the gate to investigate.
The on-duty flight chief responded and allowed three patrolmen to pro-
ceed on foot. The individuals reported seeing a strange glowing object
in the forest. The object was described as being metalic in appearance
and triangular in shape, approximately two to three meters across the
base and approximately two meters high. It illuminated the entire forest
with a white light. The object itself had a pulsing red light on top and
a bank(s) of blue lights underneath. The object was hovering or on legs.
As the patrolmen approached the object, it maneuvered through the trees
and disappeared. At this time the animals on a nearby farm went into a
frenzy. The object was briefly sighted approximately an hour later near
the back gate.

2. The next day, three depressions 1 1/2" deep and 7" in diameter were
found where the object had been sighted on the ground. The following
night (29 Dec 80) the area was checked for radiation. Beta/gamma readings
of 0.1 milliroentgens were recorded with peak readings in the three depressions and near the center of the triangle formed by the depressions.
A nearby tree had moderate (.05-.07) readings on the side of the tree
toward the depressions.

3. Later in the night a red sun-like light was seen through the trees.
It moved about and pulsed. At one point it appeared to throw off glowing
particles and then broke into five separate white objects and then disappeared. Immediately thereafter, three star-like objects were noticed
in the sky, two objects to the north and one to the south, all of which
were about 10° off the horizon. The objects moved rapidly in sharp angular
movements and displayed red, green and blue lights. The objects to the
north appeared to be elliptical through an 8-12 power lens. They then
turned to full circles. The objects to the north remained in the sky for
an hour or more. The object to the south was visible for two or three
hours and beamed down a stream of light from time to time. Numerous individuals, including the undersigned, witnessed the activities in paragraphs
2 and 3.

CHARLES I. HALT, Lt Col, USAF
Deputy Base Commander

Lieutenant Colonel Charles Halt's memorandum to the Ministry of Defence describing
the events outside the two NATO bases of Bentwaters and Woodbridge, Suffolk.
The security policemen's encounter took place in the small hours of the 26th – not
27th – December 1980. (US Air Force)

A sketch by Mike Sacks based on a description by one of the witnesses to the craft that landed outside the twin USAF bases of Bentwaters and Woodbridge, Suffolk, in December 1980. From the first book on the case, *Sky Crash: A Cosmic Conspiracy* by Brenda Butler, Dot Street and Jenny Randles, Neville Spearman, 1984.

22. EXEMPT FROM DISCLOSURE

The American National Investigations Committee on Aerial Phenomena (NICAP), founded in 1956 by Thomas Townsend Brown, a former US Navy physicist, and directed by Major Donald E. Keyhoe, became the most prestigious and influential UFO group in the world. No other UFO organization before or since has so consistently and effectively challenged official attempts to debunk the subject.

NICAP's membership included numerous retired military officers and scientists and – as it later transpired – CIA and other intelligence personnel (a fact acknowledged in an undated CIA memorandum).

It was no secret that a former CIA director, Rear Admiral Roscoe H. Hillenkoetter, became a member of NICAP's Board of Governors. Among those with covert CIA connections who had infiltrated key positions in NICAP was Colonel Joseph J. Bryan III, founder and original Chief of the CIA's Psychological Strategy Board. Others included a former member of the agency's Psychological Warfare Staff, Count Nicolas de Rochefort, who became Vice-Chairman of NICAP, and Karl Pflock, a former CIA briefing officer and author of two books on the Roswell incident. Todd Zechel, a former Army Security Agency officer, has revealed many other names, which are published in my book *Above Top Secret*.

According to Zechel, Major Keyhoe was deliberately ousted by the CIA infiltrators in 1969, after which John L. Acuff (with alleged CIA affiliations) took over as director. NICAP eventually became so ineffective that it was dissolved, and its files were taken over in 1973 by Dr J. Allen Hynek's newly formed Center for UFO Studies (CUFOS).[1] Hynek, as we learned earlier, was a consultant on UFOs to both the CIA and the US Air Force. It is difficult to avoid the corollary that CUFOS was likewise infiltrated.

SATELLITES AND UFO IMAGERY INTELLIGENCE

'Satellite and space exploration programs should give us new, valuable information on UFOs, affording definite evidence as to their reality,' declared Admiral Hillenkoetter, speaking from his position as a member of NICAP, in 1957.[2] His declaration proved to be prescient. Considerable data on UFOs – including imagery – have been gathered by spy satellites, although much of these remain classified at levels higher than Top Secret.

From 1968 to 1969 Dr Irena Scott, a physiologist and an investigator for CUFOS, worked for the Defense Intelligence Agency (DIA), where she was security cleared for two of America's photo-reconnaissance spy satellite programmes – Keyhole and Talent. 'The history of the Keyhole program,' says Jeffrey T. Richelson, author of *America's Secret Eyes in Space*, 'is a history of one of the most significant military technological developments of [the 20th] century and perhaps in all history.'[3]

In 1968 Scott was working with a section of the DIA known as Air Order of Battle, Soviet/East Europe Division, Eastern USSR Branch. 'Our work involved identifying all the flying objects over the area, such as aircraft and missiles, for each incoming mission, and then making a report to the CIA,' Scott writes.

> The CIA was the recipient of all our reports, as far as I know. In July 1968, because of a possible UFO sighting made by myself and my sister, I mentioned the subject to the people I worked with. To my surprise, no-one ridiculed me. This was because, sometime before I had entered this section, they had reported a UFO on the Keyhole photography. I was able to see these photographs. However, they were classified, so I didn't write down identifying information.
>
> The object on the photograph was shaped like a saucer with a raised dome in the center. It was over water. One could tell by the wave pattern on the water that the object was not in the water. This water was inland or near the USSR, and I think it was probably the Black Sea . . . It was to the west of a mountain range having a secret Soviet military installation on the other side. The object was photographed on at least two occasions (photography from different [satellite] passes around the Earth). It was in a slightly different place during each of these passes, but was in the same general area.
>
> Because it was seen on more than one mission (a mission [or orbit] is 90 minutes), I made copies of it and photographically changed the object's size, until I had photographs of the object that were the same size, but from different viewpoints. I examined these in stereo, in order to more clearly view the shape of the object. It appeared to be saucer-shaped with a dome [which] appeared to be quite tall in comparison to the brim – almost like a high top-hat, or like the Kecksburg, Pennsylvania, object standing on end. I don't know whether this was

actually the shape of the object, or whether the shape had been distorted by my method of photography.

The supervisors of this area told me that they had reported the object to the CIA as a UFO ... Although the CIA almost always accepted their professional opinion about the identity of objects, [they] did not accept this report. The CIA told them that what they saw was an imperfection on the film. The DIA argued that, since it was photographed on two different occasions (I recall at least three pictures – there may have been three missions or two pictures from another mission), it couldn't be a photographic imperfection ... To further check, they sent the film to densitometry specialists. These people analyzed the film, and reported that a real object had been photographed [but] the CIA again told them the photographs were not of objects ...[4]

PROJECT SNOWBIRD

On 29 December 1980, during the period of the Rendlesham Forest events, Betty Cash, her friend Vickie Landrum and the latter's seven-year-old grandson Colby were driving near Huffman, a suburb of Houston, Texas, when at about 21:00 a fiery object was seen in the sky. It quickly descended to tree-top level above the road, and hovered in front of them over 100 feet away. Flames appeared to be shooting down from the object. Betty stopped the car, and the two adults got out and watched. Colby pleaded with them to get back inside, which they did, though Betty spent more time outside than the others.

Each witness described the object somewhat differently. Betty, for example, thought it had no distinct shape, while Colby was certain it was diamond-shaped. The bursts of flame coincided with sounds 'like a flamethrower', and a 'roaring' as well as a 'beeping' noise lasted throughout the encounter. The car was so hot that Betty was unable to touch the door with her bare hand. The witnesses followed the object in the car and noticed that about twenty-plus helicopters, many of them twin-rotor Chinooks, appeared to be escorting the object – though never getting closer than about three-quarters of a mile. After stopping three more times to watch the spectacle, Betty drove the others home, and arrived at her own home at 21:50. Horrific physical symptoms – evidently resulting from irradiation – then became apparent (see pp. 345–6). The other witnesses, who spent less time outside the car, suffered some similar symptoms, though to a much lesser degree.[5]

The presence of helicopters suggests that the object was an experimental device which had malfunctioned, the main purpose of the helicopters being to ensure that in the event of a forced landing the area could immediately be sealed off by troops. Some sources state that the craft – 'Project Snowbird' – was either a nuclear-powered prototype space shuttle, or a 'lighting device' with an auxiliary conventional rocket engine that had got into difficulties. An interesting explanation was given by two US military intelligence agents during a two-hour television debate – *UFO Cover-Up? Live* – transmitted from Washington and Moscow in 1988. The agents, 'Condor' and 'Falcon', their faces blacked out and voices electronically modulated, claimed that the object 'was an alien craft piloted by military aircraft pilots [and] they found that the aircraft did not respond to certain controls [and] radioed that they thought the craft was going to crash ... However, this craft did not crash.'[6]

The agents almost certainly were Robert M. Collins ('Condor'), a former US Air Force captain who retired from his assignment at the Plasma Physics group at Sandia National Laboratories, Kirtland AFB, in 1988, and Richard C. Doty ('Falcon'), a special agent assigned to the Air Force Office of Special Investigations.[7] In a book by Collins and Doty, *Exempt from Disclosure* (2005), Collins suggests that the craft was 'a very primitive attempt by the US government to find a fast-track, secret way to get us into space and off to the stars using anti-gravity [but] according to the [Los Alamos National Laboratory] contact ... there were problems with the materials [and] propulsion system. Edward Teller had supposedly identified the [alien] power system as far back as 1957 ...'[8] (One of my sources learned that plasma physics is the key to alien propulsion technology.)

In 1982 former US Air Force intelligence officer Steve Lewis, who spent twelve years investigating UFOs for the military, both in the US and abroad, said that only a fraction of information accumulated by the military has been released. He disclosed that the Air Force believes that the very bright, sometimes blinding, lights associated with UFOs are related to their propulsion system, enabling them to travel faster than light.[9]

Betty Cash and Vicki Landrum were left in no doubt that the craft was American, and sued the US Government for $20 million damages. The case was dismissed on the grounds that no such craft was owned, operated or in the inventory of the Air Force, the Army, the Navy or NASA. There is a great deal more information on this important case – including testimony from other witnesses – and essential reading is *The Cash-Landrum UFO Incident* by John F. Schuessler, a retired NASA technician who heads the Mutual UFO Network.[10]

On 29 December 1998, Betty Cash died of health problems associated with the injuries that she sustained from her close encounter – exactly eighteen years earlier.

CONDITION ZEBRA

Merle S. McDow worked at the US Navy's Atlantic Command Support Facility in Norfolk, Virginia, with a team who briefed Rear Admiral Harry DePue Train II, Commander-in-Chief, US Atlantic Fleet (and in charge of all NATO forces in the Atlantic). 'My job,' said McDow, who held Top Secret SCI (Sensitive Compartmented Information) clearance, 'was to make sure that any incoming and outgoing audio/video information that came into the Command Center was recorded and duly logged for reference, in case they needed it later.' One day in early May 1981, a condition 'Zebra' – the Navy's highest alert – was announced.

On most occasions, 'Zebra' would be a drill – but this was the real thing. A warning came from NORAD that an unidentified object had entered the Atlantic Area of Operations (AOR) from the north. 'We launched planes from as far north as Greenland to Naval Air Station Oceana [Virginia],' said McDow, in his testimony for Steven Greer's Disclosure Project. 'This event lasted almost an hour. You could hear the pilots' live voice transmissions ... Planes were able to close a couple of times, and were able to see that the object was not an aircraft that we were familiar with.'

During the event, KH-11 satellites took photos of the object. 'From the photograph I remember,' continued McDow, 'the shape was more like a cylinder [with] abrupt ends [which] did appear to be reflecting sunlight and you could clearly tell it was metallic ... What was really bugging Admiral Train was that this thing absolutely had complete control of the situation and could be anywhere that it wanted to be in a matter of seconds ... Train was scrambling and authorizing planes [from] the north and south to literally track it and force it down.' It went from Nova Scotia to Norfolk, Virginia, in one sweep of the radar. Eventually, the craft shot off at phenomenal speed.

Later, two men in suits arrived and confiscated all records, including tape and written logs, and questioned McDow, warning him in an intimidating manner never to disclose what he had heard or seen to his colleagues or to anyone off-base.[11]

Commander Will Miller, US Naval Reserve (retired), told me that he had tried to get some confirmation for the incident from Admiral Train in person. 'My disinterest in this subject is profound,' Train simply intoned.[12]

THE NATIONAL SECURITY AGENCY

The American National Security Agency (NSA) is the world's largest electronic intelligence (ELINT) eavesdropping empire and, according to a report by Congressional auditors, classifies somewhere between 50 million and 100 million documents a year! 'With more secrets than are held by the CIA, the State Department, the Pentagon, and all other agencies of government combined,' writes James Bamford, author of two books on the Agency, 'NSA likely holds the largest body of secrets on Earth.'[13]

I am informed that, of the roughly half-dozen so-called 'intelligence disciplines' (major sources of 'raw', or unevaluated, intelligence), the NSA is the sole US Government authority and executive for the collection and reporting of signals intelligence (SIGINT): it treats all other disciplines or source categories as 'collateral' – for example, human intelligence (HUMINT) and imagery intelligence (IMINT), the latter acquired by aircraft and satellites (such as the KH-11).

Like the other federal agencies that have consistently and routinely collected and reported UFO-related intelligence, the NSA is also tasked to collect and report SIGINT about, for instance, the reactions of foreign air forces and air-defence forces to UFO incursions. Until the 1980s, however, few outside the intelligence community were aware of the fact. 'Please be advised that NSA does not have *any* interest in UFOs in *any* manner,' they told researcher Robert Todd in 1976.[14]

Thanks to Citizens Against UFO Secrecy (CAUS), some UFO-related documents originating with the NSA were released in January 1980. The Agency admitted that many more were 'exempt from disclosure'. Later that year, NSA representative Eugene Yeates admitted in a court hearing that the NSA had found many documents on UFOs that were relevant to the FOIA request. Lawyer Peter Gersten, representing CAUS, under terms of the Freedom of Information Act (FOIA), filed suit against the NSA in the US District Court, Washington, DC, to obtain 135 documents then admitted to being withheld by the Agency. After studying a twenty-one-page 'above' Top Secret affidavit in camera, Judge Gesell ruled that the Agency was fully justified in withholding the documents in their entirety. The case was dismissed.[15,16]

In 2005, NSA released a considerably less-censored version of the 1980 document, which had been classified TOP SECRET UMBRA (see pp. 347–8). 'Umbra' was the code word for a communications intelligence (COMINT) 'compartment', in use until 1999.[17] It is not a level of classification per se, but rather the communications intelligence category-three (COMINT CAT III) code word or caveat associated with top-secret material, restricting access still further to those with a 'ticket' to the right 'compartment' relating to that particular intelligence matter. Just to confuse the issue SCI can also include sub-compartments – e.g. TOP SECRET GAMMA GUPPY. Above all, however, access is determined by 'need to know' (NTK). As a source explained to me: 'One only shares SCI with other SCI'ers, but only if the other SCI'er has an NTK. NTK is the basic, bottom-line rule regardless of all the spider-webs of administration . . .' For simplification, here are some basic US Government definitions:

— TOP SECRET: Information, the unauthorized disclosure of which could reasonably be expected to cause exceptionally grave damage to the national security.
— SENSITIVE COMPARTMENTED INFORMATION: Information bearing special controls indicating restricted handling within present and future intelligence collection programs and their end products.
— SPECIAL ACCESS PROGRAM: Program imposing 'need-to-know' or access controls beyond those normally provided for access to Confidential, Secret, or Top Secret information.[18]

A Washington source who has read the uncensored affidavit assured me that it does not contain any sensational information about crashed craft or aliens, and that the deleted portions relate mostly to the 'sources and methods' by which the information was acquired. However, he remains in no doubt that the UFO subject ranks as the most sensitive in the US Government.

A US NAVAL/AIR FORCE INTELLIGENCE LINK

Robert F. Dorr, an Air Force veteran and leading aviation author, has reported some intriguing information relating to a small Air Force unit located in the mid-1970s at the US Naval Air Station at Patuxent River, Maryland. 'I've uncovered several clues,' he wrote in 1977, 'that suggest that America's secret UFO program – and the campaign to ridicule military personnel who've seen UFOs – is located in a fenced-in stucco building adjacent to the mud flats along Maryland's Patuxent River.

At the Patuxent Naval Air Test Center, a number of strange things are going on – Navy squadron VX(N)-8 operating a fleet of P-3 Orion electronics [intelligence] aircraft to investigate mysterious phenomena in the world's oceans, an Air Force radar surveillance outfit reporting *directly* to the Pentagon, and a cluster of civilian-garbed Air Force intelligence people (on a Navy base!) are all working behind those high mesh fences in a top-security area. 'This is the headquarters for it all,' a naval officer once told me. 'The Bermuda Triangle, even experiments aimed at making contact with intelligent life in the Universe. There's a guy in charge, in that building, who reports directly to the top.'

'These "leads" *are* circumstantial,' concedes Dorr. 'Although Capt. Charles R. Gillespie, the commander at Patuxent, couldn't be interviewed, [and] his public affairs officer, W.M. Frierson Jr, denied that any UFO-related activity is taking place there, [the] likely truth is that any national cover-up, if there is one, probably involves all the services and several government agencies in different locations. [However] even the most ardent UFO believers have difficulty explaining how such a big secret could be held, so tightly, for so many years, by so many people . . .'[19]

A TOP SECRET UFO WORKING GROUP

As revealed by former *New York Times* reporter Howard Blum in his book *Out There*, a top-secret group, known as the UFO Working Group, was established in the USA in December 1987. Its seventeen members included various military and scientific intelligence officers, who met regularly at the Pentagon 'Tank' to evaluate UFO sightings and related issues.[20] The Tank is the Joint Chiefs of Staff (JCS) Conference Room, located in the National Military Command Center (NMCC).

Although Blum states that the Working Group was established in December 1987, I have learned that meetings were held well before then. The header of a memo leaked to Canadian researcher Grant Cameron states that an 'Advanced Theoretical Physics Conference' was held from 20 to 25 May 1985, at the BDM McClean Secure Facility, Virginia. In the space stipulating 'Specific information to which access is requested' is typed: 'Top Secret/Restricted Data Sigmas as required.' Cameron was also given names of most of the attendees. Later, I received a complete list of attendees from another source.

According to my information, the project was the brainchild of John Alexander, a former Army colonel, and the committee was nominally sanctioned by the Army Science Board and Army Laboratory Command. The research effort, I am told, appears to have been a 'major engineering project' under Admiral Bobby Ray Inman, former CIA Deputy Director, Director of Naval Intelligence and Director of the National Security Agency.

Several attendees have confirmed for me that the meetings at BDM were related to what later became known as the UFO Working Group. One attendee was Dr Robert M. Wood, a now retired aeronautical engineer whose career included forty-three years with McDonnell Douglas. He now devotes much of his time to UFO research.

'I was there,' Dr Wood confirmed to me in 2005. 'The 1985 meetings were held in the basement at BDM. The idea was to pool our knowledge of UFOs to see what we could conclude. Several people made presentations, mostly not very classified. I was out of the room for a few minutes while some special subject was discussed. All my notes were classified at the time, and they have probably been destroyed.'

Other attendees included Ronald Blackburn, Milt Janzen and Don Keuble (Lockheed Aircraft); Howell McConnell (NSA); Dr Harold E. Puthoff (a physicist and former NSA officer who has been involved in several other top-secret UFO-related projects, such as 'remote viewing', employing psychics); Ed Speakman (Army Intelligence); and Bill Wilkinson (CIA).

THE NATIONAL MILITARY COMMAND CENTER

The NMCC is the Pentagon's primary nerve centre responsible for generating Emergency Action Messages (EAMs) to launch-control centres, nuclear submarines, reconnaissance aircraft and battlefield commanders worldwide.[21] Anthony L. Kimery is an award-winning editor and journalist who has covered global security, intelligence and defence issues for two decades. In 1989 he revealed that, according to an Army source who worked with the Joint Chiefs of Staff (JCS) at the NMCC during the 1970s, a secret, centralized command structure dealing with UFOs has been in operation since the mid to late 1970s, and (in 1989) continued to handle the UFO problem from the ranks of the NMCC.

'Based on testimony provided to this reporter by the former JCS source and others,' reported Kimery, 'military and political leaders have for more than ten years considered the UFO reality serious enough to warrant a consolidated oversight mechanism and planning force, on a par with management for global conflict. To be a matter of military preparedness directed at this high command level, the UFO situation is clearly perceived by the government as a threat worthy of continuous, in-depth monitoring and surveillance and, if the need arises, military confrontation . . .'[22]

TOP SECRET BRITISH RESEARCH

In previous books, especially *Alien Liaison* and *Beyond Top Secret*, I detailed information relating to top-secret investigations into UFOs conducted by the Royal Air Force Provost and Security Services (P&SS) in a 'lodger unit' within the Flying Complaints Flight (FCF) cell, sometimes referred to as the 'low-flying section'. The P&SS is the British equivalent of the US Air Force Office of Special Investigations (AFOSI), long involved in UFO investigations. As explained to me by a former member of the P&SS, the FCF is a unit of RAF Police Criminal and Security Investigators who investigate any report related to flying complaints – especially UFOs:

'Investigators of the RAF Police are in fact the "Special Branch" of the Air Force. Their training and qualities are superior to those of the civilian [Police] Special Branch, and even MI5, [and] are so respected throughout the world that MI5 send their own operatives to receive RAF tuition. All in all, there is no better unit to investigate UFO complaints . . . The covert capability of the RAF Investigator is so notorious that they have operatives attached to MI5/MI6, also New Scotland Yard, as well as overseas intelligence organizations.'

Another P&SS investigator revealed in conversation with my informant that from 1963 to 1965, while in charge of personnel security at the Government Buildings, Bromyard Avenue, London W3, where the FCF was then based, he became aware of top-secret research into the subject:

'I had access to every Top Secret file there was,' he said, 'except low flying, because they dealt with UFOs. I knew they dealt with low flying, but they had a special team [which] also dealt with UFOs. It was a small one . . . they had their own separate doors and entrance. We could get in anywhere, CI [counter-intelligence], anywhere, but not in that bloody department. I remember they used to have an Air Ministry guard in the passage – you couldn't get past them. And they had the doors locked from the inside. We could see the Provost Marshal's top-secret files, but yet I couldn't get into the place dealing with UFOs . . .'[23]

The FCF was later based at RAF Rudloe Manor in Wiltshire, then the headquarters of the Provost and Security Services. The Rudloe Site (where

I was arrested by Ministry of Defence Police in 1985 for snooping around its perimeter, and interrogated by Royal Navy personnel and then the civil police) is located near Corsham, 100 miles from London. Until recent years, it was the UK Government's Emergency War Headquarters, with a huge underground bunker, known by various code names, such as BUR-LINGTON, SUBTERFUGE and TURNSTILE, which could accommodate over 4,000 people, including, of course, the Cabinet.

I learned via a source who had been contracted to conduct certain scientific research into UFOs at a unit (presumably FCF) in Rudloe Manor that in 1978 alone – one of the busiest years on record for UFO sightings – £11 million had been appropriated to deal with the problem.

In the 1970s Dr Robert F. Creegan, former Professor of Philosophy at the State University of New York, made a number of trips to Britain to discuss aspects of the subject with various involved parties. 'I did get the impression,' he told me, 'that "pressure" applied by officials in the United States was one of the causes for a British policy of giving so little information vis-à-vis the UFO problem.' In an article for an American journal, he was more forthcoming:

'It was made evident to me that the British at that time desired to please the US establishment. And it was strongly hinted that US officials [were] making frantic efforts to suppress public interest . . . UFOs alarm the establishment because, whatever theory is correct, a major loss of control is apprehended, associated with reports of objects which affect mechanisms of control and which deeply puzzle and confuse both the public and many of its would-be leaders . . .'[24]

REFERENCES

1. Good, Timothy, *Above Top Secret: The Worldwide UFO Cover-up*, Sidgwick & Jackson, London, 1987; William Morrow, New York, 1988. See also *Beyond Top Secret*.

2. 'Will Sputniks Solve Flying Saucer Puzzle?' *The Washington Daily News*, 18 November 1957.

3. Richelson, Jeffrey T., *America's Secret Eyes in Space: The US Keyhole Satellite Program*, HarperCollins, 1990.

4. Scott, Irena, *Ohio UFOs (and many others)*, Vol. 1, Greyden Press, Columbus, Ohio, 1997, pp. 115–17.

5. 'Burns Follows UFO Incident', *The APRO Bulletin*, Vol. 29, No. 8, 1981, pp. 1–4.

6. *UFO Cover-Up? Live*, produced by Michael Seligman with LBS, 14 October 1988.

7. Good, Timothy, *Alien Liaison: The Ultimate Secret*, Century, 1991. Published in the US as *Alien Contact: Top-Secret UFO Files Revealed*, William Morrow, 1993.

8. Collins, Robert M. and Doty, Richard C., *Exempt from Disclosure*, Peregrine Communications, 865 Helke Road, Vandalia, OH 45377, 2005, p. 177.

9. *The APRO Bulletin*, Vol. 30, No. 7.

10. Schuessler, John F., *The Cash-Landrum UFO Incident*, Geo Graphics Printing Co., La Porte, Texas, 1998.

11. Greer, Steven M., *Disclosure: Military and Government Witnesses Reveal the Greatest Secrets in Modern History*, Crossing Point, PO Box 265, Corzet, VA 22932, 2001, pp. 238–45. Additional information supplied by Commander Will Miller Jr, USNR (retired).

12. Personal interview, Tampa, Florida, 12 April 2005.

13. Bamford, James, *Body of Secrets: How America's NSA and Britain's GCHQ Eavesdrop on the World*, Century, London, 2001, p. 516.

14. Letter from the NSA's information officer, 20 February 1976.

15. Fawcett, Lawrence and Greenwood, Barry J., *Clear Intent: The Government Coverup of the UFO Experience*, Prentice-Hall, Englewood Cliffs, New Jersey, 1984, pp. 181–2.

16. Memorandum Opinion and Order Granting Motion for Summary Judgment in the US District Court, District of Columbia: *Citizens Against UFO Secrecy* (Plaintiff) v. *National Security Agency* (Defendant), 18 November 1980.

17. Arkin, William M., *Code Names: Deciphering US Military Plans, Programs, and Operations in the 9/11 World*, Steerforth Press, Hanover, NH 03755, 2005, p. 538.

18. US Government Accounting Office, GAO/NSIAD-96-64, Defense Industrial Security.

19. Drake, Rufus (Robert F. Dorr), 'Operation Ridicule', *UFO Report*, Vol. 4, No. 6, October 1977, pp. 16–19.

20. Blum, Howard, *Out There: The Government's Secret Quest for Extraterrestrials*, Simon & Schuster, New York, 1990.

21. www.globalsecurity.org

22. Neilson, James (Anthony Kimery), 'Secret US/UFO Structure', *UFO Magazine* (US), Vol. 15, No. 9, 2000, p. 28.

23. Good, op. cit.

24. See *Above Top Secret* and *Beyond Top Secret*.

The US Department of Justice claim form filed by three witnesses who encountered an experimental, apparently nuclear-powered craft, which irradiated them near Huffman, Texas, on 29 December 1980. *(From The Cash-Landrum UFO Incident by John F. Schuessler, Geo Graphics Printing Co., La Porte, Texas, 1998)*

(11. Description of Accident cont.)

---

flames emanating from the bottom. Claimant stopped her automobile since
the object was now blocking the road. Claimant and the two passengers
proceeded to leave the vehicle and look at the object which was now hovering
at treetop level approximately 135 feet from the people. Claimant experienced
intense and excruciating heat which appeared to be caused by the object.
After approximately five minutes claimant returned to her automobile and the
object appeared to move further away. Claimant proceeded to drive along
the road where approximately three miles away she observed what appeared to
her to be approximately 23 military-type helicopters, several of which
appeared to be double rotary type, in the general vicinity of the object.
Finally there came a time when both the object and helicopters disappeared.

(13. Personal Injury cont.)

Her eyes closed completely and she could not see for several days. The
red blotches became blisters of clear fluid. Claimant was unable to eat
and continued to suffer nausea, vomiting and diarrhea. Four days after the
incident, claimant entered Parkway General Hospital in Houston, Texas where
she was treated and remained for twelve days. Furthermore claimant suffered
severe loss of hair and loss of fingernails. After being discharged, she
continued to suffer swellings, headaches and loss of appetite. A little
over a week later she returned to the hospital for an additional fifteen days
of treatment. During the following year claimant continued to have medical
problems including, but not limited to, recurring blisters, constant headache
and back pains, weight loss, chronic diarrhea and bowel problems.
Claimant experiences intense pain when she takes a hot bath and must take
cold baths. In October, November and December of 1981 Claimant was treated
at the Lloyd Noland Foundation, Inc. (Hospital & Clinic) Fairfield, Alabama for
various ailments associated with her encounter with the object. As of the
date of this claim, claimant remains constantly tired continues to experience
recurring headaches, chronic diarrhea and associated bowel problems.

SUMMARY OF MEDICAL EFFECTS: Erythema, acute photophthalmia, impaired vision,
dystrophic changes in the nails, stomach pains, vomiting, diarrhea, anorexia,
loss of energy, lethargy, scarring and loss of pigmentation, excessive hair
loss, and hair regrowth of a different texture.

DIAGNOSIS: Radiation damage confined to the skin and the immediate subcutaneous
area. The type and dosage of radiation is unknown-possible radiodermatitis
secondary to ionizing radiation.

DEGREE OF PERMANENT DISABILTY: Unknown at this time

PROGNOSIS: Unknown at this time

~~**TOP SECRET UMBRA**~~

UNITED STATES DISTRICT COURT
FOR THE DISTRICT OF COLUMBIA

CITIZENS AGAINST UNIDENTIFIED)
FLYING OBJECTS SECRECY,)
)
       Plaintiff,)
)   Civil Action No.
     v.)   80-1562
)
NATIONAL SECURITY AGENCY,)
)
       Defendant.)
)

IN CAMERA
AFFIDAVIT OF EUGENE F. YEATES

County of Anne Arundel)
) ss:
State of Maryland)

     Eugene F. Yeates, being duly sworn, deposes and says:

     1. (U) I am the Chief, Office of Policy, of the National Security Agency (NSA). As Chief, Office of Policy, I am responsible for processing all initial requests made pursuant to the Freedom of Information Act (FOIA) for NSA records. The statements herein are based upon personal knowledge, upon my personal review of information available to me in my official capacity, and upon conclusions reached in accordance therewith.

     2. (U) This affidavit supplements my unclassified affidavit executed on September 30, 1980 regarding all documents which have been located by NSA pursuant to plaintiff's FOIA request but which have been withheld wholly or in part by NSA. I submit this affidavit _in camera_ for the purpose of stating facts, which cannot be publicly disclosed, that are the basis for exempting the records from release to the plaintiff.

     3. ~~(S-CCO)~~ At the beginning of each paragraph of this affidavit, the letter or letters within parentheses designate(s) the degree of sensitivity of information the paragraph contains.

~~**TOP SECRET UMBRA**~~

Approved for Release by NSA on 11-03-2005
pursuant to E.O. 12958, as amended

Two pages from the 'above' Top Secret 21-page affidavit by the National Security Agency (9 October 1980) giving reasons why certain information pertaining to UFO reports remains exempt from disclosure. When first released, a great deal of information in the affidavit was deleted; years later, the NSA declassified additional portions, such as may be seen here (page 11). *(National Security Agency)*

~~TOP SECRET UMBRA~~ NSA25X1
NSA25X3

   c. Twelve NSA-originated COMINT reports target
the communications links and systems of ☐
Two documents, in summary format, report the decrypted text
of military communications. Two of the records are in message
format and report the decrypted texts of ☐ communications which relate that an unidentified flying object was
sighted in the air by a ☐ unit. One report
contains a summary of ☐ activity based upon communications in reaction to an unidentified flying object along the
☐ Two documents report on communications
transmitted between ☐ and ☐
☐ who report visual observations of luminous spheres. One
report is a summary of a transmission/between ☐

☐ Finally,
four documents in this group of twelve were intercepted from
other non-military communications targets. One document is based
on the intercepted transmission of a ☐
reporting a bright light. The second record is based on the
intercept of a transmission of an ☐ to
a ☐ station seeking a report on any shining phenomena or
falling meteorites observed on specified dates. The third and
fourth reports are a summaries of on-going debates on UFOs among
☐ based on intercepted communications transmitted
on ☐ nets.

   d. Five of the NSA-originated COMINT reports
target government net communications ☐ All five of these
documents are based on intercepted military communications
between ☐ units and ☐ commanders reporting observations of luminous objects in the sky.

11

~~TOP SECRET UMBRA~~

N M C C

THE NATIONAL MILITARY COMMAND CENTER

WASHINGTON, D.C. 20301

THE JOINT STAFF

21 January 1976
0630 EST

MEMORANDUM FOR RECORD

Subject: Report of UFO - Cannon AFB NM

Reference: AFOC Phonecon 21055 EST Jan 76

The following information was received from the Air Force
Operations Center at 0555 EST:

"Two UFOs are reported near the flight line at Cannon AFB,
New Mexico. Security Police observing them reported the UFOs
to be 25 yards in diameter, gold or silver in color with blue
light on top, hole in the middle and red light on bottom. Air
Force is checking with radar. Additionally, checking weather
inversion data."

J.B. MORIN
Rear Admiral, USN
Deputy Director for
Operations, NMCC

A memorandum from the Pentagon's National Military Command Center reporting
the observation of UFOs at Cannon AFB, New Mexico, in January 1976.
(National Military Command Center via William L. Moore)

23. INTRUSIONS AND INCURSIONS IN THE USSR

At around 04:00 on 20 September 1977, over 170 witnesses, including border guards and militia, observed a large, glowing cigar-shaped object which was raining down beams of light. It hovered for some fifteen minutes before heading off towards the Finnish border with the USSR. Soviet Air Force Colonel Boris Sokolov, who headed the Ministry of Defence's investigation into the case, revealed that the object had been seen over a wide area for at least four hours before the foregoing observation.[1]

'I found out that a large group of military men had witnessed the event about several hundred kilometres from Petrosovodsk, in one of the border regions,' Sokolov told television producer Lawrence Moore in 1994. 'When they tried to report it, using their usual field communications – they had telephones and cable lines, radio and short-wave – none of the links had worked. After the incident, which had lasted for several hours over Petrosovodsk, and a little shorter period of time over the border area, all communications were suddenly restored.'[2]

'INSTITUTE 22'

So concerned was the military about such a potential threat that a unique, state-funded, military and scientific research project was initiated, involving the cooperation of the Ministry of Defence and the USSR Academy of Sciences. The top-secret investigation, established in 1978, was later code-named 'Institute 22'. 'The Armed Forces were ordered to study what, if any, influences possible UFOs might have on the proper functioning of military technical equipment,' explained Alexander Plaksin, one of the scientists involved in the project. 'No-one was told the purpose of the reports.'[3]

'The Ministry issued an order which named special officers in military units and regions that were given the responsibility of watching out for abnormal phenomena,' explained Colonel Sokolov. 'Over six million participated, and during this period the rank-and-file personnel changed three times . . . and the whole of the Soviet Union was involved.'[4]

Yuri Andropov, the former short-term Soviet President and long-time chief of the KGB (now the SVR – Foreign Intelligence Service), had an acute interest in the subject, and kept a file in his desk. According to one of his aides, Igor Sinitsin, it was Andropov who ordered the thirteen-year programme, which required four million soldiers to monitor sightings.[5] (The six-million figure cited by Sokolov may have included civil servants.)

'Thousands of reports involving millions of witnesses were funnelled to Sokolov, including forty or more incidents in which Russian warplanes engaged UFOs,' reports television journalist George Knapp, who interviewed Sokolov in Moscow. 'Three of those planes crashed and two pilots were killed. In one disturbing case, UFOs manoeuvred over a Russian nuclear-missile base and manipulated the launch codes.'[6]

That incident – which occurred on 4 October 1982 at an intercontinental ballistic missile (ICBM) silo at Byelokoroviche, Soviet Ukraine – brought the world to the brink of nuclear war. At around 18:00, soldiers and villagers saw a large, geometrically-shaped object, apparently nearly 3,000 feet in diameter, hovering in the sky over the silo. Lieutenant Colonel Vladimir Plantonev, a missile engineer, described the UFO as having a completely even surface, with no visible portholes.[7] Simultaneously, inside the missile silo, an emergency warning light indicated that a nuclear missile had switched to launch mode. 'The communications officer said that somehow, something had entered the correct code,' reported Knapp. 'But Moscow had not ordered a launch, nor had any personnel in the bunker touched the control panel. For fifteen agonizing seconds, technicians frantically scrambled to stop the launch. Then, without explanation, the launch sequence was aborted.' No faults with the equipment were found by investigators from Institute 22.[8]

AIR DEFENCE INCIDENTS

According to Paul Stonehill, on an unspecified date in 1982 a Soviet MiG-21 jet disappeared during a routine flight in a militarized zone of Byelorussia. 'The following day, the aircraft reappeared from nowhere and landed. The on-board clock indicated the time of its disappearance, as if it had vanished. The plane could not have remained in the air without refuelling. The pilot claimed he knew nothing of the incident.'[9]

A Defense Intelligence Agency (DIA) message in December 1989, previously classified Secret, refers to a number of UFO reports by Soviet Air Force personnel, of which the most interesting involved a MiG-23 (NATO code name Flogger):

In the spring of 1984, a friend [censored] was sent by the regimental commander to intercept an object which had been observed flying near Mikha Tskhakaya [Gruzinskaya] airfield at a supersonic speed. However, the object did not make a sonic boom as it flew north to south over the base. The pilot, flying a MiG-23/Flogger in full afterburner at Mach 1.2 was unable to close on the object.

By the time both MiG-23 and unidentified object approached the coastline of the Black Sea, the Flogger was approaching Mach 1.6. The pilot activated his infrared search and track system (IRSTS) approximately 12 km from the target and observed the largest bloom he had ever seen on his indicator. The pilot immediately reported this information to the controller.

By the time he reached a speed of nearly Mach 2, the pilot had to break off the intercept due to low fuel. The pilot never acquired a visual identification of the object. The MiG's altitude during the chase was 5,000 m.

Another report in the DIA message cites an undated incident involving an 'ellipse-shaped object' sighted by several aircrews more than 20 kilometres from their position, during night flights in the Azerbaijan area. 'The aircrew were unable to acquire a radar contact on the object. All of the pilots [who] observed the object were instructed to land immediately. The crews were ordered never to discuss the object they had observed.' (See p. 365.)

In October 1991, following a request from Russian cosmonaut Pavel Popovich, the KGB/SVR declassified a number of documents from its so-called 'Blue Folder'. This material was obtained by Vadim K. Ilyin from the late Vyacheslav Shtyepa, of the Ufological Committee of the Russian Geographical Society. One of the documents relates to an encounter sometime in 1984 in the Turkestan Military District, when radar at an anti-aircraft unit near Astrakhan tracked an unknown target flying along the Caspian Sea coastline at 2,000 metres altitude.

The spherical-shaped target did not respond to interrogations. 'Two fighters were scrambled, but all attempts to shoot it down failed,' reports Ilyin. 'Moreover, when the object was fired at, it descended to 100 metres above the ground [thus] making further firing by the fighters impossible . . . despite the firing, the speed of the UFO did not change.' Photographs were taken from the ground as the object passed over the locations of several military units.

When the UFO approached Krasnovodsk, a helicopter gunship was sent up in another attempt to shoot it down. Immediately, the UFO climbed swiftly to an altitude beyond the helicopter's reach. After using up all their shells, the helicopter pilots landed, and the UFO made a sharp turn and disappeared out to sea.

Another incident occurred in Krasnovodsk in 1985, according to the Blue Folder, when an air-defence radar station tracked an unknown object at an altitude of 20,000 metres. 'Its diameter was about 1,000 metres!' reports Ilyin. 'The object did not move, but after some time a small disc [with] a diameter of approximately five metres flew out of the large object [and] landed at the Krasnovodsk spit.' A flotilla of patrol-boats headed to the landing site, but when they were some 100 metres from the small UFO, it took off and flew to a distance of about a kilometre. Patrol-boats approached the UFO again, and again it flew away from them. This happened five times. Finally, the smaller object shot skywards and was seen (on radar) to rejoin its 'mother-ship', whereupon the giant craft disappeared into space.[10]

In 1996, General Igor Maltsev, former Chief of Staff for Air Defences, disclosed to George Knapp that the Russian Air Forces had a standing order that UFOs were not to be fired upon because 'they may have tremendous capacities for retaliation'. Knapp also learned from another source that the Russian Air Force continues to study the UFOs in a classified programme code-named 'Thread 3'. 'The officer, who was the coordinator of the study, said the Russian military had long ago concluded that UFOs represented technology from an advanced civilization, possibly extraterrestrial.'[11]

INTRUSIONS AT MILITARY BASES

On the night of 28–29 July 1989, unknown disc-shaped objects were reported by Soviet Army personnel at a weapons depot and at another military base in the district of Kapustin Yar, Astrakhan. 'It was determined,' says the hitherto secret KGB case summary, 'that the reported characteristics of the observed UFOs are: disc 2–5 metres diameter, with a half-sphere on top, which is lit brightly. It moved sometimes abruptly, but noiselessly, at times coming down and hovering over the ground at an altitude of 20–60 metres. The command of [censored] called for a fighter [from the base at Akhtubinsk] but it was unable to see it in detail, because the UFO did not let the aircraft come near it.'

One witness, Private Bashev, said that as the object flew over him, it 'divided itself into three shining points and took the shape of a triangle'.

Ensign Valery N. Voloshin, communications officer on duty, observed the object for two hours, together with Private Tishchayev. 'One could clearly see a powerful blinking signal [like] a camera flash in the sky,' reported Voloshin.

> The object flew over the unit's logistics yard and moved in the direction of the rocket-weapons depot, 300 metres away [and] hovered over the depot at a height of 20 metres. The UFO's hull shone with a dim green light . . . While the object was hovering over the depot, a bright beam appeared from the bottom of the disc, where the flash had been before, and made two or three circles, lighting the corner of one of the buildings [see plate section] . . . then the beam disappeared, and the object, still flashing, moved in the direction of the railway station . . . Then it returned to the rocket-weapons depot and hovered over it . . .

At 01:30, the object flew in the direction of Akhtubinsk before disappearing.[12] (See p. 363.)

There are two parallels in this case with the Rendlesham Forest incident, in that the craft 'divided itself', and directed beams of light at the weapons depot. To me, these and many other similar intrusions are clear evidence of a comprehensive, strategic surveillance of the stockpiles and capabilities of our weapons.

THE LANDINGS AT VORONEZH

During the last two weeks of September 1989, in Voronezh, Russia, a UFO was observed by thousands of people, over thirty of whom claim to have witnessed landings (on at least four occasions) of an unknown craft, together with a giant, silver-suited humanoid and a 'robot'. One of these landings occurred in the city's South Park. This sensational story attracted worldwide attention – most of it inaccurate and ridiculous.

Jacques Vallée, the well-known author who investigated the case, reported that various engineers and authorities (including the KGB) had established that an unknown object, leaving impressions in the ground indicating an approximate weight of 11 tonnes, had indeed landed, and that an increase in background radiation (as in the Rendlesham Forest case) was detected at the site.[13]

OFFICIAL SOVIET RECOGNITION – AND A TRAGEDY

In an official statement, General Igor Maltsev, Chief of the General Staff of the PVO (Air Defence Forces), admitted that over a hundred observations of UFOs, mostly by pilots, had been reported to him on 21 March 1990. In referring to one such case, he stated that:

> The UFO was a disc with a diameter of 100 to 200 metres [and] two pulsating lights were positioned at its sides . . . During vertical movement it rotated and was perpendicular to the ground [and] rotated around its axis and performed an 'S-turn' flight, both in the horizontal and vertical planes. Next, the UFO hovered above the ground and then flew with a speed exceeding that of the modern-day fighter by two or three times [and its] speed was directly related to the flashing of the side lights: the more often they flashed, the higher the speed . . . The movement of the UFO was not accompanied by sound of any kind, and was distinguished by its startling manoeuvrability [as though] completely devoid of inertia.[14]

On 26 April 1990, President Mikhail Gorbachev was questioned about the subject during a meeting with workers in the Urals. 'The phenomenon of UFOs is real,' he proclaimed, 'and we should approach it seriously and study it.'[15]

General Ivan Tretiak, then Deputy Minister of Defence, argued sensibly that if it was proven that some UFOs were from a more developed civilization than our own, 'any fight with such objects and their crews – before a clarification of their intentions – would be futile'.[16] Alas, this warning was not heeded in the following instance.

Turkmenistan is one of the Turkic republics of the former Soviet Union. According to military witnesses, on 25 May 1990, during daytime, a giant disc-shaped craft, estimated to be 300 metres in diameter, reddish-orange in colour and with what looked like portholes around the rim, hovered at some 1,000 metres above the town of Mary.

'The airspace in that region was under strict control at the time, due to the war in Afghanistan,' reported my friend Nikolay Lebedev, an engineer, journalist and one of Russia's leading UFO investigators.

> All Soviet Air Defence forces were divided into regional Air Defence armies: the area around Mary was under the control of the 12th Air Defence Army, whose Air Defence division was under the command of Colonel Anatoli Kurkchy.

When informed about the UFO, Kurkchy gave the order to fire three ground-to-air missiles at it. The UFO made a slight horizontal manoeuvre, and three beams of light which had been coming from its port side disintegrated the missiles. Colonel Kurkchy then gave the order to scramble two 2-seat interceptor aircraft. But at a point about 1,000 metres from the disc, they appeared to be thrown to the ground, killing the pilots and destroying the aircraft.

Kurkchy was immediately removed from his post by the Army Command, and proceedings[17] were instituted against him by military prosecutors of the 12th Air Defence Army. However, according to my source, who spoke to the military prosecutor's department, the investigations were suddenly halted, and all information connected with the event was made secret. Later I learned that the squadron in which the four pilots served was disbanded.

Nikolay's article on the tragedy appeared in a St Petersburg evening paper, though the editor deleted some relevant details.[18] Many interesting telephone calls ensued, one of which was from General Kremenchuk of the local Air Defence staff, who flatly denied the story. Had it been true, he said, he would have learned about it. He promised to call the Air Defence division in the Mary region, and asked Nikolay to call him back the following week. 'General Kremenchuk informed me not only that the Air Defence division had no record of any incidents connected with UFOs or crashed aircraft, but that there was no one in the service by the name of Colonel Kurkchy.'

Another call came from a lieutenant-colonel (name known to me) serving under Kremenchuk. 'Although unable to confirm or deny the information contained in my article,' said Nikolay, 'he told me that Colonel Kurkchy did in fact exist, and was now commander of the Air Defence division in the large island of *Novaja Zeml'a* (New Land). This Arctic territory has the second largest proving ground for nuclear weapons in the Commonwealth of Independent States (CIS), [thus] it was impossible for me to get an interview with Kurkchy.

'I should add that if military personnel are required to remain silent about top-secret matters, the KGB compel such personnel to sign an official document which includes a warning that, in the event of the security oath being broken, they will be executed without any preliminary judicial inquiry.'[19]

RUSSIAN RADAR COMPLEX ATTACKED

Shortly after midnight on 13 September 1990, at a radar station near Kuybyshev (now reverted to its original name of Samara), 800 kilometres east-south-east of Moscow, Major A. Duplin observed a large target at a range of no more than 100 kilometres. At 00:10, the target was observed on the screen to 'scatter', and then, at 42 kilometres range, it changed into a strong signal representing an isosceles triangle. As the target came closer, the underground command post ordered a team to investigate, headed by Captain P. Lazeiko. As the men came out of the underground bunker, an unknown object passed directly over them, at a height of no more than 10 metres.

'We could see it clearly, since the perimeter of the base is always lit by searchlights,' explained Lazeiko. 'The bottom of the object was smooth, but not mirror-like: it was like a thick layer of soot. We did not notice any openings, portholes or landing gear, but we saw three whitish-blue beams of light. The corners of the object were slightly rounded.'

According to Senior Sergeant B. Gorin, Commander of the Guard, who was in the guardroom, Corporal A. Blazhis, a sentry, could not be contacted at post No. 4. At 00:20 Gorin sent two soldiers to investigate. There was no sign of Blazhis. On learning this, Gorin gave the order 'To arms!' and organized a search. Half an hour later it was reported that Blazhis had disappeared, together with another sentry, A. Varenitsa.

'After this report,' said Major Duplin, 'I decided to scan the unidentified object [on radar], which had apparently landed near the fence by the short-range radar post [No. 12]. I had time to notice on the radar screen that just after the triangular object disappeared [from radar coverage] sources of [radar] radiation could still be seen at the ends of where the triangle had been.'

Captain Lazeiko reported that as he ran up to post No. 12, he saw a flash, and the aerials' antennae appeared to be on fire, 'as if made of wood'. Another witness, Corporal S. Dudnik, described the event as follows:

I was standing on duty at post No. 6 and saw the arrival of a large, black triangular flying object, each side about 15 metres in length. It landed – not too quickly – with a soft rustling sound. The thickness of the triangle was about three metres. The flash, which knocked down the aerial behind me, came from the centre of the side of the object. There were no openings that I could see, but it seemed to be aiming at the target – and I was directly in the firing line! Strangely, I did not come to any harm ...

P. Beshmetov ran up to Dudnik when the fire started. 'He was standing near the barbed wire barrier with his Tommy-gun directed to the large triangle, which was 100 metres from the barbed wire [see sketch, p. 364]. I prepared to shoot, too,' said Beshmetov. 'The triangle took off after one-and-a-half hours, and the Commander of the Guard ordered all the soldiers back to their posts and to check the barrier. The colour of the radar truck [was] dark green, but afterwards its paint became black and blistered. Some parts of the truck had melted. The upper aerial had broken away [and] was three metres away from the truck. All its steel parts had melted, with the exception of the aluminium dish itself ...'

When I came up to the storehouse, out came Corporal Blazhis. He was very surprised to see me walking along his post. I asked him where he had been for such a long time. He began to laugh, and said that as he was going to phone to report to Sergeant A. Romanov, he suddenly lost his memory ... Simultaneously, A. Varenitsa, the other missing sentry, also appeared at his post. He too remembered nothing, and is convinced that all the time he remained at his post. In his opinion, it was as if we all appeared to them in an instantaneous film – suddenly soldiers appeared with Tommy-guns.

'The watches of corporals Blazhis and Varenitsa were one hour and fifty-seven minutes slow, and one hour and forty minutes slow, respectively. In addition, the serial numbers of Blazhis' Tommy-gun and bayonet were completely wiped out.' The ground at the site appeared as if it had been subjected to an explosion. According to witnesses, the object did not actually land, but hovered just above the ground.

These extraordinary events were reported by Captain D. Rudzit in the military newspaper *Za Rodinu* (Red Star), and taken up by the national newspapers.[20] Later that month it was explained in the press that the deputy chief of *Za Rodinu* had been summoned to the headquarters of the military district commander, General Makashov, and that Captain Rudzit, the military correspondent who first reported the story, now denied the incident. In November, all interest in the story dissolved when General Ivan Tretiak, Deputy Minister of Defence, debunked it as a 'hoax thought up by a staff member of the newspaper in order to attract readers ...'[21]

Nikolai Lebedev learned from Emil Bachurin, another investigator, that the story was not a hoax. A colonel known to Bachurin was invited to the radar complex not long after a visit there by a Ministry of Defence commission on 18 September. 'The colonel was informed that the upper aerial of radar post No. 12, and its instruments, were taken away by the commission, to be studied by the Scientific Research Department of the Ministry of Defence,' reports Lebedev. 'The colonel personally was shown videotapes from the radar screen, and the site where the incident had taken place. After having spoken to all the witnesses, he concluded that the incident did indeed happen as initially reported.'[22]

REPORTS BY COSMONAUTS AND AIR FORCE PILOTS

On 28 September 1990, two weeks after the Kuybyshev incident, cosmonauts on board the *Mir* space station, Gennadi M. Manakov and Gennadi M. Strekalov, were asked by journalist Leonid Lazarevich about 'the most interesting natural phenomena' to be seen on Earth from space.

'Well yesterday, for example,' responded Manakov, 'I saw – if one may call it that – an unidentified flying object. We had just passed over the Newfoundland region . . .'

> It was a great, silvery sphere [and] it was iridescent [at] 22:50. There was an absolutely clean, clear sky. It is difficult to determine, but the object was at a great altitude over the Earth – perhaps 20–30 kilometres. It was much larger than a huge ship [and] had a regular shape, but what it was, I don't know; perhaps an enormous, experimental sphere, or something else[23] . . . I was observing it for about six or seven seconds, then it disappeared. . . . It was simply hovering over the Earth.[24]

Many sightings have been reported by Soviet cosmonauts (see, for example, *The Soviet UFO Files* by Paul Stonehill, details of which appear in the reference section).

On 8 October 1990, two huge unidentified targets were tracked on radar over the vicinity of Grozniy, near Tbilisi, Georgia, according to S. Prokoshin, commander of the local air-defence unit. An interceptor jet was sent to investigate. 'At 11:27 I was given the co-ordinates of the target, and the task of locating it,' reported the pilot, Major P. Riabishev. 'According to the command unit, the object was at an altitude of 4.5 kilometres. The weather was cloudless and visibility fine, but the search proved to be in vain. I informed the command unit, and then made a turn and headed back to base. Suddenly, something forced me to turn round.'

Behind me and to the right, I saw two cigar-shaped objects, of considerable dimensions. The length of the first was about two kilometres, the length of the second about 400 metres. They were positioned one beside the other and were clearly visible. The small object [was] reflecting the Sun; while the larger one looked dull ... the UFOs were moving sideways at great speed. I made a turn and began to approach them, but suddenly both targets disappeared instantly from my field of vision, although traces of the targets remained on the radar screen.[25]

During the Geneva summit conference of November 1985, President Ronald Reagan told Soviet leader Mikhail Gorbachev 'how much easier his task and mine might be in these meetings that we held if suddenly there was a threat to this world from another species from another planet outside in the universe. We'd forget all the little local differences that we have between our countries, and we would find out once and for all that we really are all human beings here on this Earth together . . .'[26]

And, as mentioned in Chapter 18, President Mikhail Gorbachev confirmed that sentiment during the same summit conference, 'The US President said that, if the Earth faced an invasion by extraterrestrials, the United States and the Soviet Union would join forces to repel such an invasion . . .'

REFERENCES

1. Good, Timothy, *Beyond Top Secret: The Worldwide UFO Security Threat*, Sidgwick & Jackson, London, 1996, pp. 276–7.
2. *Network First: UFO*, produced (with Livia Russell), written and directed by Lawrence Moore, Central Productions for Central Television, 10 January 1995.
3. *Soviet UFO Secrets Revealed*, produced for the History Channel by Bill Brummell Productions, Inc.
4. *Network First: UFO*.
5. Walsh, Nick Paton, 'KGB chief ordered 4m soldiers to keep watching the skies for UFOs', *Observer*, 23 March 2003.
6. Knapp, George, 'UFOs Over Russia: Don't Believe Everything You Hear', *UFO Magazine* (US), Vol. 14, No. 4, April 1999, pp. 24–31.
7. Stonehill, Paul, *The Soviet UFO Files*, Bramley Books, Quadrillion Publishing Ltd, Godalming, Surrey, GU7 1XW, UK, 1998, p. 81.
8. *Soviet UFO Secrets Revealed*.
9. Stonehill, op. cit., p. 91.

10. Ilyin, Vadim K., 'KGB's "Blue Folder" reveals shootings, landings in USSR', *MUFON UFO Journal*, No. 403, November 2001, pp. 8–9.

11. Knapp, op. cit., p. 28.

12. KGB file: 'Communication on Observation of Anomalous Event in the District of Kapustin Yar (28 July 1989)', translated by Dimitri Ossipov, *Aura-Z*, Vol. 1, No. 1, March 1993, pp. 19–20.

13. Vallée, Jacques, with Castello, Martine, *UFO Chronicles of the Soviet Union: A Cosmic Samizdat*, Ballantine, New York, 1992, pp. 40–61.

14. *Rabochaya Tribuna* (Workers Tribune), Moscow, 19 April 1990.

15. *Sovietskaya Molodezhi* (Soviet Youth), 4 May 1990.

16. Foreign Press Note, published by the CIA's Foreign Broadcast Information Service (FBIS), 2 January 1991.

17. Under Paragraph 1, Item 5 of the Turkmenistan Criminal Procedures Code.

18. *Vecherni Petersburg*, 17 November 1991.

19. Lebedev, Nikolai, 'Important Developments in the Former Soviet Union', *Alien Update*, ed. Timothy Good, Arrow, London, 1993, pp. 184–6.

20. *Pravda*, 11 October 1990.

21. *Literaturnaya Gazeti*, 7 November 1990.

22. Lebedev, Nikolai, 'The Soviet Scene 1990', *The UFO Report 1992*, ed. Timothy Good, Sidgwick & Jackson, London, 1991, pp. 73–8.

23. *Sovietskaya Molodezhi*, 2 November 1990.

24. *Rabochaya Tribuna*, 16 October 1990.

25. *Rabochaya Tribuna*, 20 October 1990.

26. *Daily Telegraph*, London, 5 December 1985.

On the night of 28–29 July 1989, disc-shaped objects were reported by Soviet Army personnel at a weapons depot, and at another military base in the district of Kapustin Yar, Astrakhan. This sketch shows a disc as it beamed a ray at the rocket-weapons depot, during a two-hour observation by Ensign V. Voloshin and Private Tishchayev. The proportions of the craft are not quite accurate in this sketch – the top section consisted of a half sphere. (AURA-Z, *No.1, March 1993*)

The introduction to a previously secret KGB report on the event.
(Magazin 2000, *Verlag Michael Hesemann, D-40211 Düsseldorf*)

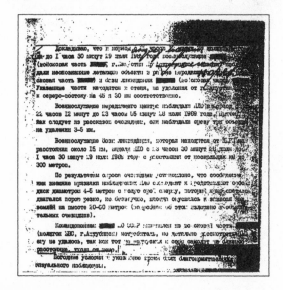

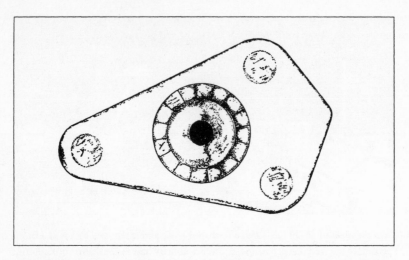

A sketch of one of the aerial devices seen over Belgium by several thousand witnesses, including Belgian Air Force pilots, between 1989–1990. This one was seen over Mazy on 11 December 1989. *(Gerard Grede)*

A sketch by investigator Nikolai Lebedev of the triangular craft that landed at a Russian radar complex near Kuybyshev/Samara on the night of 13 September 1990. During this event, a radar post was severely damaged by a beam of light which passed through Corporal Dudnik – with no apparent effect – and two sentries disappeared temporarily. *(Nikolai Lebedev)*

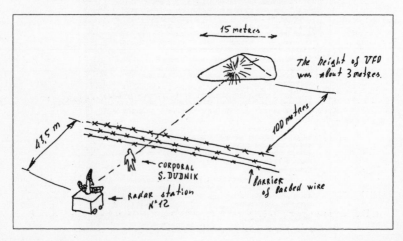

OBJECT. ▮▮▮▮▮▮▮▮▮▮▮▮▮▮

8. ~~(S/NF/WN)~~ UNIDENTIFIED OBJECT. IN THE SPRING OF 1984, A FRIEND ▮▮▮▮▮▮▮▮▮▮▮▮▮▮ WAS SENT BY THE REGIMENTAL COMMANDER TO INTERCEPT AN OBJECT WHICH HAD BEEN OBSERVED FLYING NEAR MIKHA TSKHAKAYA AIRFIELD AT A SUPERSONIC SPEED. HOWEVER, THE OBJECT DID NOT MAKE A SONIC BOOM AS IT FLEW NORTH TO SOUTH OVER THE BASE. THE PILOT, FLYING A MIG-23/FLOGGER IN FULL AFTERBURNER AT MACH 1.2 WAS UNABLE TO CLOSE ON THE OBJECT. BY THE TIME BOTH MIG-23 AND UNIDENTIFIED OBJECT APPROACHED THE COASTLINE OF THE BLACK SEA, THE FLOGGER WAS APPROACHING MACH 1.6. THE PILOT ACTIVATED HIS INFRARED SEARCH AND TRACK SYSTEM (IRSTS) APPROXIMATELY 12 KM FROM THE TARGET AND OBSERVED THE LARGEST BLOOM HE HAD EVER SEEN ON HIS INDICATOR. THE

~~SECRET~~

~~NOFORN WNINTEL~~

PAGE:0023

PILOT IMMEDIATELY REPORTED THIS INFORMATION TO THE CONTROLLER. BY THE TIME THE REACHED A SPEED OF NEARLY MACH 2, THE PILOT HAD TO BREAK OFF THE INTERCEPT DUE TO LOW FUEL. THE PILOT NEVER ACQUIRED A VISUAL IDENTIFICATION OF THE OBJECT. THE MIG-23'S ALTITUDE DURING THE CHASE WAS 5,000 M. ▮▮▮▮▮▮▮▮▮▮▮▮▮▮

C. ~~(S/NF/WN)~~ ELLIPSE SHAPED OBJECT. DURING NIGHT FLIGHTS IN THE AZERBAJDZHAN AREA, SEVERAL AIRCREWS REPORTED AN ELLIPSE SHAPED OBJECT FLYING MORE THAN 20 KM FROM THEM WHICH EMITTED A LIGHT IN ONE DIRECTION. ▮▮▮▮▮▮▮▮▮▮▮▮ THE AIRCREW WERE UNABLE TO ACQUIRE A RADAR CONTACT ON THE OBJECT. ALL OF THE PILOTS WHICH OBSERVED THE UNIDENTIFIED OBJECT WERE INSTRUCTED TO LAND IMMEDIATELY. THE CREWS WERE ORDERED TO NEVER DISCUSS THE OBJECT THEY HAD OBSERVED.

COMMENTS: ~~(S/NF/WN)~~ ▮▮▮▮▮▮▮▮▮▮▮▮▮▮▮▮▮▮▮▮▮▮▮▮▮▮▮▮▮▮▮▮

//IPSP: (U) PT 1820.//.
//CONSOBJ: (U) 324//.
ADMIN
PROJ: (U) 140110.
INSTR: (U) ▮▮▮▮▮▮
PREP: (U) ▮▮▮▮
ACQ: (U) WASH DC (891022).
WARNING: (U) REPORT ~~CLASSIFIED S E C R E T WARNING~~
~~NOTICE-INTELLIGENCE SOURCES AND METHODS INVOLVED-NOT RELEASEABLE TO~~
~~FOREIGN NATIONALS.~~
~~DECL-OADR~~
BT

#0224

NNNN

A Defense Intelligence Agency report on sightings and interceptions of UFOs by Soviet Air Force pilots in 1984. *(Defense Intelligence Agency)*

24. THE BRAZILIAN THEATRE

According to information supplied in 1999 to Rubens Villela, a Brazilian meteorologist, the Brazilian Air Force (Força Aérea Brazilia) detects an average of five UFOs a day. 'They know how to distinguish radar echoes by their speed, sometimes 40,000 km/h and 600 metres or more in size,' he revealed to me.

In 1977, Lieutenant-Colonel Uyrange Hollanda, then a captain in the Intelligence Service of the First Air Force Command (1 COMAR) in Belém, was sent to investigate disturbing reports in Colares and other remote areas of north-east Brazil. Code-named Operação Prato (Operation Plate), the investigations lasted four months. During this time, Hollanda's team, together with a team of intelligence officers, interviewed people from thirty villages in the area who had been burned and temporarily paralysed by beams of coloured light directed at them from unknown flying objects. At least two people died as a result of these attacks.

On numerous occasions, Hollanda and his team themselves experienced sightings, occasionally involving close approaches by structured craft. In November 1977 an object suddenly appeared above the men. 'I was terrified,' Hollanda told investigators Bob Pratt and Cynthia Luce. 'Suddenly a big disc-shaped object 30 metres in diameter was hovering directly above us! It made a noise like an air conditioner [and] a sound like a bicycle sprocket when you pedal backwards. It was emitting a yellow glow that would grow and dim, every two or three seconds [and] we could see small yellow lights in the middle of it.' Eventually the object shot off towards the sea, the lights having turned to a light blue.

Hollanda's team interviewed fishermen from Colares who had seen USOs going in and out of the water, and blue lights moving around underwater. Hollanda himself observed one such USO. The team also took hundreds of photographs of the objects, mostly at night-time, using special filters and ultraviolet and infrared film. Eight different shapes of object could be discerned from these images. On one occasion another shape was seen by Hollanda and his men, near Baía do Sol. 'It was maybe 100 metres long with windows in it,' he said, 'and (flying saucers) would come out of it and later go back in ... Shortly after we began seeing these things, our eyesight started to deteriorate, slowly at first. We ended up, most of us, having to wear glasses.'

Operation Plate was classified, and Hollanda was forbidden from speaking publicly while in the Air Force. 'The Brazilian government and the Air Force were not interested in publicizing the subject, because three questions often were made to the government and the Air Force: Who are they? Where do they come from? What do they want? And the Air Force did not have any answers...'[1]

THE DEVIL'S GRAVEYARD

In late 1981, incidents of objects flying in and out of the Amazon River were reported some 400 miles to the west of Colares, in an area known as the 'Devil's Graveyard'. 'All the evidence points to a base beneath the Amazon,' said Charles Tucker, director of the Indiana-based International UFO Investigative Bureau, who had led an expedition to the area to investigate reports of objects which were flying in and out of the river (12 miles wide and 200 feet deep in places). These objects had buzzed fishing vessels and passenger boats so close that witnesses had seen water dripping from the metallic skin of the strange craft; they had burned a thirty-seven-year-old female farm worker with a beam of light, necessitating hospital treatment, and knocked out a hunter with a shock from a powerful light beam after he tried to shoot at one of them.

One night, schoolteacher Noemi Rodrigues was on board a boat when the water began to swirl and bubble. It was, she said, 'as though a huge burst of air was escaping from the river. Suddenly, from the centre of the turmoil, a saucer-shaped craft shot from the water. A wave of air and water surged toward us, shocking and frightening people. The craft left the water without lights, although we could see it by the moonlight. Then it settled about 10 feet above the water and a brilliant light surrounded it.' After following the boat for twenty to thirty minutes, the craft banked and dived into the water. 'It happened in a flash,' said Noemi. 'There was a rush and a swirl in the water, and it was gone.'

The Devil's Graveyard forms an elongated triangle, the three corners of which are anchored by the towns of Obidos, Monte Alegre and Santarés – all on the banks of the Amazon. 'There have been hundreds of sightings here,' declared a police commissioner. 'On various occasions, high-placed military personnel have come to document what has happened. We are

convinced that UFOs actually take off and land at an underwater base.'
Retired Brazilian Army General Alfredo Moacyr Uchôa commented: 'Our
Air Force has impressive evidence that an underwater UFO launching site
exists in this area.'[2]

General Uchôa, whom I met in Rio de Janeiro in 1988, was a former
deputy director of the Military Academy of Brazil. He had many close
encounters, including communication with UFOs, in the late 1960s and
early 1970s – always in the company of witnesses – in the vicinity of
Alexânia and Goiânia, near Brasilia. Uchôa learned that many groups visit
Earth. 'Most, but not all, mean us no harm,' he declared in one of his
books. 'But others don't care about us; they are indifferent. They want to
study our planet, our living conditions, our animals, our plants and so on,
without paying any attention to us as responsible men. So, sometimes they
can be aggressive . . .'[3]

A UNIQUE SURGICAL PROCEDURE

On the night of 12/13 January 1996, the North American Aerospace Defense
Command (NORAD) tracked a number of uncorrelated targets over the
western hemisphere, one or more of which had penetrated Brazilian
airspace. NORAD contacted CINDACTA, the combined military-civilian
agency controlling airspace in Brazil, who immediately alerted the Army
Command (ESA) in Três Coraçoes.

On the morning of 13 January, a witness claimed to have seen a cigar-
shaped craft, apparently seriously damaged, flying slowly at low altitude.
He gave chase in his pick-up truck for some 10 miles, and came upon a
site strewn with debris, which was being collected by armed soldiers. He
was ordered to leave and later warned by two men in civilian clothes not
to talk to anyone about what he had seen.

A week later, in the small hours of 20 January, two witnesses reported
a 'submarine-shaped' craft, apparently in difficulties, with smoke or vapour
emanating from it, at only 15 to 20 feet above the ground, heading in the
direction of Varginha. At daylight, a number of strange creatures were seen
wandering about by witnesses in various parts of the town. Initially, firemen
from the Varginha City Fire Department (which is run by the Military
Police) were called out, followed by the Army, and two of the creatures
were captured separately, without resistance. One of the creatures is
believed to have been shot and killed.

One creature was taken to ESA, while another, injured one was taken first to the local regional hospital, and later to the more secluded Hospital Humanitas, as confirmed by numerous witnesses. The injured creature was examined by fifteen doctors at the Hospital Humanitas. Among the Brazilian military personnel present were Lieutenant-Colonel Olimpio Vanderlei Santos, Lieutenant Tibério, Captain Ramírez and Sergeant Pedrosa of S-2 Military Intelligence, who filmed some scenes with a camcorder.[4]

Dr Roger Leir is an American podiatrist (chiropodist) and private pilot who has authored several books, including *The Aliens and the Scalpel*, about alleged alien implants he has surgically removed from a number of people.[5] (In the US, podiatrists are trained in orthopaedic and general surgery.) The implants are small objects exhibiting unusual properties and are believed to have been inserted into witnesses during abduction. In 2002, Dr Leir visited Varginha and interviewed several medical personnel at the Hospital Humanitas who had attended the injured alien creature, as well as a doctor who had performed surgery on it. Dr Leir, whom I know as a trusted colleague, has since written a truly remarkable book about his experiences and investigations in Varginha – *UFO Crash in Brazil* – and has generously allowed me to quote lengthy extracts from his interview with the medical personnel. This extraordinary interview (which I have abbreviated in part) was witnessed by Ubirajara F. Rodriguez, a lawyer and university professor who is the foremost researcher into the case, together with his son Rudolfo, acting as interpreter, and Phil Serrins, who accompanied Dr Leir on the research trip.

'The doctor and his colleagues will be referred to as "MP" (Medical Personnel) and I will be designated as "Dr L",' begins Dr Leir.

'It was obvious this was going to be an emotionally charged interview. The expressions on their faces appeared strained. It should be understood that my emotions were also on edge . . .'

MP: There were military guards posted at the doors and they weren't letting anybody in or out. Once you were in there you couldn't get out, not even if you had to go to the bathroom.

Dr L: What was happening inside the surgical area?

MP: Everybody was in a state of panic [and] mass confusion. The military was very dominating. We knew they brought a patient in through the back door of the hospital, and brought them directly into surgery. We thought there must have been a really bad accident on the base . . . we were told not to talk about this to anyone once it was all over. We were preparing for a surgery but no one knew what kind of surgery or who the patient was. They had taken the patient directly into one of the operating rooms.

Dr L: Can you tell us what your speciality is?

MP: Yes, it's orthopaedic surgery.

Dr L: Please go ahead and tell us what happened next.

MP: I was asked to begin a surgical scrub and to prepare for a fracture reduction, and was simply told it was a leg. The answers came from one of the military officers. I noticed two armed officers were guarding the entrance to one of the operating suites and assumed the patient was already on the table being prepped for surgery. It was also a bit disconcerting to see military personnel armed with weapons and live ammunition inside the operating areas of our hospital. We did not have this experience with any of the previous accident cases.

Dr L: Were you presented with any kind of medical record of the patient or did anyone tell you the full extent of his injuries, or even the vital signs?

MP: No, there was no information available. Everybody was acting really strange [and] exchanges of conversation [were] in a very low tone so you could not hear what they were talking about . . . We were handed sterile towels and dried our hands. Next, the military guard opened the operating room doors and we were told to enter. The patient was already on the table and covered to the neck with a sterile drape sheet. Two of the nurses were preparing to gown us. I noticed they had a look of terror in their eyes. I approached the operating table with my colleague. At first glance I noticed the patient was quite small.

When I first saw the face of the individual lying there I was in a state of shock. It was far from a human face. The eyes were large and red, and staring at the ceiling with a blank stare. We were all dumbfounded. One of the military officers of a high rank told us the victim on the table had suffered a fractured leg and we were to 'fix it'. I asked him for some details regarding the patient and was told I was not there to ask questions but only to perform the requested task. He also told us to do the best job we could [and] to solve any problem that might arise, no matter what the nature . . . Any questions or requests would be relayed through the military personnel on the other side of the operating room doors.

One of the things we decided to do was to get a better look at the surgery site and at the same time examine the patient. It was at this point that we realized this creature was probably not of this world. Earlier in the day we had heard some rumours about an unusual creature [and] military activity around town.

The being was less than five feet tall. It was bi-pedal with two arms. The colour of the skin was a dark brown, which appeared rather shiny; like it was oily or wet, but in fact the skin was dry [and] looked reticulated, like large scales, but when you touched it, the demarcations of scales were not present. It was smooth to the touch.

The head was large, much too large for the size of the individual. There were three bony protuberances on the top of the head, one in each parietal area and one central. They extended from the frontal to the occipital portions, like ridges. There was no hair present either on the head or the rest of the body. The head was also larger in its upper portion than lower toward the jaw area.

The eyes were large, slightly upturned toward the lateral aspects, oriental-looking. They were red in colour and looked like two glimmering pools of liquid. For some reason, all of us did not want look into this creature's eyes and refrained from doing so.

There was a very small remnant of a mouth and two little openings with a slight ridge where the nose should have been. There were no noted ears, only small openings that looked like vestigial ear canals. The neck was narrow and appeared it would not have enough muscular strength to support such a large head. The upper portion of the torso was slight of build, with an obvious ribcage. There were no noted breasts, areola or nipples. The abdomen was similar to that of a human, with the absence of a navel. [No genitalia were detected.]

The upper thigh portions were muscular and out of proportion to the rest of the torso. This was totally different from the arms, which were thin and emaciated. The hands ended in four fingers with no thumb. The fingers were strange and different from human fingers. The creature was able to move each of his fingers so that they could articulate with each other, and by doing so, was able to probably perform all the functions we could with the use of our thumbs. We were not able to tell whether these fingers were multi-jointed or [if] for some reason the bones were flexible, enabling the fingers to perform their desired functions.

The upper leg and thighs ended in what appeared to be similar to a human knee joint with an oversized patella. The lower portions of the leg were also similar to that of a human. The entire lower extremities were heavily endowed with muscles. It crossed my mind that wherever this creature had come from, the gravity might have been much more than here on Earth.

The foot was narrow and fleshy. There were three short fleshy toes that looked more like pads than toes. There were no visible toenails or fingernails. There was an additional appendage that hung down from the medial side of the foot. This vestigial appendage was elongated like a finger and ended in what appeared to be a claw about three quarters of an inch long. Later, we found that when the being walked, it would move this appendage so it would became parallel to the rest of the foot. This allowed it to ambulate in a normal human-like manner.

Dr L: Did you examine the site of the injury?

MP: Yes. It was in the upper thigh and involved a compound fracture of the femur. The bone was protruding from the skin and there had been some bleeding around the site of the wound, which had clotted and was dry ... To our surprise the blood was dark red, just like our blood. When examined under the microscope we found the cellular structure to be very similar to human blood, with the exception of the platelet count being much higher in number. We also found that the blood would coagulate immediately upon release from a blood vessel. We were not able to determine whether this was due to the high platelet count or whether the creature was in a different atmosphere than it was used to.

Dr L: Were there X-rays taken and did you view them?

MP: Yes. They were up on the view screen in the surgery room. It showed a clear view of the fractured bone ... and I believed it could be treated in the same manner as we treat human fractures.

Dr L: Was the bone also similar to ours?

MP: Yes, with the exception that it was pinker in colour and contained numerous lacunae or holes, giving it the appearance of osteoporotic human bone. Another difference was its tensile strength: it was much stronger than human bone. We did not find it necessary to use stabilization devices to fixate the fracture site. Once the bone ends were approximated, the fracture defect seemed to stabilize and could not be moved apart.

Dr L: Was the patient awake or conscious, and was there any attempt at communication?

MP: The patient was apparently awake. It kept moving its head but mainly stared upward at the ceiling. We did make an attempt to communicate verbally, but did not receive an answer. We were concerned as to whether it was feeling any pain, but we really had no way of knowing. When we examined the fracture site it did not jerk away, scream, or give any sign of discomfort.

Dr L: Was the patient given any kind of anaesthetic for the procedure?

MP: We had decided not to use a general anaesthesia because we didn't know anything about its metabolism. We thought perhaps any of our gases might kill the thing. We were even afraid to administer oxygen, because no one knew what kind of an atmosphere it was used to. We decided to try a small amount of local anaesthesia and see if there was any untoward effect. Fortunately there was not, and that is how we were able to do the procedure.

Dr L: Did the patient at anytime make any noise, cry out in pain, or object to the treatment?

MP: No. It remained very still. Its respirations were shallow, as if it needed very little air to sustain life.

Dr L: Could you detect a heartbeat or pulse?

MP: We tried to determine exactly that, and we could not tell. Sometimes we thought we could hear a heartbeat and then at other times it was absent; we found the same with the detection of a pulse . . .

'At this point we decided to take a short break in the questioning,' said Dr Leir. 'The room was steeped in silence. We all looked at each other with wonderment in our eyes. The medical personnel sat silently, immersed in deep thought. Their faces seemed strained and ashen in colour . . .' Ten minutes later, the interview resumed.

MP: When we had finished the surgery, we were still highly tense. We did not know how the patient was going to respond. We were also afraid that if something untoward happened to the creature, we would get the blame from the military and the punishment might be severe.

These thoughts were going through my head. Suddenly, out of nowhere, the room began to fill with a greenish mist. We all stepped back from the operating table. We did not immediately know the origin of this mist and feared it might be toxic. One of the operating-room nurses began frantically banging on the operating-room door. A voice on the other side inquired if we were finished with the surgery. We told them we were essentially finished, but there seemed to be a greenish gas collecting in the room and we did not know the origin . . . we were told to find the origin of the greenish substance and let them know. We did not know at this point whether it was a gas, vapour or mist, but finally realized it seemed to be emanating from the creature lying on the table. In deep fear, I walked slowly closer to it and approached the head of the table.

Without consciously realizing it, my gaze caught the eyes of the being. His eyes were glowing red, and appeared as two swirling pools of liquid. They were pulling, pulling me in, deeper and deeper. All at once, giant portions of information came pounding into my head. These were like 'thoughtgrams' – large blocks of information, over and over again, like someone hitting me over the head with a hammer. I was also becoming dizzy and slightly nauseated.

Dr L: Undoubtedly you survived this ordeal. Can you tell us what was in those thought messages?

MP: All that I am willing to tell you at this time is what the creature told me about human beings. I also want to tell you he 'downloaded' a tremendous amount of knowledge into my head. It caused me to have headaches lasting for over two weeks following the event.

Essentially, he told me his race felt very sorry for the human beings for basically two reasons. The first is that all humans have the same potential and abilities to perform the very same things his race could do – those things we find so marvellous and magical but did not know how to do. For example, he told me that in cases where there is injury or disease of the body, it would not be necessary to confine one of his species to a special treatment facility such as the one he was confined in at the moment. He told me they either individually or [collectively] could produce all the healing necessary to repair their bodies.

The second reason they felt sorry for us was that we did not seem to realize we were spiritual beings only living in a temporary shell, and we were totally disconnected from our spiritual self . . .

Dr L: What happened to the creature after you left the room?

MP: We checked on the being from time to time. It seemed stable and had a fantastic rate of healing: the wound healed completely in less than twenty-four hours. This was also true of the bone. It was in 'satisfactory medical condition'.

The military took the creature out the back door of the hospital.

Dr L: There certainly must have been records originally. What happened to them?

MP: We believe the military confiscated all the records, X-rays, laboratory data and materials used . . .

'With that, we concluded the interview,' writes Dr Leir. 'I looked intently at the physician. He was sitting in a chair, slightly bent at the waist. Perspiration had formed on his brow and was streaking downward through his sideburns. Tears were running down his cheeks, his hands were extended in front of him, shaking, and he was trembling and distraught. I gently placed my arm around his shoulder and silently gave him a hug . . .'[6]

A military police officer who had handled a creature with his naked hands, Corporal Marco Chereze, died about three weeks later. His family was told that he had died from 'a toxic substance', but the results of the autopsy were never revealed. However, detailed information is now revealed in Dr Leir's book, and he suggests that Chereze may have died from a virus similar to the Ebola type.[7]

The body of a dead creature (presumably the one which had been shot) was, according to several sources, autopsied by pathologists at the Department of Medicine, University of Campinas (UNICAMP), headed by Dr Fortunato Badan Palhares, a leading expert in the field. What became of the creatures – of which up to seven were reported to have been seen? It seems that one was loaded on to a US Air Force transport at São Paulo International Airport on 20 January, and the same aircraft returned to Campinas Airport two days later – presumably to collect the autopsied body. Perhaps coincidental, too, was the visit to São Paulo and other parts of Brazil, early in March 1996, by Warren Christopher, the US Secretary of State, together with Daniel S. Goldin, Director of NASA.[8]

During his visit to Varginha, Dr Roger Leir was shown documents pertaining to certain agreements between NASA and the Brazilian Government which 'allow for any material coming from space that is found in Brazil to be turned over to the government of the United States'.[9]

A few sightings of strange creatures in the vicinity of Varginha continued sporadically until May 1996.

As to the official position on the incident, in 1997 British television producer Bruce Burgess eventually managed to coax a statement from Major Eduardo Calza, a senior officer based at the ESA Army base. 'If some of the descriptions by the witnesses of the incident seem a little outlandish,' declared Burgess, 'the official military version is bizarre in the extreme.'

Witnesses to these events, explained Calza, had simply mistaken 'an expectant dwarf couple' and 'a mentally handicapped dwarf' for alien creatures . . .[10]

REFERENCES

1. Good, Timothy, *Unearthly Disclosure: Conflicting Interests in the Control of Extraterrestrial Intelligence*, Century, London, 2000, pp. 187–200.
2. Mullins, Joe, and Michelini, Chuck, 'Secret UFO Base Under the Amazon River', *National Enquirer*, 20 October 1981. I am well aware that the *Enquirer* is a tabloid renowned for inventing stories. However, the late Bob Pratt, who conducted many investigations into UFO reports in various countries – especially Brazil – for

the paper, assured me that the stories published at that time were, ironically, quite accurate.

3. http://www.bobpratt.org/uchoa.html

4. Good, op. cit.

5. Leir, Dr Roger K., *The Aliens and the Scalpel: Scientific Proof of Extraterrestrial Implants in Humans*, Granite Publishing, PO Box 1429, Columbus, NC 28722, 1998/1999.

6. Leir, Dr Roger K., *UFO Crash in Brazil: A Genuine UFO Crash with Surviving ETs*, The Book Tree, PO Box 16476, San Diego, CA 92176, 2005, pp. 75–85.

7. Ibid., 137–47.

8. Good, op. cit.

9. Leir, *UFO Crash in Brazil*, pp. 8–9.

10. *The Brazilian Roswell*, a documentary directed by Bruce Burgess and produced by Jackie Stableforth, Transmedia Productions, London, 1998.

25. OPEN SKIES

In the late 1980s, reports of less conventionally shaped flying objects – typically triangular – began to increase around the world. In November and December 1988, two dramatic instances of aircraft being 'absorbed' into large UFOs occurred, in full view of witnesses, in the US Commonwealth of Puerto Rico, the second of which involved a large triangular craft.

At 19:45 on 28 December, numerous people in Cabo Rojo, south-west Puerto Rico, saw a massive, blindingly bright yellow light in the sky. 'Suddenly, I saw two planes coming, each one at the side of this thing,' said a witness, Mañuel Mercado. 'One of the jets came and crossed in front of the UFO to the left, and the other crossed from left to right. The jets seemed to be trying to intercept that thing, to force it to change its course.

'Then, when they got next to it, we thought they would collide. The object stopped in mid-air – and the jets seemed to go inside it. And that was the last we saw of them. Then that thing veered back, and that's when we noticed that it looked like a triangle. When it veered and stopped [over the Samán lake], it divided itself [into two triangles], and one of the sections shot away at great speed to the east and the other took off to the north.'

On my first trip to Puerto Rico, in August 1990, Jorge introduced me to most of the witnesses, including Mercado. In my opinion, they were truthful.

The jets involved in both incidents were F-14 Tomcats, probably from an aircraft carrier twenty to twenty-five miles away. A week after the incident, Jorge Martín spoke to a US Navy source. 'There are radar tapes that show what happened, and they were classified at once and sent to Washington, DC, to be analysed,' the officer disclosed. 'We were able to see what happened on the radar systems of the ships that were anchored nearby. We saw when the smaller targets on the radar, which represented the jets, merged with a bigger one. A lid has been placed on the whole incident . . .'[1]

BRIEFINGS

Shortly after midnight on 18/19 July 1990, the base perimeter at Fort Allen, a US Army Reserve Base in Juana Díaz on Puerto Rico's southern coast, was suddenly illuminated by a powerful white light. According to information leaked by an officer to Jorge Martín, all personnel at the base that night were in the barracks, except for those on duty.

An officer gave an order over the intercom for 'everyone to stay indoors and not to come out of the barracks or any other base facilities under any circumstances'. The light was very bright, but when the order was given the officer was already looking out of a window. 'In an area towards the coast, just over the base,' he said, 'there was a brightly lit object, circular and metallic-looking, as if it was made of aluminium. It had what seemed many windows in its central [rim], with yellowish-white lights revolving in them. At the underside of the object there was a round turbine-like protrusion with many coloured lights around it, and from underneath the object came a very bright beam of pinkish-white light, as if searching for something. That same light was the one illuminating the perimeter.'

Suddenly came the sound of jet engines, and two planes – believed to be F/A-18 Hornets – flew at high speed over the base. 'As soon as the jets headed in the direction of the UFO,' continued the officer, 'the object departed at speed to the west with the sound of rushing wind, followed by the jets. Those planes must have been scrambled from Roosevelt Roads Naval Station [some 60 miles to the east], from an aircraft carrier participating in the UNITAS manoeuvres at Roosevelt Roads and on Vieques Island, because normally there are no F/A-18s Hornets based in Puerto Rico.

'Something big is happening here,' the officer revealed. 'Recently, all the military personnel in Fort Allen were shown several video films which informed us about the reality of UFOs. They showed us an old black-and-white film about a UFO crash that supposedly happened in New Mexico many years ago. We all saw the craft, which was semi-buried in the ground at a 45-degree angle, and there were several bodies of the crew ... about five feet tall, thin, very pale, and had large bald heads [and] big round eyes and small nose ... They also showed us another video of UFOs filmed by them around the island.'

They wanted us to know that UFOs are real, but they wouldn't elaborate when asked for more details. You know, it seemed to me that they wanted us to know that UFOs are real and that the beings were not perfect: they are fallible, their craft crash and they also die – they are not invulnerable. Apparently, they wanted to condition us to the idea that they exist, and to accept the possibility of some day having to liaise with them.

The officers wouldn't say that these were alien craft, or anything like that, just that they were real and that the Government is keeping a close eye on them. Finally, they told us that they are expecting something big: they wouldn't explain what, but it had to with all this, and if that happened we would have to deal with the situation, and with the people – the public.

This event was later confirmed by two independent military sources who approached Jorge Martín and the investigator John Timmerman in San Juan the following month. 'Apparently,' reported Martín, 'special military groups on the island have been receiving official briefings on the UFO situation since 1988, the year in which the jet fighters were abducted by the huge triangular-shaped UFOs in Cabo Rojo and San Germán.'[2]

Other military personnel have been exposed to similar films. Lieutenant Colonel Ellison Onizuka was one of the astronauts who perished in the *Challenger* Space Shuttle disaster in January 1986. In conversation with Clark C. McClelland, the aerospace engineer who worked at the Kennedy Space Center (alluded to earlier), Onizuka revealed that while on military training at McClellan Air Force Base, California, about eight or nine years before his astronaut training, he and others were directed to report to a viewing room.

'As they were seated, the room darkened and a movie began without the usual official introduction by a USAF officer,' reports McClelland. 'They were all startled when a view of a facility similar to a medical examination room appeared on the screen, and small bodies were observed lying on slabs ... The small, strange-looking creatures were humanoid in shape [with] large heads, large eyes, slight torsos, arms, and legs.'

'Clark,' said Ellison, 'My God, these highly trained officers and I were shocked by what we saw ... We were all caught off-guard. Perhaps it was a test of our psyche to determine our overall reaction.'[3]

5/6 NOVEMBER 1990

One of the most spectacular events during this period involved the multiple sightings reported by military and civilian pilots, as well as by witnesses on the ground, in many European countries, on the night of 5/6 November 1990.

Jean Gabriel Greslé is a former French Air Force and Air France pilot. Having himself seen UFOs on several occasions while flying, as well as being one of Europe's finest UFO researchers, he is well qualified to differentiate between conventional and unconventional flying objects. At 19:00 on 5 November, he was standing outside a gym with six of his martial-arts pupils in Gretz-Armainvilliers, some 25 kilometres east of Paris, when an astonishing event occurred. Jean took me to the actual site, enabling me to visualize the event more precisely.

'Suddenly,' he said, 'this enormous device came into sight. My first impression was of a huge crane with a lot of lights. It was at a distance of about 800 metres and height of 300 metres. One witness saw it level off and turn. The trajectory was downward, towards us. It projected two huge, divergent beams of light, not quite touching the ground. The light was peculiar: I can only explain it as *lumière morte* – 'dead light'. The moisture in the air wasn't scattering the light. Normal light is scattered by water droplets in the atmosphere.

'It must have been at least 1,000 feet long, with a thickness of about 200–250 feet, and had triangular substructures and many, many lights. I ran around a tree to watch it as it turned its back on us, and the lights dimmed very quickly, which is surprising, because the beams must have been at least a kilometre in length – then it disappeared in the cloud. Janine, one of my pupils, caught a glimpse of the rear section, which was trapezoidal in shape. It carried with it what I can only describe as a "zone of silence", because as it flew over us – at never more than 100 mph – we suddenly didn't hear the nearby traffic. And I had the impression that my mind was blanked out ... Other witnesses saw it too, in nearby areas. It was absolutely incredible – like a city floating through the clouds!'[4]

At the same time, a flight of three Royal Air Force (RAF) Tornado GR.1 jets was transiting from the UK to RAF Laarbruch, Germany, flying through controlled airspace above the North Sea at 18:00 local time, when a large 'aeroplane-shaped' object appeared to the right side of the planes.[5] The aircraft were travelling at Mach 0.8 (about 600 mph). 'Out of nowhere, a mysterious craft emerged on their wing tips and overtook the jets,' reports Nick Pope, who headed the Ministry of Defence (MoD) UFO research effort from 1991 to 1994. 'The object was massive and covered with blue and white lights. For a brief moment, the craft flew ahead of the Tornados, before accelerating away into the distance at an unimaginable speed ...

The control centre was unable to help. Nothing had shown up on its radar. Officially, at least, the craft had never existed.'⁶

The MoD 'signal' states that two other Tornados had seen the object and 'possibly [identified] it as a stealth aircraft'.⁷ That a stealth aircraft would be so large, and covered with blue and white lights, seems improbable. What is certain is that several sightings were reported by RAF pilots that night. In an informal conversation with a friend of mine shortly after the sightings, a senior RAF officer based in Germany revealed that two terrific explosions were heard in the Rheindalen area on two separate occasions that night.

Following the second explosion (at 22:00), the crew of a Phantom jet reported UFOs heading north in 'finger' formation. Separately, said the RAF source, two Tornados over the North Sea encountered two large round objects, each with five blue lights and several other white lights around the rim. As the Tornados closed to investigate, one of the UFOs headed for one of the jets, which was forced to take violent evasive action to avoid a collision. The two unknowns then headed north until they were out of sight. Nothing showed on the Tornados' radar.

In 1991, following a request for some information which I could use, the senior officer wrote a report in letter form for my friend, and gave me permission to quote from it, 'providing the source would be protected'.

'Our version begins at 19:00 hours [local time] on the evening of 5 November with reports at [RAF] Rheindalen of a "sonic boom",' he wrote:

> We confirmed that, at that time, two of our Phantom aircraft were carrying out practice intercepts at a very high level over Germany, under positive radar control ... Simultaneously, the crew of one of the Phantom aircraft reported a UFO sighting, described as a large formation of aircraft all in reheat in finger formation ... disappearing to the north. The crews gave chase, but did not establish further visual or radar contact ... Subsequently, the NATO Air Defence Organization reported that there were several high-speed contacts during the course of that evening in the same area (Western border of Germany/Southern Belgium) as the sightings. We shall probably never know exactly what our crews saw, or our people on the ground heard ...

Among the civil pilots reporting sightings that night was a British Airways captain who told investigator Paul Whitehead that he saw two 'very bright mystifying lights' while flying over the North Sea. Later he spoke to a Tornado pilot who, together with another Tornado from the same squadron, had been 'approached by bright lights' which 'formated' on the Tornados. The accompanying Tornado pilot was so convinced that they were on a collision course with the lights – apparently nine were seen – that he 'broke away' and 'took violent evasive action' (as confirmed by the senior RAF officer).[8]

31 MARCH 1993

In his book *Open Skies, Closed Minds*, Nick Pope reports that he arrived at his desk in Whitehall on the morning of 31 March 1993 to find that there had been a major wave of UFO sightings in Britain the previous night. The reports – involving many police and military witnesses – described triangular-shaped craft uncannily similar to those reported by about 2,000 witnesses exactly three years earlier in Belgium during a wave of sightings in 1989–90.

Most sightings had occurred between 01:00 and 01:30, Nick soon discovered, with a peak at 01:10. 'By lunchtime,' he said, 'it became obvious that I was right at the centre of the biggest wave of UFO sightings ever reported in Britain ... Other reports reached me from the Irish Republic, and in the days that followed I heard of sightings in France, and, significantly, Belgium.'

A report came in from a military patrol guarding RAF Cosford, near Wolverhampton, and another from Rugeley, Staffordshire, where five members of the same family observed a huge diamond-shaped object, about 200 metres across, flying slowly above them at an estimated height of less than 300 metres. 'They also reported a low, humming sound of the frequency you'd experience standing in front of the speakers at a pop concert, feeling the sound waves passing through the body,' Nick explained. (This effect has been reported on many occasions.)

> Perhaps the most interesting report came from RAF Shawbury in Shropshire, to the north of Shrewsbury. The meteorological officer there saw the most astonishing sight of that whole amazing night. An object in the sky, at first stationary, moved erratically towards him at a speed of several hundred miles an hour. At one point it fired a beam of light at the ground, which swept the countryside from left to right, as though it were looking for something in the fields and hedgerows. The sighting ... lasted for five minutes, long enough for the witness to estimate the size of the craft to be about that of a Jumbo jet ... He heard the same low-frequency hum the family from Rugeley had heard.

What were the Ministry's answers? There was no unusual civil or military aircraft activity that night that came remotely close to fitting anything that had been seen ... So the official findings (mine) read: 'Type of craft – unknown; origin of craft – unknown; motive of occupants – unknown.'⁹ (See also pp. 431–2)

ILLEGAL ALIENS

In the small hours of 8 March 1997, Sarah Hall, a journalist for the *Folkestone Herald*, was driving through the village of Burmarsh, Kent, returning to her home in Hythe. 'I think it was about three o'clock a.m.,' she reported to Chris Rolfe of UFO Monitors East Kent (UFOMEK). 'I was driving back from dropping some friends off, and [as] I was coming down the road, I felt weird. I saw something in front of me, and I thought, "Oh my God, what the hell is that?" and sort of slowed down, because I thought it was coming at me. And it stopped in front of me, probably three to four hundred yards away.' The object was hovering above a large field, between Burmarsh and Dymchurch, not far from the coast.

It was just this huge triangle thing, which was a lot bigger than an aeroplane ... It had lights all around the outside, and this disc attached to its back, and a big light on the front. I pulled up to stop, and as I did, it shot off. Literally ... And it stopped again, sort of another five hundred yards away from me, and it did that four times ... sort of moved for about five or six seconds, stopped for two seconds, then moved again for another five or six seconds, and so on. The object was moving westwards, and all the time it was making this weird humming sound ... like the sound you hear when you stand under overhead power cables.

It was really peculiar; it was, I wouldn't say shiny, but looked more sort of shimmery. The lights were really bright; a very bright one at the front, and when it shot off, I saw lights in each corner, which were white in colour. The ones around the outside were a sort of yellow-white, and there was also a circle of lights in the middle, of the same colour as the outside ones.

The object was an equilateral triangle, about double the size of an airliner, maybe as big as a football field. It wasn't very thick, but seemed thin along the edges [with a] sort of mound in the middle. When I first saw it, the point was facing me, but when it shot off, it sort of – I don't know – it must have swivelled, but I don't remember it swivelling, because I could see it side-on then, and I could see underneath as it shot off, and there was this circle of white lights. I probably got a good look at it literally for a matter of seconds, and then it flicked off and then stopped for a few seconds, and then it flicked off and so on; I would say twenty-five seconds, if that. I saw it for quite a long time in the distance . . .

All the time, I had the feeling of the hairs standing up on the back of my neck . . . I felt really scared, as I drove home. I think I arrived home maybe half-past three, I don't remember. But I woke everyone up and told them what I'd seen, and had a drink to calm me down. I was really shaken by the whole thing.[10]

Sarah Hall wrote up her experience for her newspaper under the pseudonym 'Sophie Wadleigh'. I spoke to her by telephone not long afterwards: she certainly sounded as though she had been quite shocked by the experience. In due course, other witnesses came forward who said they had seen a strange aerial device in the area, between 02:10 and 03:30. The home of Michael Howard, then Conservative Home Secretary, in Lympne, lay a mile and a half from Sarah Hall's observation point. Chris Rolfe learned that two local firemen had seen the same object directly over Howard's house, and word spread that a fire appliance had been called out at around the same time. Then, while I was chatting to UFOMEK investigator Jerry Anderson, following a talk I had just given in Canterbury in February the following year, a man approached Jerry and revealed that he was a neighbour of Michael Howard. He told Jerry that he and his wife had been woken up in the early hours by a commotion coming from the Home Secretary's house.

'There were a lot of people running around and shouting, and the neighbour believed them to be the armed police guards on duty there to protect Mr Howard,' wrote Stuart Miller and Chris Rolfe. 'There was a helicopter hovering above, with a searchlight scanning the area. Tellingly, the neighbour told Jerry that the searchlight was not pointing down but was scanning the skies level with the helicopter, and above it as well.'

Evidence firmly suggests that a security clampdown followed the incident. Jerry Anderson experienced problems with his answering machine, then someone claiming to be from the TV Licensing Department came to the door of his home while he was away, asking his wife if they had a licence. The Licensing Authority confirmed that no checks were being made in that area at the time. And in early 1999, both Jerry and Chris received in the post a tape recording of a telephone conversation on the Burmarsh case which they had had a year before.[11]

The national press did not latch on to the story until August that year, following the Conservative defeat in the general election. 'Howard's tough line on aliens – he deported scores when he was Home Secretary – had evidently upset beings far beyond our planet,' commented the *Sunday Times*.[12] Another article appeared in the same newspaper early the following year. 'So there really was something of the night about Michael Howard,' weighed in Sebastian Hamilton:

> Senior Tory spin doctors say they were aware of the story [in] a local newspaper, while Howard's agent has admitted halting publication of further detailed reports about the incident by complaining to the editor ... Eight separate reports were filed with local UFO spotters of a triangular craft, grey in colour, hovering in an area 15 miles around Howard's home ... Neither the local police nor the Ministry of Defence have any record of an incident that evening ... A police spokesman, however, said it might have been dealt with by Howard's own police protection team.[13]

In a letter to investigator Dr Colin Ridyard, PC Roy O'Connell of the Kent County Constabulary stated, perhaps tellingly: 'Under normal circumstances, this department would at once be made aware of any such "security incident" ... The only incident that we are aware of and to which I am sure you refer, was satisfactorily dealt with and could have no bearing on your investigations into UFO activity.'[14]

Had the former Home Secretary been aware of the incident?

'Mr Howard had more important matters to deal with than UFOs,' one source told the *Daily Mail*. 'He knew about the reports, but I doubt whether he was very concerned about them.'[15] 'I am just astonished by all this really,' Howard told the *Kentish Express*. 'While I probably was at my home that night, as I often am, I certainly didn't see anything. It is all ridiculous . . .'[16]

After three requests for a statement from Mr Howard, then leader of the Conservative Party, I eventually succeeded in obtaining the following odd response: 'I was and remain completely unaware of any such incident.'[17]

THE PHOENIX LIGHTS

On the evening of 13 March 1997 – a week after the Burmarsh incident – thousands of eyewitnesses across the state of Arizona reported having seen a mile-long, V-shaped formation of lights flying relatively close to the ground. First to report a sighting was a former police officer, who described 'bright red-orange lights in the shape of a boomerang', heading south. The lights appeared to be connected, as though belonging to one enormous object. Commercial pilots reported them, and fighter jets at Luke Air Force Base, near Phoenix, took off in pursuit, using afterburners.

'For several minutes the city stood still as these lights swept overhead on their way to Tucson, where truck drivers called one another on their CB radios, and families on the dark freeway stopped and stared in awe at the passing giant formation,' writes Dr Lynne Kitei, author of *The Phoenix Lights*.'[18]

In fact, people had been reporting sightings of odd lights in the Phoenix area since January. But the air display on the night of 13 March left few doubts that something truly phenomenal was occurring. At 20:30, for example, Mike Fortson observed a massive, black, chevron-shaped object with a translucent surface, estimated to be a mile long, which 'floated' along noiselessly at about 30 to 40 mph. Others reported 'an enormous triangular mass with lights on each of the corners' appearing to be 'city blocks' in width.[19]

A female operator at Luke Air Force Base volunteered the information to one witness that their switchboard had been deluged with reports: later the base denied having received any calls about the object. According to a report telephoned by witnesses to Peter Davenport, director of the Seattle-based National UFO Reporting Center,[20] Lockheed Martin F-16C jet fighters of the Arizona Air National Guard were scrambled from Luke AFB and intercepted the object over downtown Phoenix, photographed it with gun cameras and returned to base.

'Davenport states that the sources went on to describe how the base had been "locked down", how the pilots of the fighters had proceeded in approaching to within one mile of the object, and how their targeting radar had been "neutralized" by the object,' reports Kitei. 'Apparently, they provided copious details about the object, citing precise times, the names and ranks of the pilots, contents of radio conversations with the pilots while they were in the air, and many other aspects of the events that night. Unfortunately, Davenport's staff was unable to corroborate any of the claims, despite the fact that the callers were stationed at Luke AFB. Within a few days, Davenport received another call. This time, one of the sources reported that he was being transferred to Greenland.'[21]

Another report came from a retired pilot in the Phoenix suburb of Scottsdale, whose background included ratings in Boeing 747 and DC-10 airliners. He told Dr Kitei that he was with several other people when a formation of orange lights came into view. 'We thought we could see some kind of structure to it as it went by perpendicular to us. One thing we were sure of, it was huge, at least a mile in area, and it was silent.'[22] Another witness, Tim Ley, gives a highly detailed report of his observation, with other members of his family, in Sunnyslope, a small mountain valley near Phoenix, shortly after 20:00, as a giant craft slowly approached them.

'My first impression was that it was about 100 feet up in the air,' writes Ley. 'The outline of the structure was so perfectly balanced, sharp-edged and geometrical. What we saw reminded me of a carpenter's square set at 60 degrees. Each of its two arms had two lights set in them, evenly spaced from the centre front light, with the last two lights on each arm set in the structure just in front of the squared-off ends.'

The object, which appeared to be at least two city blocks long, passed slowly directly above the family. 'It was ridiculously close, and there was no noise,' Ley's report continues.

> When it began to pass over, I felt a nervousness in my body, almost like stage-fright [and so did] my family ... the kids started jumping up and down and talking about how there was no sound, and mentioning the movie 'Independence Day' and exhibiting symptoms of hysteria ... We all continued to stand outside and watch the object [as] it finally reached the gap through the mountain peaks ... My wife said she saw a dome-shaped bulge in the middle, on top of the craft, which appeared to be picking up some of the city and parkway lights below and reflecting them off its surface [and] we later thought it must be a peculiarity of the visual stealth that at certain angles of view, you can see the light reflect off of it.[23]

Although the sightings did not register on radar at Sky Harbor International Airport, air-traffic controllers who had been on duty testified publicly that they had seen the object or objects. 'I have never seen anything like this in my flying or controlling days,' said Bill Grava.[24] Videotapes were taken by members of the public from several different areas, some of which appear to show military high-intensity flares, which a spokesman for the Air National Guard said had been dropped along the Barry Goldwater Gunnery Range by A-10 Thunderbolt IIs from the Maryland Air National Guard that night, as part of a training exercise called Operation Snowbird. This was widely promoted as 'the explanation' for the phenomena.[25]

Perhaps coincidentally, on April Fools Day an item about the Phoenix Lights appeared on *CBS Evening News with Dan Rather*. 'He stressed that you didn't have to be in a cult or spaced-out to believe in UFOs,' reports

Kitei. 'He declared that millions of Americans do, and believe as well that the government is somehow covering it up. Rather said they had asked the Pentagon, and had been told that it could not substantiate the existence of UFOs, nor did it harbour the remains of UFOs. The Air Force quit investigating UFOs in 1969 . . .'[26]

A JOURNALIST ASSAULTED?

It was 30 May 1997. Georgina Howell had finished four days researching a Scottish wildlife story for the *Sunday Times* in the Orkney Islands, off the north-east coast of Scotland. She was waiting at Kirkwall Airport to board the 11:50 British Airways Flight 8773 to Aberdeen, connecting with a London-bound flight. 'The weather was brilliantly sunny and clear,' she wrote in the *Sunday Times* the following year. 'When we were called to board the small propeller plane, I was the last one out of the terminal building and walked slowly across the tarmac.'[27]

'I was thinking, "I probably won't see Orkney again, so I'll just take a last look around,"' Georgina explained to me. 'And up to my left, at about 45 degrees above the sea – above a windsock, but I couldn't tell how near or how far – was this very clear "angle" [chevron] in the sky. It appeared to be silvery metal, and as I walked across the tarmac it sort of flashed in the sun. It was like two sides of a triangle, with space in between. I tried to see if it was a plane, or perhaps two planes superimposed by perspective, and it obviously wasn't that. I thought it might have been a piece of airport equipment, on a pole, but in fact it wasn't. So I thought, well, when I get to the plane I'm going to get the air hostess out on the tarmac and ask her what it is.

'Just at that moment, I hit the tarmac with my face. I felt I couldn't do anything to protect myself whacking down on the tarmac and wasn't able to put my hands in front of my face. I was fully conscious as I went down.'[28]

'Although I had a cut lip, scraped nose, a black eye and bruising above the eye, my hands and arms, and the tape recorder I was carrying in my left hand, were unscathed,' wrote Georgina in her article. 'Several people came to my aid and helped me up. After a minute or so I told them, "I was looking at *that*!" and pointed to the sky where I had seen the angle, but there was nothing there. Apparently nobody else had seen it.' Neither had the object been picked up by Air Traffic Control.

Later, Georgina learned about the giant chevron-shaped object seen above Phoenix on 13 March. 'Whatever happened that day has certainly changed my opinion about UFOs,' she wrote. 'The subject used to bore me. Now I think about the incident frequently and I want to know what these things are. I will go on asking questions about them for the rest of my life.'[29]

POLAND

At 17:00 on 15 March 1997 – two days after the 'air display' at Phoenix – an object was seen to explode in the air before crashing to the ground near the town of Wegorzewo, in Poland's Suwalki province. Reportedly, its remains were immediately taken away by soldiers.

'The Army denied all knowledge of the incident at the time,' reports investigator Robert K. Lesniakiewicz, 'but since then, Army spokesman Colonel Zdzislaw Czekierda of the General Staff has publicly stated that the General Staff of the Polish Army have had a special division which gathered and evaluated all information about UFO sightings and close encounters with aliens since the early 1980s.' The reports were normally classified secret or top secret, according to another investigator, Robert Bernatowicz.[30]

DEFENSE AIRBORNE RECONNAISSANCE OFFICE

The Defense Airborne Reconnaissance Office (DARO) – under the aegis of the National Reconnaissance Office – once handled the US military's Unmanned (or the more politically correct Uninhabited) Air Vehicle (UAV) programme. While in Washington, DC, in 1998, a friend arranged for me to meet Major General Kenneth R. Israel, US Air Force Director, DARO, to discuss matters of mutual interest.

On the afternoon of 6th May, I was escorted up to the DARO reception area in the Pentagon, before the scheduled half-hour meeting. Two notices caught my attention: 'No Classified Here' (meaning no talk about classified information), and the other, 'DARO Welcomes Mr Good'. At 15:30 precisely, I was ushered into a small conference room. To my surprise, about eight young DARO officers greeted me: I had been expecting a one-to-one with General Israel. Instead, DARO had put on a media presentation (I hold a press card). I was asked to sit at the head of the table.

We all stood up when the general entered. After introducing himself to me, we exchanged pleasantries about England. He then delivered a mini-presentation on the functions of DARO. 'Right now, Timothy,' he began, 'we're interested in tunnels in North Korea.' He showed a videotape of the Global Hawk UAV, and afterwards said, 'Over to you, Timothy.' The young officers sat with pencils poised above their official notebooks.

I explained that the purpose of the meeting was to seek guidance in my research on 'the subject', pointing out that it is evidently of major concern to military and intelligence officials, and that UAVs were of related interest. 'Timothy,' he responded, 'I have never encountered *anyone* who has seen a UFO, and I know of no individual or organization within this building that takes the subject seriously.' I began to suspect a charade. He went on to say that he had never read a book on the subject, at which point I took out from my briefcase a signed copy of *Beyond Top Secret* – which I believe he knew I would be bringing – and presented him with it.

General Israel thanked me and held the book up. 'Wow, look at this,' he said to the officers, '*Beyond* Top Secret!' Then, glancing through the pages, he commented that obviously I had done a lot of careful research, and he didn't wish to belittle my work. On noticing pictures in the book of frames from the 8mm film of an alien craft taken by George Adamski, in the presence of my friend Madeleine Rodeffer and a few others, at Silver Spring, Maryland, on 26 February 1965 (see plates), he looked impressed. 'How do they explain these away?' he said. 'They look real to me.'

The general asked if I had ever seen a UFO. I mentioned one fleeting sighting, the event of 15 December 1980 in north-west Kent/south-east London, because it related to the events outside the twin RAF/US Air Force bases at Bentwaters and Woodbridge later that month. He expressed vague interest, and mentioned that he had flown Douglas RB-66 Destroyer (reconnaissance) aircraft from Bentwaters and RAF Alconbury.

General Israel then showed another short videotape, of the Dark Star UAV. We discussed its similarity, in side-planform, to flying saucers. I said that the Dark Star was often cited as an explanation for many UFO reports. He laughed. 'Dark Star has only flown twice, and it crashed on its second flight!' (The problems were subsequently ironed out.)

Just after the meeting was adjourned, General Israel mentioned to me that if anyone in the Pentagon knew anything about the UFO subject, it would probably be the Air Force Office of Special Investigations (AFOSI), since the phenomenon seemed to him to be more of a policing problem rather than one affecting national security. (AFOSI's main duties are counter-intelligence and criminal investigations, sometimes including deception, referred to euphemistically as 'special plans'.) I said I was aware of their long history of involvement, but refrained from telling him that I had learned

that, up to 1989 at least, over a hundred AFOSI personnel had knowledge –
in varying degrees – about the actual alien presence. As for UFOs being a
policing rather than a national security problem, it is evidently both.

'CAT AND MOUSE'

On 19 October 1998, four different radar stations in China's northern
Hebei province picked up an unknown moving target in airspace directly
above a military flight training base near Changzhou city. To observers at
the base, the UFO first appeared like 'a small star', and then grew larger
and larger, presumably as it descended to a lower altitude. The object was
described as having a mushroom-shaped dome on top and a flat bottom,
covered with bright, continuously rotating lights. At least 140 people on the
ground saw the object.

A base commander surnamed Li reported the observation to his
superiors, and a Shenyang JJ-6 armed interceptor trainer was scrambled to
intercept the object, once checks showed that no other civilian or military
aircraft were in the area. The two pilots reported that the object closely
resembled something they had seen in foreign science-fiction films. When
they flew to within about 4,000 metres (13,200 feet) of the UFO, over Qing
county, it abruptly shot upwards. As reported on numerous occasions, the
object played 'cat and mouse' with the fighter, repeatedly outdistancing it
and then reappearing just above it.

The report said that at one point the pilots requested permission to fire
at the object with their cannon. Permission was denied by ground control.
Eventually the JJ-6, short on fuel at 39,000 feet, was forced to return to
base. The UFO then disappeared before two more modern interceptors
became airborne.[31]

Two Turkish Air Force (THK) pilots of 122 Squadron ('Scorpions')
had taken off at 12:30 on 6 August 2001 from their base at Izmir in a
Cessna T-37B Dragonfly jet trainer. While practising manoeuvres over the
Gulf of Candarli, Aegean Sea, First Lieutenant Ilker Dinçer and his pupil,
Lieutenant Arda Gunyel, were suddenly surprised by an extremely bright
object, shaped like something between a disc and a cone, with a kind of
pod on the lower part. Ground control and Combat Operations Centre
were immediately informed, but nothing was detected on radar.

The UFO approached the T-37 at high speed, on a head-on course.
Next, it positioned itself alongside, then behind, and finally above the jet.
'Object is now over us. It is literally dogfighting with us,' radioed Dinçer. 'I

repeat, radar negative,' the pilots were informed. The UFO played 'cat-and-mouse' with the jet for a while, before disappearing at high speed.

The report made headline news in Turkish newspapers, forcing the THK to issue a press release. The object had been a weather balloon, they said. However, no weather balloons were in the area at that time, and even if they had been, no balloon is capable of keeping up with the speed of an aircraft, or of performing the types of manoeuvres described.[32,33]

In June 2003 it was leaked to the press that Turkey's National Intelligence Service (MIT) had received a top-secret request from the CIA for details of all the latest UFO reports. MIT accordingly asked the Turkish Air Force, Turkish Airlines and other establishments to submit their reports. MIT, which had previously only collected such reports, subsequently recommended that the Air Force should establish an official investigative body, headed by a colonel.[34]

UFO CHASE NEAR WASHINGTON, DC

At 01:00 on 26 July 2002, two F-16 Fighting Falcon jets from the 113th Air National Guard wing, on 'strip alert' at Andrews AFB, were scrambled by NORAD (North American Aerospace Defense Command) to investigate a radar track near Washington, DC.[35] The unknown traffic was apparently slowly approaching the Temporary Flight Restriction Area designated after the terrorist attacks on 11 September 2001. Major Mike Snyder, Command Spokesman for both NORAD and the US Air Force Space Command, commented that the target's 'radar signature, speed, and elevation fit the criteria of a small private aircraft'. The radar target then faded from NORAD detection systems, the F-16s found nothing and returned to base, and that was that.[36] Or that, at least, was the official version of events.

Gary Dillman, working a late shift about 6 miles south-east of Andrews AFB, heard and saw *two* pairs of jets take off from the base at 01:00. As he continued to watch them, until 01:30, he became convinced that something unusual was going on. 'Most of the time he could see only one fighter strobe [light] at a time in the distance, sometimes two, but the aircraft were circling, turning right, turning left, flying back and forth,' writes Joan Woodward, who has conducted the most extensive investigation into the case. 'He could not hear them. Occasionally, one pair of fighters returned to the Andrews area, and then flew back to the east-southeast again. When asked whether he thought these fighters landed and were replaced by another fresh pair, Dillman thought they had not, because he would have heard their take-off sounds – with which he is very familiar – but he could not totally rule out the possibility.'

At 01:30, Dillman called WTOP news radio and informed them that something extraordinary was going on. Woodward's report continues:

> Just after his call to WTOP, Dillman looked toward the southwest (toward Waldorf, Maryland) and saw a glowing, round, hard-edged, orange object 25–30 degrees above the horizon coming toward him on a downward path [which] became brighter and larger. When the object was at about 20 degrees elevation, a fighter appeared out of the clouds coming from either north or east of the object. The fighter turned toward the object, which responded with a smooth, curving, banking turn to the south, away from the fighter that was now following it. They both flew south, then curved toward the east . . .[37]

'At 01:40, this entire sequence of events was repeated,' Joan Woodward informed me. 'Dillman saw the orange object appear in the south-west sky as above, but this time a fighter was already following it.'[38]

Meanwhile, in nearby Waldorf, Maryland, at roughly 01:40, Renny Rogers, alerted for the second time by the roaring of what sounded like more than two jets, went outside. 'He saw a bright, pale-bluish light in the north-northeast moving at what he considered to be a phenomenal rate of speed,' Woodward reports:

> The light was about 35 degrees above the horizon when first seen and its path dropped precipitously an estimated 2,000 feet and came back up slightly, after which it flew in a fast, straight line from north-north-east to east-southeast, where it was [temporarily lost from sight] . . . It moved in an effortless, floating manner but at very high speed, and it was silent . . . the light appeared to be just a light source [and] it was constantly brightening and dimming on a 1.5 second cycle. Rogers ran toward the south [and] found the blue light in the southwestern sky . . .
>
> Rogers saw his neighbour, Mike, who had come outside, and called to him. A fighter came from the north over Rogers' house in level, straight-line flight in obvious pursuit of the light . . . The aircraft was dipping its wings from side to side as it flew and continued to do so as it followed the blue light, and Rogers' impression was that the aircraft was constantly correcting its course. The fighter was not [on this occasion] using its afterburner. The blue light was much faster than the pursuing jet . . .

'These events took place beneath the cloud cover at 5,500–6,000 feet, but above the scattered clouds at 3,500 feet,' says Woodward.

Coincidentally, these events occurred on 26th July, precisely 50 years after the second wave of UFO intrusions over Washington in July 1952. 'In conclusion,' adds Joan Woodward, 'we have military fighters flying at less than 6,000 feet altitude in the middle of the night over residential areas, using afterburners, without apparent concern for the dense civilian population underneath ... unknown objects flying near our most sensitive areas, and our modern fighters are no more able to intercept and identify them than were the fighters of 1952.'[39]

'There is no question that something was going on that early morning that NORAD/USAF did not want known to the general public,' Joan wrote to me. 'And they changed the tower logs at Andrews AFB to hide it, and refused to answer some very innocuous questions.'[40]

*

In March 2007, former Arizona Governor Fife Symington III admitted to having seen an enormous triangular craft during the extraordinary air display over Phoenix on the evening of 13 March 1997. A cousin of the late Senator Stuart Symington, a former Secretary of War for Air (p. 82), the Governor had hitherto publicly ridiculed the incident. 'Unless the Defense Department proves us otherwise,' he stated during a CNN interview (21 March 2007), 'it was probably some form of alien spacecraft.'[41]

REFERENCES

1. Martín, Jorge, 'US Jets Abducted by UFOs in Puerto Rico', *The UFO Report 1991*, ed. Timothy Good, Sidgwick & Jackson, 1990, pp. 192–204.

2. Martín, Jorge, 'Puerto Rico's Astounding UFO Situation', *The UFO Report 1992*, ed. Timothy Good, Sidgwick & Jackson, London, 1991, pp. 103–5.

3. Filers Files #41, 2005. www.georgefiler.com

4. Personal interviews, Paris, 12 December 2000, and Gretz-Armainvilliers, 15 November 2004.

5. Foxhall, Richard, 'The 1990 Tornado UFO Sighting', *UFO Magazine* (UK), August 2002, pp. 58–64.

6. Pope, Nick, 'Britain's Real X Files, *Daily Mail*, 2 February 2005, p. 13.

7. MoD signal from RAF West Drayton, 061340Z Nov 90.

8. Whitehead, Paul, 'Special Report to FSR', *Flying Saucer Review*, Vol. 36, No. 2, 1991, p. 10.

9. Pope, Nick, *Open Skies, Closed Minds*, Simon & Schuster, London, 1996, pp. 134–40.

10. Rolfe, Chris, 'The Kent Flying Triangle', *UFO Magazine* (UK), September/October 1997, p. 22. Chris Rolfe can be reached at ufomek@hotmail.co.uk

11. Miller, Stuart, with Chris Rolfe, 'Something of the Night', *UFO Magazine* (UK), January 2004, pp. 4–11.

12. 'Alien revenge hits Howard', *Sunday Times*, 24 August 1997.

13. Hamilton, Sebastian, 'Tories hid Howard's "alien visitation"', *Sunday Times*, 18 January 1998.

14. 'Howardgate', *UFO Magazine* (UK), March/April 1998, p. 6.

15. Derbyshire, David, 'Take us to your leader', *Daily Mail*, 19 January 1998.

16. 'Howardgate', op. cit., p. 8.

17. Letter from the Rt. Hon. Michael Howard QC MP, Leader of the Opposition, House of Commons, 24 September 2005.

18. Kitei, Lynne D., MD, *The Phoenix Lights*, Hampton Roads, Charlottesville, VA 22902, 2000/2004, pp. 1–2.

19. Ibid., p. 20.

20. National UFO Reporting Center, PO Box 45623, University Station, Seattle, WA 98145. Hotline number (for recently observed events): +001 (206) 722 3000. www.nuforc.org

21. Kitei, op. cit., p. 23.

22. www.qtm.net/~geibdan/a1999/aug/b7.htm. See also Kitei, op. cit.

23. Kitei, op.cit.

24. Ibid. op. cit., p. 48.

25. Ibid., pp. 64–5.

26. Ibid., p. 31.

27. Howell, Georgina, 'One glance at the shining metallic object in the sky changed this writer's life for ever', *Sunday Times Magazine*, 9 August 1998, pp. 10–13.

28. Telephone interview, 7 July 1998.

29. Howell, op. cit., p. 13.

30. Lesniakiewicz, Robert K., 'UFOs, Alles-Stones and Stone Balls', *UFO Magazine* (UK), May/June 1998, pp. 48–9. In May 2006, I participated in a private debate and a public UFO conference in Wroclaw, Poland. One of the participants was Major Józef J. Makiela, a retired Polish Air Force (Reserve) pilot, who confirmed that the subject is taken very seriously by the military.

31. *Agence France-Presse*, Shanghai, 5 November 1998.

32. Metehan Demir, 'Turkish Jet's Dogfight with UFO', *Hürriyet*, Ankara, 8 August 2001. Translated by Esen Şekerkarar.

33. Thouanel, Bernard, *Objets Volants Non Identifiés*, Michel LAFON, Paris, 2003, p. 203.

34. *Vatan*, 2 June 2003; *Sabah*, 2 June 2003; *UFO Magazine* (UK), August 2003, p. 57.

35. Letter from Joan Woodward, 19 April 2006.
36. Young, Kenny, 'UFO Violates DC Airspace', *MUFON UFO Journal*, No. 413, September 2002, p. 11.
37. Woodward, Joan, 'The Washington, DC, Jet Chase of July 26, 2002', *International UFO Reporter*, Vol. 27, No. 4, Winter 2002–2003, pp. 3–7, 22–5.
38. Woodward letter, 19 April 2006.
39. Woodward, 'The Washington, DC, Jet Chase', op. cit.
40. Woodward letter, 19 April 2006.
41. Kean, Leslie, 'Symington confirms he saw UFO 10 years ago', *Prescott Daily Courier*, 18 March 2007.

26. CONFLICTING TRAFFIC

On 11 June 1985 a Chinese Civil Aviation Administration Boeing 747 on the Peking to Paris flight encountered a UFO that almost forced the captain to make an emergency landing. Flight 933 was over Lanzhou, the capital of Gansu province, when the object was seen by Captain Wang Shuting and his crew, at 22:40.

The UFO flew at very high speed across the path of the airliner at its altitude of 33,000 feet, reportedly illuminating an enormous area. Huge in diameter, it was elliptical in shape, with an extremely bright spot in the centre and three horizontal rows of bluish-white lights on the perimeter, giving the impression of 'different levels'. The official news release, which attracted worldwide attention, stated that no passengers reported the two-minute sighting.[1]

In August 1985 an Olympic Airways flight from Zurich to Athens had a near miss with unknown traffic near the Italian/Swiss border, and more UFOs were seen in that month by the crew and forty-five journalists aboard a Boeing 737 bound for Buenos Aires. The pilot said the UFOs veered away each time he headed towards them.[2]

CALIFORNIA

It was 10 September 1985. British pilot David J. Hastings was flying from San Francisco to New York and back for his US type-conversion in a six-seat Cessna 337 Super Skymaster (C337), together with his instructor, David Patterson, an ex-US Army Air Forces pilot, who owned the plane. At 12:05, on the leg from the Grand Canyon to Bakersfield, California, they were climbing to 10,500 feet on Airway Victor 209 under radar control, with the Mojave Desert coming into view, when it happened.

'We both suddenly realised that we had fast traffic in our twelve o'clock [position],' reported Hastings in *Pilot* magazine. 'We pushed and ducked beneath the coaming [ledge above the instrument panel], waiting for the bang of a mid-air collision. A shadow flashed over us but there was absolutely no sound. We slowly raised our heads and asked, "What the heck . . . ?" '

We then both felt that there was something moving to port but could not see anything. So strong was the feeling that I unstrapped and moved aft to get my normal print camera, and after strapping back in I took two shots out of the port window. We called Centre to check if they had any conflicting [traffic], and the answer was no . . .

On getting back to base we took the film to a one-hour photo shop – and there it was. One shot had nothing but the scenery, but the second had the blurred image of a UFO [see plates]. Several organizations have studied the film, including the US Navy, but as yet no one has really come up with the answer as to what it was we nearly hit that morning.[3]

ALASKA

Of the many reports of encounters with Japanese airliners, the most dramatic so far is that reported by the crew of a Japan Air Lines Boeing 747 cargo flight on the night of 17 November 1986. Flight 1628, en route to Anchorage, Alaska, from Reykjavik, Iceland – the middle leg of a Europe-to-Tokyo flight – was entering US airspace at 39,000 feet, and Captain Kenju Terauchi and his crew were making final preparations before their descent to Anchorage Airport. Suddenly they noticed some unusual lights accompanying them.

As indicated on the plane's radar, the unidentified air traffic (UAT) initially appeared in front of the 747 at a distance of approximately 7 to 8 nautical miles, for about 12 minutes, and then positioned itself on the port side of the plane, remaining there for at least 32 minutes. Terauchi said 'the two small ships and the mothership' moved quickly and stopped suddenly. He caught a brief glimpse of the main object's walnut-shaped silhouette, judging it to be 'two times bigger than an aircraft carrier' (see plates).

The pilot was instructed by air-traffic control to descend to 4,000 feet and make turns, but the objects continued to follow the plane for 32 minutes before vanishing. US Federal Aviation Administration (FAA) authorities claimed that the objects were tracked on radar, but had not registered on the radar tapes.[4] The story received worldwide media attention.

John Callahan was FAA Division Chief of the Accidents and Investigations branch at the time of the incident. Together with the Associate

Director of the FAA, Callahan was sent to Atlantic City, New Jersey, to review all the evidence, including military radar data (which subsequently went missing). 'We wanted to see everything the controller saw [and] hear everything he heard. And we wanted it all tied together; the radar, the digital radar, and the sound,' explained Callahan, in a statement for the Disclosure Project in 2000. 'It took us two days to look at all the data.' The investigators returned to FAA Headquarters in Washington, DC, with a video recording of all the data.

Vice Admiral Donald Engen was FAA Administrator at the time. At the debriefing, Engen asked to see the video. 'He started watching it,' said Callahan, 'and after about five minutes he told his staff to cancel meetings. So he watched the whole thing, just over half an hour. And his take was, "Don't talk to anybody until I give you the okay".' The next day, a meeting was arranged in the FAA's 'round room', at which a great amount of material was presented. 'They brought in three people from the FBI, three people from the CIA, and three people from Reagan's scientific study team. I don't know who the rest of the people were . . .

'We let them watch the video . . . They were all excited – the only way a man would be if that was his job. [One of the CIA agents] actually swore all these other guys in there that this never took place: we never had this meeting . . . I said [that] if it's a UFO, why wouldn't you want the people to know? [And] he says if they came out and told the American public that they ran into a UFO out there, it would cause panic across the country. So therefore, you can't talk about it.'

Much of the material presented at the meeting was confiscated by the group. However, Callahan managed to retain the original video, the pilot's report and the FAA's first report.[5]

Captain Terauchi suffered considerable humiliation following the event, and was given a desk job for an extended period.

PARIS

Weather conditions were fine on 28 January 1994, as an Air France Airbus A320–111 (Flight AF3532) on the Nice–London route was cruising at 11,700 metres in the vicinity of Coulommiers in Seine-et-Marne, just east of Paris. At around 13:10, the chief steward, who happened to be on the flight deck at the time, pointed out what he thought was a weather balloon to Captain Jean-Charles Duboc and his co-pilot and First Officer Valérie Chaufour. At first, Duboc thought it was an aircraft banking at a 45-degree angle, but all three soon agreed that the object did not resemble anything with which they were familiar.

The excellent visibility and altocumulus clouds allowed Duboc to estimate that the object was at an altitude of 10,500 metres, and at a distance of approximately 46 kilometres. Taking into account its apparent diameter, they deduced that the object was very large. It appeared to change from a dark 'brown bell' to a lens shape before disappearing almost instantaneously on the left side of the airliner, 'as though it had suddenly become invisible'.

Captain Duboc reported the *objet volant non identifié* (OVNI) to Reims air-traffic control centre, where it was confirmed as unknown traffic. Following standard procedure, Reims reported the OVNI to the military Air Defence Operations Centre (CODA) at Taverny. A few days later, Jean-Jacques Velasco, who heads SEPRA, the French Government's official UFO study group, visited CODA and studied a read-out of the radar information. It had recorded a fifty-second track showing unknown traffic, at the exact same time and location, as it crossed the trajectory of AF3532. The object – calculated to be 250 metres long – disappeared from radar at precisely the same time as this was reported by the crew.[6,7,8]

From 1977 to 2003, SEPRA received some 6,000 reports of OVNI sightings, of which 110 were reported by civil or military aircrew.[9]

MANCHESTER

Returning from Milan on 6 January 1995, two British Airways pilots, Captain Roger Wills and First Officer Mark Stuart, flying a Boeing 737 with sixty passengers on board, reported a near miss with an unknown structured craft on their approach to Manchester's Ringway Airport. The alarming incident occurred in the dark at 18:48, and is described in the official summary, extracts from which follow:

> The B737 pilot reports that he was over the Pennines about 8 or 9 NM SE of Manchester Airport at 4000 ft ... While flying just above the tops of some ragged [cloud] both he and the first officer saw a lighted object fly down the RH [right hand] side of the ac [aircraft] at high speed from the opposite direction. He was able to track the object through the RH windscreen and side window, having it in sight for a total of about 2 seconds. There was no apparent sound or wake.
>
> The first officer instantly 'ducked' as it went by [and] looked up in time to see a dark object pass down the right side of the ac at high

speed; it was wedge-shaped with what could have been a black stripe down the side ... It made no attempt to deviate from its course ... There was no known traffic in the vicinity at the time and no radar contacts were seen ...

In its report, the Civil Aviation Authority's Joint Airmiss Working Group (JAWG) concluded that: 'Despite exhaustive investigations the reported object remains untraced ... The Group were anxious to emphasise that this report, submitted by two responsible airline pilots, was considered seriously and they wished to commend the pilots for their courage in submitting it ...'[10]

CHINA

In February 1995, a Chinese pilot preparing to land his aircraft at a Guizhou province airport, in south-west China, was forced to take violent evasive action when unknown traffic approached him head-on. According to a news report, his Boeing 737 was at an altitude of 2,400 metres and starting its landing approach when the anti-collision system detected an object rushing towards the plane. At 1,852 metres from the 737, the object could be seen changing from a rhomboid to a circular shape, and changing colour from yellow to red.

The pilot landed safely, though the UFO remained on the aircraft's radar screen for some time before disappearing in the south. The Guizhou control tower confirmed that no other planes were in the area.[11]

In 1995 it was reported that the China UFO Research Organization (CURO), though described by Wang Changting, one of its leaders, as an 'independent, unofficial, civil, academic body', was then housed at the Military Weapons Industry Academic Department of the state China North Industries Group in western Beijing. By that year, the group had collected over 5,000 reports of UFO sightings in Chinese airspace. 'We also study the application of UFO phenomena to the national economy,' Wang revealed intriguingly, 'such as new materials and new technologies.'[12]

ARGENTINA

At 20:10 on 31 July 1995, Aerolineas Argentinas Flight 734, a Boeing 727 with three crew and 102 passengers on board, was in the landing pattern for the airport at San Carlos de Bariloche, Rio Negre province, when

Captain Jorge Polanco was forced to make a sharp manoeuvre to avoid colliding with unknown traffic. 'I suddenly saw a white light which was bearing right down on us really fast before it halted about 100 metres away,' he said. The UFO then made a turn and flew parallel to the 727.

The object had two green lights at each end, and a flashing orange light in the middle. 'As I came in to land on my final approach, the lights of the runway and airport suddenly went out,' said Polanco. 'I had to climb back to 3,000 metres, always accompanied by the OVNI [*objeto volante non identificado*] ... When the lights came back on the ground, and I recommenced my descent, the OVNI then disappeared at tremendous speed.' The object was also seen by a Gendarmeria Piper PA-31-310 flying 600 metres above the 727. The airliner landed an hour late.

Polanco spent some time on the flight deck recovering from the experience. 'We saw something similar to the image of an inverted flying saucer, as large as a Boeing 727,' he said, 'and with very powerful illumination that was blinding us.' A reporter from *La Naçion* on board the plane witnessed the object, and airport officials confirmed that the airliner had been prevented from landing on its first attempt due to the sudden appearance of a strange object, just at the moment when the airport was blacked out. Furthermore, instruments in the control tower were affected. 'All the airport's radio support was suddenly cut off,' said airport chief Major Jorge Orviedo, 'and there was a blackout in the whole city.'[13,14]

It will be recalled that, following the UFO interception in Iran by jet pilots in September 1976, the UFO followed one of the jets back to Mehrabad Air Force Base and did a low-level fly-past, causing a power blackout at the base for several seconds.

In briefing notes on the safety implications of UFO close approaches for the Joint Airmiss Working Group in February 1995, former British Airways captain Graham Sheppard commented:

'It would not be surprising to discover that, in the past, unexplained aeroplane losses have been caused by instinctive manoeuvring to avoid a conflicting UFO ... the commercial sensibilities of the airlines should now be set aside along with the media's inability to give serious treatment to the subject. Otherwise this discrete and notifiable hazard to aircraft safety will continue to be concealed and thus gratuitously omitted from the briefing syllabus ...'[15]

A SWISS AIRMISS

Near misses with UFOs continued to be reported by airline crews around the world, if sporadically. At 17:07 Eastern Daylight Time on 9 August 1997, a Swissair Boeing 747-300, Flight 127 to Zurich, was on the Philadelphia to Boston leg when, over Long Island, New York, a cylindrical 'glowing white' object, about the size of the fuselage of a small light aircraft, came directly towards the airliner at very high speed. The 747 was in level flight at 23,000 feet at the time of the incident, and cruising at 390 mph indicated (570 mph true air speed) in a cloudless sky. The pilots, Captain Philippe Bobet and First Officer Kurt Grunder, were interviewed separately in Boston on the following day by officials from the National Transportation Safety Board, the FAA and the FBI.

'. . . when turning [my] head from left to straight ahead, and while talking to passengers on PA, I spotted an unidentifiable flying object,' reported Bobet to Swissair flight operations officials in Zurich. 'The path of the UFO was from [the] opposite direction, slightly right. Estimated horizontal distance: between 100 and 200 feet above aircraft. At the same time, I saw the First Officer plunging his head down towards his knees. The F/O mentioned later that he thought we would get hit by the object. UFO speed appeared to be very high.' The duration of the event was about a second.

No noise could be heard from the object, and there was no trail or wake turbulence. It did not trigger the 747's electronic traffic/collision avoidance system (TCAS), indicating that if it was an aircraft, it was not using a transponder. Nor was the object tracked on radar. The most logical explanation that comes to mind is that it must have been a guided missile. Only thirteen months earlier, a Boeing 747 of Trans World Airways (Flight 800) disintegrated off the coast of Long Island, killing all on board. Although the official explanation blamed an explosion in the central fuel tank, rumours persisted in the aviation business that the 747 had been hit by a missile. Don Berliner and Robert J. Durant, authors of a book on the Swissair event, are sceptical in the case of Flight 127. '[The pilots] could easily have seen fins or wings, but saw none,' they report. 'To the best of our knowledge, there are no small- to medium-sized missiles without such flight-control surfaces. Nor was there any evidence of an exhaust [and] a missile would have been "seen" by the radar that was tracking Swissair 127 . . .'

The object was officially explained as a weather balloon, which had been spotted by a United Airlines flight in nearly the same location and at the same height – but seventy-two minutes after the Swissair incident. 'No weather balloon could have been airborne at that time because they only last for one hour, and by the time of the United report, a total of eleven hours would have elapsed since the last [known] launching,' conclude Berliner and Durant.[16]

CHILE

In 2003, members of the Defence Committee of the Chilean Chamber of Deputies analysed, for the first time, information on UFOs (OVNI). During its session on 26 August, they heard testimony – largely concerning reports from pilots and air traffic controllers – from the Comité de Estudios de Fenómenos Aéreos Anómalos (CEFAA), and from the director of OVNIVISION, another Chilean research group. Deputy Arturo Cardemil, Chairman of the Defence Committee, told the media that UFOs had sometimes disrupted air-traffic operations.[17] And, occasionally, they continue to do so. The following reports – if true – are among the most disturbing commercial cases I have studied.

DUBLIN/IRISH CHANNEL

At 20:30 on 4 January 2004, an Aer Lingus Boeing 737-448, EI-BXD, with 135 people on board, was approaching the east coast of Ireland, 15 nautical miles from the Ashbourne VOR (Very High Frequency Omni-Directional Range) beacon, before landing at Dublin Airport. The QDM (the Q-code term for a magnetic heading to a beacon) was 190 degrees, and the QDR (to fly from a beacon) 010 degrees. The chart position of the airliner was 53 degrees 31 minutes north, and about 6 degrees west. The 737 was being followed in for landing on Runway 10 by a British Midland Airbus A330-200 at a distance of 6 miles. Both aircraft were at an altitude of 3,000 feet AMSL (above mean sea level), and speeds were 250 knots.

According to Dermot Butler and Carl Nally, Ireland's leading UFO investigators, as the 737 approached the Slane area, some 30 miles north-west of Dublin, the A330 crew observed unidentified traffic take off vertically from a field. The object had very bright strobe-lights, and was triangular in shape. 'The triangular UFO began to circle the 737, and the crew of the 737 experienced a power drain on their aircraft,' reports Carl Nally, who is a private pilot:

At this point, the A330 could observe a purplish glow surrounding the Aer Lingus 737. As the UFO flew in front of the 737, at the same altitude and a short distance in front of them, the Captain requested a vector [heading] to avoid collision. Even though they were on a VOR track, air traffic control (ATC) gave the 737 an eight-degree vector to avoid the UFO, as ATC had the UFO on radar. This is a very unusual procedure, as it upsets other aircraft following behind, and may require vector changes to all aircraft, incoming and outgoing.

The 737 Captain filed a 'near miss' with ATC. The UFO angled off to the port side, and a huge wake turbulence was experienced as the 737 was violently shaken and the outside air temperature rose to +164 degrees Centigrade, as the huge UFO scorched through the air – as shown on the systems display digital readout. This lasted about 15 seconds. The only other phenomenon that can cause this effect is lightning. All of this was witnessed by the Airbus crew, who also experienced the wake turbulence. The UFO headed southeast at great speed.

When the Aer Lingus 737 landed, the crew could not raise the speed brakes [spoilers], on the wings, more than a quarter the distance up. They were then requested to go to Stand 132 by the Air Marshal. The aircraft was examined, and the wings found to be badly damaged, as if dented by a hammer. There was also aircraft skin damage and hydraulic damage to the speed brakes, caused by the UFO wake. The pilots were then told to go home for two days.

The second encounter with an airliner is reported to have occurred at 22:30 that same evening, involving an Airbus A330-200, leased from AtlasAir (USA) and chartered by Air Tours (Tack No./Call Sign, Tour Jet.N), with 213 people on board. As in the previous incident, the plane was approaching the east coast, bound for Dublin Airport, when the crew observed a flashing strobe light over the Slane area. Carl Nally's report continues:

As they throttled back to 230 KTS [knots] at 2,500 feet, the UFO took on a triangular shape [and] was now in front of the aircraft and gave off a continuous, very bright flashing light (like a camera flash). The crew were advised by ATC to vector 10 degrees to avoid the UFO. As they began to take up the new heading, the UFO began to circle the aircraft in a very aggressive manner. The crew were terrified, and expected a collision with the UFO, which was approximately 360 feet in span. The Captain filed a 'near miss' with ATC.

As the craft continued its aggressive manoeuvres, the aircraft's interior lights grew dim (power drain), and at this point the Captain drew the attention of the passengers to the 'strange craft' circling the aeroplane. The passengers had already been observing this, and were now beginning to feel panicked.

This scenario went on for about 8 to 10 minutes. At one terrifying point in the confrontation, the wake turbulence from the huge UFO shook the aircraft violently and activated the 'wind shear' warning device (which also records the stress on the aircraft and pitches the aircraft down to compensate and avoid stall). All through this episode, other aircraft in the area were observing the encounter and listening in to the radio transmissions between ATC and the Airbus. The plane was vectored in on finals to Runway 10, and just two minutes before landing, the UFO took off southeast and shot into the distance.

'After landing and completing their flight logs,' reported Carl, 'the crew corresponded with the other pilots about the experience. The general consensus was that the area north of the VOR, i.e. the Navan/Slane area, has become an area where UFOs have been a regular occurrence over the past three to four years. Most pilots won't talk about their observations/ encounters for fear of repercussions from employers. As usual, ATC have denied any UFO activity in the area.'[18]

The crews were badly shaken by these experiences, and the Aer Lingus 737 (EI-BXD) was taken out of service, according to Dermot and Carl, who later reported the story to the press. 'This story hasn't got an ounce of credibility,' said Irish Aviation Authority spokesperson Lilian Cassin. 'There is no way that air-traffic control would give a vector around an unknown object . . . If the aircraft was damaged in the way they say it was, a report would have been filed [and] there was no incident requiring attention.'[19]

The stories are difficult to believe. I do not doubt the integrity of Carl and Dermot, and I can understand that the crews concerned do not wish their identities to be revealed, but I find it incomprehensible that not one passenger has come forward by now, particularly since the captain of the A330-200 is said to have alerted the passengers. In November 2004 I met Carl and Dermot in Dublin, together with Graham Sheppard and his wife, Margaret, to discuss the case in depth. Later I gave an interview to a local newspaper, which reported that these were among the most compelling aerial encounters I was aware of. An appeal in the same article for passengers to contact Carl and Dermot has led nowhere to date.[20]

Carl and Dermot conducted an exhaustive investigation, contacting Aer Lingus, Dublin Airport authorities including Aer Rianta Police and Fire personnel, FLS Aerospace (aircraft maintenance), and the local Beaumont Hospital (which had been put on emergency alert on the evening of the incidents). Excerpts from some replies to Dermot Butler follow:

— **FLS Aerospace**: '. . . any enquiries relating to Aer Lingus aircraft must be made directly to the Airline.'[21]
  Chief Airport Fire Officer (Aer Rianta): 'As it is our policy not to comment on a specific call-out regarding a specific airline, I suggest that you contact Aer Lingus.'[22]
— **Aer Lingus**: '. . . in order to find out about what happened to Aer Lingus Boeing 737-400 EI-BXD, I need the flight number and where the flight was travelling from.'[23] [Unfortunately these were not known.]
— **Beaumont Hospital, Dublin**: 'With regard to your enquiry about an incident in January . . . it would be more appropriate for you to direct this to the Authorities at Dublin Airport.'[24]
— **Irish Aviation Authority**: 'Any questions relating to the Dublin Airport's emergency services will have to be addressed to Aer Rianta. Likewise, your questions about aircraft EI-BXD should be addressed to the aircraft's operator, Aer Lingus.'[25]

There are indications that the responses by various authorities are disingenuous. Aer Lingus, for example, could easily have identified the flight number of EI-BXD had they chosen to do so. Although no passengers have come forward, neither has anyone come forward to say that they were on that plane at the time and that *nothing* happened at all. Furthermore, Carl and Dermot, and a well-qualified friend of mine in the aviation business, encountered stumbling blocks when attempting to access the aircraft's maintenance logs. Regarding Beaumont Hospital, Dermot received a 'no comment' when he asked if Dublin Airport had put them on an emergency standby. Subsequently, he received written confirmation that the external emergency services (ambulances and fire engines) *were* called in to the airport on the night in question, although, curiously, no press release to this effect – a standard procedure – was forthcoming.

It needs to be pointed out that neither Carl nor Dermot actually met any of the pilots involved in the incidents: the story came to them from two airline pilots whose information they have come to rely on over the years. These sources are prepared to testify, should the need arise.

When I went to Dublin on 8 November 2004 for the meeting with Carl and Dermot the following day, I made a point of flying with Aer Lingus (A321, EI-CHP, Flight EI157). I had written a short letter to the pilots, asking if they were aware of the incidents and giving contact numbers of the principal researchers, as well as Graham Sheppard and myself. I handed the letter, in an open envelope, to the flight attendant and asked if she would kindly take it to the flight deck. She returned shortly afterwards, looking agitated. 'They're not accepting that,' she said brusquely. 'May I ask why?' She merely repeated what she had said.

The 737-448 re-entered service with Aer Lingus following maintenance or repairs (or both), and was cancelled from the Irish registry in November 2004, and then sold to Thai Airways for the use of HRH Crown Prince Maha Vajiralongkorn, with its new registration – HS-HRH.

Another incident is reported by Dermot Butler and Carl Nally to have occurred to another commercial aircraft in the small hours of 30 June 2005 (or thereabouts – the co-pilot is reluctant to give the precise date), following sightings of unidentified lights over Dublin Airport. The co-pilot is known to Carl and Dermot but does not wish any identifying information to be published. A UFO some 30 feet wide and 10 feet high approached dangerously close to the aircraft at its altitude of 3,000 feet. Intense waves of heat and wake turbulence were experienced. After heading in the direction of Malahide, the unknown craft returned and began further harassment, causing the plane to become uncontrollable for a few minutes.

London Air Traffic Control Centre (LATCC) was contacted shortly afterwards and confirmed the presence of unauthorized traffic. A strobe light on the UFO induced feelings of dizziness and nausea, and the co-pilot vomited several times, but then suddenly both pilots felt strangely relaxed. 'The craft then started getting aggressive with us, coming for us and then flying away at great speed. How it didn't hit us I don't know, as it seemed inches away, not feet,' the co-pilot claims. 'At one time I had to bank the plane to the starboard. It was so much of a turn that the aircraft went nearly sideways up.'

> We reported to London: '[Flight] needs assistance ... We have a hostile craft and we have made dangerous manoeuvres to avoid it. Repeat, we need emergency assistance. It's trying to take us out of the sky' ... The captain spoke to the passengers, to say we were going through bad weather, and not to worry ... [ATC] called us and said they were scrambling the RAF ... The UFO came at us again ... I really thought we were dead. Twenty-five minutes later the RAF [Tornados] showed up at a safe distance from us. There was nothing we or they could do ... It was just so damn fast.

The commercial aircraft was escorted by the Tornados to a certain UK airport, the UFO accompanying them all the way. 'We were told by certain people not to say a word of what happened, and were reminded again in a very unfriendly manner,' claims the co-pilot.

Did this terrifying event really happen? Dermot and Carl, at least, believe so. Additional information on this and the previous cases has been published in their book, *Conspiracy of Silence.*[26]

ARGENTINA AND MEXICO

In the last week of July 2005, just as an airliner was making its final approach to the local airport at Santa Rosa, La Pampa, Argentina at 19:30, the airport control tower operator noticed an unknown, luminous object moving slowly and parallel to the aircraft. The flight plan operator was alerted by the tower operator, and they both saw the object stop in its tracks. It then emitted a brilliant flash of blue-white light, moved again, emitted another flash, and then vanished. At no point was the object seen by the airliner's crew.[27]

In the first week of October 2005, the crew of a Magnicharter Boeing 737-300 (XA-MAA) encountered a highly luminous, disc-shaped object. The event is reported to have occurred at 12:30 in the air corridor of the Mexican state of Oaxaca, at an altitude of 20,000 feet, in perfect weather conditions.

The crew said that the object emerged from a cloud and then entered another, at an estimated distance of 10 nautical miles from the aircraft. Earlier, another Magnicharter airliner reported a strange, static sphere above the World Trade Centre air corridor in Mexico City.[28]

UFO HOVERS OVER O'HARE INTERNATIONAL AIRPORT

Of the several incidents regarding unidentified conflicting traffic reported subsequent to publication of the first edition of this book, the most interesting occurred at Chicago's O'Hare International Airport on 7 November 2006, when a mysterious, saucer-shaped craft was seen hovering over a terminal, in restricted airspace, for several minutes at around 16:30, just before sunset.

The incident was witnessed by a group of airline and airport employees, including pilots. They described a grey disc-shaped object, estimated up to 7.3 metres (24 feet) in diameter, without any lights and making no noise. It was defined under an overcast sky, just below the 580-metre (1,900-feet) cloud base. It then shot up, leaving a clear hole in the clouds which took several minutes to close over.

Although the object was dismissed by a Federal Aviation Administration spokesperson as a weather phenomenon and purportedly was not seen by airport control tower staff nor tracked on radar, the eyewitnesses were certain, as reported by Paul Simons, that 'this was not a plane, helicopter, weather balloon or any other craft known to man'.[29]

*

At the time of writing, these were the latest reports involving airliners to come to my attention. While most incidents do not involve harassment, some UFOs evidently pose a threat to aviation safety. Moreover, if the alleged incidents reported by the pilots in Ireland, for example, did in fact occur as described, we can begin to appreciate perhaps at least one of the reasons why governments are so determined to keep the lid down.

REFERENCES

1. *People's Daily*, 28 July and 9 August 1985.
2. *Sunday Express*, London, 25 August 1985.
3. Hastings, David J., 'Across the USA in a Cessna Skymaster', *Pilot*, June 2000, pp. 56–9.
4. Good, Timothy, *Beyond Top Secret: The Worldwide UFO Security Threat*, Pan, 1997, pp. 280–3.
5. Greer, Steven M., *Disclosure: Military and Government Witnesses Reveal the Greatest Secrets in Modern History*, Crossing Point, PO Box 265, Corzet, VA 22932, 2001, pp. 79–85.
6. *Les OVNI et la Défense: A quoi doit-on se preparer?* (UFOs and Defence: What Should We Prepare For?), an independent report by COMETA, published in *VSD* magazine, GS Press-Communication, 1999, p. 11. vsd_hs@worldnet.fr
7. Thouanel, Bernard, *Objets Volants Non Identifiés*, Michel LAFON, Paris, 2003, pp. 189–90.
8. Sage, Adam, 'Salut, Earthlings', *The Times*, London, 5 February 2003, T2, p. 7.
9. Ibid.
10. Commercial Air Transport Airmiss Reports (January–April 1995), Joint Airmiss Working Group, Civil Aviation Authority, January 1996.
11. *People's Daily*, 28 July and 9 August 1985.
12. *Sunday Express*, London, 25 August 1985.
13. *Agence France-Presse*, 1 August 1995.

14. De Vedia, Mariano, and Arenes, Carolina, 'A reporter from La Nación was in the plane when a UFO was seen over Bariloche', *La Nación*, Buenos Aires, 2 August 1995.

15. Sheppard, Captain Graham, *Safety Implications of UFO Close Approaches*. Briefing Notes prepared for the Joint Airmiss Working Group, 20 February 1995.

16. Berliner, Don, and Durant, Robert J., *Near Miss with a UFO: Swissair Flight 127*, The UFO Research Coalition, Fairfax, Virginia, 1999. ISBN 1-928957-00-05. Available from the Center for UFO Studies, 2457 W. Petersen Avenue, Chicago, IL 60659.

17. Filer's Files, #36-2003, 3 September 2003.

18. Nally, Carl, 'Aircraft Buzzed by Giant Triangular UFO over Slane', *UPRI Newsletter*, Issue 1, 2004, pp. 29–30. UFO and Paranormal Research Ireland, PO Box 7041, Harmonstown, Dublin 5, Ireland. UPRI@oceanfree.net

19. Jennings, Noelle, 'Boyne Valley UFO claims are denied', *Drogheda Leader*, 19 May 2004.

20. Jenkinson, Kevin, 'Expert on Trail of Irish UFO', *The Star*, Dublin, 20 November 2004.

21. Letter from Frank Buggie, Quality Assurance Manager, FLS Aerospace, Dublin Airport, March 2004.

22. Letter from Gerry Keogh, Chief Airport Fire Officer, 19 April 2004.

23. Letter from Fiona Carren, Customer Care, Aer Lingus, 27 April 2004.

24. Letter from Liam Duffy, Chief Executive, Beaumont Hospital, 31 May 2004.

25. Letter from Lilian Cassin, Corporate Communications Manager, Irish Aviation Authority, 27 July 2004.

26. Butler, Dermot, and Nally, Carl, *Conspiracy of Silence: UFOs in Ireland*, Mercier Press, Cork, Ireland, 2006.

27. Report from Raul Oscar Chaves, CIUFOS-LaPampa, in *Inexplicata*, The Journal of Hispanic Ufology, 14 October 2005.

28. Report from Ana Luisa Cid, *Inexplicata*, 20 October 2005.

29. Simons, Paul, 'Flying saucer punches a hole in the clouds', *The Times*, 10 January 2007. For additional information, see www.narcap.org

China Daily 27.8.85.

UFO引起廣泛興趣　全國兩萬人參加研究

新華社大連八月二十七日電　（記者趙晶春）UFO這個"宇宙之謎"正在中國引起廣泛興趣，中國數十名科學工作者新近聚會大連，第一次交流了UFO的研究成果。

UFO現象，是指"空中不明飛行物"。中國史書上對它早有記載，據瞭解，世界公認的地球上第一張UFO照片，是一九四五年在天津拍攝的。

為了揭開UFO之謎，中國在一九八一年建立了UFO研究學會，一些地方設立了分會。"中國UFO研究學會"現有會員兩千多人，加上地方分會會員，全國總共有兩萬人左右。全國還出版了《飛碟探索》、《太空探索》等雜誌。

中國UFO研究學會理事長、廣州暨南大學物理系教授梁榮麟在這次學術交流會上稱，最近五年來中國各地搜集到六百多例有關UFO的現象。

向這次會議提交的論文有四十多篇。會議選出了有代表性的論文十七篇，擬編成一本論文集，論文包括的內容有，中國人研究UFO的觀點、方法，在中國的UFO現象，UFO現象的理論著作，UFO與人體科學的關係等。

UFO是現今世界上影響頗大的一個未知之謎，支持者深信不疑，反對者則認為是虛構或幻覺。這兩種見解在國外都受到重視。世界上許多國家，包括美國、蘇聯、英國、日本和中南美洲一些國家，都建立了各種各樣的研究組織，探索UFO之謎。

An article from *China Daily* (27 August 1985) concerning a scientific conference on UFOs held in Darlian during which some forty papers were presented. 'There is great interest in China, and 20,000 people are involved in UFO research ... UFOs are an unsolved mystery, exerting a profound influence around the world.' *(China Daily)*

Chapter 4

3 UNIDENTIFIED FLYING OBJECTS

A controller receiving a report about an unidentified flying object must obtain as much as possible of the information required to complete a report in the format shown below.

Report of Unidentified Flying Object

A Date, Time and Duration of Sighting
Local times to be quoted.

B Description of Object
Number of objects, size, shape, colours, brightness, sound, smell, etc.

C Exact Position of Observer
Geographical location, indoors or outdoors, stationary or moving.

D How Observed
Naked eye, binoculars, other optical device, still or movie camera.

E Direction in which Object was First Seen
A landmark may be more useful than a badly estimated bearing.

F Angular Elevation of Object
Estimated heights are unreliable.

G Distance of Object from Observer
By reference to a known landmark wherever possible.

H Movements of Object
Changes in E, F and G may be of more use than estimates of course and speed.

J Meteorological Conditions During Observations
Moving clouds, haze, mist, etc.

K Nearby Objects
Telephone or high-voltage lines; reservoir, lake or dam; swamp or marsh; river; high buildings, tall chimneys, steeples, spires, TV or radio masts; airfields, generating plant; factories; pits or other sites with floodlights or other lighting.

L To Whom Reported
Police, military organisations, the press, etc.

M Name and Address of Informant

N Any Background Information on the Informant that may be Volunteered

O Other Witnesses

P Date and Time of Receipt of Report

The details are to be telephoned immediately to AIS (Military), LATCC.

The completed report is to be sent by the originating air traffic service unit to the Ministry of Defence Sec (AS).

A LIST OF TELEPHONE NUMBERS AND LOCATIONS IS SHOWN IN THE
DIRECTORY AT APPENDIX 'H'

14.11.91 AMENDMENT 9

Ministry of Defence instructions to air traffic controllers for the reporting of UFO sightings, as set out in the Manual of Air Traffic Services (MATS) in 1991. Details are to be telephoned immediately to the Air Information Service (Military), London Air Traffic Control Centre. *(M.R. Sutton, Editor, MATS Part I/Civil Aviation Authority)*

27. STAR WARS

One of the most frequently raised objections to the presence of actual alien vehicles and their occupants here on Earth – or anywhere else for that matter – is the assumed absence of scientific proof. First of all, it needs to be stressed that scientific evidence, per se, is in abundance: it exists in photos and films, radar and sonar records, electrical interference (sometimes on a wide scale), unexplained background radiation and/or chemical changes at landing sites, tens of thousands of military and intelligence reports, and testimony from thousands of unimpeachable sources such as pilots, astronauts, naval officers, and so on, as we have seen. However, it is true that proof remains elusive – at least, for the great mass of humanity. And that is no accident. The proof – such as recovered alien vehicles and communication with their crews – is there, but it is being denied to the general public, as well as to an overwhelming majority of scientists.

'Perhaps the most important problem with American science is that it depends heavily on the Pentagon for support,' says science journalist Terry Hansen in his book *The Missing Times: News Media Complicity in the UFO Cover-up*. 'The Pentagon's objectives are subversive to those of traditional science. In order to make progress, scientists must be able to communicate their findings to the wider community of researchers – something the Pentagon often prevents for national-security reasons. Consequently, science has become divided into *private science* and *public science*.

'The findings of private science are not available to those who don't have the necessary security clearances [and] in addition, the Pentagon has an incentive to ensure that knowledge acquired by private science is not independently discovered by public science ... There is evidence that private science understands much more about the UFO phenomenon than public science,' adds Hansen.[1] He also believes that 'to provide the impression that there is strong consensus among leading Americans that UFOs are non-existent or unimportant, intelligence officials would recruit influential people as media spokespersons. Many of the nation's most famous academics and journalists are already employed by the US government, and have signed appropriate secrecy agreements...'[2]

Hansen cites Carl Bernstein's 1977 exposé that more than 400 American journalists secretly carried out assignments for the CIA over a twenty-five-year period. 'Often, these assignments were conducted with the blessing of news-organization management ... assignments included, but were not limited to, planting disinformation and propaganda.'[3] Historical precedents for such measures include the Manhattan Project to develop the atom bomb, and the torpedoing by German U-boats of nearly 300 merchant ships off the US East Coast, with heavy loss of life, during the early years of America's involvement in the Second World War. 'Through the use of military secrecy, censorship, official denials, cover stories, and co-operative journalists,' says Hansen, 'the true story was suppressed until long after the war was over.'[4]

'The evidence is now so consistent and so overwhelming that no reasonably intelligent person can deny that something unexplained is going on in our atmosphere,' wrote Admiral of the Fleet Lord Hill-Norton, former Chief of the Defence Staff (UK) and Chairman of the NATO Military Committee, in his foreword to *Beyond Top Secret*. 'I have often wondered if the ridicule heaped on the subject in British newspapers is the reaction of ignorance, even fear of the unknown, by the third-rate journalists concerned, or whether, rather more dangerously, it has been inspired by some higher authority.'[5]

Not all the proof for alien activity on Earth is withheld by government-employed scientists. In previous books, I cite case after case involving the mutilation of animals – mostly cattle – predominantly reported in Central, North and South America. Typically, animals are found with vital organs missing: eyes, tongues, udders, sexual organs and rectal area removed with super-surgical precision, and blood completely drained (exsanguinated), with no traces of either blood or footprints (for example) on the ground. Further, in a number of cases, the animals appear to have been dropped from a certain height. Not only have unknown flying objects been reported in the vicinity; on rare occasions the animals have been observed being levitated aboard the craft.

While satanic cults and predators are blamed by officialdom for these disturbing occurrences, the scientific evidence proves otherwise. As Dr Pierre Guérin of the French Institute of Astrophysics told me in 1984: 'The testimonial facts are always doubtful, but the material facts, independent of the witnesses – in the case of the mutilations – are of a superior degree.'[6] My friend the late Dr John Altshuler, a haematologist and leading civilian expert on these mutilations, accumulated thousands of tissue samples from mutilated animals, a number of which I examined through a microscope in his laboratory. He repeatedly emphasized that no known technology on Earth could have been responsible for the mutilations.[7]

SPECIAL ACCESS

I have learned that a number of so-called 'deep black' Special Access Programs (SAPs) in the US military and intelligence community deal with alien matters. Being part and parcel of weapons and intelligence programmes, they are not classed as a discrete matter.

SAPs may be 'acknowledged' or 'unacknowledged', the latter referred to as 'core secrets', explains science and aerospace writer Bill Sweetman. Those with a 'need to know', who are briefed or 'read in' on an unacknowledged SAP, are required to deny its very existence – even a 'no comment' would be a serious breach of security. It can happen that even a general responsible for certain programmes, for instance, would not necessarily be briefed on the existence of a programme that normally should be within his jurisdiction. The wall of denial in the deep black world can thus be maintained by both deception and deliberately designed lack of cognizance, leading to apparently honest denial, says Sweetman.[8,9]

It is assumed that the US President, as Commander-in-Chief of the US Military, would automatically be briefed on the alien problem. Not so. There is no presidential prerogative – though those with a military background stand a better chance! And 'need-to-know' principles still apply. President Bill Clinton is on the record as having asked his Attorney General, Stuart Webster Hubbell, to look into the matter, and reportedly was dissatisfied with the information – or rather the lack of information – that came back.[10]

A number of former presidents, such as Truman and Eisenhower, gained access as a matter of course. Others have been briefed, in varying degrees, and some have even been exposed either to alien craft, and/or the aliens themselves – dead or alive. President Richard Nixon, for example, is reported to have arranged for his friend Jackie Gleason, the comedian and musician, to view alien bodies at Homestead Air Force Base, Florida, in 1973.[11]

In 2003 I wrote to President George H. Walker Bush, a former US Navy pilot and Director of Central Intelligence, care of a retired military friend, requesting a dialogue 'to discuss matters pertaining to aerial and submarine phenomena [since] it has been my feeling for many years that you might have more knowledge of these delicate matters than other Presidents and Directors of Central Intelligence'.

'Mr Bush appreciated hearing from you,' replied his assistant, 'and while he appreciates the spirit of your request, he must respectfully decline [owing to] the many requests he receives for personal appointments...'[12]

Regarding the present incumbent, a friend of mine who knows President George W. Bush (a former Air National Guard pilot), queried him in the White House a few years ago about the subject. 'Ask Cheney,' came the terse reply (referring to Dick Cheney, the current Vice-President).

It has long been rumoured that President J.F. Kennedy, whose Navy career included commanding the motor torpedo boat PT-109 in the Second World War, was well informed about the subject. In *Alien Base*, for instance, I allude to his secret meeting in Washington, DC, with George Adamski, who had been contacted by extraterrestrials and who liaised with a number of high-ranking military personnel and politicians at the time, including those in the UK (such as Lord Dowding and Lord Mountbatten, on one occasion). In addition to holding a passport bearing special privileges, Adamski held a US Government Ordnance Department card which gave him access to all US military bases and to certain restricted areas. He told my friend Madeleine Rodeffer that Kennedy had a meeting with extraterrestrials at a secret Air Force base in Desert Hot Springs, California.[13]

In early 2006 I received some important information from an impeccable source who was close to Kennedy and a member of the White House Staff at the time that Kennedy had been granted 'special access'. My source does not wish to be identified. 'As you would expect from any ex-military officer,' he explained, 'a strong sense of patriotism and loyalty exists, even after retirement and a long passage of time. However, the following may be helpful...'

Around 1961/62 President J.F. Kennedy expressed a wish so see the alien bodies associated with an alien crash-site. He had obviously been informed of their existence and wished to see for himself the evidence. General McCue was in charge of the arrangements at the time and Air Force One was used to take Kennedy and other top brass on this visit. The purpose of the flight was closely guarded; however, the reason for Kennedy's flight became evident to senior personnel on board, through unguarded comments and the whispering which went on. Remember, even the pilots were members of the White House Staff, ex-military and trusted implicitly.

The whispering or muted talk was mainly about the metal-like material from the crash site and the unique properties of this; apparently very light, flexible and seemingly indestructible, of unknown origin . . . and nothing like it on Earth.

Originally the alien bodies were located at [Wright-Patterson] and later removed to Tyndall Air Force Base, Florida, near [Panama City] . . . According to information received, the alien bodies were taken to Florida when Kennedy went to see them [at] a medical facility. They have probably been moved around over time.

'Since any alien evidence has been covered up for as long as rumour has existed,' continued my source, 'the US authorities are unlikely to admit their complicity or make information available to you. There will probably be no official record of the AF1 [Air Force One] visit as this was Top Secret at the time . . . There is clearly an international agreement in force between all governments to withhold information on alien and UFO phenomena.'

ALIEN LIAISON

'I have recently become troubled and interested in the mounting series of reports and indications of unreported or unidentified airborne vehicles,' begins a letter written in 1992 by a friend of mine, then Counsel to the Senate Appropriations Committee for National Security matters.

I would be very interested in discussing these matters with individuals who you believe may shed light on the nature and/or origin of such technologies, and the history and nature of any relationships that have been developed between entities of the United States Government or other organizations with such phenomena. I am prepared to engage in such discussions under whatever ground rules might be necessary and can ensure that the identity of the sources of such information will be completely protected . . .

The letter (see p. 430) had been sent to the late Karl T. Pflock, former Deputy Assistant Secretary of Defense and CIA intelligence officer, who later wrote two books on the Roswell incident (see Chapter 5). He did not respond. At the time, I was assisting the Senate writer by recommending certain people I knew who had either had experience of, or inside knowledge about, the subject matter, to contact him. In time, and with assistance from others, he amassed a great deal of hearsay evidence, but was never able to gain access to the most sensitive information being withheld in the military and intelligence communities. As Robert Crowley, former CIA Deputy Director of Operations, confirmed to my agent, Andrew Lownie, in 1986: 'UFOs are the most sensitive subject in the intelligence community.'

As far as Congress is concerned, in 1962 Arthur Sylvester, Assistant Secretary of Defense, Public Affairs, told the press at a briefing that, if deemed necessary for reasons of national security, information about UFOs would not be furnished to Congress, let alone the American public.[14] This is not to say that no one in Congress is aware of the problem: I know of several who are well informed.

During a dinner party in 1989, an Executive Branch employee revealed to Anthony L. Kimery, the award-winning editor and journalist referenced earlier, who covers global security, intelligence and defence issues, that he had seen a top-secret National Security Council report in which high-level references to the National Security Agency were made. The report had been prepared as a briefing paper for the new administration of President George H.W. Bush, at the Department of State's Bureau of Intelligence and Research (INR) office. Allegedly, the report referred to the operation of a government facility dealing specifically with the alien situation, located somewhere along the northern New Mexico border.

'The source said the report indicated that this "facility was deep underground",' writes Kimery, 'and had to do with the development of a "super-computer", along the lines of artificial intelligence, utilizing alien technology apparently provided by alien beings themselves, who, the source said, "I got the impression were running the show" . . .' As mentioned in Chapter 6, I have learned that the facility is (or was) located in the nuclear-weapons storage area within the Manzano Mountains.

'The source has been responsible for providing crucial information to support a number of stories on covert operations and national security matters [which have] been published in some of the nation's most influential newspapers and magazines,' Kimery points out. 'Those present at the dinner, including a man previously attached to the Joint Chiefs of Staff, believe he did see the document . . .'[15]

According to an analyst with the Army's Intelligence and Threat Analysis Center (ITAC), Kimery learned, significant black budget monies are regularly funnelled through ITAC to deal with the UFO problem. 'Some of these funds are earmarked for secret programmes run by the NSA; both the NSA and CIA are said to work closely with the ITAC.'[16]

In 1989, on my behalf and that of Lord Hill-Norton, investigator Bob Oechsler spoke by telephone to Admiral Bobby Ray Inman, whose former posts include that of Director of the NSA as well as Deputy Director of the

CIA and Director of Naval Intelligence. At one point in the recorded conversation, Oechsler asked: 'Do you anticipate that any of the recovered vehicles would ever become available for technological research – outside of the military circles?'

'I honestly don't know,' responded Admiral Inman. 'Ten years ago the answer would have been no. Whether as time has evolved they are beginning to become more open on it, there's a possibility ...' [17] When the story came out, Inman claimed to a reporter that the subject of the conversation had been submarines, not aliens.

In *Unearthly Disclosure*, I reveal information acquired via high-ranking source indicating that a number of alien craft have been recovered, and that elements of the military and scientific intelligence community have been engaged in developing, with alien assistance, the highly advanced propulsion systems that power these craft. Is it possible that the United States has now developed such craft, capable of space travel? Circumstantial evidence suggests that this is indeed the case.

Ben R. Rich, who died in 1995, headed Lockheed Martin's 'Skunk Works', which developed Stealth aircraft, among others. On 23 March 1993, Rich gave a presentation at the University of California at Los Angeles (UCLA) School of Engineering Alumni, and among those present was Jan Harzan, an IBM engineer/executive and UCLA graduate. 'He cut off the presentation at the F-117 stealth fighter, and said that anything since then he was not able to talk about due to national security reasons,' Harzan related to me. 'His last slide was a black disc zipping off into outer space, and he ended the talk with these words: "We now have the technology to take ET home."'

After the presentation, a group of fifteen to twenty people – including Harzan and another person known to me – gathered around the great man for informal discussion. 'We now know how to travel to the stars, and it will not take us a lifetime to do it,' revealed Rich at one point. 'We have found the error in the equations, and we now know how to travel to the stars.'

'He was very vocal that the blanket of secrecy that he and his people had been forced to work under was no longer necessary,' Harzan continues, 'and that this technology should be brought out from the "Black" world and put to use in the "White" world for the benefit of humanity ... My feeling is that he was ready to go public.' [18]

STAR WARS

'UFOs are as real as the airplanes that fly over your head,' declared the
Hon. Paul Hellyer, a former Canadian Minister of Defence (1963–7) under
Prime Minister Lester Pearson, and Deputy Prime Minister under Pierre
Trudeau, during an extraordinary half-hour speech he delivered to the
Toronto Exopolitics Symposium Conference on UFOs, held at the Univer-
sity of Toronto on 25 September 2005.[19]

Although well aware of UFO reports during his tenure as Minister of
Defence, Hellyer did not became really interested until reading *The Day
After Roswell* by Colonel Philip J. Corso, former head of the US Army's
Foreign Technology Division, and later a member of President Eisenhower's
National Security Council (Chapter 5).

In his book, Corso describes weapons incorporating alien technology,
including advanced particle-beam weapons. Among the early weapons
systems developed for this purpose were 'Saint' and 'Blue Gemini', which
were 'outgrowths of USAF 7795, a code number for the USAF's first satellite
programme [which was] designed to locate, track, and destroy enemy
surveillance satellites or, more importantly, orbiting UFOs . . . Both of these
weapons, under the cover of other missions, of course, were eventually
deployed, and today they form one of the lines of defence in an anti-missile
and anti-UFO surveillance system.'

Corso also claimed that the Strategic Defense Initiative (SDI), or 'Star
Wars' (currently known as the Missile Defense Shield), a space-based
defence system ostensibly first designed to protect the USA from an all-out
nuclear attack by the USSR, was developed – with the USSR's knowledge –
to counter an alien threat.[20] Dr Rimili Avramenko, a senior engineer in the
Russian SDI programme, contends that information from the ongoing
study of UFOs has been incorporated in his own country's SDI programme. In conversation with reporter George Knapp, for instance, he
referred to one programme as 'the weapon of the aliens'.[21]

'We both knew who the real targets of SDI were,' Corso revealed. 'It
was the UFOs, alien spacecraft thinking themselves invulnerable and invisible . . . swooping down at will to destroy our communications with EMP
[electro-magnetic pulse] bursts, buzz our spacecraft, colonize our lunar surface, mutilate cattle in their own horrendous biological experiments, and
even abduct human beings for their medical tests and hybridization of the
species . . .'[22]

'The secrecy involved in all matters pertaining to the Roswell incident was unparalleled,' continued Hellyer. 'The classification was, from the outset, above Top Secret, so the vast majority of US officials and politicians – let alone a mere allied Minister of Defence – were never in the loop.

'Furthermore, when the alien technology was fed to US industry, at no time was the source revealed. Colonel Corso had the perfect cover: it was foreign technology that he was providing – ostensibly something picked up from the Soviets or the Germans. No questions were allowed and no explanations given. And, as you might expect in a country with three separate military services, the Army, Air Force, and Navy did not share their secrets . . .'

After reading Corso's book, Hellyer telephoned a friend, a retired US Air Force general, to verify Corso's claims. 'Every word of it is true – and more,' declared the general. 'We then spent twenty minutes or so discussing the "and more"', continued Hellyer, 'to the extent he could without revealing classified material. What he said was just as fascinating and compelling as the book.'

There is a problem for Earthlings. Within hours of the crash at Roswell, US General Twining designated the visitors as 'enemy aliens'. It appears . . . that it has remained as official US policy ever since. At that time, however, it was an enemy about which the US could do nothing, because the visitors were so technically superior . . . The rationale was that ordinary people couldn't cope with the news and might easily panic. Reference was made to Orson Welles' Halloween broadcast [October 1938] depicting a Martian invasion, which had been so realistic that a sort of panic ensued. The best way to prevent a recurrence was to keep the public in the dark . . . This policy resulted in what has probably been the greatest and most successful cover-up in the history of the world.

But much has happened in the more than half-century that policy was adopted. The most important change has been in US military capability. The US has developed the aliens' own weapons – lasers and particle guns – to the point where they can be used against the visitors from space . . . The Bush Administration has finally agreed to let the military build a forward base on the Moon [in 2018], which will put them in a better position to keep track of the goings and comings of the visitors from space, and to shoot at them, if they so decide . . .[23]

I must emphasize here that not all alien species are hostile. It is evident that some appear to be millennia ahead of us in terms of their ethical development. Yet, evidently, we are in conflict with some races. Given that the universe appears to be teeming with life at different stages of evolution, we should not be surprised. Furthermore, I have long subscribed to the hypothesis that *Homo sapiens* is a genetically modified species, deriving from the colonization of Earth by an alien race millennia ago. Some of these races, in my view, are still based here. The centuries-old phenomena prevalent in certain areas of our planet such as the Bermuda Triangle – disappearances, space–time warps and so on – indicate the existence of highly advanced technology. And it would appear that our presence in or near these areas is not always welcomed.

As I revealed in *Unearthly Disclosure*, based on information provided by a high-ranking source in the late 1980s, some aliens posed a threat to the environment because they were 'messing around with tectonic plates' in the Pacific Ocean, and 'the presence of the alien ships in our oceans was causing – or at least contributing to – the warming of the waters'. Supposedly, the aliens had been requested by those few in the military who had access to them to vacate their undersea bases. The request was ignored. Further compounding the issue, there appeared to be a conflict of interests between resident alien races here on Earth.

Are we, as a number of sources claim, already at war with some of these beings? Robin Cole, cited in Chapter 10 in connection with his research into the involvement in UFO monitoring by Britain's Government Communications Headquarters (GCHQ), which liaises hand-in-glove with its American counterpart, the National Security Agency, relates a telling comment by a GCHQ Signals Intelligence analyst in the 1990s. 'I've got something really serious to tell you,' she told her brother on returning home from work one day. 'We've known for years that we're at war with these beings.' No further details were given.[24] Anecdotal it may be, but the woman appeared very concerned.

In my opinion, the US Air Force Space Command (AFSPC) is the military unit charged with the operation to counter an alien threat.

'Ladies and Gentleman, the war in space has begun,' announced General Lance W. Lord, Commander of AFSPC, at an international conference in 2004. 'Space superiority for us has got to be something we work [at] very hard, and has to be considered equally as important as air superiority.'[25] He didn't mention aliens, of course, but his comments are apposite, nonetheless.

In 2002, Gary McKinnon was arrested in London under the Computer Misuse Act for having hacked (with relative ease) into numerous military networks, specifically to uncover information being withheld by the US Government on UFOs. No charges were brought against him, but in 2005 he faced extradition proceedings by the US Government. Currently (June 2006), the case is the subject of an extradition request which has successfully, so far, gone through the initial court process and is now the subject of an appeal. If extradited, McKinnon faces up to sixty years in a US jail.[26]

For McKinnon, the most important information he uncovered related to AFSPC. 'I found a list of officers' names under the heading "Non-Terrestrial Officers",' he told journalist Jon Ronson. 'It doesn't mean little green men. What I think it means is, not Earth-based. I found a list of "fleet-to-fleet transfers", and a list of ship names. I looked them up. They weren't US Navy ships. What I saw made me believe they have some kind of spaceship, off-planet.'[27]

'On finding the first image on my PC,' Gary told me, 'the Earth – or at least a blue and white planet with no continents visible – filled two-thirds of the screen. Midway between the "camera" and the planet hung a cigar-shaped object with geodesic domes above, below, and to the left and right. I didn't see any rivets, seams or telemetry antennae.'[28]

'Space is our final frontier,' declared Canadian Prime Minister Paul Martin at the United Nations General Assembly in September 2004. 'What a tragedy it would be if space became one big weapons arsenal . . .'

Paul Hellyer has joined forces with three non-governmental organizations to ask the Parliament of Canada to hold public hearings on the extraterrestrial problem. He is to be commended for his courage in braving the ridicule which he knew would attend his speech.

'I'm so concerned about what the consequences might be of starting an intergalactic war, that I just think I had to say something,' admitted the retired Defence Minister. 'The time has come to lift the veil of secrecy, and let the truth emerge, so there can be a real and informed debate, about one of the most important problems facing our planet today . . .'[29]

Certainly, an informed debate is long overdue. But has the time yet come to lift the veil of secrecy – in its entirety? I think not. Due to a few leaks, we may have some good hints, but lacking a 'need to know', we can only guess at what precisely is being withheld from us.

In the conclusion to my last book, I suggested that whatever threat is posed by certain alien species, we have more to fear from our own kind, and that official disclosure might be just the sort of shock we need. But based on what I now know, I believe that a full revelation would be destabilizing. Disclosing prematurely the facts about such a situation would run the risk of social upheaval on an unprecedented scale.

In this event, gradual disclosure – the planned agenda – is by far the wisest course.

REFERENCES

1. Hansen, Terry, *The Missing Times: News Media Complicity in the UFO Cover-up*, XLibris Corporation, 2000, p. 299.
2. Ibid., p. 141.
3. Ibid., p. 63.
4. Ibid., pp. 147–8.
5. Good, Timothy, *Beyond Top Secret: The Worldwide UFO Security Threat*, Sidgwick & Jackson, London, 1996, p. xii.
6. See *Above Top Secret* or *Beyond Top Secret*.
7. Good, Timothy, *Alien Liaison: The Ultimate Secret*, Century, 1991. Published in the US as *Alien Contact: Top-Secret UFO Files Revealed*, William Morrow, 1993 and *Unearthly Disclosure*.
8. Sweetman, Bill, 'On Black Special Access Programs'. www.ufoskeptic.org/black.html
9. *USA Today*, 6 September 2000, cited by Bill Sweetman in 'Extraterrestrial Visitation: Some Thoughts on Keeping it Secret', UFO Special Access Programs. www.ufoskeptic.org/secret.html
10. Aldrich, Gary, *Unlimited Access: An FBI Agent Inside the Clinton White House*, Regnery, Washington, DC, 1996.
11. See *Alien Liaison/Alien Contact*.
12. Letter from Linda Casey Poepsel, Assistant to President Bush, Office of George Bush, Houston, Texas 77024, 2 July 2003.
13. See *Alien Base*.
14. Corso, Colonel Philip J. (Ret.), with Birnes, William, *The Day After Roswell*, Pocket Books, 1997, p. 264.
15. Neilsen, James (Anthony Kimery), 'Gov't. Source Describes UFO Brief', *UFO Magazine* (US), Vol. 4, No. 2, 1989, p. 10.
16. Neilson, *UFO Magazine*, Vol. 15, No. 9, October/November 2000, p. 29.
17. See *Alien Liaison/Alien Contact*.
18. Email, 8 February 2006.
19. 'Paul Hellyer Speaks', *UFO Magazine* (US), Vol. 20, No. 5, December/January 2006, pp. 36–9.
20. Corso, op. cit., pp. 264–7.
21. Knapp, George, 'UFOs Over Russia: Don't Believe Everything You Hear', *UFO Magazine* (US), Vol. 14, No. 4, April 1999, p. 28.
22. Corso, op. cit., p. 267.
23. 'Paul Hellyer Speaks'.
24. Redfern, Nick, 'View from a Brit: British Intelligence Deep Into UFO Matters,' *UFO Magazine* (US), Vol. 19, No. 4, August/September 2004, pp. 20–1.

25. 'Harnessing the Power of Space', a keynote speech by General Lance W. Lord, Commander, Air Force Space Command, at the MILCOM International Conference, Monterey, California, 1 November 2004.
26. Personal interview, London, 19 May 2006.
27. Ronson, Jon, 'Game Over', *The Guardian/Guardian Unlimited*, 9 July 2005.
28. Personal interview, London, 5 June 2006.
29. www.rense.com

Two excellent books which address the history of UFOs and officialdom, in a wider context, are *UFOs and the National Security State*, Vols I and II, by Richard M. Dolan, Hampton Roads Publishing Company, Charlottesville, VA 22902 (2000/2006).

United States Senate

COMMITTEE ON APPROPRIATIONS
WASHINGTON, DC 20510-6025

December 10, 1992

Mr. Karl Pflock

Dear Karl:

As you know I am Counsel to the Senate Appropriations Committee for National Security matters.

I have recently become troubled and interested in the mounting series of reports and indications of unreported or unidentified airborne vehicles. I would be very interested in discussing these matters with individuals who you believe may shed light on the nature and/or origin of such technologies, and the history and nature of any relationships that have been developed between entities of the United States Government or other organizations with such phenomenon. I am prepared to engage in such discussions under whatever ground rules might be necessary and can insure that the identity of the sources of such information will be completely protected.

Thank you for any help you can give me in pursuing this inquiry.

Sincerely,

A letter to Karl T. Pflock, a former Deputy Assistant Secretary of Defense, CIA officer and author of two books on the Roswell incident. The letter has been censored by the author in accordance with the writer's instructions.

LOOSE MINUTE

D/Sec(AS)12/7(JC106/93)

22 April 1993

ACAS

SIGHTINGS OF UNIDENTIFIED OBJECT

1.   I do not normally concern you with the UFO aspect of Sec(AS)'s work but in the light of previous conversations we have had, you may wish to be aware of a recent particularly unusual incidence of UFO sightings over the UK, involving descriptions that match some of the reported characteristics of the so-called "Aurora".

2.   The sightings took place over a period of about 3 hours early on Wednesday 31 March. Most of them were in Devon and Cornwall, South Wales and Shropshire. There is a number of factors which make these sightings unusual; firstly, there is a good deal of commonality in the description of the object, and considerable commonality in the times of many of the sightings - around 1.10 am (although several occurred in locations some distance apart at about the same time indicating the possibility of more than one phenomenon); secondly, none of the usual explanations put forward to explain UFO sightings seem applicable; and thirdly, the reliability of the witnesses, a good many of whom were police officers and military personnel. Our latest information indicates that at least seventy people witnessed something, and I have attached a small selection of the reports.

3.   My staff have made extensive efforts to find an explanation for these sightings, including discussions with air defence and both civil and military ATC authorities; generally it has been confirmed that nothing unusual was seen, and no requests for clearance for any "unusual activity" have been acknowledged to have been received. However the ATC radar at Burrington recorded some slow moving contacts over North Devon at the same time as some of the sightings in that area were reported. Despite this coincidence West Drayton suggest these recordings could be attributed to clutter. The only other main ATC radar (Clee Hill) which might have picked up contacts in the area in which sightings were reported was in fact not working on primary radar during the period of the sightings and therefore only aircraft working Secondary Surveillance Radar could be seen. Routine checks have advised us that there were no military aircraft operating at the time.

4.   Some of the reports state that the object was moving at a very high speed, while some say that it was hovering or moving very slowly. Many of the reports refer to the object being very large, flying low and making a low humming sound. My staff have spoken to a number of the military and police witnesses, many of whom commented that the object was unlike anything they had ever seen before; a

A minute from the Ministry of Defence's Head of Secretariat (Air Staff) to the Assistant Chief of the Air Staff (ACAS) regarding the Secretariat's conclusions on the events reported at RAF Shrewsbury and elsewhere in the small hours of 31 March 1993 (see pp. 384–5). (*Crown copyright*)

Met Officer at RAF Shawbury reported seeing the object projecting a narrow beam of light at the ground at a height of 400-500 feet and estimated its size at somewhere between a C130 and B747 when it passed over his head at an estimated 4000 feet.

5.   In summary, there would seem to be some evidence on this occasion that an unidentified object (or objects) of unknown origin was operating over the UK.   Given recent speculation about Aurora by both media and MPs it is surprising that so far this has not been taken up by the Press or, indeed, again by MPs.   Frankly, I can see little that we can do to follow it up.   If there has been some activity of US origins which is known to a limited circle in MOD and is not being acknowledged it is difficult to investigate further. I would however be interested in your views in the light of your earlier interest about Aurora.   I attach a copy of a letter I sent to the US Embassy not long ago which I am assured has been disseminated to all "interested Agencies" in the US.

Head of Sec(AS)

Index